Lonely Places, Dangerous Ground

Also in the series

William Rothman, editor, *Cavell on Film*

J. David Slocum, editor, *Rebel Without a Cause*

Joe McElhaney, *The Death of Classical Cinema*

Kirsten Moana Thompson, *Apocalyptic Dread*

Frances Gateward, editor, *Seoul Searching*

Michael Atkinson, editor, *Exile Cinema*

Paul S. Moore, *Now Playing*

Robin L. Murray and Joseph K. Heumann, *Ecology and Popular Film*

William Rothman, editor, *Three Documentary Filmmakers*

Sean Griffin, editor, *Hetero*

Jean-Michel Frodon, editor, *Cinema and the Shoah*

Carolyn Jess-Cooke and Constantine Verevis, editors, *Second Takes*

Matthew Solomon, editor, *Fantastic Voyages of the Cinematic Imagination*

R. Barton Palmer and David Boyd, editors, *Hitchcock at the Source*

William Rothman, *Hitchcock, Second Edition*

Joanna Hearne, *Native Recognition*

Marc Raymond, *Hollywood's New Yorker*

Lonely Places, Dangerous Ground

Nicholas Ray in American Cinema

Edited by
Steven Rybin
and
Will Scheibel

Cover: James Dean in *Rebel Without a Cause* (Warner Bros., 1955), directed by Nicholas Ray. Courtesy of Photofest.

Published by State University of New York Press, Albany

© 2014 State University of New York

All rights reserved

Printed in the United States of America

No part of this book may be used or reproduced in any manner whatsoever without written permission. No part of this book may be stored in a retrieval system or transmitted in any form or by any means including electronic, electrostatic, magnetic tape, mechanical, photocopying, recording, or otherwise without the prior permission in writing of the publisher.

For information, contact State University of New York Press, Albany, NY
www.sunypress.edu

Production by Eileen Nizer
Marketing by Anne M. Valentine

Library of Congress Cataloging-in-Publication Data

Lonely places, dangerous ground : Nicholas Ray in American cinema / edited by Steven Rybin and Will Scheibel.
    pages cm — (The SUNY series, horizons of cinema)
Includes bibliographical references and index.
Summary: "Examines the director's place in the history of Hollywood and the institution of cinema"—Provided by publisher.
  ISBN 978-1-4384-4981-4 (hardcover : alk. paper)
  ISBN 978-1-4384-4980-7 (paperback : alk. paper)
  1. Ray, Nicholas, 1911–1979—Criticism and interpretation. 2. Motion picture producers and directors—United States. I. Rybin, Steven, 1979– editor of compilation. II. Scheibel, Will, 1983– editor of compilation.

PN1998.3.R39L66 2014
791.4302'33092—dc23
                                                   2013008318

10 9 8 7 6 5 4 3 2 1

To Jessica Belser and Andrea Scheibel

Contents

Figures   xi

Acknowledgments   xvii

Introduction: Nicholas Ray and the Potential of Cinema Culture   1
Steven Rybin and Will Scheibel

1. Looking for Nicholas Ray   9
   Jonathan Rosenbaum

2. Nicholas Ray: The Breadth of Modern Gesture   19
   Joe McElhaney

3. Economies of Desire: Reimagining *Noir* in *They Live by Night*   29
   Ria Banerjee

4. *Knock on Any Door*: Realist Form and Popularized Social Science   41
   Chris Cagle

5. "I've Got the Queerest Feeling" about *A Woman's Secret* and *Born to Be Bad*   49
   Alexander Doty

6. Something More than *Noir*   63
   Steven Sanders

7. *On Dangerous Ground*: Of Outsiders 73
   R. Barton Palmer

8. *Flying Leathernecks*: Color and Characterization 85
   Tony Williams

9. *The Lusty Men* and the Post-Western 97
   Neil Campbell

10. Citizen Nick: Civic Engagement and Folk Culture in the Life and Work of Nicholas Ray 109
    James I. Deutsch and Lauren R. Shaw

11. A Teacup and a Kiss: Staging Action in *Johnny Guitar* 123
    Murray Pomerance

12. "You Can't Be a Rebel If You Grin": Masculinity, Performance, and Anxiety in 1950s Rock-and-Roll and the Films of Nicholas Ray 139
    Paul Anthony Johnson

13. Places and Spaces in *Rebel Without a Cause* 151
    Robin A. Larsen

14. Nicholas Ray's Wilderness Films: Word, Law, and Landscape 163
    Susan White

15. *Bigger Than Life*: Melodrama, Masculinity, and the American Dream 177
    Will Scheibel

16. Ray, Widescreen, and Genre: *The True Story of Jesse James* 189
    Harper Cossar

17. Disequilibrium, or: Love Interest (On *Party Girl*) 209
    Adrian Martin

18. *King of Kings* and the Politics of Masculinity in the Cold War Biblical Epic 219
    Jason McKahan

19. "As Surely as a Criminal Would Die": Nicholas Ray's *The Doctor and the Devils* *Larysa Smirnova and Chris Fujiwara*	231
20. The Pedagogical Aesthetics of *We Can't Go Home Again* *Steven Rybin*	241
Postscript: The Class: Interview with Nicholas Ray *Bill Krohn*	251
Nicholas Ray: Chronological Filmography	267
Works Cited	269
Contributors	281
Index	285

Figures

Figure 1.1	A hero to some, a pariah to others, Ray sought and relished the role of outlaw, of maverick (Mark Goldstein Collection).	10
Figure 2.1	*On Dangerous Ground* (RKO Radio Pictures, 1952): The hand and the act of gesturing are embedded in the very form and structure of the film, and Ray frequently frames in such a manner that the hand becomes dominant (frame enlargement).	20
Figure 3.1	*They Live by Night* (RKO Radio Pictures, 1948): Keechie and Bowie radically reconceptualize what operating as a couple within the *noir* world means (frame enlargement).	30
Figure 4.1	*Knock on Any Door* (RKO Radio Pictures, 1949) exemplifies the social problem film's tendency to adapt film aesthetics to popularized social science discourses circulating in late 1940s (frame enlargement).	42
Figure 5.1	*A Woman's Secret* (RKO Radio Pictures, 1949; pictured) and *Born to Be Bad* (RKO Radio Pictures, 1950; fig. 5.2) indicate that, from the beginning of his career, the bisexual Ray was interested in queering the American studio film in various ways (frame enlargement).	50
Figure 5.2	*Born to Be Bad* (RKO Radio Pictures, 1950) (frame enlargement).	50

Figure 6.1	*In a Lonely Place* (Santana Productions/Columbia Pictures, 1950): Ray uses a high-key light on Dix's face to emphasize his enthusiastic, perverse pleasure as he graphically describes how he believes the strangulation of Mildred would have taken place (frame enlargement).	64
Figure 7.1	*On Dangerous Ground* (RKO Radio Pictures, 1952) expresses Ray's "force of personality" not only textually, but also, if in an indirect fashion, through the shaping of the context of production, which was in every sense "for him" (frame enlargement).	74
Figure 8.1	*Flying Leathernecks* (RKO Radio Pictures, 1951) contrasts two types of star personae who epitomize different aspects of post–World War II cinematic masculinity: John Wayne and Robert Ryan (frame enlargement).	86
Figure 9.1	*The Lusty Men* (Wald-Krasna Productions/RKO Radio Pictures, 1952) reveals much about national and regional identity, and how concepts of home appeal in differing ways, through memory and nostalgia, to fixing roots in a particular time and place (frame enlargement).	98
Figure 10.1	In light of his years working almost exclusively with amateurs in the U.S. Department of Agriculture's Resettlement Administration and the Works Progress Administration productions, Ray became a master of coaxing impressive and often unexpected performances out of Hollywood actors (Nicholas Ray Archive/Nicholas Ray Foundation).	110
Figure 11.1	In *Johnny Guitar* (Republic Pictures, 1955), scenes ostensibly coherent in themselves turn out to be only preparations for higher-order treatments of the same motifs; expressions on faces rebound and reflect one another; colors express sentiments (frame enlargement).	124
Figure 11.2	*Johnny Guitar*: The carriage of that teacup, as well as Johnny's (Sterling Hayden) calculated civilities of language as he addresses the men,	

	show that like Vienna, he may have two sides, combative and civilized, rough and delicate (frame enlargement).	125
Figure 11.3	*Johnny Guitar*: They will struggle verbally, their faces moving in and out of shadow, and then come together and kiss, kiss as though no time has passed, kiss as though there is no tomorrow (frame enlargement).	135
Figure 12.1	*Rebel Without a Cause* (Warner Bros., 1955): James Dean's Jim Stark simply apotheosizes the typical Nicholas Ray protagonist, creating the most lasting and influential pop iteration of Ray's chronicles of a fractured American masculinity (frame enlargement).	140
Figure 13.1	*Rebel Without a Cause* (Warner Bros., 1955): After Jim (James Dean) chases Judy (Natalie Wood) as she sprints around the pool edge, they land on a chaise in the gazebo. As Jim puts his head in Judy's lap, she wipes his face with a handkerchief, and Plato (Sal Mineo) continues to play child, rolling on the floor into a sitting position against their legs that indicates they should be his parents (frame enlargement).	152
Figure 14.1	Joseph Cotten as Henty in "High Green Wall" (Revue Productions/*General Electric Theater* series, 1954): Henty has left "the jungle of the civilized world," the sole survivor of a doomed expedition into the Amazon (General Electric Theater press release/Susan White Collection).	164
Figure 15.1	The marketing and reception of *Bigger Than Life* (Twentieth Century-Fox, 1956) as an exploitative social problem movie about prescription drug addiction can be read as an attempt to conceal or repress the more unspeakable (or "melodramatic") social problem the film wants to address: masculinity in crisis. (Frame enlargement)	178
Figure 16.1	In *The True Story of Jesse James* (Twentieth Century-Fox, 1957), Ray fashions the CinemaScope format toward more laterally	

	oriented set-ups, whereas *Johnny Guitar*'s outdoor shots rely on more vertical compositions that emphasize height rather than width (frame enlargement).	190
Figure 16.2	*Johnny Guitar* (frame enlargement).	196
Figure 16.3	*Johnny Guitar* (frame enlargement).	196
Figure 16.4	*Johnny Guitar* (frame enlargement).	196
Figure 16.5	*The True Story of Jesse James* (frame enlargement).	197
Figure 16.6	*The True Story of Jesse James* (frame enlargement).	197
Figure 16.7	*The True Story of Jesse James* (frame enlargement).	197
Figure 16.8	*The True Story of Jesse James* (frame enlargement).	197
Figure 16.9	*Johnny Guitar* (frame enlargement).	198
Figure 16.10	*Johnny Guitar* (frame enlargement).	198
Figure 16.11	*Johnny Guitar* (frame enlargement).	198
Figure 16.12	*The True Story of Jesse James* (frame enlargement).	199
Figure 16.13	*The True Story of Jesse James* (frame enlargement).	199
Figure 16.14	*The True Story of Jesse James* (frame enlargement).	199
Figure 16.15	*Johnny Guitar* (frame enlargement).	202
Figure 16.16	*Johnny Guitar* (frame enlargement).	202
Figure 16.17	*Johnny Guitar* (frame enlargement).	202
Figure 16.18	*The True Story of Jesse James* (frame enlargement).	203
Figure 16.19	*The True Story of Jesse James* (frame enlargement).	203
Figure 16.20	*The True Story of Jesse James* (frame enlargement).	203
Figure 16.21	*The True Story of Jesse James* (frame enlargement).	204
Figure 16.22	*The True Story of Jesse James* (frame enlargement).	204
Figure 16.23	*The True Story of Jesse James* (frame enlargement).	205
Figure 16.24	*The True Story of Jesse James* (frame enlargement).	205
Figure 17.1	*Party Girl* (Metro-Goldwyn-Mayer, 1958): Nicholas Ray is a director who is dear to many cinephiles, but he proves hard to get a grip	

	on. . . . We cannot tell, sometimes, whether we are really watching the films themselves or the images we project onto them. . . . (frame enlargement).	210
Figure 18.1	Ultimately, the realization, marketing, and reception of *King of Kings* (Metro-Goldwyn-Mayer/ Samuel Bronston Productions, 1961) was grounded in the filmmakers' effort to gain respectability among religious middle-class audiences by forging a humanist image of Christ, and simultaneously, increase filmic appeal by engaging the gospel text from a contemporary worldview (Jason McKahan Collection).	220
Figure 19.1	Ray's attraction to *The Doctor and the Devils*, then, can be seen as a stage in his progressive approach to the theme of the artist's death, including also his acting role as the American ambassador who abstains—that is, withdraws, or plays dead— in *55 Days at Peking* (Samuel Bronston Productions, 1963) (frame enlargement).	232
Figure 20.1	Both dressed in red (the signature color of rebellion in Ray's cinema, after the red jacket James Dean wears in *Rebel Without a Cause*), Tom Farrell and Ray are united not only by their costumes but also by the fact that both of them are blind in their right eye (frame enlargement).	242
Figure P.1	Ray in the short film *The Janitor* (Film Group One, Amsterdam, with Cinereal Films, West Berlin, 1974; frame enlargement).	252

Acknowledgments

This collection would not have been possible without the efforts of Murray Pomerance as the Horizons of Cinema series editor for SUNY Press. We owe him our deepest gratitude for his faith and enthusiasm, as well as his honest, encouraging advice from the project's inception. Thanks also to James Peltz, Associate Director at SUNY Press, and Jen Stelling, Acquisitions Editorial Assistant at SUNY Press, for keeping it running smoothly; to our anonymous referees for their comments; and to our dream cast of authors for their wonderful essays.

I owe a deep debt of gratitude to all of the mentors and professors who have taught me so much about cinema over the last several years: Matthew Bernstein, David A. Cook, Ryan DeRosa, Keith M. Harris, Adam Knee, Evan Lieberman, Susan Linville, Nina K. Martin, Karla Oeler, Alessandra Raengo, and George Semsel. My fellow film professors at Georgia Gwinnett College, Stacy Rusnak and Rodney Hill (now at Hofstra University), are wonderful colleagues and were a great source of professional support while this book was completed. Will was an excellent collaborator, and I thank him for his tireless work on the collection and his passion for the subject. I also thank my family for their emotional support. My work on this book is dedicated to Jessica Belser, who has given so much joy to my life.

—Steven Rybin

I would first like to thank Joan Hawkins, Barbara Klinger, and Gregory A. Waller, part of the film and media studies team at Indiana University–Bloomington, who have guided my thinking and research on Nicholas Ray in highly productive directions. In particular, Barb is an ongoing source of constructive criticism, intellectual inspiration, and personal and professional support. Alexander Doty, who also contributed an essay to this collection, passed away just before the manuscript went into production, and I hope somewhere he knows what an impact his teaching and scholarship made on me. From the Indiana University Department of English, Edward P. Comentale has introduced me to valuable literary and theoretical perspectives on popular culture. My former mentor Christoph Lindner, currently at the University of Amsterdam, has been a helpful colleague and friend, and I am indebted to him for his generous insights over the years. Collaborating with Steven on this book was a pleasure, and at every stage I appreciated his meticulous hard work, his expertise and good sense, and, most of all, his love for Ray's films. Finally, I would like to thank my parents for reminding me I can always come home. My work on this book is dedicated to Andrea Scheibel, who has enriched my life in more ways than I am able to do justice here.

—Will Scheibel

Introduction

Nicholas Ray and the Potential of Cinema Culture

STEVEN RYBIN AND WILL SCHEIBEL

THE DIRECTOR OF CLASSIC FILMS SUCH AS *They Live by Night*, *In a Lonely Place*, *Johnny Guitar*, *Rebel Without a Cause*, and *Bigger Than Life*, among others, Nicholas Ray was the "*cause célèbre* of the *auteur* theory," as critic Andrew Sarris once put it (107).[1] But unlike his senior colleagues in Hollywood such as Alfred Hitchcock or Howard Hawks, he remained a director at the margins of the American studio system. So too has he remained at the margins of academic film scholarship. Many fine scholarly works on Ray, of course, have been published, ranging from Geoff Andrew's important *auteur* study *The Films of Nicholas Ray: The Poet of Nightfall* and Bernard Eisenschitz's authoritative biography *Nicholas Ray: An American Journey* (both first published in English in 1991 and 1993, respectively) to books on individual films by Ray, such as Dana Polan's 1993 monograph on *In a Lonely Place* and J. David Slocum's 2005 collection of essays on *Rebel Without a Cause*. In 2011, the year of his centennial, the restoration of his final film, *We Can't Go Home Again*, by his widow and collaborator Susan Ray, signaled renewed interest in the director, as did the publication of a new biography, *Nicholas Ray: The Glorious Failure of an American Director*, by Patrick McGilligan. Yet what Nicholas Ray's films tell us about Classical Hollywood cinema, what it was and will continue to be, is far from certain.

After all, what most powerfully characterizes Ray's films is not only what they *are*—products both of Hollywood's studio and genre systems—but also what they *might be*. When viewed through the eyes of those who love them, Ray's films reveal themselves as fascinating visions of the world and alternative systems of seeing and feeling. Ray is a great director not because his films arrive to us as fully realized masterworks; as Jacques Rivette once suggested, even Ray's best films do not have the polish of a privileged master (Hitchcock, for example). These films instead call for us to bestow on them, in Rivette's words, "not indulgence, but a little love" ("Imagination" 104). Ray is a great filmmaker, in part, because of the way his works reward the close attention of viewers ready to see in them, and ready to imagine alongside them, the possibilities at work in the margins of the Hollywood studio film. As Rivette's colleague François Truffaut proposed, in an especially polemical moment, if one proved unable to provide this "little love" to Ray's at times unwieldy films, at the same time one proved oneself unworthy of cinema ("Certainty" 108).

This is not to say that Ray's films constitute a sloppy and undisciplined body of work. Nevertheless, it is telling that even his great films are about the search for a different or better home and world, an alternative system of loving and thinking. In *They Live by Night*, it is the search for an ideal romance against the rural backdrop of the open road pockmarked by the vestiges of the Great Depression; in *Rebel Without a Cause*, the search by a trio of suburbanite teenagers for a home more in line with the affective and existential challenges posed to them by late adolescence; and in *Bigger Than Life*, a sensitive intellectual's exhaustion with the static suburban environment in which he lives. And, in the only film Ray made that was explicitly about Hollywood and one that to a great extent functions as an allegory for his own career in the industry, *In a Lonely Place*, it is the search for a different cinema in which a screenwriter imagines a practice of Hollywood filmmaking without compromises, beholden only to love.

The chapters in this collection explore in various ways Nicholas Ray's own place in the history of the Hollywood institution and in the larger institution of cinema. Few American filmmakers of the 1950s invested genre conventions and familiar narrative frameworks with as much idiosyncrasy as Ray; and few imagined, with equal passion, that such normative tropes could be harnessed to create an alternative vision of things. Ray made films that fall in well-traveled generic territories, including the "lovers on the lam" film (*They Live by Night*), the morally ambiguous shadings of *film noir* and the crime picture (*In a Lonely*

Place, On Dangerous Ground, Party Girl), the landscapes of the American West (*The Lusty Men, Johnny Guitar, Run for Cover, The True Story of Jesse James*), the frontlines of World War II (*Flying Leathernecks, Bitter Victory*), the domestic angst of American suburbia (*Rebel Without a Cause, Bigger Than Life*), an almost ethnographic fascination with exotic cultures (*Hot Blood, Wind Across the Everglades, The Savage Innocents*), the spectacular period epic (*King of Kings, 55 Days at Peking*), and even early-career ventures into the "women's picture" (*A Woman's Secret, Born to Be Bad*), and the social problem film (*Knock on Any Door*). Yet Ray's best films ultimately exemplify his ability to capture that idiosyncratic (and sometimes entirely accidental) gesture, glance, or movement that threw the trajectory of the conventional Hollywood film off course—or at least inflected that trajectory with a sensibility that, for as long as the film itself was on the screen, fundamentally refigured it.

The philosophy behind this collection is that Ray's films continue to possess this vital power, and that as experiences they continue to possess the ability to intervene in the histories we write, in the criticism we craft, and the society we critique. Indeed, Ray's films might be more vital today than they ever were given that appreciation of initially neglected works, such as *Johnny Guitar* and *Bigger Than Life*, has only intensified with time. Thus, this collection demonstrates the value of Ray's work to our present-day cinema culture. Even if Ray's films were a crucial part of this culture in the United States and France in the 1950s and 1960s, the relative dearth of academic scholarship on Ray (compared to other directors at work in Hollywood at the time) suggests contemporary film studies has forgotten some of the pleasures and insights from which it was born. However, Ray's films are not simply a part of an already articulated film history; nor do they formally "cue" us to discover a meaning already hidden within. Instead, they invite us to become collaborators (much as Ray did with his actors), revealing meaning as viewers bring their own passions to the screen. His films are not simply a part of our culture, then; they have much to teach us about what the phrase "cinema culture" *means*—what the potential of such a culture might *still* mean to us. What does it mean to have an encounter with cinema, with its history, with its most personal visions and tumultuous collaborations? What was possible in the Classical Hollywood cinema during its transition (still ongoing) to the contemporary? How do Ray's films—and their pleasures—teach us to write about history, theory, and genre? The authors in this book probe how intimate engagements with Ray's films reveal the ongoing, dynamic potential of cinema culture to a contemporary academic audience. In this respect,

Ray's films, like their director (a teacher near the end of his life), have much to show us about what a cultivated cinema culture in and beyond academia might still achieve, indeed what it might *be*.

The collection begins with Jonathan Rosenbaum's revision of his 1981 essay, "Looking for Nicholas Ray," on the myths and legends that surround Ray's career and his post-Hollywood sojourns into independent and experimental filmmaking. Rosenbaum's essay shares priceless anecdotes from his contact with Ray in the 1970s, and reflects on the director's body of work as a whole. Next, in chapter 2, "Nicholas Ray: The Breadth of Modern Gesture," Joe McElhaney takes both a wide and focused look at several Ray films, finding both concrete and figurative gestures in Ray's films that relate to a specific postwar American film context in which the human figure must increasingly bear the weight of the contradictory social forces being enacted in the films.

The next several chapters bring new critical perspectives to Ray's earliest, and in some cases his most critically neglected, films. In chapter 3, "Economies of Desire: Reimagining *Noir* in *They Live by Night*," Ria Banerjee explains how Ray's young lovers in his first film reconceptualize what it means to live in a *noir* world, developing an alternative way of negotiating the geography of *noir* and defining its parameters. Meanwhile, in chapter 4, "*Knock on Any Door*: Realist Form and Popularized Social Science," Chris Cagle points to Ray's early intervention into the social problem genre as a pivotal text in the analysis of popularized social science in social realist cinema. Rather than reading through genre to locate the "real" Nicholas Ray, Cagle studies Ray's relationship to the social problem genre in its own right. And in chapter 5, "'I've Got the Queerest Feeling' about *A Woman's Secret* and *Born to Be Bad*," Alexander Doty claims that two of Ray's most forgotten films, often framed as mere genre efforts in a career of more distinctive masterpieces, are in fact examples of Ray's ability to queer the traditional American studio film, opening spaces for some degree of nondemonized representation of different gendered and sexual identities.

Several of the authors investigate Ray's complex work with genres. In chapter 6, "Something More than *Noir*," Steven Sanders looks at the multigeneric nature of *In a Lonely Place*, arguing that Ray's celebrated collaboration with Humphrey Bogart and Gloria Grahame is both a representative example of the *noir* genre and a film whose rich implications go well beyond *noir*. R. Barton Palmer, in chapter 7, "*On Dangerous Ground*: Of Outsiders," turns his attention to another of Ray's acclaimed *noir* films. Palmer, following Jacques Rivette's praise of the "mistakes" in *On Dangerous Ground*, locates in the film's roughness an

oppositional, against-the-grain quality that represents Ray's own "force of personality." If *In a Lonely Place* and *On Dangerous Ground* are two of Ray's most highly regarded genre films (and two of his most personal works), *Flying Leathernecks*, by contrast, has been both poorly received by Ray *auteurists* and generally neglected in scholarship on the director. Tony Williams redresses this situation in chapter 8, "*Flying Leathernecks*: Color and Characterization," reading Ray's intuitive use of color in this World War II film and the relationship of the director's choices in color to the ideological positions carved out by the film's two central characters, played by John Wayne and Robert Ryan.

The next two authors interpret how Ray's films mirror, shape, and were shaped by myths and experiences in rural America. In chapter 9, "*The Lusty Men* and the Post-Western," Neil Campbell frames Ray's film about rodeo cowboys as a key forerunner of what he defines as the "post-Western," a type of modern film of the New West, symptomatic of the nation's postwar desire for stability and consensus and a renewal of family values (epitomized in the American Dream of homeownership). *The Lusty Men* reinvigorates old myths by helping to develop a new narrative form for a new age, but Ray's work on this and other films also reflects his pre-Hollywood experience of America. In chapter 10, "Citizen Nick: Civic Engagement and Folk Culture in the Life and Work of Nicholas Ray," James I. Deutsch and Lauren R. Shaw examine Ray's various jobs with the U. S. government in the late 1930s and early 1940s, work that brought Ray into contact with many important currents in American folklore, music, and theater. Examining archival documents and primary sources, the chapter tracks how Ray's federal service influenced his subsequent career in film.

No collection on Ray is complete without an analysis of Ray's work with actors, and two chapters address performance and the cinematic context of performance in Ray's work. In chapter 11, "A Teacup and a Kiss: Staging Action in *Johnny Guitar*," Murray Pomerance argues that Ray's vibrant Western is an example of the director's facility, in tune with his actors, with filmic orchestration and symphonic form. Looking at key gestures, expressions, colors, and other motifs, Pomerance discusses how Ray worked out lines of complex action and resolution with his actors to form not one more familiar genre film but rather a distinctive, unforgettable cinematic melody. In chapter 12, "'You Can't Be a Rebel If You Grin': Masculinity, Performance, and Anxiety in 1950s Rock-and-Roll and the Films of Nicholas Ray," Paul Anthony Johnson approaches Ray's work with actors, informed by the director's interpretation of the Method, echoed by performative currents at play in rock-and-roll. In turn, as Johnson points out, rock-and-roll embodied the ethos of revolution and rebellions of several of Ray's leading men, including James Dean, Farley Granger, Robert Ryan, and Sterling Hayden.

Ray's sense of place and space provides a stirring filmic world in which his actors shape actions. In chapter 13, "Places and Spaces in *Rebel Without a Cause*," Robin A. Larsen uses phenomenological film theory to explore how the representation of American institutions (such as the school, the home, and the police) expose not only the values of the 1950s but also existing structures that continue to demand conformity and inspire rebellion. In chapter 14, Susan White's essay, "Nicholas Ray's Wilderness Films: Word, Law, and Landscape," the spaces and places in question are the deserts, jungles, swamps, and landscapes of films such as *Bitter Victory*, *The Savage Innocents*, and *Wind Across the Everglades*. Importantly, White also turns her critical analysis of wilderness to a short film Ray directed for the *General Electric Theater* television series in 1955, "High Green Wall."

If Ray was an important figure in Hollywood genre filmmaking, he nevertheless also made crucial contributions to other aesthetic forms crucial to 1950s Hollywood cinema. Will Scheibel examines Ray's deployment of "male melodrama" in chapter 15, "*Bigger Than Life*: Melodrama, Masculinity, and the American Dream." Scheibel argues that *Bigger Than Life*, Ray's critically maligned collaboration with James Mason, tackles the subject of prescription drug abuse as a way to diagnose much deeper masculine insecurities running through popular discourses of the 1950s. In chapter 16, "Ray, Widescreen, and Genre: *The True Story of Jesse James*," Harper Cossar studies Ray's use of new widescreen technology. Ray's *Jesse James* film, his fourth foray into the Western genre and his fifth widescreen film, is for Cossar an example of how Ray served the tropes and strictures of the Western genre in the newly widened Cinema-Scope frame, adapting his approach to close-ups and camera movement to the new format.

Ray's final films in the mainstream industry are examined in a pair of essays. In chapter 17, Adrian Martin grasps Nicholas Ray as a transitional figure in his piece "Disequilibrium, or: Love Interest (On *Party Girl*)." As Martin states, Ray's work, and *Party Girl* in particular, offered "fugitive glimpses" of the modern cinema to come, a crucial part of Ray's appeal to French New Wave filmmakers such as Godard and Truffaut. *Party Girl* is, for Martin, representative of the way Ray's most special works give cinephiles, critics, and especially budding filmmakers intuitions of what the future of their art is to become. If *Party Girl* offers glimpses of the future, Jason McKahan's chapter 18 tells us how Ray films were also firmly grounded in the present. In "*King of Kings* and the

Politics of Masculinity in the cold war Biblical Epic," McKahan sheds light on how the critical reception of the film was framed by discourses of film authorship (through a likening of the film's Jesus figure to an earlier Ray rebel, James Dean) and cold war masculinity. McKahan's essay also underscores how the filmic appeal of *King of Kings* was increased by engaging the gospel text from a contemporary worldview.

Although he was a Hollywood director for most of his career, Ray's "late works" were produced not in Hollywood, but in other, alternative modes, many of them only in a state of unrealized potential. In chapter 19, "As Surely as a Criminal Would Die: Nicholas Ray's *The Doctor and the Devils*," Larysa Smirnova and Chris Fujiwara investigate draft scripts of Ray's adaptation of Dylan Thomas's *The Doctor and the Devils*, written in collaboration with Gore Vidal. They posit this unrealized adaptation functions as a kind of "ghost film" in Ray's *oeuvre*, haunting the films that were actually realized and expressing Ray's ambivalence about his own position as an artist in exile. A work that Ray did realize in his years of exile as a college teacher is examined by Steven Rybin in chapter 20, "The Pedagogical Aesthetics of *We Can't Go Home Again*." Rybin shows how the film participates in the relationship forged between experimental cinema and film studies pedagogy on college campuses in the 1960s and 1970s, offering Ray's students an artistic frame through which to realize their own potential as artists and human beings. The collection closes with a Postscript, a generous contribution by Bill Krohn, "The Class: Interview with Nicholas Ray." One of the final interviews with Nicholas Ray, and never before published in its entirety in English, this collection's postscript is a frank document of Ray's final years. Joining Ray on the set of his final film as director, the short *Marco*, Krohn observes the director working with a new set of students at the Strasberg Institute in New York.

Rather than "applying" conceptual paradigms from critical theory and cultural studies to Ray's films, the authors of the diverse chapters collected in this volume aim to rediscover Ray through close analysis of his films in their various contexts, as works of art, as industrial products, and as cultural artifacts. Together, the authors consider what this rediscovery means for contemporary cinema studies, ranging from studies of film authorship, style, genre, and history, to technology, performance, and politics, to studies of gender and sexualities, film as social document, popular music, and cinephilia. Ray has yet to receive the sustained scholarly attention he deserves. We hope to have corrected that mistake and show how Nick Ray might help academic film studies "go home" to reimagine its culture.

Note

1. Because Ray's films receive copious citation in this volume, we have made the editorial choice not to cite release years inside the chapters but instead to provide a full filmography at the book's end.

1

JONATHAN ROSENBAUM

Looking for Nicholas Ray

From the December 1981 issue of *American Film*. I was quite unhappy with the way this article was edited at the time, which reversed the meaning of a few sentences and made various cuts, and based on what I can remember about all this now, I've tried to restore portions of what I originally wrote, in essence if not verbatim.

—J. R.

❦

FOR BETTER AND FOR WORSE, the life of Nicholas Ray has become the stuff of legends. Ray has been sentimentalized, analyzed, worshipped, dismissed, and debated for what he was and did to such a degree that it has become difficult to hold him in focus.

During his Hollywood career, from 1947 to 1958, he directed seventeen features, from *They Live by Night* to *Party Girl*—a body of work that includes films such as *In a Lonely Place*, *On Dangerous Ground*, *Johnny Guitar*, *Rebel Without a Cause*, and *Bigger Than Life*.

From 1959 to 1969, Ray lived mainly in Europe, where he directed his last three commercial features, all of them in 70mm: a film about Eskimos shot in the Canadian arctic, Greenland, and British and Italian

Figure 1.1. A hero to some, a pariah to others, Ray sought and relished the role of outlaw, of maverick (Mark Goldstein Collection).

studios (*The Savage Innocents*), and two spectaculars produced by Samuel Bronston in Spain, *King of Kings* and *55 Days at Peking*.

Ray's last ten years, from 1969 to 1979, were spent mostly in the United States, during which time he brought only one feature anywhere close to completion: the unorthodox *We Can't Go Home Again*. *Lightning Over Water*, a film about his last months, on which he collaborated with German director Wim Wenders, was completed after he died of brain cancer.

Like the myths surrounding immoderate poets from Arthur Rimbaud to Dylan Thomas, the tall tales that trailed in the wake of Nick Ray have continued to haunt the film communities on both sides of the Atlantic. A hero to some, a pariah to others, Ray sought and relished the role of outlaw, of maverick. He created an outsized portrait of himself during his final years that perhaps no film of his, finished or otherwise, could have expressed or contained. For sixteen years, he directed films that were bigger than life. After that, Ray led a life that was at once larger and smaller than the films he didn't direct.

The first time I met Ray was at the Paris Cinémathèque in the spring of 1973. We were at a private screening of the unfinished *We Can't Go Home Again*, made with several students at Harpur College in

Binghamton, New York—a radically experimental, multi-image statement of political alienation, filmed partly in 8mm, Super 8, 16mm, Super 16, and 35mm, where images are combined with a video synthesizer into one crowded fresco. And I saw him again when he showed the film to a bewildered audience at the Cannes Film Festival shortly afterward.

Then, late one rainy morning in Paris, I found him huddled in front of the Café aux Deux Magots, completely soaked and looking rather pathetic. I had already heard talk about the large doses of alcohol and amphetamines he had recently been consuming, and they had visibly taken their toll. Wearing a black eye patch over his right eye—whose sight had been lost because of an embolism he had suffered in Chicago a few years earlier, while filming portions of the 1969 *Conspiracy Trial* for a never-completed project—he seemed more vulnerable than ever at sixty-one, and virtually a derelict.

There seemed to be only one thing to do. I invited him inside for a drink; he warmly accepted, and promptly ordered a tequila with a beer chaser. I was in the midst of writing an article about him at the time (for *Sight and Sound*) and was full of questions. Yet despite his friendliness and willingness to help, most of my queries were met with protracted pauses and blank stares. There were a couple of significant exceptions to this. When I mentioned having attended a civil rights camp at Highlander Folk School in the summer of 1961, he was full of warm memories about this institution dating back to the 1930s. He also perked up when I remarked that many of his films reminded me of musicals, such as the knife fight in *Rebel Without a Cause*, which made me think of *West Side Story*—at which point he said that he'd dreamed of doing *Romeo and Juliet* as a contemporary musical long before *West Side Story*. And when I mentioned *Johnny Guitar* as another example, he briefly recalled with some pride having done all the dissolves for that film inside the camera.

My biggest disappointment was failing to get him to speak about Frank Lloyd Wright, whose fellowship at Taliesin he had attended in 1933 when he became part of Wright's first batch of students. Having grown up in a Wright house in Alabama that was built only six years later, I assumed this would spark some interest, but he was almost completely nonresponsive and uncommunicative on the subject.

When we got up to leave, Ray invited me to accompany him to the novelist James Jones's place on the Île St.-Louis; I regretfully had to decline because of a prior commitment. It was still raining fitfully along Boulevard St.-Germain as we walked together for several blocks. I offered the shelter of my umbrella, but he politely refused, saying that he had a phobia about umbrellas and their pointed ends because of his single eye.

I later discovered that my conversation with Ray was typical of countless ones he had had with young admirers over the years, when his responses were often minimal or separated by protracted pauses. His early fans included members of the French New Wave—Godard, Rivette, Truffaut, Rohmer, and others—who in the 1950s filled the pages of *Cahiers du cinéma* with extravagant panegyrics for the personal passion they found in Ray's movies, scrawled like a swirling signature across the studio stamps of Columbia, Fox, MGM, Paramount, Republic, RKO, and Warners. Prior to that, a generation of young English critics, headed by Penelope Houston and Gavin Lambert (who later worked for Ray as a scriptwriter), had applauded his debut as a film director, at age thirty-seven, with *They Live by Night*—which, like the subsequent *Rebel Without a Cause*, dealt with a romantic teenage couple on the run.

Shortly after I saw Ray in Paris, he directed and acted in a semicoherent avant-garde sketch about a theater manager for a Dutch movie called *Erotic Dreams*, but then wasn't able to edit the results.[1] The following fall, when he was back in the United States on the East Coast, Tom Luddy of Pacific Film Archives invited him out to Berkeley for a retrospective of his films. "He came out for three weeks," Luddy recalls, "and then it became apparent that he had no place to go, and that he wasn't returning to where I'd invited him from, and he felt like staying. So he stayed on."

Eventually, Ray had the uncompleted *We Can't Go Home Again* shipped out west. Then, as Luddy tells it, "two guys showed up, students, and talked Francis [Coppola] into giving them the editing rooms for *The Conversation* from midnight to eight in the morning. And Nick would sleep in the screening rooms at Zoetrope in the daytime, and then emerge around midnight to edit *We Can't Go Home Again* on Francis's machines."

Over the next month or so, however, many problems cropped up. The old Zoetrope was in a warehouse district of San Francisco, and had a very complicated burglar alarm system that had to be disengaged every time someone went out between midnight and eight. "Whenever Nick went out for drinks and stuff, he *always* managed to trip the burglar alarm," recalls Luddy. "Every time it cost money. And large expenses started appearing for phone calls made between midnight and eight, and the burglar alarm kept going off, and then the editing machine broke and the editors complained, and it became impossible for Francis to support him there."

Luddy called some friends in a film collective called Cine Manifest—the group that later made the independent feature *Northern Lights* (John Hanson, 1978)—which was also located in the warehouse district.

"I was minimizing to them the problems they would encounter with Nick and encouraged them to help him. They had an extra space, and they allowed him to have a couch there and an editing table. He continued working there for a while, and it didn't work out too well: disorderliness, chaos, drinking. I used to go back there to see him, and he'd be zonked out with a gallon of White Almadèn Mountain Rhine wine. Things would break—he'd get into funny situations with things like keys and doors."

Luddy continued, "Then he managed to find a situation in Sausalito for a while which was very odd. It was a big warehouse space with sewing machines and seamstresses, and in the middle of this—there were no partitions—was suddenly a couch, a refrigerator, an editing table, tins of film, and Nick Ray. Right in the middle of a clothing factory!"

Nick would sometimes sit there nearly passed out and say, "Tom, you don't know where I can find $36,000 do you?" I'd say, "No, Nick, you asked about that last night." And he'd say, "How about six dollars? If I had six dollars, I could buy a hamburger and a bottle of Almadèn."

"When I first saw *We Can't Go Home Again*," Wim Wenders told me, "Nick showed it to me on an editing table." (Wenders was editing his film *The American Friend* at the time, in which Ray played the part of an art forger.) "I thought it was pretty revolting. I mean, I was shocked by the amateurish aspect of it, also the sense of destruction that was in there—both together."

"Since then, I've seen it six or seven times," Wenders went on. "Finally, I got to see a new print—at least the image was new, the sound track [sic] was just as lousy as ever—where the image was really brilliant and absolutely mind-blowing. You just have to imagine the sound in order to appreciate it, and you realize just what a great movie is hidden in there. Not even hidden, it's there—you see it."

There are many Nick Ray stories that make the rounds. One involves Ray driving a car in Paris's Latin Quarter during the student uprisings of May 1968 and picking up a couple of radicals. At one point, goes the story, he reaches into his glove compartment, pulls out a gun, and says, "James Dean gave this to me, and I'm passing it on to you because you'll know what to do with it."

Another story is that in the very last shot of *Rebel Without a Cause*, after all the characters have gone, the lone figure who's glimpsed walking up to the planetarium is Ray himself. "You think it's the astronomer, but actually it's Nick," Wenders said. "At least he said to me it was him. In a way, it's no different from his appearance in *We Can't Go Home Again*, trying to kill himself twice. It is in a way on the same level. Because it is totally different from the walk-ons Hitchcock would do. It made me realize how highly private, or, rather, personal his films always were."

"To what extent was *We Can't Go Home Again* a group project?" I asked Tom Farrell, one of Ray's students in Binghamton who worked on the film—and who also served in several capacities on *Lightning Over Water*, including as an actor. "Well," he said, "Nick was the guiding light because we were all students. It was all new to us. We listened to him because of his experience. We were all in awe of him, at least for a time, and then gradually people got turned off by Nick's megalomania. He had a free labor pool, you know, and at the beginning everyone was willing to work all day long. But he took advantage, he was asking too much of everyone."

"I think in America there is a certain puritanism that an artist has to comply with," Chris Sievernich, the German producer of *Lightning Over Water*, told me, "It's reflected in contracts—you can get fired for being drunk or for using obscene language. In a way, I think, in Europe, there's somehow more generosity towards the freaky artist, the drunken artist, the crazy artist. In America there's a tendency for a person like that to be clean and straight and have a straight sense of business. You can fight with your lawyer, but you never hand out bad words to your producer. Nick just wasn't that type—he was a man of discussions, of endless, riotous discussions."

"Even in the good old days," said Laslo Benedek, director of *The Wild One* (1953) and an old friend of Ray's, "when he worked with Bogart [on *Knock on Any Door* and *In a Lonely Place*] and made regular, commercial Hollywood films, he had the reputation of being a difficult director—meaning he didn't take orders willingly from the production department. But as long as these people made money, one could get away with that."

"As much as Nick said that the artist has to expose himself," Tom Farrell insisted, "he was deathly afraid of exposing himself. And when he realized afterwards that he *had* exposed a lot of himself, he tried to keep it from being seen. Without Wim, *Lightning* never would have been finished because Nick would not have allowed it to be shown. It was another of those things—he had a block against showing his own work."

Is that why he never finished *We Can't Go Home Again*? Farrell thinks so: "Even when he talked about finishing during the course of that film, you could tell he was afraid to do it. Because for the first time, Wim actually offered to put up the money, to raise it—he had the resources. And for a while Nick was excited about that, about the possibility of finally finishing. And he had no excuse not to, for Wim offered that. But then he was afraid, he was withdrawing."

A related interpretation of Ray's character can be found in John Houseman's *Front and Center*, the second volume of his memoirs. As someone who worked extensively with Ray in theater and radio, and produced two of his best early features, *They Live by Night* and *On Dangerous Ground*, Houseman has a sense of Ray's origins that is more detailed than most:

> From his year's apprenticeship with Frank Lloyd Wright, Nick had acquired a perfectionism and a sense of commitment to his work which were rare in the theater and even more rare in the film business. But in his personal life he was the victim of irresistible impulses that, finally, left his career and his personal relationships in ruins. Brought up in the Depression, one of a generation with a strong anti-Establishment bias, he had been taught to regard hardship and poverty as a virtue and wealth and power as evil. When success came to him in its sudden, overwhelming Hollywood way and he found himself, almost overnight, living among the rich and powerful with a six-figure income of his own, he was torn by deep feelings of guilt, for which his compulsive, idiotic gambling ($30,000 lost in one night in Las Vegas) might have been a neurotic form of atonement. (178–79)

What about all of Ray's unrealized film projects during his final years? There was an adaptation he wrote with Gore Vidal of a Dylan Thomas film scenario, *The Doctors and the Devils*, in 1965, not long after he opened a restaurant and nightclub in Madrid. The film was to be produced by Ray himself in Belgrade, with Warner Brothers providing part of the backing. But according to film historian Bernard Eisenschitz, who is researching a detailed biography of Ray (subsequently published in French in 1990 and in Tom Milne's English translation in 1993), "The project fell through, apparently because the director walked out when the sets had already been built and Maximilian Schell had been signed for the leading role." Among several European projects in the late 1960s was *In Between Time*, a thriller to star Terence Stamp that was prepared over the better part of a year with fledgling French producer Stéphane Tchalgadjieff (who went on to produce major works by Robert Bresson, Marguerite Duras, and Jacques Rivette, among others, including *The Devil, Probably* [1977], *India Song* [1975], *Out 1* [1971], and *Duelle* [1976]).

"He was a great liar," said producer Chris Sievernich, who knew Ray only during the final months of his life: "He lied about everything one could lie about—it was a game somehow, I always felt. He just wanted to try out people. I think he conned a lot of people into money and projects and advances on projects. He traveled around, you know, and since he was Nick Ray, it was fairly easy to survive, I believe, within the European film community, where he was highly respected and regarded."

Perhaps the most often discussed unrealized Ray projects in the United States were his film about American justice (which led him to Chicago to film the *Conspiracy Trial* and material relevant to the murder of Fred Hampton, where he met his future wife, Susan Schwartz) and *City Blues* (with Rip Torn and Marilyn Chambers) in the mid-seventies. Yet despite Ray's intermittent work as an actor in *The American Friend* (Wim Wenders, 1977) and *Hair* (Milos Forman, 1979)—playing a U.S. army general—none of his countless plans for directing films ever took shape. Even after he joined Alcoholics Anonymous and stopped drinking in 1976, it was too late for his luck to change; as many have pointed out, he had simply burned too many bridges by then.

In *Lightning Over Water*, Ray in his Spring Street loft in Soho describes to Wenders the film he would like to make—the film that he initially hoped *Lightning* would be: "This is a film about a man who's an artist, sixty years old. He's made a lot of money in the art world on his early paintings. He's not been able to sell his current output, and he has another great need, besides money, which is to regain his own identity as fully as he can before he dies. He is fatally ill with cancer and knows it. To regain his own paintings, he steals them, as well as forging his work and trying whenever possible to replace what he steals from museums with his forgeries. This is what he enjoys doing the most."

"If you look into it analytically," I was told by Benedek, who was present during part of the shooting of *Lightning*, "I think this idea for a film has something to do with all these fantasies he had about making films—at a point where he knew subconsciously that this *was* a fantasy." According to Sievernich, "He lived on his projects. I think in a way he was very creative in developing and expanding ideas, but maybe he didn't have the follow-through energy any more. It takes a lot, once you're completely out of the grind. And I don't think he was uncomfortable with his situation; I think he enjoyed tremendously being the rebel."

When Benedek, chairman of the graduate film department at New York University's School of the Arts, invited Ray to teach a summer school directing workshop in 1977—a course that Benedek himself had designed, which involved working with actors—a cautionary meeting was held that included the two of them, the associate dean, and the head of the undergraduate film school. "Not more than two minutes went by," Benedek recounted, "when Nick said, 'Gentlemen, I know exactly why you want to see me. So let me put my cards on the table. I'm not drinking. I've been to AA and I'm still going, so let's just have this question out of the way.' Of course, I was deeply moved by this, because I knew it wasn't easy."

After that course, Ray was offered a regular job at NYU teaching third-year film production students. By that time, he had already been operated on for lung cancer. "The trouble was, his health deteriorated much faster than he or we thought it would," Benedek said. "It was difficult for him to keep the schedule of assigned hours. What helped a great deal was that three or four students really fell in love with him, picked him up at home, took him to school, and helped him physically in every way."

"And what happened in class was that—I must tell you—he was absolutely brilliant," said Benedek: "His function as a teacher was in a way limited by his physical weakness, and concentration for two hours was very difficult for him. But certain people profited a great deal, and were inspired by him—mostly the kind of students who didn't keep asking, 'What do you think will sell now in Hollywood?'—nor the ones who thought they knew it all. The freedom and respect that he gave to actors was actually—I don't want to be highfalutin'—but it was a spiritual teaching. Anyone who was willing to take that benefited a great deal from Nick."

The last time that I saw Nick in a social situation was in December 1977. Along with two mutual friends, we decided to meet for dinner at the Spring Street Bar, less than half a block from Ray's Soho loft.

When Ray arrived, I found the change in his appearance and manner startling. In place of the gypsy-like outfits he had favored in Paris, he was dressed in a conservative blue suit, wearing glasses instead of an eye patch, and his speech patterns were reasonably brisk. He was full of enthusiasm for at least a couple of film projects, and most of the conversation remained light and inconsequential.

I reminded him that I'd grown up in a Frank Lloyd Wright house, and sparked by this information, and with much encouragement on my part, he proceeded to relate the story of his tempestuous falling out with Wright—a rift that was apparently patched up to some extent afterward.

It was a classic Nick Ray anecdote, full of macho hyperbole, bluff, and braggadocio. It involved a fairly modest architectural suggestion or question on Ray's part that had provoked the full wrath of the great man's conceit. This curious thing about this tale now, as I try to remember it less than four years later, is that the actual details of the encounter between Ray and Wright remain only shadowy sketches. What persists with extraordinary vividness is Ray's *performance* of those details, using mainly his voice and his hands—a kind of expressionist *mise-en-scène* of temperaments and emotions, abrupt and staccato and full of his and Wright's sound and fury, delivered with remarkable restraint and economy in a few bold gestures.

Only much later did it occur to me that by finally fulfilling my request for an anecdote about Wright, Nick was at the same time exposing the vanity of my desire to hear one in the first place. What he actually gave me had nothing permanent about it, and that was both its poignancy and its power. With a few deft strokes, he had created an imaginary Nick Ray movie, as passionate as *Johnny Guitar*, that quickly vanished into empty space.

Note

1. Editors' note: The title of Ray's sketch is *The Janitor*, and Bill Krohn also discusses it in the postscript to this volume; the Dutch film *Erotic Dreams* is occasionally referenced in Ray scholarship by its alternative title, *Wet Dreams*.

2

Joe McElhaney

Nicholas Ray
The Breadth of Modern Gesture

In the films of Nicholas Ray, people stagger, trip, fall. *Rebel Without a Cause* famously opens with the image of a drunken Jim Stark (James Dean) falling down on the sidewalk and curling into a fetal position. But Ray's characters also get back up again, or they are helped back up. At the end of *Rebel*, and after the death of Jim's friend Plato (Sal Mineo), a distraught Jim, again on the ground, clutches the legs of his father (Jim Backus) standing next to him. "Stand up," his father gently instructs him. "I'll stand up with you." As the father says these words, he gently pulls Jim up to an unsteady vertical position.

All of these images of falling and rising give voice to the constant problem of equilibrium in Ray's work. How does one keep things in balance (including one's own body) when engaged in a violent, anxious struggle to understand the relationship between oneself and the world? Such a struggle is far from unique to Ray. It is central to postwar cinema, American and otherwise, and is manifested in several ways. Jacques Rancière, for example, argues that the act of falling in Roberto Rossellini's films of this period is a way for Rossellini to "fix the indiscernible presence of the incorporeal in the corporeal in the movement of an

Figure 2.1. *On Dangerous Ground* (RKO Radio Pictures, 1952): The hand and the act of gesturing are embedded in the very form and structure of the film, and Ray frequently frames in such a manner that the hand becomes dominant (frame enlargement).

ascending, descending, or falling body" (130). The same year that *Rebel Without a Cause* was released (1955), Jacques Rivette published "Notes on a Revolution" in *Cahiers du cinéma*. For Rivette, the violent content of much of this new American cinema was symptomatic of the desire to not simply testify to the contemporary world but also to create a new type of modern filmmaking in which "violence is the external sign of rupture" ("Revolution" 95). Classical filmmaking is giving way to a modernism that is paradoxically tied to a much earlier form of cinema, to a silent era prior to the streamlined developments the Hollywood studio system fostered. These new postwar filmmakers are involved in "the rediscovery of a certain breadth of gesture, an externalizing of the roughest and most spontaneous emotions; in short, the rediscovery of naïveté" (96). In this brief essay, Rivette isolates several filmmakers as being major examples of this trend: Robert Aldrich, Richard Brooks, Samuel Fuller. But it is the "spontaneously poetic" (96) Nicholas Ray who, for Rivette (and indeed for an entire generation of French critics and filmmakers), best exemplifies this new cinema. Two years prior to this essay, in a review of *The Lusty Men*, it is Ray alone who is praised by Rivette for Ray's "search for a certain breadth of modern gesture" ("Imagination" 105).

The gestures at work in Ray—violent, "naïve," and rupturing the classical surface of these films—are not simply those the actors give life to. They are also expressed in the editing rhythms and through a camera with its frequently nervous and unexpected framings and movements. In *The Lusty Men*, Wes Merritt (Arthur Kennedy) tells his wife Louise (Susan Hayward) that he wants to leave their ranch and join the rodeo, an ambition Louise strongly opposes. They are sitting on their bed in medium shot as Wes makes his announcement and in the midst of this he takes off his hat and casually places it on the bed. While still arguing with Wes, Louise quickly and angrily grabs his hat and throws it on the floor. The camera follows this gesture with a close, rapid panning movement that intensifies Louise's anger but also short circuits Wes's attempts at casualness in placing his hat on the bed. In *Party Girl*, the criminal lawyer Thomas Farrell (Robert Taylor) violently throws a cigarette lighter down on the table at a gangster, Louis Canetto (John Ireland). As Farrell performs this, the camera's tilting movement literally follows the lighter, in medium shot, as Farrell tosses it down on the table. Written descriptions do not render such moments with the kind of force they have in the film itself. Ray's methods are neither the classical ones of a Howard Hawks, in which the elegant gestures and movements of the actors are handled in discreet medium shots; nor are these the methods of a Fritz Lang, where gesture is typically iconic and in which the hand in close-up (particularly via the insert shot) assumes a privileged function within Lang's rigorous formalism.

It is highly unlikely, for example, that either Hawks or Lang would have allowed for the cutting in relation to gesture that occurs at one point in *Johnny Guitar*. As Emma (Mercedes McCambridge) and her gang stride into Vienna's, the saloon's dealer Eddie (Paul Fix) reaches for his gun. The gesture is handled in two separate shots, the first a medium shot, as Eddie sits at a table playing cards and his right hand reaches for the gun. In the middle of this gesture, there is a cut to a closer shot of Eddie; but in the second shot, both left and right hands reach for the gun. It is a strange kind of discontinuity at work here, "sloppy" in comparison with Hawks or Lang: "The editing is jerky," François Truffaut noted in an otherwise favorable review of the film ("Certainty" 142). But the surprise of the cut here, which works to both mismatch and slightly overlap a simple action, gives the gesture an indelible nervous intensity. Throughout Ray, the framing, editing and, movement of the camera constitute a form of cinematic gesturing, a physical "writing" with the camera that occurs in tandem with the gestures of the actors. In *On Dangerous Ground*, as Brent (Ward Bond) is about to slap Mary (Ida Lupino), the camera is placed in the position of her face until the hand of the policeman Jim Wilson (Robert Ryan) comes into the frame and abruptly pulls Brent's hand away. A shot designed to mirror this one occurs near the end of the film. As Mary touches Jim's face, the reverse angle once again is placed in the position of the face that is about to be touched. Mary's blindness, however, complicates reading both of these shots as simple point of view. Brent's hand and all that surrounds it are fully visible in the first of these "point-of-view" shots; and in the second, the eyeline match necessary to confirm that Jim is seeing Mary touching his face exactly from the same position as the camera is complicated by Mary's own eyes searching off, unable to make direct eye contact. The camera at such moments neither records dramatic action nor insinuates itself into a clearly defined point-of-view/eyeline match structure. Instead, the camera becomes a type of physical being, a point of mediation for the bodies of the actors. In his review of *Bigger Than Life*, Éric Rohmer argues that Ray's approach to the image is closer to that of a painter "because by slightly slowing the pace or by accelerating it a bit too much, by inserting a pause that lasts perhaps not more than a fraction of a second, he is able to give the simplest gesture an eternal quality, thereby making it as expressive as it is handsome" (143).

Accelerations, pauses, fractions of seconds. And the eternal. When Eddie reaches for his gun, does the editing slow down time or accelerate it? It is difficult to say. We are dealing with characters caught up in paradoxes of time, who live intensely in the present moment even while such moments are predicated on relationships to pasts and futures that are not simply personal but historical and cosmic. The apocalyptic commentary in the Griffith Observatory sequence from *Rebel Without a Cause* could not be more explicit about this, with its references to the "trivial problems of man" when placed in relation to "the immensity of our universe, and the galaxies beyond" and in which "man, existing alone, seems himself an episode of little consequence." The voice-over narrator at the beginning of *The Savage Innocents* draws attention to the fact that the Eskimos of the Atomic Age continue to hunt with bow and arrow, within a land of "eternal" ice and in which one-third of the year is spent in darkness: "She knows the future because she knows the past." This is the narrator speaking again, much later in the film, about the grandmother (Anna May Wong), who insists on being left alone by her family in the frozen landscape to a certain death, after she has ceased to be useful: "And her knowledge of life allows her to understand. She accepts without bitterness nature's eternal tragedy: that the flesh may perish so that the flesh may live." The grandmother sits alone on the ice, her body almost entirely immobile, as she submits to being killed by a polar bear. This cruelly achieved wisdom may be the logical end point of Ray's characters and of their relationship to the world. But how did they get to such a point in the first place?

"Live fast, die young, and leave a good-looking corpse" is the much-quoted line uttered in *Knock on Any Door*, and it epitomizes this need in Ray to exhaust one's entire physical being within a highly compressed period of time and a world seemingly there for the taking. The Scottish/Irish folk ballad "I Know Where I'm Going" serves as the plaintive and ironic love theme to Ray's first film, *They Live by Night*. However, in order to know where one is going in this world, in order to move or gesture with any kind of assurance, one must first be grounded, both physically and emotionally. In *Rebel Without a Cause*, Jim asks a group of high school students directions to the school, and they respond by pointing him in totally contradictory ways, a silly prank that is nevertheless indicative of the film's depiction of an unsettled adolescent landscape. In *The Lusty Men*, a problematic competitive horse is named Politician because "he doesn't know where he's going." It is symptomatic of this world, then, that characters often have difficulty simply in walking. Jeff (Robert Mitchum), early in *The Lusty Men*, walks across the rodeo yard at dusk, papers flying around him, with a limp brought on by his rodeo injuries; this limp becomes a permanent condition for Farrell in *Party Girl*, who walks on crutches (often theatrically, especially in the courtroom) and whose duties include defending the gangster Rico Angelo (Lee J. Cobb), who is suffering from incipient paralysis.

In two of Alfred Hitchcock's most notable films from this period, *Rear Window* (1954) and *Vertigo* (1958), James Stewart portrays a character also suffering from a limitation in his physical mobility. Such a limitation is also clearly meant to serve as metaphor for a neurosis no less paralyzing in its nature than what one finds in Ray's characters and in which the act of falling, particularly in the latter film, assumes great importance. However, Hitchcock places and contains this "unstable" psychology within a brilliantly precise, carefully constructed conception of the cinema. Ray's films, on the other hand, often "stumble" in a manner that echoes not only the gestures and movements of its actors but also the shape and movement of the films themselves. The producer John Houseman's feeling that *On Dangerous Ground* was made up of "two halves that never really came together" (*Front* 326) is symptomatic and does not take into account the degree to which that film (and indeed much of Ray in general) is organized by another logic, one built on a kind of poetic and musical structure of visual echoing and rhyming effects. *Time*'s review of *The Lusty Men* complained that its screenplay developed a "limp" (qtd. in McGilligan 238), the reviewer failing to recognize that this limp becomes a metaphor for (if not a structuring principle of) Ray's approach to filmmaking, one with little patience for observing the niceties of classical construction and dramaturgy. Bernard Eisenschitz's claim for *In a Lonely Place* that "Ray lets scenes be guided by the characters' moods, by the revelation of imperceptible shifts in their relationships" (141) is one that could be applied to any number of Ray's films.

Nevertheless, the desire for order and "normality," most strongly articulated through the formation of the couple, the family, and through homeownership, is a perpetual thread in Ray. It is a desire articulated with a full poetic force even as the films simultaneously demonstrate the impossibility of just such a desire. The failure of the violent Dix (Humphrey Bogart) in *In a Lonely Place* to understand the logic of a grapefruit knife, straightening its curved form and holding the knife in his hand in a fistlike, stabbing gesture as he attempts to section the grapefruit, lays the seal of doom on his marriage proposal to Laurel (Gloria Grahame) even before the proposal itself is uttered. In both *Run for Cover* and *Party Girl*, women reach for something on the stove (coffee in the former film, cocoa in the latter) and burn their hands; in *Party Girl* the burning of her hand prompts Vicki (Cyd Charisse) to go into the bathroom for a bit of first aid only to discover that her roommate, lying in a pool of blood and water in the bathtub, has slit her wrists. The world of domestic interior spaces is marked by a constant fragility where the characters often literally lose their balance and must hold on to whatever is most immediately at hand. The young sister of the murdered girl in *On Dangerous Ground* holds on to a wooden stud in the family living room, standing very still with her face almost blank, as though this bit of architecture is the only thing that offers comfort in the aftermath of witnessing her sister's murder. The Avery home in *Bigger Than Life* is one in which Ed Avery (James Mason) doubles over in pain and holds himself on the refrigerator door; or, the same night, falls as he tries to leave the house, clutching the door frame as he does so, inadvertently pressing down on the buzzer as his wife Lou (Barbara Rush) puts her hand over his, trying to pull him away.

"I'll never get close to anybody," Judy (Natalie Wood) defensively declares in the opening of *Rebel Without a Cause*. Plato's body in the opening at the police station is withdrawn, as he hugs himself in a posture that equally indicates a need to keep people away. But, in fact, the need to be touched and to reach out toward someone is crucial to this cinema: Jim's reaching out to Judy, standing precipitously on the edge of a cliff after her boyfriend's car has just plunged into the ocean, is an emblematic moment from the film. The first extended sequence between Bowie (Farley Granger) and Keechie (Cathy O'Donnell) in *They Live by Night* culminates with a farewell handshake. Bowie extends his hand toward her in a conventional manner but Keechie reacts by delicately placing her hand, fingers close together, in his. She looks down at their hands, pulls hers away as though suddenly aware of the spontaneous intimacy of what she has done, while Bowie keeps his hand extended for just a second before also withdrawing. This beautiful moment condenses the need in Ray, both defensive and acute, to be physically close to another person, even as the social and material world continually interferes with such a need. The most shocking bit of violence in *They Live by Night* occurs when Bowie rebuffs the jeweler (Will Lee). Oblivious to the fact that Bowie, sitting in a parked car, is in the midst of a bank robbery, the jeweler leans into Bowie's rolled-down window (where the jeweler rests his hands) and attempts to continue a friendly conversation with Bowie from the day before. Unable to get rid of the lonely man, Bowie makes a karatelike chop at the jeweler's knuckles and then pushes him to the ground. The look of pain on the jeweler's face as he withdraws his hands implies a hurt that is more emotional than physical, as though he cannot comprehend this aggressive rejection.

Throughout Ray, gesture is so often poised between violence (if not murder) and tenderness. *On Dangerous Ground* is perhaps the most sustained of the films in terms of this idea. The opening images of a woman's hands reaching for a holster on a bed, the camera tilting and panning as she does so, the hands tenderly caressing the holster and then, tracking with her as she walks across the room to put this around her husband, establish the film's concerns with great clarity. As she puts the holster around her husband, Ray cuts to a medium two-shot of them in which we see their faces for the first time and are able to observe the tenderness and eroticism of this act, the wife running her hands along her husband's back and chest as she helps him: "Oh, Pete. I don't like bein' alone." From this moment on, the intense need to be physically touched, and in any manner, manifests itself in various ways: the pharmacist (Jimmy Conlin) giving a massage to the shoulder of the policeman Pop (Charles Kemper); the playful punch under the chin that Pop gives to Jim as he says goodbye to him; the clear state of arousal that Myrna (Cleo Moore) experiences in being assaulted by her boyfriend, Bernie (Richard Irving), proudly displaying the bruises to Jim; or the equally intense psychosexual arousal that Bernie expresses as he goads Jim into hitting him. The hand and the act of gesturing are embedded in the very form and structure of the film and Ray frequently frames in such a manner that the hand becomes dominant. As Jim moves toward Bernie in Bernie's hotel room, for example, Bernie is seated at the rear center of the shot and Jim is at the far left; but Jim is framed only below the chest, his arm poised at his waist waiting to strike and his face is out of the frame, so that his hand assumes prominence in the foreground as he moves slowly toward Bernie. This shot is echoed later in the film with our first extended glimpses of the young killer Danny (Sumner Williams), holding a knife in the far left of the frame, his face not yet visible.

The presence of Mary (arriving almost exactly halfway into the running time) crystallizes many of the issues at stake. Her blindness, while authentic, also serves as a metaphor for a world dominated by characters who have seen too much, who cannot process the horrors that they witness, and flail "blindly" at the events around them. Jim is clearly the central figure in this regard, and his out-of-control responses to what he witnesses as a policeman are strongly played out through physical violence. "What did I tell you about being so free with your hands?" Captain Brawley (Ed Begley) warns Jim early in the film. When Jim begins beating Bernie, the moment of physical contact is not directly shown but instead Ray films Jim's punching gestures from a low-angled position, the victim not even in the shot, so that Jim seems to be hitting at something abstract, literally absent at the moment. The connection Jim eventually makes with Mary is predominantly one of sustained acts of nonviolent touching that are tied to a deepening of perception on his part. Throughout the film, the words "hands," "alone," and "lonely" recur, as though there is an implied link between them, and the first meeting between Jim and Mary is dominated by these words. "May I touch your hand?" she asks Jim, and she strokes it for a few seconds as they talk. Mary literally feels her way around the interior spaces of her home, largely thanks to Danny's organization of this space for her. At the center of this space is the tree trunk that Danny has brought in for her (and which distinctly evokes the wooden stud in the home of the murdered girl), and both Jim and Mary hold on to this as she hesitates in telling him the truth about her brother. "If only I could see you," she tells Jim as she touches his face.

When Jim must finally confront Danny, he attempts to calm him by saying, "I don't have anything except my hands." This ironic echo of the earlier assault on Bernie, where Jim likewise "only" had his hands, points to a transformation on Jim's part, in which his hands are now graced with the potential for healing and being healed. Such potential is quickly thrown off course as Danny escapes and runs to the top of a cliff only to fall to his death, his hands giving out as he attempts to clutch a rock. Brent's response to this fall, though, is what lifts this moment to another dimension. Unprepared for just how young Danny is, and finally looking at him for an extended moment, Brent picks up and carries the boy back to the authorities. Ray will return to this image of one man carrying another in *Bitter Victory*, *Wind Across the Everglades*, and *The Savage Innocents*. But the *Pietà*-like nature of this moment in the earlier film is remarkable for the implication of the profound and immediate ability of Brent to forgive the young man who murdered his daughter. The film, like Jim himself, is driven by a need to cleanse, to redeem. After Jim has had sex with Myrna and beaten her boyfriend, he returns to his apartment (where a crucifix sits on the dresser, amidst athletic trophies) and washes his hands, aggressively using a towel to dry them off, as though he is unable to wipe away the sense of dirt and guilt.

King of Kings is a culmination of some of the underpinnings of *On Dangerous Ground* and the other films but played out within the logic of a religious epic. Here Ray was working within the economic and production circumstances that would eventually be central in destroying his career as a director in Hollywood. In one sequence, the extended hand of Jesus (Jeffrey Hunter) passes over a physically disabled boy and the boy's hands and feet heal in close-up; the boy gets up, tries to walk, falls, but (like a typical Ray character) gets back up again. In a sequence in a market square, a madman runs toward Jesus, clutching at him. But by embracing the man, Jesus causes him to slowly fall to the ground, where the madman kisses the hand of Jesus. And it is Robert Ryan who plays John the Baptist, crawling up a prison wall to reach Jesus at the window before John falls back down, the hands of Jesus twice shown in close-up as they attempt to reach out to John: all of this reaching out, touching, healing, falling and getting back up, and falling again, all of this need for a profound connection to the world expressed through the physical. The name given to the central female character of *On Dangerous Ground* cannot be unintentional, a "cleansing" of Myrna into Mary, and it is Mary who is the one character shown praying at the end of the film over the dead body of her brother. But Mary herself also must fall, and in Jim's presence, when she is no longer able to negotiate her way around the living room, due to Danny's death. The very objects he created for her, that allowed her to "see," now impede her movements, render her blind once again, and she stumbles and falls to the floor. Mary redeems Jim but her saintliness must be brought down to earth in order for the two of them to eventually become a couple.

The controversial ending Ray insisted on, in which Jim returns to Mary, allows for the film to give itself over to a romanticism that underpins Ray's body of work but is articulated with a fullness here that is in other resolutions aborted or kept in check. But it is not their embrace on the stairs inside of her home that is the ultimate romantic image of the film. It is the image of their hands coming together in the same space, in close-up as she descends the stairs, moving toward him. In a mobile medium shot, she first slides her hands along the railing and then begins reaching out to him with her right hand. He does not, however, speak to her at this moment, using his voice to guide her. Instead, in a reverse shot, he holds out his hand and she intuitively feels for it, the point of contact occurring in close-up, as she slides her hand into his. This moment harkens back to the first tentative handshake between Bowie and Keechie even while it more clearly looks ahead to Jim reaching out to Judy as she stands at the edge of a cliff. But we might also think ahead even further, to John the Baptist attempting and failing to touch the hand of Christ. In each of these examples, it is not simply the need to touch someone else that is important. To touch also involves the gesture of reaching out, of saving or attempting to redeem someone else who is threatened with falling, either morally, physically, or both. But who is redeeming whom in *On Dangerous Ground*? The playing field has, by this point, become relatively equal and their embrace gives both of them a stable (rather than dangerous) ground. However, the final image of the film is one without any human figures in it as Ray dissolves from a close-up of Jim and Mary kissing to a panning shot across the cold, snowy landscape. While the dissolve could easily be read in romantic terms, as an indication of the powerful and transcendent love of the couple, the bleakness of the landscape itself equally suggests a movement toward the inexorable workings of time and the natural world, where the "infinite problems of man" finally dissolve into questions of the eternal.

3

Ria Banerjee

Economies of Desire
Reimagining *Noir* in *They Live by Night*

*F*ILM NOIR IS A GENRE OF INSIDERS. The twisted male protagonist, the *femme fatale*, the mob boss, and the two-bit criminal are recognizable stock figures from genre-defining films such as *Double Indemnity* (Billy Wilder, 1944), *The Maltese Falcon* (John Huston, 1941), and *Criss Cross* (Robert Siodmak, 1949), where these and other characters are knowing participants in the social codes of their diegetic worlds. Rarely does a *noir* begin like Nicholas Ray's first feature film *They Live by Night*, with the assertion that the two main characters have not been "introduced" to the depicted story world. Evil, the consciousness of which suffuses such a world, comes from characters' familiarity with its rules and any attempts to leave crime behind ends in a failure to recapture their own lost innocence. The legitimate, domestic life—depicted so well in another Ray film, *In a Lonely Place*, in the couple Brub and Sylvia—remains a problematic and contested space that is at once alluring to the stock *noir* figure, but also repellent as a symbol of the passivity and boredom of a legitimate union. *They Live by Night* is unique in this regard,[1] as Keechie and Bowie radically reconceptualize what operating as a couple within the *noir* world means. They hope for an escape—not with the desperate, cold sweat of Walter Neff and Phyllis Dietrichson in *Double Indemnity*, but with the fey insouciance usually associated with

Figure 3.1. *They Live by Night* (RKO Radio Pictures, 1948): Keechie and Bowie radically reconceptualize what operating as a couple within the *noir* world means (frame enlargement).

a romance. Never "introduced" to *noir*, they operate outside its conventions and upend the assumptions associated with *noir* love. Closeness drives apart Cora Smith and Frank Chambers in *The Postman Always Rings Twice* (Tay Garnett, 1946), but Bowie and Keechie's closeness is tangibly strong and establishes an alternate economy of desire that admits only the couple. By contrasting the "must be"s of *noir* with the "could be"s the lovers utter, the movie presents an alternate system where desire is not always damaging and hope is not eternally hollow. The film's greatest achievement is to do this without ever abandoning the cinematic conventions of *noir*, and the heightened tragedy of Bowie and Keechie lies in the final reassertion of the dictates of the genre.

Accidents of Release: *They Live by Night*'s Production History

Avoiding censorship was only one of the problems Ray faced in making this movie. In February 1946, producer John Houseman came upon a treatment of Edward Anderson's novel *Thieves Like Us* (1937), which had been previously rejected by the Production Code Administration (PCA). Ray's biographer Patrick McGilligan calls it "a Woody Guthrie song in cinematic form" (117), and thinking this project might be interesting to his friend, Houseman offered Nick Ray the chance to work it into a script that would get past the censors. In August 1946, as McGilligan reports, the PCA rejected Ray's treatment as "'unacceptable' and 'enormously dangerous,' in large part because of the 'flavor of condonation' attached to the character of the young criminal Bowie." Furthermore, "Joseph I. Breen . . . [wrote] a letter condemning Ray's adaptation as 'invidious'" (120). The PCA could not stomach the overarching sense of complicity and guilt that the script highlighted, nor the way it pinned Bowie and Keechie's predicament on rents in the social fabric rather than a result of their individual moral failings.

The year 1946 was the beginning of the end of the Golden Age of Hollywood cinema, when escapist fantasies were no longer doing well with audiences but "problem" pictures and what would later be referred to as *noir* films began to do better (McGilligan 125; J. Harvey ix). As critic Robert Warshow tells us, the gangster became "the 'no' to that great American 'yes,'. . ." which is "stamped so big over [the] official culture and yet has so little to do with the way we view our lives" (106). Sylvia Harvey has suggested that this sense of off-kilter instability in *noir* reflects the frustration of GIs returning home from World War II (39). Not coincidentally, many *noir* protagonists are war veterans (including Dixon Steele from Ray's *In a Lonely Place*, which would come out a few years later); in an interesting metatextual twist, *They Live by Night* was also Farley Granger's first movie after his discharge from the war. The prevailing mood across the country was dark, and low-budget genre films seemed to be fulfilling the mimetic functions of art vis-à-vis life by centering their diegetic worlds at a nexus between robbery, murder, gambling, and prostitution. "*They Live by Night* came about as a result of [MGM head] Dore Schary's wanting to try to make a series of low-budget films with new directors," notes John Francis Kreidl (27), which also included Edward Dmytryk's *Crossfire* (1947) and Joseph Losey's *The Boy with the Green Hair* (1948). The intention was to make a simple B-grade revenue-earner by capitalizing on the emerging popularity of postwar crime films.

What followed was anything but quick and easy. After the PCA's first round of rejection, Charles Schnee, a former lawyer, was called in to work on Ray's 196–page script to pare it down and soften its tone. In June 1947, after many changes, cuts, and more than a year of editing and revisions, the PCA tentatively approved the film. Its working title,

Your Red Wagon, was changed to *The Twisted Road*, and remained thus during filming. However, Howard Hughes's takeover of RKO meant that the new management was wary of older projects, and another year passed before *They Live by Night* was finally renamed and readied for release. David Thomson, film critic of *The Guardian* and a friend of Ray's, blames Hughes for the delay: "RKO owned *They Live by Night*, and Howard Hughes owned RKO and didn't know what to do with the film" ("Nick" 4). That the movie was eventually released is something of a miracle, and Nicholas Ray must be among those few directors whose first film premiered after his second and third productions hit screens, premiering in London in spring 1949.

Kreidl observes that "[s]uch accidents of release dates often have strange positive or negative effects on the careers and reputations of directors; but in Ray's case it seems to have worked to his benefit as the simultaneous appearance of *They Live by Night* and *Knock on Any Door* gave him the immediate reputation of being skilled in showing both sensitivity and toughness" (27). European audiences swooned over this and subsequent films such as *Johnny Guitar* and *Bitter Victory*, with Truffaut calling Ray a "poet of nightfall" ("Certainty" 108). One of the most oft-cited bits of criticism about Ray's work also from this period is Jean-Luc Godard's 1958 proclamation in *Cahiers du cinéma* that "[t]here was theatre (Griffith), poetry (Murnau), painting (Rossellini), dance (Eisenstein), music (Renoir). Henceforth there is cinema. And the cinema is Nicholas Ray" ("Stars" 118). Critical appreciation often compares Ray's debut to another landmark first feature film by another Midwestern American director, *Citizen Kane* (Orson Welles, 1941), although Ray was ten years older than his more famous contemporary. *The Guardian* calls *They Live by Night* the "finest American directorial debut after *Citizen Kane*" ("1000 Films" 7), and McGilligan admits that the comparison was not far from Ray's own mind while filming, spurring his determination to make a movie that was just as good as *Kane*.

The resulting film is a mixed bag of surprises: while never achieving the formal stylistic heights of Welles's masterwork, *They Live by Night* radically reshapes any simplistic conception of *noir*. Less heavily stylized, it nonetheless contains the first aerial shots ever taken from a helicopter: in the opening shot, it follows the three escaped convicts traveling down the road on a sunny day in their getaway car, the blades of the helicopter blowing their hair and clothes around as if in a gale. Neil Jordan, who cites *They Live by Night* as the first movie that made him want to become a filmmaker, notes the "rainy eroticism" of a scene between Bowie and Keechie in the barn, and the technical innovation of the tight, claustrophobic framing that Ray observed being used in newspaper comic strips.

But Jordan's highest praise is for that marvelous opening shot: "Ray just came in and said 'We're going to get a helicopter,' as if it was perfectly normal" (qtd. in Donaldson 10). Biographers note that this combination of an easy manner and a radical, engaged mind was one of the hallmarks of this director.

Thematically, too, in *They Live by Night*, perhaps for the first time, the *noir* style is drenched in the conditional. Bowie and Keechie are young, but their fight is not only a romantic desire to leave the world of their drunk and degenerate relatives. At each stage of their journey, they ask what the other wants, if the other will stay, if the other will continue to love them—and at each stage they enact their desire with the reply, "I want to." Their repeated use of this mode of question and answer creates a linguistic code whose rules are not shared by the *noir* world at large so that, as Kreidl states, "[i]n each case, these films strive toward a resolution, no matter how painful, rather than move rigidly toward a foregone conclusion, as in a classic *film noir*" (30). By basing each step on such an affirmation of desire, Bowie and Keechie create an alternate economy of desire that is very different from the usual *noir* collation of desire with lust and criminality. As the next section shows, *film noir* often uses the metaphor of railway tracks to indicate how the central couple is on a journey from which they cannot diverge.

Hope and the Economy of Desire in *They Live by Night*

In almost every *film noir*, everyday existence is tedious and deadening. Characters routinely refer to the world outside the *noir* circle as a place ideal for the criminal to hide, but it is ultimately dissatisfactory. When Keechie first meets Bowie, he tells her if he "wasn't so hot," he would like to open up a small filling station and garage somewhere. His desire is not unique because *noir* protagonists often long for the quiet life they cannot have. Keechie, thinking that she sees right through Bowie, tries to explode his romantic idealization of life on the right side of the law: "It'd be too slow for you. You want to live your life fast. You don't know what you want." She would have been right if Bowie had been the typical *noir* hero whose ambivalence toward ordinary life compels a move toward the illicit or illegal, such as with Walter Neff or Professor Richard Wanley in Fritz Lang's *The Woman in the Window* (1944). But Bowie is atypical just as is Keechie, her sexual desire for Bowie markedly different from the barroom loves of the formulaic *femme fatale*.

In the standard *noir* formula, the blossoming of love is short-lived and intense, and once the crime has been committed, the couple finds itself facing an inalterable structure of retribution without a means of escape. As Barton Keyes (Edward G. Robinson) tells his protégé in *Double Indemnity*, it is not like taking "a trolley ride together where each one can get off at a different stop. They're stuck with each other. They've got to ride all the way to the end of the line." The criminal act that was so transgressive at first becomes yet another preordained trajectory in a humdrum existence, and the boredom and dissatisfaction that haunted the couple at the beginning of the plot reassert themselves. The relationship falls apart as trust crumbles, ending with the ultimate resolution: death. Even an early *noir* like *Dead Reckoning* (John Cromwell, 1947), whose ending points to what R. Barton Palmer calls the "relentless determinism" (36) of the typical *noir* plot, equates safety and security with boredom, and crime with thrill.

They Live by Night simultaneously reiterates this idiom and distances itself from it. As noted previously, the most crucial difference is indicated in the opening sequence itself, which shows Keechie and Bowie smiling at each other as if in their own private world, with the scrolled words: "This boy . . . and this girl . . . were never properly introduced to the world we live in." The film later implies this might be caused by the circumstances of their childhood, but more crucial than the question of why, is the consideration of what "world" is being invoked. Although Bowie's interaction with the extant world is limited because of his time in jail, his inexperience seems to be chiefly of a sexual nature. Keechie, too, is repeatedly described as a level-headed girl who can manage as required; the gaps in her knowledge are also related to the things "most girls" like to do with their "fellas": Bowie is not Sam Spade, and Keechie no Brigid O'Shaughnessy. The use of the word "introduce" in the opening sequence thus carries with it the implication of a special type of society—and indeed, Keechie and Bowie harbor no illusions about the *noir* world of their fathers (mothers are all but absent here), but they remain unaffected by it. Through Keechie, Bowie realizes that his jail-bred dependence on T-Dub and Chickamaw is a snare, and with her, he creates a new world whose idiom is different from that of the "world" of the film. The rules of this *noir* world are not unclear to them; instead, and more problematically, they are immaterial to the lovers.

This difference asserts itself linguistically at the outset when they first meet. Bowie's bad foot means that he has to stay behind while Chickamaw and T-Dub carry on to the Mobley house to find shelter (the drunken Mobley is Chickamaw's brother and Catherine's father). They send Keechie in an old pickup truck to go get the boy, who has been hiding behind some shrubs. Hearing her engine stalling, Bowie approaches to see a figure almost entirely obscured by a large hat. Indeed, the first time Cathy O'Donnell appears on screen she is in such heavy shadow that she is unrecognizable, and her small angular silhouette looks almost masculine. The conversation that follows is worth repeating, both for its verbal acrobatics and the tart sweetness of their first exchange:

BOWIE: You having trouble?

KEECHIE: Could be.

BOWIE: Who are you? You live around here?

KEECHIE: Could be.

BOWIE: You haven't had a couple of visitors lately, have you?

KEECHIE: That wouldn't be a sore foot making you limp, would it?

BOWIE: Could be.

KEECHIE: I got some other stuff to pick up. Get in or we'll both get pneumonia.

Noir dialogue typically falls on the ear like staccato hail, a breathless exchange that formally reflects the tense nature of the genre. This small snippet is certainly clipped, but Keechie's calm repeated "could be"s have a hypnotic rhythm that Bowie, by the end, catches and repeats.

This conditional tense is not normally part of the *noir* idiom. In the typical *noir*, there is no "could be" about trouble, and characters are fully "introduced" and integrated into the diegetic world. But in *They Live by Night*, this and subsequent speeches clear a space that the two characters inhabit alone, separate from their drunken fathers and uncles, even distanced from the deceitful Mattie and other female bit roles. These two enjoy each other's company with a familiar openness and gladness. Their sexual relationship, which Keechie's pregnancy clearly asserts, is similarly removed from the night club atmosphere inherent to the sensuality of the *femme fatale*. Alcohol, often used in *noir* as a marker of a certain kind of hard living, is entirely absent from their lives. Bowie has a gun (and one cannot forget that he actually killed a man when he was sixteen and running with a carnival), but he is clearly not comfortable using it; the pair even buy a pale-colored convertible, which is a stark contrast to the ubiquitous black town car used by criminals in this and other *noir* films.

With these key indications as markers of their otherness, Keechie and Bowie distance themselves from the entire represented world in the film. As mentioned before, the typical *noir* world holds itself in opposition to the other, larger humdrum one; here, that distinction collapses. People walking in the park or riding horses or playing golf are just as immaterial to the lovers as Chickamaw and T-Dub. Once in the city, Keechie and Bowie decide to make a day of it by going out to eat "just like other people"—echoing the distance that *noir* insists on between those inside and "other people" outside this world. However, once they are outside, they see people riding, and Bowie wonders, "Why do they do it; they're not going anyplace!" Seeing some people playing golf, he again says, "That's something else I never could figure, how anybody could get interested in patting a little ball around!" Keechie laughs, "If they stood on their heads it wouldn't bother me if they were having a good time." Bowie keeps musing: "People sure do act funny, though. You having a good time?" Keechie replies, "Such a good time." This seemingly banal exchange late in the movie actually marks how complete their personal system of signification is, and how little they are interested in understanding "people." Not only are they unlike the criminals of the *noir* world (a little later, the mob boss who runs the supper club easily outmaneuvers Bowie and demands he leave the restaurant), they also mark themselves distinct from the world at large. Suddenly, the carefully wrought distinction between "worlds" disappears and the sunny law-abiding larger world is exposed as being fully implicated in the seedy *noir* subculture.

Importantly, even in their first conversation, neither Keechie nor Bowie sounds tentative or hesitant: the space that opens up between them is not evanescent, nor is it convulsive in the way that *noir* relationships most often are. Here, there is no sense of doomed escape that haunts all *noir* protagonists, the sibilant whisper of failure egging on the likes of Fred MacMurray's Walter Neff or Robert Mitchum's Jeff in *Out of the Past* (Jacques Tourneur, 1947). For a brief while, it seems like Bowie and Keechie will succeed at running away from the deterministic *noir* end because they do not try to subvert the inevitable but sidestep it completely. They remain fundamentally innocent even though they are not childish or uncomprehending.

Keechie and Bowie's ability to manipulate significations and alter meanings runs deep. In their private world, the connotations of objects change, such as in the case of the watch from Zelton. Bowie buys a watch for Keechie as part of the ruse to get inside and learn the layout of the Zelton Bank, which he then helps rob. He only has the chance to give Keechie her present after he gets into a car accident and Chickamaw delivers him, hurt, back to her for safekeeping. The watch, already a stereotypical present from a "fella" to his "girl" as well as the reminder of a crime, should have carried a doubly negative association—Keechie and Bowie are not in any normal relationship, and knowledge of his crime turns her into an accessory and puts her in significant danger. But instead of this, the lovers turn the watch into a symbol of their special relationship. Before giving it to her, Bowie says, "I bought something for you there in Zelton. It's a little ol' watch. Do you want it?" Keechie replies in their characteristic idiom: "Do you want to give it to me?" When he replies "Yes" in all seriousness, she smiles, "Then, yes, I want it." Gift giving, normally an insidious and unidirectional imposition of coded social behavior (gift givers are rarely asked if they want to give a gift; their right to give a gift is mostly taken for granted), is turned here into a series of questions, a sequence of happy conditionals. Instead of setting the time to any other clock, they even decide to change time:

BOWIE: What time do the hands say?

KEECHIE: Five minutes to two.

BOWIE: That's close enough.

Later, Keechie also buys Bowie a watch for Christmas. Then, too, they do not match the hands of the watch to an external timepiece, but intend to set it to match each other's. We are never told if Bowie actually does set the time on his watch; subsequent events put all thought of watches out of the couple's heads.

Sylvia Harvey points out that in *film noir*, "the expression of sexuality and the institution of marriage are at odds with one another, and . . . both pleasure and death lie outside the safe circle of family relations" (42). In *They Live by Night*, this paradigm is reversed in an interesting way. Although Bowie and Keechie are married in the film at a $20 wedding hall (a move made partially to placate the PCA, which repeatedly found the film script "unacceptable" and full of too much "loose sex") enough hints remain to suggest that the two were intimate previously. Furthermore, Bowie's sour expression prompts Hawkins, the officiator, to observe that the young man does not seem to approve of the service he provides. Although getting married has been his own idea, Bowie immediately agrees that he finds the marriage hall a cheap and tawdry place. Hawkins, unmoved by Bowie's disapproval, explains, "My way of thinking, folks ought to have what they want. 'Long as they can pay for it.'" Hawkins sees himself as providing a service for people who need it, selling a little bit of hope that people are willing to pay for.

Hawkins, in other words, is the consummate shopkeeper who sells an idea more than the product itself, and in keeping with the stereotype, he inhabits the liminal space between the *noir* world and the world of "other people."

Keechie and Bowie, however, are not really buying the same thing that he is selling: after they are officially declared man and wife, Keechie kisses her new husband with a romantic abandon that looks completely out of place in their situation and their own recognition of it. Her gesture returns them to a private space, one that they continue to inhabit even after they have left the seclusion of their lodging house for a small bed-and-breakfast in the city. But Hawkins returns at a crucial juncture, when Bowie asks for help running away to Mexico. The latter refuses to help him despite the pile of money offered him:

> HAWKINS: Maybe I did help you before, but not now. I believe in helping people get what they want as long as they can pay for it. I marry people 'cause there's a little hope that they'll be happy. But I can't take this money o' yours. No, sir. In a way I'm just a thief the same way you are, but I won't sell you hope when there ain't any.
>
> BOWIE: No chance?
>
> HAWKINS: None at all.
>
> BOWIE: No place for her and me?
>
> HAWKINS: I don't know of any, son.

Hawkins is money-minded, keeps to the letter of the law, and is not averse to underhandedness when it suits him, and in all this he exactly reflects the characteristics of the "world" to which Bowie and Keechie have not been "introduced." Hope is what Mary Astor's Brigid O'Shaughnessy desperately clings to in *The Maltese Falcon* until Sam Spade sends her on her very last trip to the police station. Brigid recognizes the falseness inherent in her hope even as she simultaneously refuses to let it go: and this is the type of hope that a man like Hawkins sells. Because Bowie and Keechie are looking for something more real, their hope cannot be realized within the filmic world.

The pathos of their situation deepens because Keechie and Bowie so easily sustain their alternate idiom and believe, until perhaps the very end, that they will continue to do so. However, they fundamentally misapprehend the situation they are in. Bowie carries on his person, at all times, a little pouch that contains a paper clipping that T-Dub had given him in jail. It reports that the Supreme Court freed a criminal because there was "no due process of law." Bowie does not seem to understand what the legal phrase means, and instead is convinced that he could see a lawyer in Tulsa who would get him out of his jail sentence. Even Keechie is prey to a similar misunderstanding: pleading with him not to go on a second heist, she says that there are people who run away from the law, hide for years, and are later forgiven after becoming law-abiding citizens. Any audience of *noir* is unlikely to believe such stories, and the couple's sidestepping of the *noir* ethos cannot save them from such a misreading of legal idiom.

The conventions of *film noir* reassert themselves through the appearance of Chickamaw and T-Dub, who force Bowie to do one last job. T-Dub says to Bowie when they reconvene, "The way things are, we gotta keep right on going," in a speech that recalls Barton Keyes's famous lines from *Double Indemnity* quoted earlier. When the young man replies, "Not me," and prepares to walk out, T-Dub drops his avuncular manner and snaps, "So to speak, you're an investment. And you're gonna pay off." T-Dub is the rough obverse of the smoothly polished Hawkins, who also sees the world in similar monetary equations. With the burly Chickamaw standing behind, T-Dub slaps Bowie repeatedly, saying, "You hear me?" At first Bowie resists but eventually is forced to reply, "I hear ya," and looks away. The scenario is a reversal of that first conversation with Keechie in the shadowy truck: here, under the harsh indoor light, these two stock *noir* characters reassert the rules of the genre, the "world" the lovers have thus far circumvented. There must be no more "could be"s; the deterministic universe reasserts itself and continues to the foretold end.

Note

1. Indeed, some critics would class *They Live by Night* as a "road movie" rather than a *noir*. This catch-all genre is built around the idea that "it's the journey itself that matters, as the people, landscapes and experience the voyager encounters along the way lead him to a kind of self-discovery" (Stephen Harvey's "The Road Movie"; see also Michael Atkinson's "Crossing the Frontiers" in *Sight and Sound*, and David Laderman's "What a Trip: The Road Film and American Culture" in *Journal of Film and Video*). Ray's first film is also often discussed in light of *Bonnie and Clyde* (Arthur Penn, 1967) as a heist film, which further distances it from *noir*, or following Kreidl, as a tragic romance. I argue, however, that genres are reinforced by those alternate depictions that question the established modes, such as in *They Live by Night*.

4

CHRIS CAGLE

Knock on Any Door
Realist Form and Popularized Social Science

THE CRITICAL RECEPTION OF Nicholas Ray's work has tended to read *through* the social problem content of his films. This *auteur* reading formation juxtaposed directorial vision and Hollywood assembly line in order to suggest that Ray's authorial voice came in counterdistinction to his social problem film scripts. "It must be remembered," Andrew Sarris admonished, "that *They Live by Night*, *The Lusty Men*, *Rebel Without a Cause*, and *Bigger Than Life* are socially conscious films by any standards, and that *Knock on Any Door* is particularly bad social consciousness on the Kramer-Cayette level" (107). Film critics after the wave of 1970s theory took the opposite approach, valuing the films precisely for their politics, yet they looked not for the stated social problem messages but rather for the "category E" ideological contradictions that might expose the seams in American postwar consensus.[1]

Rather than obscuring the "real" Nicholas Ray, the generic and ideological dimensions of the social problem add a complexity to Ray's films precisely because they cannot always be written off as irony. *Knock on Any Door* exemplifies the social problem film's tendency to adapt film aesthetics to popularized social science discourses circulating in late 1940s. Sarris castigated the film as "thesis filmmaking," but few critics,

Figure 4.1. *Knock on Any Door* (RKO Radio Pictures, 1949) exemplifies the social problem film's tendency to adapt film aesthetics to popularized social science discourses circulating in late 1940s (frame enlargement).

if any, have managed to wrestle with its thesis, an amalgam of approaches to criminal sociology developing in the first part of the twentieth century. Similarly, Ray's early work does not figure large in readings foregrounding ideological contradiction and formal expression, yet *Knock on Any Door*'s narrative inhabits its cultural contradictions as surely as *Bigger Than Life*. Arguably 1950s melodramas seem to refract their ideological meaning because the cultural politics of social conformity are legible in a way that midcentury changes in criminology are not.

Social problems films lack the consistency of some other genres, but *Knock on Any Door* exhibits certain key elements of the genre (Maland, "Social" 306–08). First, the social problem film thematically indicts existing social or political conditions with an eye to reform. Additionally, to the action and psychological subplots typical of classical narrative, social problem films add a central historical conflict that lies outside of the film. They may show narrative closure but still suggest problems that go beyond the diegesis. *Knock*'s narrative is primarily about juvenile delinquency and secondarily about the problem of justice for young criminals.

Nick Romano (John Derek) is a confused youth charged with murdering a police officer; a lawyer, Andrew Morton (Humphrey Bogart), is responsible for defending him against a murder charge. In a manner typical for the problem film, *Knock on Any Door* exhibits formal markers of didacticism, particularly in the courtroom scenes that often place the spectator in the position of the jury. Morton defends Nick on two grounds—first by arguing Nick's innocence in the face of circumstantial evidence and then, when it becomes clear that Nick was in fact guilty, by arguing that Nick's criminality springs from economic hardship. "Nick Romano is guilty," Morton tells the jury in closing argument. "He's guilty of many things. He's guilty of knowing his father died in prison. He's guilty of having been reared in poverty. He's guilty of having lived in the slums." In short, Morton's monologue lays out an environmental determinist for crime.

Politically, social problem films generally spring from a political viewpoint that is both liberal and reformist. For some critics, such as John Hill in his study of the British social problem film, this vantage means the appeal to a middle-class spectator and universalizing of middle-class values. In *Knock on Any Door* this inscription of the professional class vantage is surprisingly explicit. Structurally, the main characters fulfill two functions in the narrative. Adele (Susan Perry), Andrew Morton's love interest, is a social worker representing the reformist sentiment, whereas Andrew represents the professional class's ambivalence toward troubled teenagers: wanting to help but feeling the issue hopeless. Allegorically, charity and the law are two sides to the same necessary approach to the problem. Ideologically, the role of the lawyer character (and Bogart's star image) is to position a skeptical spectator who undergoes the transformation from doubt to belief in the urgency of reform.

The flashback structure carries both the theme and Morton's character development. The present tense narrative follows Nick's crime and indictment, as well as the trial and aftermath. During the trial, a series of four flashbacks covers key turning point moments in Nick's life: the wrongful conviction of Nick's father on a murder charge; Nick's move to a slum neighborhood; his experience in reform school and after, including his romance with Emma; and the impact on his marriage of his failed attempt to go straight. After each flashback, Morton's speeches contextualize Nick's story with their thematic importance by pointing out the deleterious effect of every key life event. Throughout much of the narrative, Nick Romano is plausibly the protagonist who is basically good yet gets caught in circumstances that lead to crime. The Warner Bros. crime cycle of the early 1930s repeated this kind of narrative, and *Knock on Any Door* initially seems to follow this trajectory. However,

Nick's ultimate guilt complicates the evidence of the flashbacks so that the spectator is asked to read both hardened criminal and society's victim in the same person. Concurrently, the flashbacks include events with Morton himself, as he moves from mentorship to disillusionment. The interweaving implicates the law with the problem of Nick's delinquency.

In making the case for the social determinism of crime, the film synthesizes several contemporary discourses of popularized social science. On one hand, the reformist sentiment in the film shows the imprint of Progressive reform sentiment. The Skid Row scene in particular uses a washed-out style shot on fast film stock, its realism invoking an iconography of urban suffering inherited from Jacob Riis's *How the Other Half Lives*. The depiction of the reform school is a muckraking portrait of abuse. (Social problem films of the 1930s, like *Hell's House* [Howard Higgin, 1932], specialized in this issue). More important, the dyad of Adele/reformer and Andy/lawyer is reminiscent of the close relation between social work, public policy, and sociology around the turn of the century.

On the other hand, the depiction of a city as a dynamic and determining social environment owes more to Chicago School sociology than to mere reformism. The Chicago sociologists made the social fabric of the American city their primary object of study and developed an "urban ecology" approach that examined simultaneously material determinants and primary and secondary group interaction (Park et al). The Chicago School serves as the basis for the kind of social-determinist theme of *Knock on Any Door*. Chicago School sociology coincided with the rise of criminology as a scientific subfield, and Edwin Sutherland's research set an agenda of differential association to explain the causes of crime. As Sutherland writes:

> the causal or genetic process through which a particular person or series of persons, regarded individually, became criminals. This is a statement of lifetime processes, running through the entire career of the person, rather than an analysis of the attitudes of a person and the characteristics of his situation at the time of the crime. ("Differential" 45)

The film's emphasis on turning points similarly abstracts Nick Romano's personal life to causal processes of character formation.

In addition to Progressive and Chicago Schools, the depiction of Nick's descent into criminality shows the possible influence of nascent labeling theory, particularly the work of Frank Tannenbaum, who saw self-fulfilling prophesy in social and self-identity as a criminal. This view echoes in Morton's monologue: "We the solid citizens of this community, we photographed and labeled this boy years ago." This version of labeling theory had neither the disciplinary self-critique nor the subjectivist focus on social interaction that labeling theory would represent in the 1960s. Here, it is merely one model of criminal causation among multiple ones.

What is missing, however, is the functionalist approach that emerged in the 1940s and came to dominate postwar sociology of deviance. As a theoretical outlook, the functionalist work emphasized social structure and anomie—the inability for individuals to adapt to culturewide social norms (Short 615–16). Little sense of anomie appears in *Knock on Any Door*, unlike other films in the postwar problem film cycle such as Edward Dmytryk's *The Sniper* (1953). *Knock on Any Door* therefore shows an odd historical lag between the discourses it invokes and postwar social science. The one exception is the confidence the film ascribes to scientific reform. For instance, after one flashback ends on Nick's arrest, Morton discusses reform schools: "The word reform means . . . to improve. It can also mean degrade, brutalize. There are reformatories with modern methods, where the delinquents are looked upon as individuals, with individual problems. And then, there are others, like the one where Nick was sent to. . . ." Charles Maland points to problem films' faith in the solution of problems ("Social" 306), yet this confidence in "modern methods" was the hallmark particularly of postwar functionalism.

The final soliloquy of Morton's closing arguments encapsulates the theme's intellectual pluralism. The lawyer invokes labeling theory: "We're scandalized by environment, and we call it crime." He indicts "society" for the production of criminal deviance. He criticizes the press for sensationalism. He calls for tearing down the slums in order to get rid of poverty and crime, a thesis *Dead End* (William Wyler, 1937) shared ten years earlier. Here, the film's title is explained. "Knock on any door," Morton says, "and you may find Nick Romano." The phrase and the overdetermined cut to a medium shot of a teenager combing his hair are an extreme statement of social determinism.

The social problem discourses in *Knock on Any Door*, therefore, are anything but straightforward. As is often the case in popularized social science, no rigorous or consistent social model is at play, even if sociology's and criminology's intellectual history has a disproportionate impact on the depiction of crime in the problem film. Moreover, some of the lag can be explained by the continued influence of the Chicago School, since those working in the criminology-related fields in the postwar years would have learned from books such as Edwin Sutherland's *Principles of Criminology*. What gave popularized social science of deviance urgency was the confluence of a few factors. Crime, to begin with, became less frequent by the late 1940s, for largely demographic reasons (Patterson

62). Paradoxically, the declining rate could encourage a sense of urgency by contributing to a sense of the problem's ameliorability. Meanwhile, juvenile law had only recently (by the early 1930s) developed into a distinct form, urged by the Progressives (Sutherland, *Principles* 302–04). Finally, the maturation of sociology as an academic discipline gave prestige to scientized approaches to reform.

The contradictions of the social problem thesis are not merely contextual. The film's form builds in hints of self-critique. The narrative treats Nick Romano's life as abstract moments of social causation and inscribes it in the middle-class worldview of Andrew Morton, yet the narrative is ultimately not fully Morton's. The final shot, in particular, a long take in deep focus accompanied by an ending title, frames Morton's back in medium close-up as Nick walks to the electric chair. The shot is curiously de-dramatized, with Nick's emotional reaction central to the shot yet unreadable at a distance. The compositional relation between the two men suggests a moral responsibility between them, but equally Nick is a cipher whose presence indicts Morton/civil society/the spectator for their inability to understand Nick as a person. Fittingly, the nondiegetic music beginning the shot is in a style and volume more reminiscent of transitional music than of a climax.

This closing exemplifies the intrusion of Ray's directorial style. *Knock on Any Door* at points adopts a more authorial narrational stance, exhibiting what David Bordwell in *The Classical Hollywood Cinema* calls the "bounds of difference"—that is, stylistic markers that separate from the presentation of the narrative action to comment on it ("Bounds"). The high-angle shot of the final sentencing works in this manner. Whereas previously the spectator has been visually aligned with the jury, she now assumes the power and vantage of the judge. The thematic emphasis is on the responsibility of society to get criminal law and criminal reform right. At the same time, though, the high angle places the spectator in the uncomfortable position of causing Nick and Andrew's humiliation and defeat. Like other examples of spectatorial alignment, the visual and emotional identification of the scene do not align.[2]

Knock on Any Door would seem to be a key *auteur* film, then, because it shows a director who transcends the script through both narrative contradiction and stylistic flourish. However, one could equally read the approach as part of a historical tendency toward "serious" Hollywood. The distinctive combination of realism and stylization puts *Knock on Any Door* in the company of the "*films gris*" cycle RKO and the independents produced. Broadly considered, *film gris* combined *film noir* and social problem content. More narrowly, this socially relevant group of films typically fused crime story, lower-class milieu, inverted Horatio Alger narrative, stylized direction, and realist cinematography (Maland, "*Film Gris*" 16–18). Films such as *Force of Evil* (Abraham Polonsky, 1948) could tackle issues allegorically, whereas others such as *The Lawless* (Joseph Losey, 1950) were outright social problem films. These films had aesthetic influences from theater, the novel, and photography, but one of the main driving sources of their emergence was the economic emphasis on cultural prestige and low budgets in late 1940s Hollywood (Cagle 294–98).

Knock on Any Door was an in-house independent production for Columbia Pictures, and this approach matched perfectly the ascendency of Columbia in the postwar studio hierarchy. Columbia tended not to make bigger-budgeted prestige problem films (with the arguable exception of *All the King's Men* [Robert Rossen, 1949]), but it gravitated toward projects with distinctive storylines and low budgets. It even copied other studios' successes, as in *noir*-ish procedurals such as *Walk a Crooked Mile* (Gordon Douglas, 1948) and the later *City of Fear* (Irving Lerner, 1959), both using variants of realist style. *Knock on Any Door* did not meet the critical success that some other *gris* film saw, and even a problem film champion like Bosley Crowther panned the film (*Knock* 31). However, the studio latched onto the *gris* style to gain both a prestige problem–film audience and a mass genre–film audience.

The film's complex underpinnings are more than either *auteur* vision or category E contradiction. Rather, the complexities emerge from the popularization of social science as sociology and its applied subfields come into their own and influence the public discourse in diffuse ways. From this, Nicholas Ray (and the writers, producers, and others) worked to develop aesthetic strategies to relate these ideas to a spectator and, occasionally, to challenge the spectator's own position in getting a lesson. One dominant trend in film theory and the history of midcentury American cinema has been to see realism and social problem discourse as natural and problematically ideological extensions of one another. The example of Ray demonstrates that this pairing was actually historically specific and the result of deliberate work. Social problem film makers combined a realist aesthetic with stylistic flourish in order to give expressive form—imperfectly—to a set of ideas about American social life more complex than generally acknowledged.

Notes

1. See McNiven for one example of this type of film criticism; for a discussion of category E, see Comolli and Narborni.

2. Browne's reading of *Stagecoach* points to this split between specular and affective identification.

5

ALEXANDER DOTY

"I've Got the Queerest Feeling" about *A Woman's Secret* and *Born to Be Bad*

WHAT LITTLE CRITICAL WORK there is on *A Woman's Secret* and *Born to Be Bad* has generally approached these films as challenges to *auteurism* or to genre studies. Some critics label these films "lesser" Ray, finding that his *auteurist* signature on *A Woman's Secret* was compromised by writer-producer Herman J. Mankiewicz, executive producer Dore Schary, star Maureen O'Hara, and Ray's (and Schary's) growing infatuation with costar Gloria Grahame, and by executive producer Howard Hughes and star Joan Fontaine (as well as Hughes's long-standing, but unreciprocated, desire for the star) on *Born to Be Bad*. Other commentators understand these films as either failed *films noir* or failed woman's pictures—or failed attempts to combine the two along the lines of *Mildred Pierce* (Michael Curtiz, 1945) or *The Reckless Moment* (Max Ophüls, 1947). Dana Polan takes yet another critical position, finding that while a film such as *Born to Be Bad* might fail "to find a place within aesthetic systems of valuation" like *auteurism* or genre, this may say "as much about the functioning of those systems as about the value (or lack thereof) of this one film" ("Bad" 211). While *A Woman's Secret*

Figure 5.1. *A Woman's Secret* (RKO Radio Pictures, 1949; pictured) and *Born to Be Bad* (RKO Radio Pictures, 1950; Figure 5.2) indicate that, from the beginning of his career, the bisexual Ray was interested in queering the American studio film in various ways (frame enlargement).

Figure 5.2. *Born to Be Bad* (RKO Radio Pictures, 1950) (frame enlargement).

and *Born to Be Bad* do reveal signs of competing authorships and (sub) genres that might be understood as diluting the impact of Ray-as-*auteur*, critically pressing on the figures of Susan Caldwell/Estrellita and Marian Washburn in *A Woman's Secret*, and Christabel Caine in *Born to Be Bad*, foregrounds aspects of unconventional gender performance and non-normative sexuality that compellingly link these films to many of Ray's more canonical works, such as *In a Lonely Place*, *Rebel Without a Cause*, and *Johnny Guitar*. Although Jonathan Rosenbaum mentions both Ray's bisexuality and the "celebrations of alternative lifestyles" in films such as *Hot Blood*, *Wind Across the Everglades*, and *The Savage Innocents*, he does not link them (*Essential* 334). But we might: if nothing else, *A Woman's Secret* and *Born to Be Bad* indicate that from the beginning of his career, the bisexual Ray was interested in queering the American studio film in various ways.[1]

Ray's first feature film, *They Live by Night*, pairs sensitive, pretty Farley Granger with sensitive, pretty Cathy O'Donnell in a "criminal lovers on the run" story that presages the pairing of sensitive, pretty James Dean with both sensitive, pretty Natalie Wood and sensitive, pretty Sal Mineo in *Rebel Without a Cause*. The exciting homosexual and bisexual dynamics the Mineo-Dean-Wood relationship creates make the film's eventual elimination of queerness and restoration of normative gender and/in heterosexuality—through Mineo's death and Dean-Wood being reabsorbed as a couple into the nuclear family—an even more painful conservative move. But it is a cultural and narrative move that is perhaps understandable not only because of the times (America in the mid-1950s) but also because of Ray's own ambivalence about his bisexuality. Life on the set of *Rebel Without a Cause* reportedly imitated the film's script, with Ray casting the bisexual Dean as his surrogate, and then proceeding to have affairs with both Mineo and Wood during filming.[2] Sensitive and dangerous pretty boys appear in several Ray films: Scott Brady in *Johnny Guitar*, John Derek in *Knock on Any Door*, Derek again in *Run for Cover*, Cornel Wilde in *Hot Blood*, Summer Williams in *On Dangerous Ground*, Jeffrey Hunter and Robert Wagner (as the James brothers) in *The True Story of Jesse James*, Hunter again (as Jesus) in *King of Kings*, and aging former pretty boy Robert Taylor in *Party Girl*. While the narratives and *mise-en-scène* surrounding these figures do not work up quite the same intense, triangulated bisexual charge that *Rebel Without a Cause* has, these films offer moments for the erotic contemplation of their male stars (even, or maybe especially, Hunter-as-Jesus) while also killing off most of these pretty boys in an attempt to diffuse any queer erotics that have emerged.

Neither *A Woman's Secret* nor *Born to Be Bad* center their queerness around male figures—interestingly, the only pretty boy in either film is

Born to Be Bad's painter Gabriel/Gobby (Mel Ferrer), who is homosexually coded and the only person who seems to appreciate Christabel's combination of gender masquerade and transgressive desire. As in almost every Ray film, the gender and sexuality politics of *A Woman's Secret* and *Born to Be Bad* combine conservative and progressive impulses, finding their unconventional protagonists exciting, but also frequently off-putting for various reasons. In both *A Woman's Secret* and *Born to Be Bad*, women are the locus of "genre trouble," and, therefore, of gender and sexuality trouble. While the narratives of these films lean on *noir* conventions in an attempt to establish a "good girl–bad girl" pair, their woman's picture elements trouble or refute this binary with regards to Susan, Marian, and Christabel. As a result, Susan's and Marian's bisexuality (or, possibly, lesbianism) and Christabel's transgressive female (hetero)sexuality are posited as both the narrative problem and as essential to their ability to survive and thrive in a man's world. These films do not fully demonize Susan, Marian, and Christabel by making them unproblematic *femme fatales* because of their queerness. If they fall into any category, it would be one common to both *noir* and the woman's picture (and melodramas in general), "the good-bad girl," who Andrew Spicer defines as a female character who "can appear to be cynical, willful and obsessed with money, but this stems from disillusionment with men and the frustrations of a circumscribed life" (92). He also goes on to note this figure's fundamental gender queerness because she embodies "both masculine and feminine qualities" (92).

What is made most problematic about Susan's, Marian's, and Christabel's gender and sexual queerness is how other characters respond to it by attempting to possess or to police these good-bad girls. Even characters who draw out, or who are drawn out by, the good-bad girl's queerness, such as Luke in *A Woman's Secret*, Nick Bradley in *Born to Be Bad*, and Marian herself (in terms of her relationship with Susan), finally want to control female transgressiveness, largely by domesticating it. While we might see *A Woman's Secret* and *Born to Be Bad* as companion pieces in Ray's early career for their mixture of *noir* and the woman's picture elements, their tangled authorship, and their relatively nonjudgmental representation of nonnormative women, this chapter focuses on *A Woman's Secret*, offering a wider and more complex range of queerness: bisexual, lesbian, and heterosexual. What this film does not have are queer male figures such as Gobby and Nick; Luke Jordan might be understood as queered through his triangulated relationship with Marian and Susan, although he is not represented as possessing queer qualities himself. Also, for a while, the effete, upper-class Brook Matthews, who is first seen traveling with his mother in *A Woman's Secret*, seems destined for inclusion in the roll call of queer(ed) men in Ray films.

There is no conventional "rise to stardom" montage for singer Marian Washburn (Maureen O'Hara) in *A Woman's Secret* because during the performance that is supposed to make her a star, she begins to sing in a way that "doesn't sound like her," giving her "the queerest feeling." At the time, neither Marian nor her doctors can explain this "queer feeling" except as some sort of "rare laryngitis." Luke (Melvyn Douglas) responds to Marian's "queer feeling" by telling her to "keep quiet . . . [y]ou say another word and I'll slug you." At its inception, Marian's queerness seems to be marked as a problem: it is connected with the end of her career and classified as a physically and mentally debilitating sickness. It is also one of those mystery maladies that cannot be clearly named (at least not in a mainstream film), but one that calls forth repressive violence in straight men. On the other hand, her queer malady allows Marian to regain her independence because she will no longer being managed by Luke or judged by men like voice teacher Paul Camelli. The next time Marian has queer feelings, they will lead her into becoming both voice teacher and manager for another female singer.

The queer feelings that accompany the transformation of Marian's voice are reignited when she encounters Susan (Gloria Grahame). Tellingly, this happens very soon after a scene in which Marian and Luke banter about marriage in a way that leaves them in a state of indecisive stasis:

MARIAN: You're proposing to me?

LUKE: No.

MARIAN: Afraid I'll accept?

LUKE: Afraid you won't.

This "take-it-or-leave-it" indifference to heterosexuality that forms the basis of Marian's and Luke's relationship is established even earlier when Marian sings "Let Him Go, Let Him Tarry," accompanied at the piano by Luke. "Let him go, let him tarry/Let him sink or swim/He doesn't care for me/Nor I don't care for him," goes the beginning of the song's chorus, and even though there are lines about marrying "a far nicer boy," the song keeps returning to its title assertion. Marian and Luke's conversation following this song is about her future success in which Luke will play a part as manager and cheerleader, but not, it seems, as lover or husband. Later, after Marian receives the bad news about her voice from Camelli, and she and Luke reconfirm their near-platonic relationship with their "indifference to marriage" repartee, the pair encounters a tired and hungry Susan leaving an audition. Initially filmed in a three-shot on the stairs with Susan between Luke and Marian, Luke quickly drops out of the frame as Marian moves Susan over to a bench and invites her back home for some food. Susan, as it turns out, has a prodigious appetite.

What follows is *A Woman's Secret*'s reworking of the Svengali-Trilby story in which Marian is Svengali and her protégée Susan a bisexual(izing) Trilby figure. Cullen Gallagher's analysis of the film is one of the few to examine the film's queerness in any detail. Gallagher attributes the "bisexual undercurrents" in the film to the performances of its female stars, especially to O'Hara, who brought with her a star persona that mixes masculinity and femininity, and, therefore, was able to suggest an erotic "undercurrent" in the mentor/protégée (or alternately, mother/daughter) relationship between Marian and Susan. While Marian/O'Hara is important to the bisexual dynamics in *A Woman's Secret*, Susan is the one who simultaneously seduces Marian and Luke by singing a love song, "Paradise." "Paradise," as it turns out, is the last song we hear Marian sing on a record that Luke smashes when it becomes clear that she will never sing like this again—that is, sing like the (heterosexual) woman he can flirt with and whose career and life he can manage.

With Marian's coaching, Susan will sing something like Marian did. A post-"queer feeling" Marian will not only manage Susan's career, but will live with, and through, her protégée. This sets in motion a triangulated, bisexually-charged, narrative centered on the women: to varying degrees that change over time, Marian desires both Susan and Luke; Susan desires both Luke (and other men) and Marian. As it plays out in the film, Marian and Susan working and living together also evokes specifically lesbian butch-*femme* coupling—although, more accurately, Marian is actually a *femme*-butch to Susan's butch-*femme*. Their combined personal and professional relationship also invokes notions of lesbianism as a narcissistic doubling around "the feminine" (or "the *femme*") that blurs the lines between identification and desire in ways that the narrative finally marks as disturbing and unhealthy as Marian becomes increasingly obsessed with molding the working-class Susan into a suitably "classy" performer and devoted domestic partner.

Initially, however, Susan draws both Luke and Marian into a bisexual triangle with what might be understood psychoanalytically as the voice of the pre-Oedipal erotic mother who "regresses" her listeners into the polymorphously perverse and prelinguistic space of the Imaginary. Marian is pulled from her kitchen back into the living room by the siren sound of Susan's voice as Luke accompanies her on the piano. While the lyrics of "Paradise" (its Symbolic language, if you will) are insistently heterosexual, the editing and shot compositions, coupled with Susan's deep, throaty voice, build a more compelling queer erotic charge during the sequence. Earlier shot patterns in this sequence have laid some of the bisexual groundwork by smoothly moving between three-shots of Luke-Susan-Marian and two-shots of all potential pairings (Luke-Marian, Marian-Susan, Luke-Susan). Susan's story of the "scandal" with a man that drove her from Azuza breaks this editing pattern by focusing on a close-up of Marian's anxious face, establishing a new pattern that alternates shots of a male-female couple (Luke and Susan) with shots of a woman (Marian) intensely looking on from the outside.

In this context, we might understand the new editing pattern here as either an attempt to reestablish heterosexuality after the initial threat of bisexuality/lesbianism or, conversely, as representing the threat of heterosexuality to a more fluid, all-embracing bisexuality. In any case, the sequence tellingly returns to a three-shot when Susan suggests singing a song for them, but then once again isolates an anxious-looking Marian in close-up before returning to a three-shot that finds Marian hastily leaving the frame for the kitchen to get Susan more food. Framed by the kitchen door, Marian will appear in medium shots that alternate with two-shots of Luke and Susan at the piano. Once Susan begins singing, the editing pattern relies on individual close-ups of Luke and Marian as they become more and more compelled by Susan's voice, establishing the possibility of heterosexual, bisexual, and more specifically lesbian erotics. Things resolve themselves bisexually as Marian moves from kitchen to fireplace as Susan begins to divide her eye contact between Luke and Marian. Marian enters what becomes a three-shot (angled from Susan's position) and stands next to Luke at the piano, putting her arm across his shoulder and exchanging tender looks with him and with Susan. In effect, Ray and his collaborators create a bisexual "paradise" out of music, editing, *mise-en-scène*, and the exchange of looks that finally overwhelms the song's heterosexualizing lyrics.

Susan's song triggers a complicated mixture of identification and desire in Marian, who quickly becomes a jealously possessive Svengali figure once she begins coaching Susan into having the singing career she was denied. Parts of the *noir*-ish "Who shot Susan—and why?" multiple flashback crime investigation (largely those sections Luke narrates)—as well as an oddly curtailed scene at the end of Susan attempting to reseduce Brook Matthews, her rich lover (from her hospital bed, no less)—attempt to represent Susan as a cold, manipulative, self-serving "fatal woman" who almost ruins many people's lives. However, the woman's picture aspects of the film offer a counternarrative of Susan as a somewhat naïve, good-hearted "working girl" from Azuza trying to make her way in a world ready to exploit and control her. In this register, Susan's "calculating" and "selfish" qualities might be understood as tactics she develops for her survival and self-preservation. Indeed, the film opens in woman's picture "troubled relationship" territory and only (and arguably) moves into *noir* when we hear a gunshot behind closed bedroom doors. Besides establishing Susan as emphatically not a *noir femme fatale*, *A Woman's Secret*'s *in medias res* opening also suggests that a queer reading of the film—or a more specifically bisexual or lesbian reading—is the "preferred" one. Susan may be a *femme*, but she is not *fatale*, except possibly to herself, as it turns out.

As the film opens, Susan is singing the song that has also become her stage name: "Estrellita." Again, although the lyrics speak of a "he," the line "my heart is yours alone" calls forth a slow dissolve between a glamorous close-up of Susan and one of Marian, who is sitting in their shared apartment impatiently looking at her watch. Toward the end of the number, Marian moves across the room to turn off the machine on which she has been recording Susan's voice on a disc (perhaps as a replacement for the one Luke has smashed?). Marian sits down, and another slow dissolve overlaps Marian's body with that of Susan coming in the front door. Midway up the stairs to the second floor, Susan stops and complains about how difficult work has been. Marian asks Susan if she is "hungry." We later discover Susan's "hunger" is what initially prompts Marian to invite her home, where Susan seduces Marian (and Luke) with her rendition of "Paradise." This talk of "hunger" also tellingly initiates a series of shot–reverse shot close-ups that move between isolating the two women and including part of the other woman in the frame. What follows looks like, sounds like, and reads like a classic domestic argument about career versus relationship. Susan says she is "through for good," which Marian (willfully?) misunderstands as Susan only needing a professional break. After Marian suggests that the two of them "can go away someplace," Susan calls Marian "the biggest fool I've ever met" for not understanding "what [she's] talking about."

When Susan brings up Luke Jordan, Marian's reaction suggests that Susan's anger is, in part, triggered by her jealousy: "Is that's what's bothering you, Susan? I don't mean anything to Luke Jordan—and there is no reason why I should. He doesn't owe me a single thing—not anything at all." But it appears that jealousy of Luke and Marian's relationship is less behind Susan's anger than Marian's possessiveness: "Oh, but I do, don't I? You made me what I am, didn't you?" Threatening to abandon her career and the domestic life with Marian that comes with it, Marian's intense "Stop it, Susan!" cuts off Susan. Rushing up the stairs crying, Susan enters a bedroom (we only ever see one), soon followed by Marian.

As the door closes behind Marian, we are left to wonder what exactly is going on in there that the film cannot show. If anything, the sound of a gunshot, followed by the sight of Marian (in black) kneeling beside Susan's prostrate figure (clad in white) only intensifies a butch-*femme* "lover's quarrel" reading of what we have just seen. In her autobiography, Maureen O'Hara interestingly misremembers her character shooting Grahame's character "in a jealous rage," and juxtaposes this with talk of Grahame's real life sexual transgressions (126).

Of course, the patriarchal forces of law and order—and of classical narrative—will not really be able to deal directly with the queer lover's quarrel and shooting that we see in the film's opening scenes. There will be one "woman's secret" that will not get out into the public spaces of the film once the case is "solved." Luke suggests as much when he tells Inspector Fowler, "I'm surprised you didn't realize what an odd friendship that was." But on some semimanifest, semilatent level, the film realizes, and reveals, the oddity of this "friendship," and is simultaneously fascinated by it and as disturbed as Luke is by Marian's expression of her "queer" feelings earlier. So the narrative "slugs" the queerness back as best it can, which, finally, is half-heartedly. The provocatively queer erotic charge of Marian and Susan's relationship—as well as Susan being the apex of bisexual triangles—leads to violence. Actually, with the film's fractured chronology, it has all "begun" violently, and we are given two versions of what happened: Marian's *noir*-lit lying flashback that casts her as the perpetrator (to protect Susan? to expiate guilt about her relationship with Susan?), and Susan's evenly-lit domestic melodrama flashback that shows what happened was the result of Marian trying to stop Susan from shooting herself. As it turns out, Susan's desperation on the staircase was a red herring. Neither her desire to end her career nor her relationship with Marian motivated her suicide attempt. A telegram Susan received from her secret husband Lee Crenshaw, whose immanent visit would ruin her relationships with Marian and Brook, and, possibly, would mean the end of her career, throws her into a panic.

Speaking about the final scenes that work to separate Marian and Susan and pair them with men (Luke and Brook, respectively), Cullen Gallagher finds that "*A Woman's Secret* betrays every one of its nuances and subversions, and reverts to the staid, conformist melodrama it was originally trying to avoid." Although the end of the film allows for conventional readings (the queer women are chastised, separated, and heterosexualized; or, more heteronormatively, each woman gets her "happy ending" with a man), I contend that the end of *A Woman's Secret* shifts the queerness from lesbian or bisexual to female heterosexual queerness. Marian and Susan's "odd friendship" is almost exposed in the glaring light of a hospital room—with its connotations of "disease" and "sickness" as well as "cure"—by the combined force of straight men (Luke, Inspector Fowler) and straight women (the Inspector's wife). But rather than fully reveal the queerness of the "friendship" and deal with it once and for all, the narrative (as it would have to in 1949) decides to police and redirect these queer energies. Mrs. Fowler's parting shot to Susan is particularly pointed: "So nice to meet you, Mrs. Crenshaw." But as soon as Mrs. Fowler and the others have left the room, "Mrs. Crenshaw" turns her attentions to luring Brook to her bed as the scene fades out—hardly normative married woman behavior. So while we leave Susan in a heterosexual space, it is a space queered by her nonnormative desires. I also contend that in its abruptness—not to mention its hospital room *mise-en-scène*—this seduction scene presents Susan's actions more as being outrageously funny than as the evil machinations of a hard-boiled *femme fatale*.

As for Marian and Luke, after she is released from the police station, the pair proceed to a *noir*-lit street where Marian begins to call the narrative shots by telling Luke that he needs to get a couple of things "straight": they are not going to any rehearsals or helping any fainting girls. As a cab pulls up, Marian continues to take the initiative and rhetorically asks Luke, "There's no law about being romantic in a cab, is there?" Borrowing Marian's question from their earlier conversation, Luke asks, "Are you proposing to me?" Not answering directly, Marian pushes Luke into the cab ("in you go") and—still on the street and looking into the cab window—suggestively orders the driver to go "[o]nce around Central Park, very slowly," before getting into the backseat of the cab, removing Luke's hat, and initiating their fade-out kiss. Rather than a marriage proposal, what Marian offers here is more along time lines of a sexual proposition. If Marian is going to be in a relationship with a man rather than a woman, it seems as if she is still going to be the more butch partner—all of which still leaves open the possibility that Marian is bisexual and has merely moved from a relationship with a woman to one with a man. On the other hand, since Susan's bisexuality has been represented in the film by her maintaining simultaneous (and not serial) relationships with one woman (Marian) and various men (Luke, Brook, Lee), her reunion with Brook and her status as Mrs. Crenshaw, in conjunction with her bitter separation from Marian, leaves Susan's queerness more insistently coded within heterosexuality. So even though the narrative has left them with men, Susan and Marian are still unruly queer women at the end of *A Woman's Secret*.

In their final heterosexual(ized) gender queerness, Susan and Marian are linked to *Born to Be Bad*'s Christabel (Joan Fontaine). But since a combination of masculine and feminine qualities remains a part of

Marian's queer performance of heterosexuality in the taxi scene with Luke, Susan's breathy vamping from her hospital bed provides a more direct link to Christabel, who deploys a masquerade of demur, selfless femininity to conceal less conventionally ladylike passions for social status and for sex. Indeed, Geoff Andrew finds that "[i]n retrospect, Susan may seem like a blueprint for the character of Christabel" (34). Constructed to present a performance of vulnerable femininity cut to the measure of male desire and vanity, Christabel can easily take advantage of most of her lovers. The exception is Nick (Robert Ryan), who suggests that there are "two of her," the proper bourgeois woman (the "false" her) and the transgressive sexual woman (the "true" her)—and who proceeds to bring out the latter. That Nick shares his first name with the director and is a wry, tough-guy writer who evinces a degree of emotional sensitivity as well as queer artistic bohemianism by saying how much he likes visiting Gobby's studio is perhaps no coincidence.

As a (queer) painter, Gobby may be the other obvious double for Ray. Evan Davis certainly makes this case: "It is natural that Ray could have seen himself in a witty, self-consciously ambitious, confident, uncompromising character like Gobby" (2). Certainly, Gobby's studio is the epicenter of the queerness in *Born to Be Bad*. Not only is it where Nick hangs out with Gobby, but it is also where Christabel has her portrait painted by Gobby—a painting that will become the film's central, and ultimately campily celebratory, icon to her nonnormativity. This studio is also where the thorny, *noir*-like queer relationship between Gobby and Christabel is most explicitly established. Richard Dyer suggests that what is most compelling about the relationship between queer men and women in *films noir* like *Laura* (Otto Preminger, 1944), *Gilda* (Charles Vidor, 1946), and *The Dark Corner* (Henry Hathaway, 1946) is that the queer men "aestheticize" the central female characters in various ways, creating an intense yet "asexual" space that "allows queers a closeness to women uncomplicated by heterosexual lust" (124–25). Furthermore, certain queer men in *noir* can "both adore, [and] inflate, the femininity of already highly feminine women, and, by association, also suggest its artifice" (125).

Dyer's comments here accurately describe important aspects of Gobby's relationship with Christabel, as well as explaining the work his portrait is doing for those who can see queerly. What it leaves out is how queer men like Gobby can both "adore" women and (to borrow Christabel's appraisal of Gobby) "[not] care too much for women." Gobby "adores" the campy, queer artifice of Christabel's masquerade of femininity, while appearing not to care too much for the woman herself, who he is only too willing to help Curtis kick out of his mansion at the end of the film. The close, yet troubling, queer relationship between Christabel and Gobby is perhaps best summarized by something he says while she is posing for him: "I know too much about you—so you can be yourself with me."

Gobby's portrait of Christabel is his aestheticized tribute to her—or at least to how her performance of conventional heterosexual femininity allows her to be, as Nick puts it on seeing the painting, "a cross between Lucrezia Borgia and Peg o' My Heart"—that is, someone (like Susan or Marian) who borrows from both the *femme fatale* and the ingénue, while being neither. Though it might be criticized for reinscribing a "good woman–bad woman" patriarchal binary even while it suggests the limits of such binarization, this view of Christabel, courtesy of the film's two queer male figures, provides a somewhat more complicated way of understanding her than simply as an "evil woman," particularly for those straight men in the audience who might see Nick as their identification figure and those queer men who might connect with Gobby.

Christabel's lusty "sex attraction" to Nick and her platonic relationship with Gobby are marked, in many ways, as preferable alternatives to her performance of conventional femininity within traditional heterosexual contexts. On the other hand, Nick often attempts to control Christabel through her sexual desires as these desires also bring out a degree of traditionally feminine vulnerability in her, while Gobby initially counts on Christabel's wealthy connections to promote his career, and then arguably exploits her scandalous notoriety for the same reason.

Against all conventional narrative odds—at least in Ray's cut of the film, which appears to have been initially released as an "export version"—Ray allows the homosexual and the transgressive queer woman to have the last laugh—and asks viewers to put themselves in a nonnormative viewing space and laugh with them. Amidst some witty-bitchy banter, Christabel surrenders the mansion keys to Gobby, promising to get into "more trouble" to help drive up the price of her portrait, which Curtis has returned to Gobby. Driving off with a backseat filled with fur coats, Christabel has an accident that lands her in the hospital, delivering her into the arms of married Dr. Abernathy (echoing Susan's circumstances at the end of *A Woman's Secret*). A newspaper headline announcing Mrs. Abernathy's "alienation of affection" lawsuit is followed by a shot of Gobby raising the price of Christabel's portrait. Arriving at her lawyer's to discuss the lawsuit, Christabel again performs helpless femininity, resulting in an implied second lawsuit as she goes out for "cocktails" with her lawyer and we see Gobby once again raising the price of her portrait. This is where the film leaves us. One would have to go back to the pre-Code days of *Red-Headed Woman* (Jack Conway,

1932) and *Baby Face* (Alfred E. Green, 1933) to find more audacious delight being taken at female "misbehavior" at the expense of straight men. Even more, *Born to Be Bad* suggests that the transgressive woman and the homosexual man might profitably work in tandem to scam a "one born every minute" patriarchy. As Andrew puts it, "One cannot help feeling that Christabel's victims get their just desserts; certainly one of the greatest pleasures when watching the film is to hear her insinuations and see her smiling to herself. . . . In Christabel . . . do we encounter any real sense of purpose, achievement, or happiness. . . . Ray seems to have reserved most of his sympathies for the self-empowering Christabel who . . . is by far the most positive character in the movie" (42, 44–45).

While one could argue that Christabel masquerading to entrap her lawyer and doctor, Susan seducing Brook, and Marian propositioning Luke are forms of "working-within-the-(patriarchal)-system" female empowerment, the final movement of both *A Woman's Secret* and *Born to Be Bad* also share a comic, winking approach to queer female transgression that sets them apart from the generally moralizing endings of most *films noir* and domestic melodramas in which nonnormative women reform, are ruined, or die. Audiences are invited to laugh with, rather than at, the machinations of the central female characters and to take pleasure in their easy manipulation of men. On top of all this, everything at fadeout indicates that Susan, Marian, and Christabel are not interested in marriage or monogamy, which, considering the pressing cultural and narrative demands on them, makes the women in these "lesser" Ray films, finally, as profoundly rebellious as the men in Ray's more canonical works.

Notes

1. Numerous sources mention Ray's bisexuality, including Patrick McGillian's *Nicholas Ray: The Glorious Failure of an American Director*, Jonathan Rosenbaum's *Essential Cinema*, Gavin Lambert's *Natalie Wood: A Life*, and Michael Gregg Michaud's *Sal Mineo: A Biography*.

2. Accounts of the queer erotics surrounding *Rebel Without a Cause*, both on-screen and offscreen, can be found in McGillian, Lambert, and Michaud, cited in note 1 above, as well as in Larry Frascella and Al Weisel's *Live Fast, Die Young: The Wild Ride of Making* Rebel Without a Cause, Douglas L. Rathgeb's *The Making of* Rebel Without a Cause, and in a brief response from critic David Ehrenstein to an online piece on *Born to be Bad* in which he covers much ground in two sentences: "I trust you know that Nick Ray was bisexual and for many years carried on an affair with Gavin Lambert—who wrote many of his scripts. He also had an affair with Sal Mineo during the shooting of *Rebel Without a Cause* AND deflowered Natalie Wood" (quoted in Davis).

6

STEVEN SANDERS

Something More than *Noir*

"BUT WHAT SORT OF FILM IS *In a Lonely Place*? There's a strangeness to it," writes Dana Polan in his monograph on the film published in 1993 (10). He adds that in *In a Lonely Place* "we find a production that quests for ways to define itself . . . and that offers no one view but rather a series of possible images, possible identities" (10). It is quite true that *In a Lonely Place* is multigeneric, with elements of the crime melodrama, the crime suspense story, the police procedural, the domestic *noir*, even, perhaps, as Polan suggests, the screwball comedy. But why should the fact that *In a Lonely Place* is rich in implication, strange in its shifting genres and moods, and multiply interpretable because of the ways Ray reshapes its social and political materials, lead us to doubt its pedigree? Explaining why *In a Lonely Place* is a *film noir* and at the same time celebrating Ray's signal achievement in making the film, as Raymond Chandler might have phrased it in "The Simple Art of Murder," "something more than *noir*," is easy.

In a Lonely Place, released in 1950, is based on the 1947 novel of the same title by Dorothy B. Hughes, but the book and the film have significant differences. For instance, in the novel, Dixon Steele is a serial killer, whereas by the end of the film we know that Dixon clearly did not murder the woman he is suspected of killing. Furthermore, the Dixon Steele character in the novel is not a part of the film industry

Figure 6.1. *In a Lonely Place* (Santana Productions/Columbia Pictures, 1950): Ray uses a high-key light on Dix's face to emphasize his enthusiastic, perverse pleasure as he graphically describes how he believes the strangulation of Mildred would have taken place (frame enlargement).

at all, whereas in the film, he is a Hollywood screenwriter. This allows Ray to explore the theme of unfulfilled promise in both creative work and personal relationships. While comparing and contrasting the novel and feature film would undoubtedly be interesting, a description of the most significant ways in which Ray, Bogart, and screenwriter Andrew Solt proceeded independently of the book has already been provided by James W. Palmer: "From the beginning Hughes's novel exposes the reader to the tortured mind of a psychopath. . . . In the film, Dix Steele is not a psychotic killer, but a flawed man whose insecurities and violent temper, fed by the doubts and distrust of those closest to him, lead to tragedy" (201).

In a Lonely Place situates an intense drama against the backdrop of the Hollywood movie industry. The film casts Humphrey Bogart as down-on-his luck screenwriter Dixon Steele and Gloria Grahame as his neighbor and soon-to-be lover, Laurel Gray, in a departure from the conventions of the genres mentioned earlier in what might be called a fever dream of emotional free-fall. The film clearly implies that Dix's short fuse has its origin in the tendency of the movie industry to stifle creativity and reward conformity—an industry known, after all, as 'the Dream *Factory*'—and it gives us a glimpse of Hollywood's power relationships with its focus on the themes of mistrust, paranoia, and betrayal. Yet the title is a metaphor not only for Hollywood, but also for Dix's existential condition. While he is not the murderer, Laurel's recognition of the possibility that he *could be* terrifies her and drives her from him.

Shot just a few years after the House Un-American Activities Committee (HUAC) inquiries into the communist influence on Hollywood, suspicions and enemies as well as alliances were products of its aftermath. James W. Palmer writes:

> Bogart had already become embroiled in the 1947 Congressional investigation when, as a member of the Committee for the First Amendment, he flew to the hearing in Washington, D.C., with his wife, Lauren Bacall, and a host of other Hollywood luminaries to offer a show of support for the Hollywood Ten. Alastair Cooke reports that Bogart "was aghast to discover that several of them were down-the-line Communists coolly exploiting the protection of the First and Fifth Amendments to the Constitution. He had thought they were just freewheeling anarchists like himself." (204)

Palmer goes on to write:

> Bogart, shocked by the political affiliations of the Hollywood Ten and equally troubled by the strongarm [*sic*] tactics of HUAC, also became disillusioned with the film industry's wavering response to the investigations which led to compromises and the eventual blacklisting of many actors, screenwriters, and directors. (205)

Against such a background Bogart played out his role of a Hollywood screenwriter prone to be more than slightly suspicious of almost everyone, and in this context of paranoia, the scenes that bookend the film signify its meaning. First, we see Bogart's sad eyes in his automobile's rearview mirror behind the film's opening titles. This seems to suggest both his character's loneliness as well as his looking back on something, perhaps his past, as if he is afraid it might be catching up with him. And unlike a conventional Hollywood film where viewers are comforted by a happy ending, Ray provides nothing of the sort. By film's end, in a scene we will come to, the fatalism of the *noir* world Dix may have hoped he no longer inhabits has caught up with him completely.

Showdown at the Fantasy Factory

Screenwriter Dix Steele's career has been on the skids since the end of World War II. Indeed, we are told his last good film was written before the war. What is more, he has become virtually unemployable because of his abrasive personality and violent temper. We see instances of this in an early scene at Paul's, a Hollywood restaurant where he insults a big director, calling him a "popcorn salesman" (he makes the same movie again and again), and then assaults the son-in-law of a studio boss, sending him sprawling into a banquette after Dix has heard enough of his abusive references to one of Dix's friends, a heavy-drinking has-been actor for whom Dix has a soft spot. And here in miniature is Ray's emotional portrait of the paradoxical Dix: a man sensitive enough to take in the matinee idol from bygone days (Robert Warwick) whom he respects and loans money he knows will never be repaid, and sufficiently volatile to attack a well-connected studio director who has insulted this friend.

Despite his toxic reputation at the studios, Dix is offered an assignment to adapt a potboiler novel, *Althea Bruce*, for the screen. The producer, Brody, wants to know right away whether Dix will take the assignment, so Dix invites a hatcheck girl, Mildred Atkinson (Martha Stewart), to his apartment to tell him the story of the book, thereby saving him the trouble of having to read it himself. When they arrive at the Beverly Patio apartments, they run into Laurel Gray, who occupies the apartment across the courtyard from Dix's. She walks between, rather than around, Dix and Mildred, thereby drawing attention to herself, and proceeds upstairs, lingering for a moment before she enters her apartment. With this small but effective piece of choreography, Ray establishes their mutual attraction.

Dix quickly grows bored with Mildred's recitation (replete with malapropisms). The novel is a mediocre job of work, as he suspected. Moving to his bedroom to remove his jacket, kick off his shoes, and put a smoking jacket on over his slacks while Mildred continues, Dix looks out his window and sees Laurel looking down at him from her balcony. (Later he will joke that it is unfair that she can see his bedroom from her balcony but he cannot see hers.) When Mildred finishes he asks her if she would mind taking a cab home, gives her $20, and they say goodnight. In the early morning hours, a police detective, Brub Nicolai (Frank Lovejoy), who served under Dix during the war, comes to Dix's apartment to bring him downtown for questioning. Dix believes he is being brought in for the fracas at the restaurant earlier in the evening, but he soon learns from police Captain Lochner (Carl Benton Reid) that he is to be questioned in connection with the investigation of the strangulation murder of Mildred Atkinson.

Dix seems unmoved during Lochner's questioning, and with evident sarcasm he asks if Lochner is going to arrest him for "lack of emotion." In what strikes Lochner as a troubling anomaly, Laurel provides Dix with an alibi, thus for the time being rendering moot Dix's curiously unemotional response to the news of Mildred's murder. Laurel tells Lochner that she saw Dix say goodnight at his door and then walk back into his apartment as Mildred made her way to the taxi stand around the corner. But Laurel is either lying outright or strongly slanting her testimony since Ray has been careful not to provide a shot to validate what she tells the police, and this gives us our first indication that Laurel will grow suspicious of Dix since she is, after all, shading the truth about what she has seen. After Dix leaves, Lochner tells Brub that a man who shows neither shock, horror, nor sympathy at such news, is hiding something.

Dix and Laurel soon begin a relationship. Laurel provides the stability and encouragement Dix needs to establish a disciplined work schedule, and he makes steady progress on the adaptation he has promised to write for Brody. Having set up the audience to believe that the film will follow out the storyline of a happy couple embraced by Hollywood and poised to enjoy the success the town is capable of bestowing (and that Dix so clearly desires), Ray thwarts these expectations by showing Dix's psychological complications and existential impasse to be pervasive and the suspicions of the police, in the person of Lochner, to be intractable. He calls Laurel in for a second time and his discovery that Laurel and Dix are, in his words, "inseparable," is all the more disquieting when she confirms that she is indeed in love with Dix. Lochner reveals Dix's dark and violent side, describing his history of fights and brushes with the law. Laurel strongly defends Dix, but Lochner's revelations cannot help but fan the flames of her suspicions. Laurel's (second) interview with Lochner is inadvertently revealed to Dix at a party with the Nicolais. In what may seem to the viewer like a self-fulfilling prophecy, once Dix learns of this meeting, he is enraged by what he fears most—betrayal. Dix's violence in this connection reinforces Laurel's original distrust and suspicion: when he flies into a rage and drives off, Laurel has to rush to the car and jump in to avoid being left behind. Running a stop sign, Dix has an auto accident with a college boy whom he beats up and would have killed without Laurel's intervention. Additionally, Laurel's masseuse Martha (Ruth Gillette) has told her repeatedly that she made a big mistake in ditching her wealthy former lover. For good measure, she tells

Laurel that Dix beat up his last girlfriend. Laurel fires the masseuse on the spot, but she is clearly troubled by these latest revelations of Dix's violent behavior.

For his own part, Dix is clearly on the edge, simultaneously possessive and wary. He proposes marriage, but by this time Laurel is convinced she has reason to fear him, especially after she witnesses another bout of anger when Dix learns that she has given his completed screen adaptation to Dix's agent Mel (Art Smith), who shows it to Brody. Dix attacks the loyal and kindly gent, knocking his glasses off and shaking him up badly. Even if we attribute Dix's responses to paranoia, his friends, their good intentions notwithstanding, are complicit in his alienation and mistrust. As James W. Palmer observes, "The characters surrounding Dix are compromised by their own conspiratorial behavior. Although she defends Dix during her second interrogation by the police, Laurel fails to tell Dix of the meeting. Laurel meets secretly with Sylvia Nicolai to discuss Dix's erratic behavior," and Sylvia suggests that maybe Laurel needs to get away and think things over (205). Even after Sylvia tells her, "You know he's innocent," the camera stays with Laurel and we know she is thinking, "What have I done?" Palmer continues:

> Still later, Laurel plots her escape from Dix even as she agrees to marry him. Hoping professional success might soften the impact of her betrayal, Laurel, in collusion with Mel submits Dix's completed script to the studio without his knowledge. Captain Lochner uses Brub's friendship with Dix to further his investigation. In the end Dix's isolation is complete. (205)

The motivational crux of *In a Lonely Place* therefore can be found in a series of increasingly ominous disclosures: Dix's propensity to violence that ultimately ignites Laurel's fear for her life and Dix's discovery of what he takes to be betrayal from all quarters, but especially by Laurel, that shatters him.

Auteur et Noir

Dix and Laurel occupy alternative and conflicting identities: he has a well-earned reputation as a man who is prone to violent outbursts; she is infatuated (she tells police she first noticed Dix because "I thought he looked interesting, I liked his face"), but cautious (she tells Dix she does not like being rushed), and terrified of him by film's end. Neither character can escape from or avoid his or her evolving existential condition and achieve a hoped-for redemption or happy ending. Laurel's reinvigoration of Dix's creative powers is only temporary, for, in the words of Julie Kirgo and Alain Silver, "In Ray's vision of the *noir* universe, destructive impulses such as Steele's must eventually short-circuit the sexual and creative potency that Laurel temporarily inspires" (145). At the film's end, when Dix discovers that Laurel plans to leave him on the eve of their trip to Las Vegas where they are to be married, he nearly strangles her and she knows she must take flight, even as Brub calls her apartment to tell her that Mildred Atkinson's boyfriend Kessler has confessed to the murder and Dix is cleared. This occurs in a tense scene as Dix enters Laurel's apartment and discovers that she has been packing and plans to leave him. He turns on her in all his fury and she cries out, "Don't act like this, Dix. I can't live with a maniac."

Dix tells her, "I can't let you go."

"Dix, stop, don't."

[Phone rings.]

"No, Dix, please don't."

[Dix picks up the phone.]

It is Brub: "Just got an airtight confession from Kessler."

This ironically timed and choreographed disclosure of the confession is one to which Laurel can only reply: "Yesterday this would have meant so much to us; now it doesn't matter at all." To this irony we can add others: Ray's deteriorating marriage to Grahame (the couple by this time lived apart) and Bogart's hot temper (he and his third wife, Mayo Methot, were known as "the Battling Bogarts"), and we get fact supporting fiction as the final scene builds to the ultimate irony. By adapting the themes of alienation, loneliness, and betrayal from *film noir*, Ray was able to lend themes from his own life and the lives of his two stars to the film's storyline. Dix can neither live without Laurel nor contain the nearly homicidal rage that consumes him, terrifies her, and ultimately drives them apart. The ominous closing line, written by Dix, that Laurel quotes as she watches Dix walk out of the Beverly Patio apartment complex and into the night—"I lived for a while when we kissed"—is a portent of doom, existential if not literal. Darkness serves as a metaphor for fate in this psychologically compelling film, and the darkness that Dix enters in the end suggests the fate that entraps him. As Dix exits into the night we know he has entered a world of helplessness and hopelessness in which he will never again find trust.

Under Ray's direction, the film is a complex generic mix. Ray uses genre conventions only to transcend them and in doing so to comment on more general issues of love (or the lack of it), personal integration (or its absence), alienation, mistrust, and betrayal. He embellishes the police procedural, for example, by reinforcing the attraction between Dix and Laurel in the first interview (or interrogation) scene, and later he has Dix instruct Brub and his wife Sylvia (Jeff Donnell) on how to act out the way he imagines the murder of Mildred Atkinson occurred. Ray's direction of Bogart's direction of Brub and Sylvia in this scene is a striking self-reflexive comment on the role of the director in creating often unexpected effects. Ray uses a high-key light on Dix's face to emphasize his enthusiastic, perverse pleasure as he graphically describes how he believes the strangulation of Mildred would have taken place, and this has the effect of heightening Sylvia's suspicion that there is more to Dix's involvement in the murder than meets the eye. "He's a sick person," she tells Brub, who continues to defend Dix.

Another self-reflexive moment occurs in the famous scene as Dix prepares breakfast for Laurel in her kitchen. She tells Dix how much she liked a love scene he has written, and Dix replies: "That's because they're not always telling each other how much in love they are. A good love scene should be about something else besides love. For instance, this one: me fixing grapefruit, you sitting over there, dopey and half-asleep. Anyone looking at us could tell we're in love." Dix's deep understanding of love here is that love is not something couples find, or keep, by pursuing it directly. Rather, love arises as a consequence of all the dispositions, emotions, thoughts, and actions that are (mistakenly) believed by some to be love's accompaniments rather than its constituents. Like a good love scene, *In a Lonely Place*, ostensibly about a murder case, is actually a film about Dix and Laurel's relationship. As Geoff Andrew writes, Ray "was forever exploring the nature of love in films that appeared to be about something else; *In a Lonely Place*, for example, is primarily about a relationship, and only secondarily a 'whodunit' about Mildred's death" (51).

The second convention is that of the down-on-his-luck Hollywood screenwriter who redeems himself through his own creative efforts. Ray subverts this cliché by showing Dix to be so much a creature of his conflicts, frustrations, and impulses that he is beyond such redemption. At a point in his relationship with Laurel when Dix should be moving away from alienation and toward trust and intimacy, the relationship begins to metastasize first into possessiveness, then suspicion, and ultimately into homicidal violence.

In *film noir*, style and content so thoroughly implicate and complement each other that the various contrasts that have been suggested by those who seek to define it—style *or* dark narratives? Period *or* genre?—should be seen as so many false alternatives. The great *noir* films exhibit their distinctive style in the service of narrative, using devices such as voice-over, flashback, long takes, and the entire panoply of implements in the *noir* director's toolbox to enhance narrative and thematic objectives. The style is in the telling, but what is told is more than just contingently connected to the choice of stylistic devices for the telling. The *noir auteur* then becomes the director who orchestrates all the technical devices at his command—essentially lighting, camera movement, sound, and performance—into a unified whole. In Ray's case, his special facility with his actors, his *verstehen philosophie*, allows him to enter into their emotional states in order to achieve outstanding performances from them, and is his special claim to outstanding director status. Even if, as it is sometimes said, Ray's deteriorating relationship with Gloria Grahame is the template for the Dix-Laurel romance, this hardly repudiates his capacity as *auteur*. Far from diminishing this role, it serves as evidence for it. *In a Lonely Place* may indeed be one of Ray's best instances of his emotional investment in his actors and therefore his characters.

In a Lonely Place was not only of, but also ahead of, its time. It is a stark enactment of human alienation and crisis and an early precursor of those dramas of personal disintegration and existential fate that came at the end of the classic *film noir* cycle with *Vertigo* (Alfred Hitchcock, 1958) and *Touch of Evil* (Orson Welles, 1958) some eight years after *In a Lonely Place* was released. It is as well a precursor to those self-reflexive comments on the absence of narrative closure found in the French New Wave, and to *neo-noir* with its existential bleakness and paranoid logic, from *Mickey One* (Arthur Penn, 1964) and *Seconds* (John Frankenheimer, 1966) to *The Driver* (Walter Hill, 1978). *In a Lonely Place* should also be seen as one of the most important progenitors of "anti"-Hollywood *noirs*, reminding us how important this subgenre has been, from *Sunset Boulevard* (Billy Wilder, 1950) and *The Big Knife* (Robert Aldrich, 1955) to *The Player* (Robert Altman, 1992), three of the best Hollywood *noir* films. In all four cases, Hollywood is a place, a state of mind, and, most significantly, a frame for an existential question. For example, for Altman it is how effectively can a guilty man—studio executive Griffin Mill (Tim Robbins), the killer of screenwriter David Kahane (Vincent D'Onofrio)—conceal his crime and remain free? For the others, it is how much must a man compromise his artistic integrity to survive as a creative force in the Dream Factory? And for Ray, it is as well how free must a bitter romantic who is frustrated in his ambitions and undernourished in his pleasures be to outrun his past? How far can his efforts to avoid failure and loss succeed? The answer Ray's film gives is not encouraging, and in this respect it clothes its subject in that darkness called *film noir* even as it transcends it and is thus, in its profound and disturbing study of love, possessiveness, betrayal, and loneliness, something more than *noir*.

Author's note: For research assistance and numerous helpful comments and criticisms, I am grateful to Christeen Clemens.

7

R. BARTON PALMER

On Dangerous Ground
Of Outsiders

THOUGH NOT WELCOMED BY American reviewers and failing to meet the studio's box-office expectations, *On Dangerous Ground* was received enthusiastically by the *Cahiers du cinéma* critics of the era. In fact, the film confirmed their already considerable admiration for Ray, which was based on what biographer Patrick McGilligan identifies as the principal quality of his distinctive body of work. Ray's films, he argues, "owe something to Hollywood, where he never quite fit in, and everything else to his idiosyncratic sensibility" (2). The Ray text is thus thought as generated by this dialectic of influence, by the opposition between an acceptance and perpetuation of industry conventions, but also their continual subversion in response to an extraordinary directorial personality. So imagined, Ray's career perfectly suits the scenario of creation envisioned by the *politique des auteurs*, with its enshrinement of artists who in important senses stand apart from the industry that simultaneously constitutes the ground of their activity. The *auteur*, in short, works in Sisyphean fashion to establish through communal means an unrealizable individuality. He is an outsider on the inside, and his films are personal only in a continually renegotiated sense. Speaking of *On Dangerous Ground* in a typical *Cahiers* homage, Jacques Rivette praises the

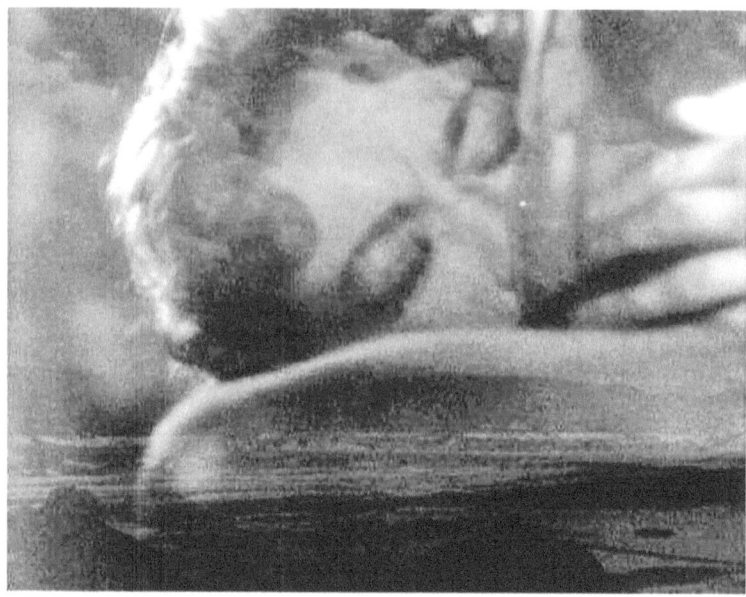

Figure 7.1. *On Dangerous Ground* (RKO Radio Pictures, 1952) expresses Ray's "force of personality" not only textually, but also, if in an indirect fashion, through the shaping of the context of production, which was in every sense "for him" (frame enlargement).

"wonderful progression of . . . ideas" the film manifests, conceding that even what seemed to be flaws redounded to the credit of geniuses like Ray: "the most simple mistakes turn out to be to their advantage, rather than diminishing their stature" ("Imagination" 104). As Rivette argues, *On Dangerous Ground*'s vivid stylizations and portrayal of character, as well as its (for the time) quite idiosyncratic narrative structure, fit well with the *politique des auteurs* and the critical preference of the *Cahiers* circle for the against-the-grain productions of Hollywood mavericks, whose "mistakes" (perhaps better, deviations from accepted industry practice) displeased insiders such as the film's producer, John Houseman, who was dubious from the start about Ray's choice of material and later disappointed by the director's rewriting of the script's conventional conclusion.

It was also a defect, Houseman opined, that *On Dangerous Ground* divides uneasily into two sections that are connected only loosely by the central presence in each of Jim Wilson (Robert Ryan), a Los Angeles detective who has become increasingly disgusted by the lowlife characters—petty criminals, prostitutes, psychopathic gangsters—that it is his job to surveil and control. While his partners are family men and thus have a life apart from the squalidness of their working lives, Wilson, for reasons that are never fully explained, has proven unable to overcome his isolation. He feels poisoned by the "garbage" he has to deal with and thus lives, as Geoff Andrew aptly puts it, "in a nightmarish hell of his own making" and "wallows in the self-pitying knowledge that he has no friends to help him" (55). Wilson and his partners take part in the pursuit of a cop killer, and in the course of that investigation Wilson treats suspects and informants with such violence that, in order to save his career, his captain sends him out to the country on another assignment. There he immediately becomes involved in yet another chase, this time of a mentally deranged youngster Danny (Sumner Williams) who has raped and murdered a local girl. In his embrace of violence and justifiable hatred, the girl's father, Walter Brent (Ward Bond), who accompanies Wilson on the manhunt through the Sierra Mountains, is clearly a doppelgänger serving as an object lesson. Persuaded by the young man's blind sister, Mary (Ida Lupino), to bring Danny in alive, Wilson struggles to capture the boy but prevents Brent from shooting him. As it turns out, Danny falls to his death before the two men can capture him. Unable to keep his promise, Wilson returns in despair to Mary, with whom he has fallen in love. They part, and he returns to the city, having failed to discover some way to curb either violence or the urge toward self-destruction in others, although he proves able to transform himself. He resumes his role as an ineffective force of moral regulation in a world that seems beyond reform and redemption, dooming him to suffer again from the impotent anger he felt from the outset. But then, in a startling reversal, he returns to Mary, and the film ends with their coupling.

This chapter confirms Rivette's understanding and valuation of Ray's "mistakes" in the film and evaluates the sense in which the production is "personal," that is, reflecting the director's control over the choice of material and its shaping. A central deviation from industry practice is the controversial ending that Ray substituted for the one that screenwriter A. I. Bezzerides provided, faithfully following the source novel, Gerard Butler's *Mad with Much Heart*. This rewriting was certainly a "personal" gesture or a "mistake," undertaken even in defiance of his screenwriter and producer. A consideration of the film's production history reveals that in general *On Dangerous Ground* expresses the director's sensibility and his intellectual obsessions, beginning with his selection of Butler's novel, a choice of text whose intellectual significance has hitherto escaped critical notice. From the outset this was an against-the-grain project, birthed by opposition.

What is surprising, however, is that in large measure the personal nature of the production was enabled by its somewhat dubious producer, who was more responsible than is usually thought for its coming to be, even in a form he found unsatisfying. Here the *auteurist* line on Ray, at least for this film, needs some substantial revision. In terms of the negotiation of creative freedom, the film belongs less to Ray and more to Houseman, who, paradoxically, was relentless in furthering a vision he did not share. Ray's substantial investment of emotion in the project seems to have focused Houseman's energies, making him not only a willing, but even a self-sacrificing partner. *On Dangerous Ground*, in short, expresses Ray's "force of personality" not only textually (that is, in terms of the choice of material and its significant rewriting), but also, if in an indirect fashion, through the shaping of the context of production, which was in every sense "for him."

A correlative of the director's emotional investment can be glimpsed in Wilson's enigmatic spiritual journey, with its surprising final act. This may also be a personal gesture, if of a different sort. In a complex sense, Wilson achieves the transcendence of self denied to Dixon Steele (Humphrey Bogart), his anomic fellow traveler in Ray's previous release, *In a Lonely Place*, whose title describes the psychological condition that Dixon never escapes (Houseman, *Front* 320). This film, many have thought, is in part autobiographical, especially since the woman whose love Steele forfeits through his uncontrollable violence is played by none other than Gloria Grahame, at the time Ray's increasingly estranged wife. That Dixon is a screenwriter facing continual difficulty in sustaining a Hollywood career argues even more strongly for an autobiographical approach. Viewed this way, the films thus constitute an interesting diptych of contrasting sensibilities (the *noir*-ish delineation of a defining pathology from which there is no exit versus a sudden transcendence of anger and anomie). A desperately truthful analogy for Ray's personal predicament is followed by a similar character's miraculous acceptance of salvific love. We might agree with Rivette that *On Dangerous Ground* indeed manifests a "wonderful progression of ideas," that it is in the words of John Houseman (and who should know better?) a film that was "made with much love." (*Front* 320).

Rebels without Causes

On Dangerous Ground would be Ray's sixth release in three hectic years of continually overlapping productions over which he was fortunate in exercising a substantial degree of control. His circumstances at the time thus very much enabled him to occupy the role of the *auteur* working within Hollywood, but not surrendering (at least no more than occasionally) either his thematic obsessions or personal style. In searching for a property to suit his interests, Ray came across and read the novel *Mad with Much Heart*, recently published by British writer Gerard Butler in 1946, and quickly decided to make a screen version. A piece of character-driven crime fiction, Butler's novel centered around a London policeman's pursuit of a mentally deficient young man whose has killed a young girl and is protected by his older, blind sister, with whom the detective soon falls in love, putting him into the kind of morally compromised situation whose imaginative possibilities were then being explored, to great popular acclaim, by, among others, Graham Greene in such novels as *The Heart of the Matter* (1948) and *Brighton Rock* (1938). The latter book, in fact, is startlingly similar to *Mad with Much Heart*. Butler's title would do nicely for Greene's "entertainment." Both these novels feature the pursuit of a psychopathic murderer and a love affair that, potentially redemptive, is soon doomed by the weight of its own psychological contradictions, religious contradictions, or both.

The appeal of *Mad with Much Heart* for Ray, just then finishing the semiautobiographical *In a Lonely Place*, must have been strong. Here was yet another story about a man with violent urges that seem an elemental part of his character, pushing him toward a pointless and unwilled self-destruction; here too, like Dixon Steele, the protagonist by happy chance finds himself attracted to a gentle woman who seems eager through her loving kindness to help him overcome the terrible anger that so easily and constantly rises to the surface. Dix struggles to resurrect his career as a Hollywood screenwriter and cope with a charge of murder that eventually proves false, but his uncontrolled outbursts turn him into a pariah; the often uncontrolled violent impulses of Butler's detective have prevented him from establishing any meaningful connection to others. In *In a Lonely Place*, Laurel (Gloria Grahame) attempts, as Andrew so well puts it, to offer Dix "an opportunity to become truly alive, so that his sense of identity and self-respect no longer depend entirely on his status in a philistine, profit-motivated, industry town" (48). With its focus on pathology and the dirty world of police work, *Mad with Much Heart* also provides its protagonist with the opportunity for renewal and transcendence through an escape from degraded urban life; here too, however, that chance is squandered.

Butler's novel was hardly a presold property in the usual sense, having never achieved bestseller status. Selling it to the studio would not be easy. Furthermore, instead of offering a simple, linear narrative, the novel was constructed around a striking contrast between a morally bankrupt modern urbanism and the natural renewal of self problematically made available by the "unspoiled" countryside, which ironically manifests its own murderous pathology. This was a thematic emphasis that would make for more an art house film than an entertainment film. As industry wisdom had it, such a novel would be worth adapting only if it offered material useful for the making of an appealing film. With its British settings, the novel would require considerable recontextualizing if the story were to be restaged as "American" in more than a superficial sense (McGilligan 190). Ray's intention from the outset was to erase the story's Englishness, which is not surprising since his oeuvre in general reveals, as Andrew suggests, "a deeply felt disillusionment with American life in general . . . expressed through his awareness of inner torment, of solitude and despair, conflict, and confusion" (1). Apart from the two large-scale studio projects he oversaw late in his career (*King of Kings* and *55 Days at Peking*), Ray's films focus clearly on various aspects of the American national character. This project was to be no different.

But from an industrial if not an *auteurist* point of view, transferring the story and characters to Los Angeles and the California Sierra Nevada was by no means an obvious move. Butler's similarly *noir*-ish crime novella *Kiss the Blood Off My Hands* (1946), adapted for the screen by Norman Foster, had just been released in 1948, and the screen version had retained to good effect the story's English setting and characters, with Robert Newton as the villain and the transatlantic Joan Fontaine as the love interest, and only Burt Lancaster as the unfortunate protagonist lending the film a North American flavor of sorts. Ray seems not to have considered seriously the possibility of following Foster in making a Hollywood British film, although there was much successful precedent for this course, particularly at the time when, because of British tax law, there was much advantage in making such hybrids for those American studios, like RKO, that had the substantial British connections to do so. At the close of the decade, RKO in fact had just signed an agreement with Britain's J. Arthur Rank for a series of coproductions, and the first result, released in 1947, had been a critical and popular success: Edward Dmytryk's adaptation of the James Hilton novel *So Well Remembered* (1945), featuring John Mills and Trevor Howard. *Kiss the Blood* was successful enough to be adapted as a *Lux Radio Theater* production, with Lancaster and Fontaine reprising their roles, about the time (1949) Ray was reading *Mad with Much Heart*. Perhaps this is how he became acquainted with the novelist. If largely unknown today, Butler enjoyed a certain popularity in the early postwar era for *noir*-ish fiction centering on the good-bad guy protagonist's relationship with a loving woman. Like *Kiss the Blood*, whose de-mobbed veteran cannot find a place in the postwar world, *Mad with Much Love* also focused on the inchoate dissatisfaction of a barely socialized character who cannot easily stay within the law he is sworn to uphold. And yet a penitential journey away from the dark city fails to relieve him of his unwilled isolation.

Despite Houseman's misgivings, then, Ray chose very well, lobbying for a source novel whose rights could be purchased relatively cheaply and that closely suited his emerging thematic interest in anatomizing, as Andrew puts it, "a violent man riven by contradictory impulses" (4). Then becoming almost a standard presence in what later critics would term the *film noir* of the period, this character type, in its various incarnations, becomes for Ray the affective center providing, to quote Andrew once again, the "raw emotional force" characteristic of other Ray dark melodramas such as *Born to be Bad, In a Lonely Place, Johnny Guitar, Rebel Without a Cause*, and, perhaps preeminently, *Bigger Than Life* (4). These portraits of alienation, pathology, and self-destruction suited an era in which what was then called "nonconformism" seemed an appropriate, perhaps justly valued *moyen de vivre* in a world deemed by many to be meaningless, unwelcoming, even degraded.

Significantly, one of Ray's most applauded productions, *Rebel Without a Cause*, draws its title, if not its narrative, from an influential sociological treatise, Robert Lindner's noted 1944 study of criminal psychopathology. As Ray may well have known, Lindner was the period's most vocal and provocative spokesman for the kind of irrepressible individuality that Ray's films both dramatize and celebrate (see, most notably, Lindner's bestselling *cri de coeur* against "organization men" in *Must You Conform?* [1946]). But Lindner's was not the only voice raised in favor of a radical individuality that gained an appreciative audience. In his immensely popular philosphico-literary exploration of this character type, *The Outsider* (1956), Colin Wilson notes his "sense of strangeness, of unreality," a disconnection which means that he "cannot live in the comfortable world of the bourgeois, accepting what he sees and touches as reality . . . what he sees is essentially chaos" (15). Estrangement and a pervasive feeling of moral numbness become the spiritual condition of the outsider; he is mired in an everydayness he can no longer embrace, dedicated to the consumption of his own poisonous emotions. Butler's bitter and disillusioned London inspector, which Ray transforms into a Los Angeles detective, is such a man. As in Greene's fiction, the narrative in which this character becomes embroiled answers to his obsessions, sensitivities, and desires, offering the possibility of self-transcendence through love, but in the end deploys a series of penitential adventures that only lead back to the narrative's beginning point.

The sophisticated and cultured Houseman was too familiar with the contemporary literary scene not to appreciate the middlebrow appeal of

Butler's contribution to the fiction of moral crisis and attendant failure, or occasional deliverance, so prominent a feature of European writing of the era (as in the novels of François Mauriac, then undergoing a kind of revival and soon to receive the Nobel Prize in 1952). And yet Houseman would only admit that he was "interested in it mainly because of Nick Ray's enthusiasm" (*Front* 317). The reason he gave was simple: Houseman saw "what drew him to the story" but "not how he proposed to turn it into a viable movie" (318). If he continued to support Ray, it was at least in part because he was eager to repeat their recent and successful partnership on an RKO production that was also a literary adaptation (*They Live by Night* provided a less *engagé* version of Edward Anderson's politically provocative novel, *Thieves Like Us*, published in 1937).

Houseman quickly dispatched *Mad with Much Heart* to the studio story department for evaluation, hoping, one supposes, for a more positive reading than he could himself provide (Houseman *Front* 317–18). But it was not to be. Like Houseman, editor William Fadiman recognized the story's appeal, but voted against proceeding further. *Mad with Much Heart*, he wrote head of production Sid Rogell, is an "unpleasant but powerful novel," which was likely "to emerge as an 'art' production that may receive critical acclaim but not sizable box-office returns" (qtd. in Houseman 317). But Fadiman's suspicion that there was latent artistic quality in Butler's novel may well have influenced his boss to not foreclose the project. Rogell wrote Houseman he agreed with his editor's judgment of the book's commercial unsuitability, but, somewhat surprisingly, he closed with a cryptic comment that was hardly discouraging: "Thanks to you and Nick for digging it up. Keep punching" (qtd. in Houseman 318).

Did Houseman get some implied message to proceed? Or did he ignore that the head of production was trying, somewhat ineptly, to say forget it? In any event, Houseman was not deterred. He must have trusted Ray's talent, but the project's forward motion was also something of a leap of faith because Ray's heavy involvement in *In a Lonely Place* made conferring with him about his "angle" for the film impossible. So, still nervous about a potentially disastrous failure, Houseman asked for a second opinion from novelist and screenwriter Raymond Chandler, who, like Fadiman, admitted to feeling no "enthusiasm" for the book, which he saw as marred by a badly motivated plot, unappealing characters, and "hardly a line of dialogue that would not be pure slop on the screen" (qtd. in Houseman 319). Tellingly, Houseman did not show Chandler's letter to studio executives including Rogell. And he did not show it to Ray. Yet again, he was not deterred, despite the utterly damning judgment of the industry's reigning expert on marketable crime fiction.

Houseman would have kept Chandler's opinions to himself only because he wanted to make sure that *On Dangerous Ground* was in fact made—and under the direction of an artist not entertaining any doubts about his choice. Once again, this indicates support he could not bring himself to articulate more forthrightly. Even more remarkable, the project avoided cancellation because he agreed to produce another property for RKO about which he had even less enthusiasm. In addition, Robert Ryan, he promised, would play the lead in Ray's film, while the producer would personally develop the screenplay. These promises mollified studio executives, who then approved what Ray had proposed. Houseman, not Ray, made the argument for creative independence. And Houseman, not Ray, paid the price: producing the flimsy melodrama of *The Company She Keeps* (John Cromwell, 1951), which he counted as the most disagreeable of his professional experiences.

A Shallow and Uneven Affair?

Fadiman's prediction of commercial failure for the project, and of a critical acclaim based on a perceived "artiness," would prove correct. Ray's enhancement of that artiness contributed to viewer indifference, which was hardly unexpected. More surprising, perhaps, Ray's most substantial alteration of his source—his reconfiguration of the story's downbeat ending—earned him a rebuke from highbrow critics. Ray substantially reworked the script A. I. Bezzerides prepared for him, earning a screen credit for adaptation, but also earning Houseman's disapproval of the changes. Not only did *On Dangerous Ground* fail to be a hit with audiences; it was accorded only a lukewarm reception from the era's most influential tastemaker, Bosley Crowther. Writing in the *New York Times*, he declared in his review that *On Dangerous Ground* represents "an obvious attempt to get something more than sheer melodrama onto the screen—something pictorially reflective of the emotional confusion of a man" ("*Dangerous*" 35). Reflecting his Hollywood-influenced view of what constitutes a well-made film, however, Houseman complained that the story was a "shallow and uneven affair," marred by "inadequate explanations of character and a not well-motivated happy ending" (*Front* 322).

Crowther's enthusiastic review of *In a Lonely Place* had emphasized that film's downbeat ending and, more generally, what he saw as Ray's wise decision to stay close to the script, itself a rather faithful adaptation of the source novel. Ray, Crowther enthused:

> moves flawlessly through a script which is almost as flinty as the actor himself [star Humphrey Bogart]. Andrew Solt, who

fashioned the screen play from a story by Dorothy B. Hughes and an adaptation by Edmund H. North, has had the good sense to resolve the story logically. Thus Dixon Steele remains as much of an enigma, an explosive, contradictory force at loose ends when the film ends as when it starts. ("Three Films" 46)

In other words, Ray plays it safe, follows the rules, and does not deviate from the excellent script from his talented collaborator. Yet Crowther is not calling him a hack, or to use the *Cahiers* term, a *metteur-en-scène*. The film is in a central way unusual. If, in part, Ray is praised for following the Hollywood convention of logical, coherent story construction, he is also lauded for violating one of the industry's most entrenched doctrines. Dixon Steele has no arc; he does not move from some inferior, incomplete form of being to self-fulfillment, thus providing the conclusion with a sense of earned stasis. Moreover, Dix does not become "knowable" as the film progresses; his fragile volatility and barely restrained homicidal tendencies, although abundantly and movingly illustrated, are never psychologized in even the simplistic manner so popular in films of the period. The narrative, it is true, locates the trigger for his self-destructive behavior in the cutthroat environment of the Hollywood filmmaking community, with its outsize egos, manipulative self-promoters, and savagely competitive success ethic. But Dix, as Crowther suggests, remains "an explosive, contradictory force" never reducible to environment or some formulaic, if decisively formative, experience. This is filmic modernism in one of its most interesting and affecting forms.

In a Lonely Place holds out the promise, never fulfilled, of a conventional form of happiness, dependent on the woman's Austenesque ability to reform her man as well as accommodate herself to his nature. As it turns out, however, the narrative merely delivers the ill-starred couple to the miserable, suspicious, and fearful loneliness that had been their condition at the outset. It seems dedicated to proving that love does not always conquer all, ending instead with the antimelodramatic gesture of withdrawal and irreconcilable separation. It concludes with a focus on the after-scene of the powerlessness of love to either ameliorate or tolerate a violence that, at the very moment of its ostensible vindication, makes clear its potentially homicidal energies. In a terrible irony, Dix is cleared of the charge of murdering his assistant just after barely restraining himself from strangling Laurel, who, he discovers, had planned to leave him.

On Dangerous Ground would take these same story materials in a radically different, if equally antigeneric direction, that pleased no one involved except Ray himself. *In a Lonely Place* traces the failure of both love and developing self-awareness to effect Dixon's deliverance, and in *On Dangerous Ground* the radical rejection of this vision of human impotence illustrates precisely what Rivette terms Ray's "wonderful progression of ideas": here the antirealistic resolution of character through a transcendental gesture that in a decisive moment erases the past and inaugurates a different, if thoroughly impossible, mode of being for the reunited lovers. This projected closure, of course, is very much in line with conventional cinematic conclusions: a reconstituted couple; an implied future in which all interpersonal problems are imagined as solved; and, perhaps most significant given the film's bipartite structure, a metonymic melding of the opposing elements from which the narrative has been constituted (here a pair of significant archetypes: the dark city and the restorative county, respective loci of innocence and experience, each of which generates its own expressively typical character). The man who sees too much becomes one with the girl whose blindness makes her reliant on her other senses; together they constitute a whole in a paradigmatically neat fashion as thoroughly conventional as the merging of pride with prejudice.

Yet in its violation of story logic this finale (for which the viewer is deliberately not prepared) seems more metafictional than fictional, more a wager the filmmaker placed on the possibility of transcending the story world and its inescapable discontents (which are thoroughly detailed with Ray's customary careful attention to *mise-en-scène*, plausible dialogue, and careful development of character) rather than a possible vision, however remote or unlikely, of character transformation. Not "the story might end with this sort of inner transformation," but rather "wouldn't it be wonderful if things ended this way, but of course that's impossible." The conclusion of *On Dangerous Ground*, which Ray wrote in defiance of both Bezzerides and Houseman, is thus a wish fulfillment that, somewhat paradoxically, denies the possibility of this wish being fulfilled. If that is so, this commentative metafictionality is a profoundly obtrusive form of authorial signature, a self-conscious writing on the given materials of commercial production and an antirealistic excess of the kind that figures interestingly, if only occasionally, in other Ray productions, especially the flamboyantly baroque *Johnny Guitar*. In *On Dangerous Ground* (whose title perhaps issues a warning to directors who might go too far), Ray is afforded by possibility of such an ultrapersonal gesture, of a defiance of all the logic of industrial common sense, by the against-the-grain work of a producer who, though believing in him, does not trust (as it turns out, for very good reason) the project he makes possible, in the process interestingly participating in the causeless rebellion that is otherwise at the heart of Ray's *oeuvre*.

8

Tony Williams

Flying Leathernecks
Color and Characterization

Directed between two later critically acclaimed films, *On Dangerous Ground* and *The Lusty Men*, *Flying Leathernecks* has generally been neglected in discussions of Nicholas Ray's early work. It preceded Ray's uncredited reworking of RKO studio productions such as *The Racket* (John Cromwell, 1951) and *Macao* (Josef von Sternberg, 1952) as a favor to studio head Howard Hughes who protected him from the blacklist (Eisenschitz 60). Suffering from a chaotic shooting schedule with director and costar (Robert Ryan) unsympathetic to the entire project, *Flying Leathernecks* might be dismissed as a work-for-hire production as opposed to earlier and later films where Ray's personality is clearly evident. According to a concept associated with the original "*auteur* theory," *Flying Leathernecks* would be an unpromising text ironically contradicting that absurd *Cahiers du cinéma* claim that *auteurs* can never make a bad film while a craftsmen can never direct a good film, something nobody takes seriously today. However, circumstances exist when personal vision and craftsmanship coexist. *Flying Leathernecks* is one such example. It is neither a recognizable work of personal cinema nor is it, as Geoff Andrew asserts, solely "one of Ray's most anonymous and

Figure 8.1. *Flying Leathernecks* (RKO Radio Pictures, 1951) contrasts two types of star personae who epitomize different aspects of post–World War II cinematic masculinity: John Wayne and Robert Ryan (frame enlargement).

conventional films" (60).[1] Although Bernard Eisenschitz, in his biography of Ray, and Andrew, in his *auteur* study, dismiss the film, they also recognize certain features that anticipate more developed accomplishments.

Despite regarding *Flying Leathernecks* as an anonymous patchwork entity involving several scripts and the interweaving of documentary footage and fictional reconstruction, Eisenschitz notes a far from anonymous use of color operating in the film:

> The cameraman William Syder uses color with a delicacy rare in such films, and rare for Technicolor at that time. Not only do the hills of California (standing in for Guadalcanal), the khaki uniforms, the aircraft, the lightly overcast skies suggest the green and beige tones associated with images of war; but also these colors are echoed in Wayne's home, where certain scenes are played out in semi-darkness or against a single splash of brightness. Similarly worthy of note is a strategic

maneuver, signposted by garishly-colored flags—red, yellow, and violet. (163)

Unfortunately, Eisenschitz does not examine the reasons *why* these colors occur in *Flying Leathernecks*, nor does Andrew. Although Andrew defines the film as "an almost entirely traditional and conservative war film, lacking a strong dramatic foundation and notable mainly for the efficient way in which the documentary footage is sewn, relatively seamlessly, into the story proper," his retrospective comments sense the presence of other distinctive elements (60). Like Eisenschitz, he does not explore these features in depth and instead sees the film as a "very dry run for *Bitter Victory*, distinguished mainly by its genuinely delicate Technicolor hues, unusual in an actioner of this kind" (172). *Flying Leathernecks* is no *Bitter Victory*. But it does contain the origins of the personality conflict present within the later film. It also subtly recognizes the dehumanizing effects of war on those who fight. *Flying Leathernecks* also contrasts two types of star personae who epitomize different aspects of post–World War II cinematic masculinity: John Wayne and Robert Ryan.

Wayne needs little introduction since he is well-known for his embodiment of American conservative values in the majority of his films.[2] Robert Ryan embodies a completely different type of star persona. While never a major star like Wayne, he is most well-known for personifying the insecure, neurotic, and disturbed aspect of a postwar masculinity defined by many of his performances in *film noir*, of which Ray's *On Dangerous Ground* contains one of his most distinguished roles. Part of the fascination of *Flying Leathernecks* involves seeing not only the contrast of two types of acting styles but also a particular symbiotic parallelism that Ray stylistically develops between both these characters, a parallelism he will perfect in *Bitter Victory*.

Despite the fact that characterization is not as realized as those in later Ray films, rudimentary features operate in *Flying Leathernecks* as prototextual elements. Anyone familiar with Ray's entire work can ignore the tight propaganda structure that Howard Hughes imposed on Ray and will easily interpret such elements as faint, subversive traces of destabilizing ghosts lurking in a Hollywood studio machine awaiting further realization at a more convenient time when restraints would not be as dominant concerning expectations of what a propaganda film should be. According to Ryan, Ray may have indulged in some over-directing on the film purely out of disgust (Nogueira and Zalaffi 55). He may also have attempted to insert some subversive tensions into the text that, if not entirely destabilizing its conservative message, at least revealed the presence of motifs that he would elaborate and refine later in his career.

History, Ideology, and Cultural Contradictions

Made in the heyday of the Korean War, a conflict anticipated in the late 1940s with the return of affirmative war films such as William Wellman's *Battleground* (1948), Allan Dwan's *The Sands of Iwo Jima* (1949), and Lewis Milestone's *The Halls of Montezuma* (1950), after the pessimism displayed in productions such as John Ford's *They Were Expendable* (1945), Wellman's *The Story of G. I. Joe* (1945), and Milestone's *A Walk in the Sun* (1946), *Flying Leathernecks* merges certain components of the Dwan and Ford films tailored to new ideological requirements. Produced by the executive producer of *The Sands of Iwo Jima*, Edmund Grainger, *Flying Leathernecks* was made at the request of the Pentagon. The head of the Marine aviation branch, General Clayton Jerome, wished to see a film applauding the contribution that Marine fliers had made to the Pacific conflict. Originally, Grainger wanted to set the story during the Korean War but the Navy's withdrawal of an aircraft carrier needed for the conflict led to the setting being changed to the World War II battle for Guadalcanal. Although Lawrence H. Suid notes that the change resulted in Marine pilots flying against Japanese rather than Korean and Chinese soldiers, "the film also suggested that the Marines were again supporting their men on the ground during the Korean police action then being fought" (124). Certain advantages resulted from this collaboration such as color archive footage. Suid notes the Navy and Marines used color film in the Pacific from the beginning of the war as opposed to the European conflict where archive footage was in black and white until after D-Day and then not on a large scale (170).

Despite being set in World War II, *Flying Leathernecks* ideologically merges aspects of the past Pacific conflict with the present Korean War, which would have been on the mind of most audiences. Its two major stars personify cinematic masculine images associated with each conflict. Wayne would be indelibly associated with *The Sands of Iwo Jima*. Major Dan Kirby in *Flying Leathernecks* also evokes the Kirby York(e) character he plays in John Ford's *Fort Apache* (1948) and *Rio Grande* (1950). However, unlike Ford's cavalry trilogy and *The Sands of Iwo Jima*, the Frontier has not been won and the conflict continues, this time with a greater loss of human personnel than in *The Sands of Iwo Jima*. Although Ryan would not make a Korean War film until Anthony Mann's *Men in War* (1957), his whole acting persona, unlike Wayne's, is one expressing doubt both over conservative definitions of masculinity and the institutions he is part of. Like *The Sands of Iwo Jima*, *Flying Leathernecks* ends with respect and understanding of the rebel for his commanding officer. But here it is arbitrary and forced suggesting a possible deliberate strategy on the part of Ray and Ryan, who both expressed dissatisfaction with this RKO project.

As Bruce Cumings notes, the issues that led to the Korean War were complex but it seems certain that America envisaged future conflict emerging several years before it actually occurred.[3] For American military and political leadership, the issue was one of selling this new war to a public slowly recovering from World War II. Several internal and external factors such as McCarthyism and the demonization of America's former ally, the Soviet Union, into being a threat to world peace, contributed to a new political strategy of reawakening a war-weary nation into accepting its new responsibilities as the guardian of the free word. Cinema would play a strategic role in this scenario since Hollywood and the Pentagon always engaged in appropriate close cooperation with certain exceptions, such as the Vietnam War. As a film from a studio Howard Hughes managed and whose Hughes Tool Company would certainly benefit from the emerging conflict, *Flying Leathernecks* would make an ideal contribution to a new version of the "Why We Fight" ideology of World War II. Like its leading star John Wayne, Edmund Grainger, first screenplay writer Kenneth Gamet, and Wayne's favorite screenwriter James Edward Grant were all war veterans.[4] Another uncredited scenarist, Bernie Lay Jr., was reworking his coauthored *Twelve O'Clock High* (Henry King, 1949) screenplay for the film, which did not involve the mental breakdown of a commanding officer (Eisenschitz 161). James Edward Grant probably wrote the final version. In addition to *The Sands of Iwo Jima*, *They Were Expendable* also influences *Flying Leathernecks*. The Marine aviation unit has to prove itself to the high command. But whereas *They Were Expendable*'s PT boats are regarded with condescension until Washington begins thinking sensibly at the end of the film, in *Flying Leathernecks* the unit has already proved itself in aerial combat missions with Japanese planes. However, the high-ranking officers in *Flying Leathernecks* needs to be convinced that the aviation unit can drop bombs on the enemy during low-level flying missions and not cause any friendly fire losses. This would become a key activity during the Korean War when American planes dropped napalm on Chinese and North Korean forces to help the outnumbered military fighting in conditions that did not resemble those of World War II. Despite its World War II structure, *Flying Leathernecks* is a Korean War film in all but name working as a propaganda tool for the Pentagon and starring an actor embodying the accepted masculine Western imagery of frontier America and now identified as *the* World War II hero after *The Sands of Iwo Jima*.

Like the doomed PT boat crew in John Ford's film, the young flyers in *Flying Leathernecks* are as expendable as their predecessors. They appear too young to have fought in World War II and one of them studied at the Harvard Business School. He is now drafted like the reluctant character William Holden played in *The Bridges at Toko-Ri* (Mark Robson, 1955), a World War II veteran wishing to remain in civilian life. Like other official Korean War films such as Samuel Fuller's *The Steel Helmet* (1950) and *Fixed Bayonets* (1951), *Flying Leathernecks* expresses hesitancy suggesting that this conflict will not be easy, something endemic to Korean War films as opposed to their World War II predecessors. Conflict between Griffin and Kirby represents a watered-down version of that between Brickley and Ryan in *They Were Expendable*, with the only difference being that Griffin is more experienced and older than Ryan. He has obviously experienced more combat missions and wishes to save as many of his men as possible. Until his final ideological capitulation to Kirby in the last sequence of *Flying Leathernecks*, Ryan's character Griffin foreshadows the doubting character of John the Baptist that he will play in his penultimate scene later in *King of Kings*. Despite his acceptance of command decisions, several medium shots and close-ups in the film reveal agony on his face as he witnesses his men die in combat. Although Griffin will not succumb to post-traumatic stress disorder (PTSD) like the officer in *A Walk in the Sun*, he is clearly on the verge of a nervous breakdown. Although Kirby does care, as we see in certain scenes and his decision to write letters to the families of deceased flyers, like Sergeant Stryker he cannot explicitly exhibit his feelings like Griffin does. Despite being hampered by ideological restraints, certain subversive cracks occur in the structure of *Flying Leathernecks* that the total structure of the film attempts to disavow. This is clearly seen in certain performative moments during the film. Although Ray and former Marine Robert Ryan may have felt themselves outnumbered by "Sheriff" Wayne and his posse of Kenneth Gamet, James Edward Grant, Howard Hughes, and actors such as Jay C. Flippen (was Ward Bond working on another film at the time?) who shared Wayne's right-wing views, they may have attempted ways to sweeten the nasty ideological pill both were forced to swallow. As Ryan said, "We often asked ourselves what we were doing on a film like this. I hate war films" (qtd. in Eisenschitz 161). These alternative ways came in the form of subversive interpretations involving deliberately stylistic color imagery and character representation.

Color and Characterization

> It might be interesting to ask different people, or the same people on entirely different kinds of days, when they're in different moods, what different colors mean to them, and to ask in such a way that they're taken off guard and respond truthfully, and not with an intellectual idea of green as envy, or green as health, or green as jealousy, or green as sanitation, or green as love.
>
> —Nicholas Ray (*Interrupted* 58)

The above statement appears in a posthumously collected series of essays based on Ray's notes during his later years as a film teacher. Although this collection appeared many decades after Ray had made the films he mentions, we have no reason to doubt that his retrospective comments represent intuitive thoughts that appeared during the time he made these films. His comments appear in a brief but rewarding section on color and reveal that his approach to this technology was as intuitive as his attempts to get fresh performances from his actors. Ray also remarks that, "A few of us have done a lot of experimenting in the use of color and its emotional connection with the audience. These experiments of mine and other directors are within most commercial films" (Ray, *Interrupted* 58). Although Ray later discovered a key text by Dr. Max Lüscher whose dust jacket announced that "the principle of the Lüscher Color Test is that accurate psychological information can be gained about a person through his choices and rejections of colors," we have every reason to believe that before, during, and later Ray's discovery of this was more intuitive than formulaic concerning the appropriate type of color needed for each particular film (Frascella and Weisel 118–119).[5] This was definitely the case with *Flying Leathernecks*.

Flying Leathernecks is a film that would appeal to the aviation and right-wing political interests of studio head Howard Hughes. Although Ray and Ryan were uncomfortable in making this film, certain strategies could be used to minimize the bitter ideological pill that both were forced to swallow while working on this production. Color is one of those strategies. Commenting later on his previous film, *On Dangerous Ground*, Ray mentioned that he overcompensated for the lack of color by letting his leading actors overplay. He also excessively emphasized the contrast between the city and the country in visual terms. Yet while his first color film *Flying Leathernecks* downplays any type of excessive performance on the part of its leading actors to elicit a more intuitive type of acting, he uses color in a muted but revealing manner. As Ray states, "The significance of objects is always lost without color. Not always, but now that we are used to color" (*Interrupted* 58). The strategy that Ray uses in *Flying Leathernecks* not only involves integrating studio and location footage with the 16mm documentary footage the Pentagon donated to this project, but also uses color in significant ways to suggest other meanings destabilizing the patriotic *Sands of Iwo Jima* message RKO wished to promote.

As noted earlier, several critics discerned the distinctive use of color in *Flying Leathernecks* but refrained from trying to excavate its meaning in the film. Blaine Allan cites *Flying Leathernecks* as belonging to a group of Ray films that involve problematic attempts to try to search for meaningful definitions of home and family, a search often doomed to failure as in *They Live by Night, In a Lonely Place*, and *Rebel Without a Cause* (27).[6] Although *Flying Leathernecks* attempts the usual type of division between a tranquil home front and violent battlefield characteristic of most generic war movies, Ray's use of color undermines this convenient type of separation as Eisenschitz notes above. In fact, both locations display echoes of wartime trauma throughout the film as selective color imagery reveals. During the introductory voice-over modeled on *The Sands of Iwo Jima*, the first image seen is a beach on the island of Oahu with blue sea, blue sky, and brown mountain range in the background. The scene changes to introduce Kirby, Griffin, and the officers of VMF 247 (Virtual Marine Fight Squad). Key colors are khaki and green. The men wear light khaki jump suits matching the colors worn by their commanding officers. A green bar table and light green walls also predominate. Kirby notices the garish cowboy boots Griffin's brother-in-law Vern, nicknamed "Cowboy," wears that combine brown, green, and yellow. Brown associates "Cowboy" with the group but green and yellow representing competing and contrasting colors suggesting instability. In *Party Girl*, John Ireland's erratic gangster wears a light green suit. Yellow anticipates the yellow shirt worn by the immature Turkey in *Johnny Guitar* as well as Buzz's T-shirt in *Rebel Without a Cause*. In these later films, both characters are sacrificial victims of violence, one lynched by a posse and the other dying in the chicken run due to peer group pressure after revealing the potentiality for friendship he could have with Jim Stark just before his tragic and unnecessary demise. In *Flying Leathernecks*, "Cowboy" is a likeable if immature character having a more stable family life than Griffin who appears to be a solitary man with no family connections. The key climactic moment in *Flying Leathernecks* is when Griffin no longer allows his heart to rule his head showing himself ready to take command by not rescuing Cowboy when a Japanese fighter attacks him. This scene is equivalent to Conway's conversion at the end of *Sands of Iwo Jima* when he takes on the role of Sergeant Stryker and orders the platoon to get back to the war. However, Ray questions this type of conversion since the audience has grown to like Cowboy and may regret the ideological necessity for his sacrificial death. By associating Cowboy with a strategic type of color coding, Ray predestines his eventual fate in the same way as the helicopter shots in *They Live by Night* foreshadow those of its doomed characters. Like Shipley and McHugh in *The Sands of Iwo Jima*, "Cowboy" becomes the film's surrogate sacrificial victim allowing Griffin to purge his personality of unacceptable feelings before finally taking on the mantle of Kirby. However, unlike these predecessors, Ray presents his death as tragic and unnecessary.

Home front sequences that usually intrude irrelevantly into war narratives are also here significantly color coded. The camera tracks right before a green framework showing each officer sending a letter home leading to several sequences revealing those back home. Lieutenant Castle's girlfriend wears a light green sweater whereas Cowboy's wife has a washed pale green dressing gown and his two children have light green pajamas. Unlike Cowboy's boots, green here represents a complementary color tone linking pilots with their loved ones. When Kirby arrives home, his wife wears a light blue dressing gown and his son has two blue pendants hanging on his bedroom wall next to a red Harvard pendant. The blue evokes the beautiful, yet dangerous, blue skies the pilots fly against, which also contain threatening Japanese opponents. Each VMF mug inscribed with the names of each flyer has a red background. They become significantly reduced in number as the film continues. Red is the color of danger in *Flying Leathernecks* as seen in the fiery demise of planes downed in combat by Japanese Zeroes as well as the red sun on the Japanese flag. During a briefing scene before VMF 247 undertakes its first low-flying mission at tree-top level, contrasting primary colors of red, yellow, and violet appear prominently in the film for the first time against familiar brown and green background colors. Red rectangles represent ground Marine positions at risk from overwhelming Japanese forces as well as friendly fire should a flyer miscalculate. Friendly fire is frequently mentioned as one reason for the high-ranking officers' hesitation over using the aviation unit to support ground troops. One design used to illustrate the mission is an arrow having a red base with a yellow tip. As well as representing a device used to illustrate strategy for the benefit of the flyers, this arrow has other ominous associations. Yellow previously appeared as the color of life jackets both Kirby and Griff wear earlier in the film. The mission is designed to save lives, but success depends on the maturity of each flyer, two of whom previously disobeyed Kirby's orders to work as a team. At the end of the briefing,

"Cowboy" jokes about his boots to the Colonel. Kirby ascribes his immature behavior to Griffin's lax commanding "Bring your troubles to Papa" attitude. As noted, these boots have clashing green, brown, and yellow colors of which the last is the discordant color. Red and yellow arrow imagery suggests that the mission could go wrong due to one immature pilot causing the death of ground Marines by friendly fire.

The home front is not exempt from tensions. Kirby gives his son a Japanese officer's sword, which he gleefully swings in the air before bedtime. Although depicted as a father's gift to his son, it not only grimly evokes what could happen to Kirby were he to fall into Japanese hands but also the fate of Lieutenant Jorgenson who when left dangling by his parachute may have had suffered more mutilations than the bullets Japanese ground troops fired into his body. Kirby takes his wife to bed while wearing a light khaki officer's uniform during a scene significantly revealing a red lamp in the left foreground of the frame against a dark background. During their farewell scene, Mrs. Kirby (Janis Carter) ominously wears a red dress.

Although *Flying Leathernecks* ideologically reworks the conflict between opposites of *The Sands of Iwo Jima* and moves toward acceptable institutional resolution, it also foreshadows darker aspects of *Bitter Victory*. Wayne's and Ryan's acting styles differ but they operate in significantly contradictory and complementary ways in the film. Several close-ups show Ryan neurotically upset over the deaths of each flyer in his unit. When Cowboy's plane descends in flames, more shots are devoted to Ryan's expression than Wayne's. But Wayne is clearly affected by these deaths reacting to them in a stoic, minimalist manner. Regret briefly appears on his face. Like Major Brand and Captain Leith, Kirby and Griff are complementary opposites, emotionally scarred by war, but restrained by combat (and the ideological forces within RKO studios) to repress their feelings. Ryan can explicitly reveal them. Wayne cannot and certainly not on the ground. During particular scenes, both characters wear similar colored outfits, which not only signify their roles as commanding officers but also suggest a symbiotic traumatic relationship that the film attempts to repress, although not entirely. Kirby and Griffin wear green trousers and light khaki shirts at different points of the film but not in the same scenes together. After witnessing the tragedy of a downed pilot's plane exploding in flames, the jumpsuits of both exhibit a dark brown texture due to the rain. When Cowboy's plane descends in flames, the last weakest link in the original squadron perishes. Griff now takes over command since he has not left the formation to help his brother-in-law. Like Jim Stark, Griff is now ready to function in the everyday world. Yet, despite the ideological restraints imposed on this film, the viewer is still left with the question, "Was it really worth it?"

Notes

1. Allan Eyles caustically mentions that "Howard Hughes, boss of RKO, reportedly paid Wayne a record $301,000 for making the picture and also arranged for the artistic sensitivity of co-star Robert Ryan and director Nicholas Ray to be as thoroughly annihilated as the enemy in the film" (127).

2. See Eyles (11–14) and Willis.

3. See Cumings. For a recent perspective see Halberstam (94).

4. According to Eisenschitz, Gamet had written war movies for Grainger such as *Flying Tigers* (David Miller, 1942) starring John Wayne. Gamet also coscripted *Wake of the Red Witch* (Edward Ludwig, 1949) (513). Wayne allowed him both to write and to direct one of his own productions, *Angel and the Badman* (1947). Grant also scripted *The Sands of Iwo Jima* with Wayne in his evocative role of Sergeant Stryker. In 1952, Grant wrote the screenplay for the pro-HUAC *Big Jim McClain* (Edward Ludwig), which Wayne both coproduced and starred in.

5. See also Lüscher.

6. As Allan writes: "As an alternative, characters have homes and attempt to maintain families under duress or warlike conditions in foreign lands. The field bases in *Flying Leathernecks* are scarcely homes, but Sweeney [Clancy, *sic*] steals at least some objects to keep up the Marines' morale. On the home front, Kirby's dilemma involves a choice between a desk job and his family, or his mission to introduce new forms of strategy for the air corps" (27).

9

Neil Campbell

The Lusty Men and the Post-Western

"A film in America is at the same time always a film about America"

—Wenders (121)

❦

During a 1979 lecture at Vassar College, following a screening of his 1952 film *The Lusty Men*, Nicholas Ray made the following remarks:

> In any case, this film isn't a Western. It's really about people who want nothing more than a home of their own. That was actually the great American dream at the time, and in all the statistical questionnaires that ask what Americans aim for, 90 per cent always gave the answer: "Owning a home of my own." And that's what the film's about. (qtd. in Wenders 119)

For Ray, the film is not a Western in any conventional sense; it is a post-Western, engaging with contemporary social, economic, and politi-

Figure 9.1. *The Lusty Men* (Wald-Krasna Productions/RKO Radio Pictures, 1952) reveals much about national and regional identity, and how concepts of home appeal in differing ways, through memory and nostalgia, to fixing roots in a particular time and place (frame enlargement).

cal changes and, in George Kouvaros's words, "bringing the tropes and iconography of classical genres into engagement with the material realities of postwar life" (151). Immediately after World War II, when the film was set and made, the United States sought stability, consensus, and a renewal of family values, epitomized in the suburban dream of homeownership. As Ray argues, this was an abiding national dream, and one that has always resonated in the West where settlement and homebuilding were marks of achievement and proof of the taming of the frontier. As a contrary pull, however, the establishment of a home on the range and a new social order in the West demanded a type of wild, rugged individualism that, perhaps by its very nature, was *unhomely*. In playing out such contradictions *The Lusty Men* reveals much about national and regional identity, and how concepts of "home" appeal in differing ways, through memory and nostalgia, to fixing roots in a particular time and place.[1]

The Lusty Men, however, is a post-Western concerned with the "troubling afterlife" (Kouvaros 161) of the mythic West, retaining traces, tropes, and iconographies from its classic Western forms that John Ford and Howard Hawks made famous, all while dramatizing a changing region, living with the specters of its mythic past and its increasingly complex future. "Post" in the post-Western always signifies, as Stuart Hall writes, "not only 'after' but 'going beyond'. . . as post-modernism is both 'going beyond' and 'after' modernism" (Hall 253). Crucially the post-Western breaks strict linearity or genre progression by interrelating between forms while extending and altering them. Hence, the classical Western and its "post-Western" forms never function in a purely binary way but interact, overlap, and interfuse in complex dialogical ways dramatized centrally in a film such as *The Lusty Men*.

In its opening scenes, Jeff McCloud (Robert Mitchum) undergoes a powerful journey whereby "every shot gradually becomes a sign in some sort of runic script, that you slowly see and hear" (119). Wim Wenders recorded the Vassar lecture for the film he made with Ray about the dying director's last months, *Lightning Over Water*. The word "slowly" explains Wenders's admiration for Ray's work, who, despite his eminence within Hollywood, made films that took time to reveal human relationships through detailed characterization and complex framing. For Wenders, Ray's film is a "song" with its visual notes and melodies, pauses, and refrains working on-screen in some of the most extraordinary sequences in film history, and most certainly, establishing the cinematic post-Western. Not surprisingly, then, *Cahiers du cinéma* critics such as Godard, Rohmer, Truffaut, and, above all, Jacques Rivette greatly admired Ray's work. Godard claims, for example, that Ray was "the cinema" itself ("Stars" 118), whilst Rivette praised "those long pauses, those turns that are at the centre of Ray's films," mixing "violence" and "meditation" in a recognition of "a new *mal de siècle* which it would be difficult for us to disown" ("Revolution" 95–96). The French saw in Mitchum's performance, and the cool shades of black and white created by cinematographer Lee Garmes, a moody disillusionment and melancholic longing that captured the spirit of the postwar age perfectly.

This admiration is fully expressed in Rivette's 1953 review "On Imagination," noting the "disconcerting" quality of *The Lusty Men*, caused by its "youthful exaggeration" wherein "everything is sacrificed to expression, to efficacity [*sic*], to the sharpness of a reflex or a look" (104). Thus, unlike Hollywood's obsession with action and fast-cutting, Ray took time to place characters in the frame and allow the camera to establish their emotional geometries, as well as being "lavish with ideas . . . ideas of *mise-en-scène* or—if I were to be shocking about it—of framing or the way shots are put together" (Rivette 104). In the most perceptive and prescient section, Rivette comments on Ray as "obsessed with the abstract" through a "certain dilation of expressive detail, which ceases to be detail so that it may become part of the plot" found in "dramatic close-ups" and a "breadth of modern gesture" contributing to "an anxiety about *life*, a perpetual disquiet" often capturing "the feverish and impermanent" even in the "most tranquil of moments" (104–05). In this respect, *The Lusty Men* marks a shift Gilles Deleuze identifies away from the "movement-image" and toward the "time-image" (or a subtle blending of the two), creating "modern political cinema" responding to a post-1945 climate of increased social and political change. Sequences of hero-derived action and the unquestioned links between the film's linear movement and narrative order associated with Classical Hollywood were placed under question because such causal relations were interrupted by a greater emphasis on time's passage.

This is apparent in the opening scenes of Ray's film, beginning under its titles, with the razzamatazz and spectacle of the rodeo parade; with bunting, patriotic bands, Indians, cowboys, wagons, and horses inviting us into the coming attraction, advertised on a screen-filling billboard as "The Wildest Show on Earth." Immediately the film signals one of its key themes, the transformation of the West into performance, simulation, and spectacle, into a perpetually self-fulfilling narrative of mythic proportions, a "wild show" acting out in the rodeo arena stories of conquest, masculinity, and control. Alongside this spectacle, a counternarrative of violence emerges through the brahma bull ride that almost cripples McCloud, filmed in documentary naturalist style with blurred shots and point-of-view camera angles. In the subsequent sequence, McCloud limps from the arena as the announcer's voice describes the next contestant quickly dispatched by a bull called "Round-trip" ("He must have bought a one-way ticket"), and as the excitement of the crowd dies away, Ray focuses on this lonesome figure, another man with a one-way ticket, walking in an extraordinary panning shot of dreamy beauty across the now desolate, windswept, shadowy rodeo grounds surrounded only by choking dust and swirling litter, looking forlorn like just another piece of trash abandoned *after* the event. This sequence, typical of what Geoff Andrew describes as Ray's "lyrical poeticism verging on the abstract" (64), conveys an absolute sense of *after*ness and melancholic loss epitomized by McCloud, a man out of time, resembling photographs from the Depression's Farm Security Administration, a figure barely holding on to the remnants of his life in the Old West. Documentary precision and pensive slowness bordering on "abstraction": these are precisely the qualities admired by the *Cahiers* critics, Wenders, and Deleuze, who all claimed that Ray, although working in the tradition of the "action-image," "was to modify the image of violence and of speed profoundly" so that his films ceased to be a "reaction linked to a situation" and were more closely "internal and natural" to the character (139). Here, stripped of "violence and speed," the once man-of-action McCloud stands *between* an older West of (apparent) certainty and masculine order (the film's interrogated culture of "lusty men") and the challenges of the emerging, contingent post-West full of the "anxiety about *life*" and "perpetual disquiet" that Rivette notes. At this liminal moment, the "lusty" McCloud, now perplexed and fretful, signifies, in our examination of the post-Westerns, the "troubling afterlife" of mythology as it shifts uneasily toward a gate over which hangs the sign "Stock Exit" as if he too is damaged, limping "stock," carrying all his possessions in a small duffle bag, with nothing else to show for twenty years of wandering the West.

Suddenly from the classical mythic time and action of the rodeo with vibrant deeds conveyed by dazzling camera work and a documentary concern for the details, skills, and courage of its participants, Ray shifts the rhythm of the film, making the audience feel the actual duration of time, measured in the ponderous and awkward gait of McCloud struggling against the wind to his exit. No past, no present, and no future, he cuts a broken, tragic figure on the edge of a changing world he barely comprehends. Ray questions the contextual conditions of the rodeo's mythic hero, exposing the tension-filled world of an emergent post-West where the center of that old mythic frame can no longer hold. Suddenly, the unsubtle mythic narratives of frontier, unquestioned patriarchy, eternal "natural" values, and Anglo-Saxon centrality are interrupted by the complexities of new cultural orders glimpsed in Ray's deceptively layered film: gender roles, economic change, mobility, and labor shifts. Although Michael Allen is right to see in the film "the frontier/civilization dialectic" and the struggle inherent within that between the "wild and the tame" (41–42), at the film's core is a set of tense and indeterminate conflicts beyond just these binary pairs, including others, such as rural and urban, male and female, past and future, and the sense of a real and imagined West itself. Ray dramatizes these tensions to demonstrate the complex nature of the postwar West as it both *comes after* and *moves beyond* its own mythological past while inevitably wrestling with its still-deep connections to such powerful cultural symbols.

In the montage sequence that follows McCloud's solitary exit from the rodeo, he hitches a ride on a truck and travels to a remote and now dilapidated farm his parents once owned. In the last shot before he walks to the house, Ray intersects the foreground with a chain-link fence, representing the West as increasingly owned, divided, and "industrialized" within a new economic order where the open range has been quantified and segmented. His journey back in time is also a quest for a stable national identity, signified by the house with a white-picket fence and, with a melodic and sentimental tone in the soundtrack, McCloud's gaze across the rural landscape, "the melody of the look," as Ray termed it (Bitsch 123). Suddenly, each gesture emphasizes an anticipation of memory, of yearning bound up in his imagination of this home place and the possibility, of rediscovering roots and belonging in a time clearly associated with his distant past. Cut adrift from his own "shiftless" family, alone with no tangible connection to "home" or any meaningful past, McCloud's journey away from the rodeo leads him back to a nostalgic memory of the only home he had ever known. Nostalgia, of course, comes from the Greek root "*nostos*," meaning returning home, carrying with it the "ache" or pain resulting from the failure to actually achieve this. McCloud's remembered home is reduced to a few saved items stored since childhood under the crawlspace of the house, amid the accumulated cobwebbed detritus of time and age. In a characteristic of many post-Westerns, this return marks an unearthing, a resurfacing, and a confronting of some hidden history or buried secret, one both personal and political.[2] Here, a toy gun, a rodeo program, and a tobacco tin containing two nickels are the remains of McCloud's buried past; each object eerily predicting the life he has apparently led.[3] "I was looking for something I thought I'd lost," McCloud says to the current owner, Jeremiah Watrus, revealing momentarily his tenuous attachment to the past and the desire to rediscover home. Of course, McCloud has literally "lost" his past and his family and these are the remnants he clings to, but he has also lost his place in time as his rodeo career ends. This tension between loss and hope is an impulse that hovers suggestively over the rest of the film, adding to its intensely woven psychological landscape. Unable to recover some antecedent sense of the homely, McCloud will soon displace this desire onto the lives of the Merritts, the couple who want, above all else, to own the McCloud house and to kindle their own ideal family life there.

Before this, however, McCloud has two important exchanges with Jeremiah concerning time and change. As he wanders the house noticing how little has changed since his childhood, stopping to survey the room where he was born, Jeremiah comments on the theme of change more generally: "Some things never do [change]. . . . There's been changes; sun's got a little hotter, a little more earth blowed away, a little less water. That's about all the changes" [*sic*]. He advocates natural, inevitable change beyond human control, demonstrating how time does indeed alter things and that, despite the desire to resist its passage, the world evolves. So when Jeremiah asks McCloud if he owns anything, the reply attests to his inert life: "What I started out with, a strong back and a weak mind." He is becalmed in time while the world shifts and swirls around him: an Old Westerner in the confusion of the New West. The second exchange is brief but vital to understanding the film. Here Jeremiah comments that McCloud's visit to the old family home is "kind of like visiting a graveyard": the death associated with the past (his parents, his dreams, the Old West) are in dialogue with the present and future; the remains of hope are the childish objects he has recovered to carry forward into the imponderability of an uncertain future. As so often in the post-Western, this attention to the *afterlife*, the *posthumous*, matters; what we carry forward from the past, from death, and how we make a life beyond that "graveyard." As we have already seen in the "Stock Exit" scene, McCloud is like a ghost himself, a man astride the spectral border of past and future, hovering between the fake glories of the rodeo and the fading memories of childhood. As the sequence ends, he is about to make another exit and climb yet another fence, when he is drawn back by Wes Merritt (Arthur Kennedy) and simultaneously drawn into a possible future defined by his displaced desires.

Almost immediately Ray's film redefines its sense of home as 1950s suburbia transplanted to rural Texas wherein the Merritts' married world is expressed through neat, domestic rituals; his hard work on the ranch, branding and rounding up cattle, and hers of cooking, cleaning floors, washing dishes, sensible bedtimes, and planning for the future. It is a world of stark capitalist decisions: earning, saving, spending, and investing. To Louise Merritt (Susan Hayward), McCloud is a "great has-been" antithetical to her primary economic rationale, for he has made money only to fritter it away. "Easy come, easy go," as she puts it. For her, he is the Old West, an anachronistic rodeo star at odds with her desired world of order and routine, of a life spent "trying to keep us straight" to produce a "decent, steady life" in the New West. Louise's role is that of family "banker," saving hard for their dream home; as Wes tells McCloud, "I just hand her my pay."[4] She is often viewed in the kitchen, preparing meals, washing floors, and planning for the future, epitomizing the idealized 1950s homemaker of Betty Friedan's "feminine mystique." In these scenes, Ray employs a claustrophobic domestic *mise-en-scène* to illustrate Louise's environment, with the characters framed in tight close-ups and McCloud pushed right up against the walls, like an awkward, corralled animal. For Louise, McCloud represents masculinity defined by rugged, individualist action, spontaneity, and ruthlessness, the very traits she abhors and is trying to condition Wes away from. Inevitably, Wes is attracted to this mythic masculinity, feeling he is unready for the emasculating "suburban" life Louise is planning, and so proceeds to exploit McCloud's knowledge to enhance his dreams of rodeo glory and the fast buck. After all, Wes's mantra is, "I know what I want," a vision encouraged by McCloud's recollection of the "buzz" that follows both the experience of the rodeo and the glitzy life it brings:

> I've come out of those chutes a lot of times—heard the crowd holler—with a horse or a bull jumpin' and twistin' underneath. I've always felt the same thing: *for a little bit there* you're a lot more than you are walking down the street, or eating, or sleeping. Maybe it's something you can't explain to a woman. [my emphasis]

When Louise asks why women would not understand this feeling, McCloud replies, "It's a different kind of buzz." For Wes, contained by the domesticated world of ranching, homebuilding, and saving, this sounds like a viable alternative. However, McCloud's "for a little bit there" suggests he has come to understand the transience of his success, calling it soon after "chicken today, feathers later."

Dissatisfaction pervades the film, with its dominant mood of "perpetual disquiet," as Rivette termed it ("Imagination" 105), creating an edgy instability that Ray captures so perfectly. Accordingly, the rootless cowboy McCloud now desires the type of life in the West that Louise represents, rather like the attraction Shane feels for Marian Starrett in Jack Schaefer's novel and George Stevens's film *Shane* (1953). As the domestic order impinges on McCloud, he says at one point to Wes, underscoring their differing views, "You stay with those lamb chops man, she cooks 'em good." In contrast, however, Wes identifies with the mythic rodeo dream, rejecting traditional labor for what Louise derides as a "short-cut" to success. He fails to comprehend McCloud's sense of lack, and so, after an initial success at the San Angelo rodeo, is quick to quit the ranch and go on the road, with a justification again related to economics and control: "My old man spent his whole life working for somebody else and all he left behind him was a big grocery bill and a worn-out saddle. . . . I know what I want and I know how to get it." He refutes Louise's efforts to domesticate him, seeing it both as emasculation of his wild spirit and a form of infantilization. At one point he says in defense of his decision to take risks, "I ain't wearing diapers." Ray's contrast between the wild "action-images" of the rodeo scenes and the attention on "time-images" and slow exchanges in enclosed spaces exemplifies the tension explored in the film, to quote Kouvaros, as "the idea of the West has lost its purchase in the modern world" (159).

As Wes's reputation grows he becomes increasingly selfish, turning against McCloud and pushing Louise away in favor of the rodeo groupies who feed off his success and wealth. This is the modern West of itinerant entertainers moving from site to site, and as a post-Western, the film embodies its diverse, shifting landscapes and economies, including the tensions between the older lifestyle of the rural and the increasingly urban and suburban pull of the larger towns and cities, and the consequences of all these factors on the everyday lives of Westerners. Rodeos in the film travel to Phoenix, Salinas, Fort Worth, Cheyenne, and Tucson, many of the Sunbelt boom towns of the New West where the "ritualized form of mass entertainment" reached its primarily suburban audience embodying what Atwood Lawrence calls "the frontier spirit as manifested through the aggressive and exploitative conquest of the West . . . deal[ing] with nature and the reordering of nature according to the dictates of this ethos" (qtd. in Allen 6). Such repetitive and endless circuits present a perverse account of the once heroic westward journey, a somewhat tarnished version of the pioneering fortitude of the Old West.

The trailer parks of the rodeo are presented as harsh, dark spaces where women perform specific, secondary roles, as doting housewives, like Jenny Logan ("I like keeping house"; "I just scream"); codependent women, like Rosemary Maddox, who admits, "All Jeff McCloud had to do was whistle and I'd come running"; or neurotic women like Grace Burgess living on the edge of despair because of her husband's tenuous occupation. Louise navigates between these roles in the course of the film, unsure of her place in this burgeoning, but complex, New West. Ray, as in all his films, is interested in gender, and, despite the relentlessly macho world of the rodeo, portrays moments when the contradictions of postwar United States are made deliberately and starkly apparent as feminine and masculine subjectivities are redefined. For example, when McCloud describes the rodeo as "just like dancing with a girl, except you let him lead," or when Louise casts aside her domesticity, puts on the only silk stockings she owns, and tries to make a stand for Wes against the predatory Babs, or when Grace Burgess comments that her husband, underneath all the bravado, is "scared" and drinks "to hide how frightened he is." Most memorably, Ray shoots a sequence at night in the trailer park where the dangers of the rodeo are recorded on Louise's face and body as she waits anxiously for news of Wes. We only hear the announcer and the crowd, gauging their response against Louise's increasing disquiet and edginess glimpsed in the shadows and *noir*-ish half-light on the periphery of this male-dominated culture.

Wes's rise to stardom at the rodeo is marked by drunken parties in hotel bars and suites, not in the rural backwaters one might associate with the cowboy life. This is a neon-lit New West of cocktails, glamour, and excess, epitomized by Babs, a twice-married rodeo groupie with a "dress cut down to her knee caps" (says Louise), whose first exchange with Wes, when he offers her a drink, is "You just pour it in 'til it runs over" and then, biting his arm exclaims, "I'm going to put my brand on you, sugar." Momentarily reversing McCloud's parallel of the rodeo as like "dancing with a girl," Babs shows female sexuality as overtly predatory in ways that Louise finds threatening to the domestic space she seeks to create around Wes.

Only the shocking realization of visceral, rodeo violence intrudes into this hermetically sealed, inward-looking community. Initially, as a result of Burgess's accident prompting Grace to disrupt one party with a powerfully critical speech: "You poor dumb fools, kidding yourselves, calling this a sport? A bunch of crazy men paying for the privilege of getting yourself killed, and my husband did it for $25 of borrowed money." Later she tells Louise, "[This is] all I've got to show for fifteen years of married life. It's not much. Get out of this while the going's good. Rodeoing'll make an old woman of you." In the harsh economics of the rodeo, as the film constantly reminds us, it can be boom and bust, as McCloud knows only too well, but more often than not it is about scratching a living at an endless circuit of dusty arenas. This reminds us that the gritty, nomadic life shades the seeming allure of the high-rolling rodeo, played out in grungy trailer parks that, as Allen writes, "closely resemble[s] the fruit camps of Louise Merritt's Depression youth," full of broken figures that "evince the tragedy and pathos of their wandering lives" (43). Figures like Booker, once a rough stock rider, but now simply a hanger-on, whose own terrible leg injury mirrors McCloud's increasingly disabled existence, who even Rosemary Maddox rather disparagingly refers to as "my wandering cowboy."

As Louise grows more frustrated with Wes's reluctance to return to their now affordable farm, she rebels against her domestic role telling McCloud, "I'm through saving his pennies and washing his socks and shirts. . . . I ain't his mother. . . . I'm tired of being the good little wife who waits things out. . . . I'd like to fry them all [men] in deep fat." In trying to win back Wes she sets up a showdown with McCloud who seizes the opportunity to tell Louise of his feelings for her. But she is clearly a loyal wife, only asking him to help her "get [Wes] away from here," and this demand leads him indirectly to his final sacrifice at the rodeo. McCloud decides to rodeo again to prove his manhood to Wes who has accused him of being "yellow" and of "freeloadin'" off his success, but unconsciously his actions demonstrate the transitory nature of the sport and the ultimate price to be paid. In a film that, as we have seen, is obsessed by money and economics, we should not be surprised that McCloud comments, "You beat the money or the money beats you." His dying words, however, say even more: "broken bones, broken bottles, broken everything. There never was a bronc that couldn't be broke. There never was a cowboy couldn't be throwed. Guys like me last forever." Of course, in one sense he is right, since the rodeo circuit goes on relentlessly circulating people and animals in its own economy even though at this point, acknowledging the "broken" life of McCloud, Wes sees beyond it and returns with Louise to make a home in Texas. However, in another sense, the film asserts a different economy, one based in marriage, family, and land-ownership, a vision reinforced as Booker and his teenage daughter Rusty (who mouths "I love you" as McCloud dies) join the Merritts, creating a new, extended family.

Unsurprisingly, McCloud dies in Louise's arms cradled like the child/lover he longs to be, yet Ray makes the reconciliation implied by this ending, with its assertion of specific American values of home and family, ambiguous because, as the reunited couple walk under the large foregrounded "Exit" sign (echoing McCloud earlier), the announcer speaks of another young rider in the shoots, appearing for the "first time on the circuit," as if keeping the tainted rodeo cowboy dream alive. Ray often commented that for every film he ever made, his personal trademark was, "I'm a stranger here myself" (Bitsch 121), and in the ambiguity of *The Lusty Men*, one senses this shadow of estrangement falling over the film. In the end, it is an unhomely or uncanny post-Western, yearning for an idea of home in whose quest is revealed only compromises, struggles, and the inherent dangers associated with its possible acquisition. Ultimately, one remembers not the resolution toward a new life, but the haunting presence of McCloud's world where everything is lost or broken. As Nicholas Royle explains the uncanny, the film finds a true unhomeliness where "another thinking of beginning" occurs precisely because "the beginning is already haunted" by the dreams and myths of the afterlife of a once-familiar West now transformed into an unfamiliar and troubling post-West (1).

Notes

1. For details, see my book *Post-Westerns*.
2. I am thinking of films such as *Bad Day at Black Rock* (John Sturges, 1955), *Lone Star* (John Sayles, 1996), *Don't Come Knocking* (Wim Wenders, 2005), and *Down in the Valley* (David Jacobson, 2005), all discussed at length in *Post-Westerns*.
3. This scene was reimagined in Wenders's film *Kings of the Road* (1976).
4. Economics are central to the film and mentioned constantly: the Great Depression, buying a home, earning wages, saving and losing money, tax auctions, bank accounts, and bookkeeping. These form a context and contrast to the "wild," carefree atmosphere of the rodeo, adding to the sense of a world undergoing rapid change.

10

James I. Deutsch and Lauren R. Shaw

Citizen Nick

Civic Engagement and Folk Culture in the Life and Work of Nicholas Ray

From 1936 to 1944, Nicholas Ray worked in various capacities for the U. S. government—with the Works Progress Administration (WPA), the U. S. Department of Agriculture's Resettlement Administration (RA), and the Office of War Information (OWI). These jobs not only brought him into close contact with many of the country's leading figures in the worlds of theater, music, and folklore; they also allowed him to take extended tours through rural areas in the American South and Midwest. These were highly formative experiences for Ray, then in his mid-twenties and early thirties. During his subsequent thirty-year career as a filmmaker, Ray regularly returned to many of the forms of cultural expression and civic engagement he had encountered during these years. This chapter explores some of Ray's most significant activities while working for the federal government, and how that service affected his career in Hollywood, particularly four lesser-known feature films from the 1950s: *The Lusty Men*, *Hot Blood*, *The True Story of Jesse James*, and *Wind Across the Everglades*.

Figure 10.1. In light of his years working almost exclusively with amateurs in the U.S. Department of Agriculture's Resettlement Administration and the Works Progress Administration productions, Ray became a master of coaxing impressive and often unexpected performances out of Hollywood actors (Nicholas Ray Archive/Nicholas Ray Foundation).

In a letter from 1939, Ray wrote he hoped that "in the near future someone will be able to cover this untouched area of America which still contains much of the lore and spirit of the frontier" (Ray, Letter). This chapter demonstrates how Ray himself fulfilled this hope in his own films by strongly promoting civic engagement and expressions of American folk culture.

Facing a country in economic depression, President Franklin D. Roosevelt knew that drastic action was needed on the part of the federal government. Along with programs designed to rehabilitate farms and put thousands of unemployed laborers back to work, the President's New Deal also extended a hand to Americans struggling to stay afloat in the performing and creative arts. "Hell!" Harry Hopkins, leader of the Federal Emergency Relief Administration, exclaimed. "They've got to eat just like other people" (Schlesinger 270). These new, unprecedented levels of federal spending in support of the arts did not come without controversy. Fears abounded that government money was being wasted or, worse still, being used to pay the salaries of communists. Yet in spite of funding cuts resulting from such suspicion, the 1930s and 1940s were a time when average American citizens were simultaneously exposed to quality, affordable theater through programs like the Federal Theatre Project (FTP) and experiencing the rich variety of folk music recorded by traveling WPA workers.

During this time of improvised solutions and surprising discovery Ray found his footing in the worlds of theater, radio, and ultimately film. Between 1936 when he first took a job with the FTP and 1945 when he contributed to the OWI propaganda film *Tuesday in November*, Ray worked for several government agencies, projects, and productions. Ray's first involvement with the New Deal came in 1936, when he was offered a job by another young Wisconsin transplant to New York. Joseph Losey had recently become director of the FTP's third Living Newspaper production and asked Ray to serve as stage manager. The offer could not have come at a better time. Ray's happy years of performing left-wing agitprop were drawing to an end as New York City's Theatre of Action was succumbing to financial troubles.

The FTP was created in 1935 as part of "Federal Project Number One" within the ambitious WPA.[1] It sought to provide meaningful employment not only for actors, but also for theater workers. Hallie Flanagan, a well-respected Vassar theater professor, was chosen to lead the FTP, and as author Susan Quinn writes, Flanagan was hopeful that "it might be possible to make theatre history, mounting cutting-edge productions that were too risky for the profit-bound theatre" (11). To address the overwhelming need for jobs in New York's theater community, Flanagan suggested that the project create topical, cabaret-style Living Newspapers that required large casts.[2]

Injunction Granted, the Living Newspaper production on which Ray served as stage manager, traced the history of American labor in twenty-eight scenes from the first indentured servants in the New World to the present struggles between labor unions and the courts. It was a massive undertaking, much larger in scale than the two previous Living Newspapers. Ray, who had to this point considered himself an actor, now found himself in charge of more than 125 performers and an equally large number of lighting and musical cues, including photographs and headlines constantly projected overhead. Ray rose to the challenge magnificently. When *Injunction Granted* opened on July 27, 1939, it drew both crowds and heavy criticism. Flanagan had made clear from the beginning that she would not have the FTP used politically; when she first saw *Injunction Granted* performed, she was furious. Many of the production's cast and crew were, like Ray, previously involved in leftist political theater and, in Flanagan's opinion, the play's treatment of labor issues was "bad journalism and hysterical theatre" (72). Reviewers like Brooks Atkinson echoed this criticism, opining, "the Moscow stylization of writing and staging . . . reduces the long struggle to adolescent gibberish," and that "if it wants to give the Federal Theatre a bad name for political insurgence it has found the most effective method" (16). However, despite the turbulence of the production's short, three-month run, *Injunction Granted* can be seen as an important shift in the future director's career. Perhaps, as Ray biographer Patrick McGilligan suggests, in offering him this position, Losey was one of the first people to recognize that Ray's talents would reveal themselves not on-stage, but off-stage.

Ray was drawn back into New Deal programming by the promise of a job in Washington, D.C. American families driven off their land by famine or eviction were relocating to government-planned communities, where musicians, photographers, artists, and performers in the RA's Special Skills Division would work with residents to foster a sense of community and living culture. The division, under the leadership of writer Adrian J. Dornbush, had assembled a diverse group of creative talent, including the renowned musicologist Charles Seeger; singer Margaret Valiant; artists Ben Shahn, and Jackson and Charles Pollock; and as of January 1937, the twenty-five-year-old Nicholas Ray.

Placed at the head of the division's Theatre Section, Ray was tasked with organizing local theater performances across the country. As he grew into this role, Ray began to experience the diversity of American life firsthand among lumberjacks and shepherds, miners and farmers. He went "wherever the earth was ruined and the people were hungry," his first wife and frequent travel companion Jean Evans later recalled (qtd. in Eisenschitz 41–42). In rural communities that dotted the Appalachians from Pennsylvania to the Carolinas, and in settlements westward through Tennessee as far as Arkansas and Texas, Ray asked Americans to tell him the challenges they were facing, which he then crafted into plays to be produced in those very same communities by local performers. Ray staged one such play, *Settlement and Resettlement*, for the June 1937 Penderlea Annual Fair, where First Lady Eleanor Roosevelt was the guest of honor.

Among the personal stories of lives uprooted, Ray also heard the music and the spoken lore that flourished in these tucked-away corners of the country. This exposure to American folk culture in the late 1930s came at a time that Alan Lomax, a folklorist and good friend of Ray's, called a turning point in the country's perception of itself. Until this point, Lomax declared, "Everything local and native had been treated as non-art. . . . Suddenly we opened up the flood-gates. The creativity of ordinary people, engaged in living in ordinary places, came into focus" (qtd. in Szwed 106). Folklorists and ethnomusicologists were moving away from simply collecting and preserving antiquarian items (à la John Lomax and Francis James Child) to a more functionalist approach (à la Benjamin Botkin, Alan Lomax, and Charles Seeger). According to Benjamin Filene, the folklorists of the New Deal "shifted the profession's mission from preserving cultural relics to exploring the processes by which culture was created and transmitted" (139). Ray was on the front lines of this exploratory mission and, with Alan Lomax's encouragement, he began carrying a Presto recording machine to document the music and stories he heard.

Ray's travels were a chance to peer into the soul of the nation, and the impression it left followed him to Hollywood. After observing Ray's work on *They Live by Night*, his first feature film as a director, producer John Houseman commented, "Nick's personal experience of hard times in the Southwest, combined with his visual sense, enabled him . . . to re-create the emotional reality of that world of shabby small towns, abandoned farms and squalid cabins and tourist camps in which the film was taking place" (*Unfinished* 283). The characters of his films, too, mirror in many ways the people he met during his time with the division. As Michael Goodwin and Naomi Wise reflect, these characters are "the sons and daughters of the American dream—but it is a dream gone sour. At the heart of Ray's cinema lies the anguish of living from day to American day" (7).

Even when Ray was not embarking on one of his numerous backcountry trips, he was surrounded by leading figures in the movement to document America's folk culture. Charles Seeger, father of folk music icon Pete Seeger, was Ray's counterpart in the Music Section of the Special Skills Division. Seeger introduced Ray to Alan Lomax, who became one of Ray's closest friends and inspirations during his time in Washington, D.C. Lomax described his friendship with Ray as being "like Damon and Pythias, like brothers." He also remarked, "I was the only person who had been out there with the Blacks, the Mexicans, the Cajuns, and all the rest. And Nick was one of the people who came and listened and took it seriously" (qtd. in Eisenschitz 45). The house that Ray, Evans, Lomax, and his wife Elizabeth shared in Arlington, Virginia, became a hotspot and stopover point for folk musicians such as Woody Guthrie, Aunt Molly Jackson, and Lead Belly.

As funding disappeared for the Farm Security Administration (which absorbed the RA in 1937), Ray began working with the WPA Recreation Division. Beginning in July 1938, he worked as a drama consultant, performing many of the same duties he had earlier with the

Special Skills Division. In his engagement with both programs, he helped foster the development of community drama, often working with amateurs or semiprofessional performers. Critic Robin Wood observed, "No one ever gives a bad performance in a Ray film" (qtd. in Rosenbaum, "Guilty" 50), to which Jonathan Rosenbaum added, "Ray's remarkable work with relatively unskilled or inexpressive players is among the steadiest pleasures to be found in his canon" (50). However, because of his years working almost exclusively with amateurs in RA and WPA productions, Ray became a master of coaxing impressive and often unexpected performances out of Hollywood actors.

During his time with the Recreation Division, Ray continued to travel the country, but quickly grew unhappy with the WPA bureaucracy. One trip to Mitchell, South Dakota, in October 1939 epitomizes both his enthusiasm for and his frustration with his WPA work. While there, he recorded thirty-eight tracks on eleven twelve-inch records, later to be deposited into the Library of Congress collection. Among the square dances and ballads, off-color jokes, and fiddle tunes, Ray's voice can be heard joking with performers, requesting certain songs, and on at least two tracks—"Irish Washerwoman" and "Turkey in the Straw"—adding his voice to those of the local musicians. Though the quality of the recordings is less than professional, Alan Lomax said, "[they] showed me that his heart was in the right place. He didn't know how to do it, but he was interested in the *real* raw guts at the bottom of the grass roots, where the shit piles up!" (qtd. in Eisenschitz 46).

Ethel M. Dowdell, South Dakota state director of the WPA's Professional and Service Division, also praised Ray's work in Mitchell, writing:

> Mr. Ray spoke of the place of public recreation in the life of a community.... Leaders discussed their problems with Mr. Ray and his advice exerted a definite influence upon the outlook on life in general of a number of the leaders. His instruction at the institute was a source of inspiration to his group and each member regarded him as a personal friend. His work was a magnificent demonstration of leadership and teaching. (WPA Central Files)

But despite praise from others, Ray was disappointed with what he had been able to accomplish in Mitchell. In a letter to Harold Spivacke, chief of the Music Division of the Library of Congress, Ray wrote:

> I was very irritated with the fact that I had only two or three hours at the most each day in which to find, make dates with, and record ... and consequently I'm quite dissatisfied with

the recordings. Another thing that displeased me was having to be confined to the Mitchell area because of my official responsibilities. . . . I have made several attempts to outline and develop in a rather comprehensive way my ideas on the origin, development, and the decline of the Folk Theatre in America. I can not [sic] do it while I am being constantly interrupted by making train schedules and carrying on my other duties (Ray, Letter).

Though dedicated to the mission of the Recreation Division and the work of his colleagues at the Library of Congress, he grew increasingly frustrated with what he felt were the limitations of his position. He missed the relative freedom the Special Skills Division afforded him, allowing him to disappear into the land for weeks at a time. Thus, when the WPA came under a renewed wave of political criticism and budget cuts, Ray left the program in July 1940.

The remainder of 1940 and the better part of 1941 were spent in New York City after separating from Evans. There he became involved in the jazz and blues scene at Café Society, one of the nation's first interracial jazz clubs, and collaborated on Alan Lomax's CBS radio folk music program *Back Where I Come From*.

After the attack on Pearl Harbor on December 7, 1941, the Roosevelt administration asked Houseman as head of the Overseas Programming Bureau to create a national radio program. From President Roosevelt's fireside chats to the live reporting of disasters, radio had proven itself to be an immensely effective medium, through which the U.S. government communicated with its people. With the creation of the OWI's Voice of America (VOA), radio became America's presence abroad. Ray and Houseman knew each other from the FTP; the latter also greatly admired *Back Where I Come From*. He quickly invited Ray, who had been rejected for military service because of a heart condition, to join the VOA.[3] Molly Kazan, wife of director Elia Kazan, also worked with the VOA and once told her husband, "Nick knows more about what's going on in the back roads of this country than anyone" (qtd. in Kazan 262). Houseman counted on this knowledge of folk culture and music that Ray was bringing to the program. "We discovered that folk music is international," Houseman commented, "and, more and more, we used to use a lot of folk music in order to convince everybody—our allies, our enemies—that we were brothers under the skin, that Americans were not remote barbarians" (qtd. in Eisenschitz 65).

The programs Ray contributed to drew heavily on his experience at CBS, bringing with him musicians who had performed on *Back Where I Come From*, including Woody Guthrie, Burl Ives, Lead Belly, Earl

Robinson, Pete Seeger, and Josh White. Because of their casual dress, they quickly became known as "Nick's barefoot guitar players." The VOA staff and performers were a tight-knit group and among them Ray cemented friendships and professional relationships that he took to Hollywood. *They Live by Night*, for example, was done in collaboration with producer Houseman and melded some of Guthrie's music with popular Depression-era songs. Another one of "Nick's barefoot guitar players," Burl Ives, would later star in *Wind Across the Everglades*.

Ray worked on a variety of VOA projects and even helped direct foreign-language programming. Like many other federal organizations Ray had worked for, however, "most of the OWI were New Dealers and leftists of one stripe or another," writes John Szwed, "so the power that they had been given to address the nation made some in Congress nervous" (196). Following the Congressional election of 1942, the political climate surrounding the broadcast became increasingly tense and in April 1943 Houseman resigned and returned to Hollywood. Ray left soon after and—at the urging of Kazan and Houseman—headed west as well. With the exception of Ray's assisting Houseman on the 1945 OWI film *Tuesday in November*, which aimed to explain the American electoral process to an international audience, this move marked the end of Ray's official engagement with federally funded theater and arts productions. However, it was not the end of his engagement with folk culture.

The Lusty Men was first developed not by Ray, but by RKO producers Jerry Wald and Norman Krasna. They had read Claude Stanush's article in *Life* about Robert "Wild Horse Bob" Crosby, and hired Stanush to develop a film treatment. Described in the article as "rodeo's greatest practitioner [and] its most spectacular showman," Crosby had "broken his right leg five times, every rib at least once, both arms, both hands and both clavicles" (Stanush 59). In other words, he was the real McCoy, the type of natural character who appealed to Ray's quest for authenticity. "Don't fuck with a natural," was one of Ray's mottoes. "If you're lucky enough to find a natural, let him run, because in him you have a free guest. I wouldn't tell a cowboy who rides fence in the southwest how to walk" (Ray, *Interrupted* 75).

Equally appealing to Ray was Stanush's detailed fieldwork. Ray biographer Bernard Eisenschitz reports that Stanush had "50 pages on 'Western dialogue and colloquialisms,' 75 on 'drought and grass problems,' 120 on 'general research, ranching and rodeo,' plus a collection of notes, amassed over a period of more than 10 years, on the modern cowboy" (175). By the time Ray started work on *The Lusty Men* in September 1951, the script had gone through several drafts, title changes, and personnel changes. Still it seemed ideal for Ray, Geoff Andrew notes, a project that was "tailor-made for the director's special interests" (64). As McGilligan observes, "Years before, during summers growing up in La Crosse, Ray had fallen in love with the rodeo; during his WPA days, he began to see the cowboy competitions as a sort of Western people's theater" (218). As a result, Ray particularly enjoyed the opportunities afforded to shoot rodeos on location, most notably the annual Pendleton Round-Up in Oregon.

The footage shot there, such as the Pendleton Round-Up's processional opening, is reminiscent of the small-town pageantry that Ray had observed and helped organize during his WPA travels. Similarly, Ray could not resist including cowboy folk music in *The Lusty Men*. In one of the early party scenes, a cowboy sits on the floor and sings three stanzas from "Chilly Winds," one of the songs of "men at work," which John and Alan Lomax had published ten years earlier in *Our Singing Country* (293–94). Ray was most familiar with this publication through his friendship with Alan Lomax.

Although several critics at the time of the film's release complained that the story seemed trite, nearly everyone praised its realistic look. Especially enthusiastic was the *New York Times*: "With a literal and candid use of camera that would stand out in the documentary field, Director Nicholas Ray has really captured the muscle and thump of rodeos. Working right through the circuit, from deep Texas to the big show in Pendleton, he has followed the genuine bronc riders and kept his cameras on them while they perform . . . [and] all are recorded faithfully" (Crowther, "*Lusty*" 12). Similarly, the *Washington Post* noted, "The virtue of this slambang [sic] picture lies in its highly authentic background, at least it seems authentic" (Coe, "Life" 29), while *Newsweek* admired the film's "raw life behind the scenes" that is "loaded with professional rodeo detail" ("New Films" 109). Latter-day critics drew parallels between Lee Garmes's cinematography and the work of "Walker Evans or the Farm Administration photographers" (Eisenschitz 185).

One of Ray's dream projects while working at RKO in the early 1950s was a film about gypsies, using the extensive research his first wife conducted. According to Eisenschitz, "Jean Evans had spent weeks gaining the confidence of the store front gypsies on First, Second and Third Avenues on the Lower East Side [of New York]. Her research was not only better than anything Ray could have hoped for; it was also, according to him, virtually unique" (258). Like the folk community of cowboys and rodeo riders in *The Lusty Men*, Ray greatly admired the folk community of gypsies. "It is easy to see why Ray was attracted to a film in which he could portray the customs and experiences of a gypsy minority living in a contemporary American city," Andrew observed, adding that "the gypsies are both wanderers and outcasts who adhere to traditional tribal rituals and who are viewed with suspicion by 'respectable' *gajo* society" (98).

Unfortunately, by the time Columbia Pictures approved the film in mid-1955, much of Evans's fieldwork had been tossed aside in favor of less rigorous research screenwriter Jesse Lasky Jr. and Roger Donoghue, a former boxer and technical consultant for Marlon Brando, James Dean, and others, conducted. The research for *Hot Blood* was often improvised, Donoghue recalled:

> I asked Jim McShane, a New York cop . . . to find me a fallen gypsy, who would tell me exactly what happens at the wedding scenes, at the death scenes, and so forth. So I met this gypsy on Second Avenue, and I taped him. Nick wired me $200 from California, and every ten minutes I would give him ten dollars. Then Nick and I, we wrote the wedding scene (qtd. in Eisenschitz 258–59).

At the same time, the studio cancelled Ray's plan to film in gypsy neighborhoods, preferring (for reasons of economy and management) to shoot on its own sound stages in California. Moreover, while the film was in production during July and August 1955, Ray was distracted by post-production work on *Rebel Without a Cause*. Casting Cornel Wilde as the gypsy king's son and adding Ross Bagdasarian and Les Baxter's nongypsy music further compromised the film's folk authenticity.

Nevertheless, Ray was pleased with the results. He stated, "I think the photography of Ray June is extraordinary. I think the folklore of the gypsies is as extraordinary as the folklore of any minority group that you can find any place in the world outside of the Aborigines. . . . The stuff that takes place in the gypsy headquarters, the trial and the marriage, should go to the Library of Congress, because that's the way it was and there is no other record of it in our film history" (qtd. in Eisenschitz 263). However, the reviewers in 1956 were much less charitable. The *Chicago Tribune* told its readers, "You must have something better to do" than see *Hot Blood*—a film that "is as boring as its title is repulsive" (Tinee A4).

Although Twentieth Century-Fox released Ray's film version of the Missouri outlaw as *The True Story of Jesse James*, Ray originally had something very different in mind for his next film. He had wanted to call it "The Ballad of Jesse James," and to "do it entirely as a ballad, stylized in every aspect, all of it shot on the stage, including the horses, the chases, everything" (qtd. in Eisenschitz 284). Not surprisingly, the studio rejected this plan—as it likewise rejected Ray's alternate plan to film in Missouri, where Jesse James was born and raised. Nevertheless, Ray managed to inject elements of the James legend, taken from Botkin's influential collection, *A Treasury of American Folklore* (Rodgers and Hirsch 1944). Botkin had served as assistant director (and then director—succeeding Alan Lomax) of the Archive of American Folk Song at the Library of Congress from 1942 to 1945, where he and Ray must have known each other. That may explain why the "somber music from Botkin's version of the 'Ballad of Jesse James' carries throughout the film," as Clinton Scott Loftin describes it, and also why Ray utilizes Botkin's "unsubstantiated tale" of "Jesse James and the Poor Widow" (79–80). In this narrative, Jesse helps an indigent widow pay her mortgage before cleverly retrieving that same cash from the pitiless banker who had tried to foreclose on the widow's farm.

The film received mixed reviews, but the *New York Times* singled out the director for praise, noting that "the real star [of the film] is a fellow named Nicholas Ray, the director. Profiting by his experience with *Johnny Guitar*, a prairie fiasco, he has admirably utilized his sprawling cast, the CinemaScope expanse and the very color itself" (Taubman 17). Botkin himself might also have approved, since according to Lawrence Rodgers and Jerrold Hirsch, he "believed fervidly that if the American people understood their interconnected history, their shared lore, and the relationships between their seemingly diverse experiences and backgrounds, they could embrace their diversity and fulfill their democratic and egalitarian ideals" (2).

Perhaps the best example of Ray's use of folk culture in any of his films is *Wind Across the Everglades*. As both Eisenschitz and McGilligan have reported in detail, the shooting on location in Everglades City, Florida, from November 1957 to January 1958 was plagued by so many problems (including Ray nearly being killed by a Cadillac convertible—driven by his suicidal girlfriend—plowing into the wall of his bedroom) that producer Budd Schulberg fired Ray two weeks before the filming in Florida was completed. "Hiring Nick Ray was my worst professional mistake," Schulberg ruefully admitted in 1980 (qtd. in Eisenschitz 317).

Ironically, only several months earlier, in September 1957, Schulberg and his brother Stuart (the film's coproducers) had enthusiastically selected Ray for the job. Schulberg commented, "We felt that Nick would have that special feeling for primitive people, for the Glades, for the poetry of it, for the folk music, for Burl Ives, the whole thing" (qtd. in Eisenschitz 320). Indeed, Ray presumably orchestrated the casting of Ives in the crucial role of Cottonmouth, the formidable leader of a gang of bird poachers in the Everglades swamps, as a nod to one of his former "barefoot guitar players."

Ives arrived in Everglades City in early December 1957—several weeks after the other cast and crew members—because he first had to finish shooting *The Big Country* (William Wyler, 1958), for which Ives would win an Academy Award as Best Supporting Actor. When he finally did arrive, Ray seemed to recover slightly from the funk into which he had descended. "The burly folksinger serenaded everyone at night," McGilligan writes, "taking up his guitar and singing favorite songs from the balcony of his room. Ray too sprang back to life" (369). Indeed, several of Cottonmouth's songs come from the same folk repertoire that Lomax and Botkin were promoting, such as "The Spider and the Fly" and "The Empty Pocket Blues."

Nevertheless, Ives's folksongs and Ray's interest in the folk culture of Florida could do only so much to resurrect the film, which *Newsweek* termed a "work of disappointing mediocrity" ("Savagery in the Swamps" 94). Bosley Crowther noted approvingly in his review for the *New York Times* that "the natural outdoor settings in the wilds of 'the glades' are for real" and that Cottonmouth was "the lustiest looking thing in the film," thanks to his "red beard and black hat, adorned with plume of an egret and wearing a cottonmouth moccasin as a wrist adornment." But the final product was still "one of the most disordered professional motion pictures we've ever seen" ("Everglades" 21).

Certainly other examples from Ray's cinematic *oeuvre* could be cited in this brief survey of Ray's reverence for and eager use of folk culture. For instance, Ray's upbringing in Wisconsin with his Norwegian-American mother and German-American father surely influenced the portrayal of the Swedish immigrants in *Run for Cover*; in fact, Ray confirmed "the Midwestern immigrant scene is something that I knew the rhythm of very well" (qtd. in Goodwin and Wise 12). Likewise, the inclusion of Depression-era radio programs in *They Live by Night* suggests Ray's earlier work in that broadcast medium. In *Johnny Guitar*, the music that Johnny plays and the Dancing Kid's persona are reminiscent of the folk culture that Ray recorded in the Midwestern states as part of his fieldwork for the federal government. And *The Savage Innocents* is often cited as an "anthropologically coherent" film that resulted from extensive research in archives and primary sources (18).

Nevertheless, these four films—from *The Lusty Men* to *Wind Across the Everglades*—are the best demonstration of Ray's lifelong fascination with what Blaine Allan calls "the ways people present themselves and their own worlds, and to different cultures' customs, habits, and rites" (24).

Notes

Author's note: With additional research assistance by Hannah K. Korn.

1. The Works Progress Administration (est. 1936) was renamed the Work Projects Administration in 1939, but retained the same acronym.

2. The term "living newspaper" was first used in Germany and Russia after World War I to describe cabaret style current-event productions. Flanagan, who had extensive exposure to international theater, had used a similar style for her earlier play *Can You Hear Their Voices?*

3. The reason for Ray's rejection by the draft board is contested. Various health issues, as well as rumors of his homosexuality, have all been suggested as possible reasons for its decision (McGilligan 80).

11

Murray Pomerance

A Teacup and a Kiss
Staging Action in *Johnny Guitar*

T HE GENERIC BIZARRENESS OF Nicholas Ray's *Johnny Guitar* may flow from the fact that he was always, and distinctly, less concerned with storytelling conventions than with the tensions and resolutions of performance. "What is an action?" is a question that riddled him continually. In a DVD introduction, Martin Scorsese admits that American audiences laughed when first they saw this film, expecting a Western that had more than the right look (and unable, we might add, to see that this was it). The *New Yorker* scathingly produced a twenty-four-line review full of factual errors, as though the film had not even been worth watching carefully (McCarten, "Kill" 62–63), and Bosley Crowther in the *New York Times* summarily labeled it a "fiasco," dubbing Joan Crawford "as sexless as the lions on the public library steps and as sharp and romantically forbidding as a package of unwrapped razor blades" ("*Johnny Guitar*" 19). Ray's approach to the Western gains truth from being personal, stylized. François Truffaut called this "a film of exceptional poetic sensibility" (Letter 281), and suggested that anyone who rejects it "should never go to the movies again" (*Films* 143).

Ray puts the most dangerous weapons in the hands of women,

Figure 11.1. In *Johnny Guitar* (Republic Pictures, 1955), scenes ostensibly coherent in themselves turn out to be only preparations for higher order treatments of the same motifs; expressions on faces rebound and reflect one another; colors express sentiments (frame enlargement).

and, as Scorsese notes, offers a film that is "operatic" in the sense of being "pitched from beginning to end in a tone that is convulsive and passionate." Perhaps, like opera itself, that evaluation is biased toward characterization; it makes as much sense to see the film as symphonic, given its very tight interweaving of motifs, its repetitions, and the freedom of Ray's camera both to attach itself to characters and to withdraw from them into self-reflexive contemplation. "I had my sights set on becoming a director of symphony orchestras," said Ray, "It was painful to admit that I had neither facility nor talent with piano, reeds, strings, or brass" (*Interrupted* 74); yet his facility was with the idea of orchestration and with the symphonic form. As with other masterpieces from Ray (for example, *On Dangerous Ground*, *Bitter Victory*, and *In a Lonely Place*, among others), the symphonic nature makes writing about only part of this film, as I will try to do, difficult. Scenes ostensibly coherent in themselves turn out to be only preparations for higher order treatments of the same motifs; expressions on faces rebound and reflect one another; colors express sentiments. As Truffaut said in his review, "This film is a string of preciosity, truer than the truth" (*Films* 141). Offered a contract to direct a Western, and turning immediately to the biographical and psychological complexities of his characters as a way of understanding their present (their diegetic) conditions, Ray built on these complexities to work out lines of action and resolution—melodic lines—through the development. What results is a picture of situations, deployments, provocations, turnings, and stalls, not a documentarian representation of social life on the frontier or yet one more exemplification of the conventional character conflict that made John Ford and other filmmakers (such as Howard Hawks, Raoul Walsh, Anthony Mann, and John Sturges) famous. "*Johnny Guitar* is a long way from Ford," writes Bernard Eisenschitz, "Its raw material is not the West, but a cinematic vision of the West" (208).

A Teacup

If we look at the opening sequence of this film, we find Johnny (Sterling Hayden) riding solo through mountainous territory to reach the town where our action will take place. The peaks are ruddy with iron, jagged, architectonic. Suddenly, he is jolted in his saddle (and we in our seats) by

Figure 11.2. *Johnny Guitar*: The carriage of that teacup, as well as Johnny's (Sterling Hayden) calculated civilities of language as he addresses the men, show that like Vienna, he may have two sides, combative and civilized, rough and delicate (frame enlargement).

the thunderous sound of an explosion far too near. Beside his path, half of the top of a mountain shoots into the air. Someone yells "All clear!" and workmen come running. They are blasting a way through these hills, making a level grade for the new railway: this information rationalizes the dynamiting in terms of the story and its setting (and in terms of social history: photographers such as William Henry Jackson had been shooting plates of the Yellowstone River and the Rocky Mountains to provide the U.S. Government Survey [later the U.S. Geological Survey] with what could be used as "blueprints" for railway development). Ray's *mise-en-scène* eclipses the idea of being informative about this important, even predominating, node in the history of technology, however. What we experience—with Johnny on his horse—is nothing less than the wholesale dislocation of his movement and purpose, by the agency of an interruption that falls on him as a complete surprise. At once, then, we are being told that this story takes place in the Western territory at the time of the laying of the railway line from the east, as well as that in this narrative territory we will not be receiving advance signals of danger or projections of what is likely to happen next. Happenings will overwhelm us, and that is all. We find ourselves inhaling a thin, powerfully charged atmosphere of reality.

This "formula" is now given immediate proof. As Johnny rides on, he hears continuing sounds of that blasting, suggesting the possibility of a prodigious (and lavish) engineering undertaking in full swing, one that involves dozens of workers scattered among these peaks. But no, the sounds are coming too quickly one after another. As he stops to look down from his path he sees that they signal gunshots, produced by a gang of four men on horseback robbing a coach far below. One passenger has been killed, and the robbers are already swiftly riding off, with Johnny gazing down to "drink" it all in, impassive as a camera, uncommitted. This icon of the cowboy-drifter passing through emergent civilization without attachments, thanks at least to his foundational presence in George Stevens's popularly received *Shane* a year before, a staple figure of the Western genre, was here merely being toyed with by Ray, as viewers would have to wait to see.

Johnny is on his way to find Vienna (Crawford), who has built a saloon just on the outskirts of town and is waiting eagerly for the completion of the railroad to bring the lucrative new civilization out her way. She is a hungry investor just at the point of having expended her funds yet still without profit: eager, alert, cautious, measuredly anxious, protective. As played by Crawford, Vienna is also a manly woman (and a womanly man), described as such by her croupier Sam (Robert Osterloh): "Never met a woman seems more like a man. She thinks like one, acts like one, and sometimes makes me feel like I'm not." Pamela Robertson sees Crawford's "camp persona" combining "features of a certain kind of artificiality with a hard professionalism. That artificiality includes the evident constructedness of her physical image—her padded shoulders, thickly drawn eyebrows, the slash of a mouth formed with dark red lipstick, and the perfect (because it is strictly regimented) body" (34). When Johnny shows up, she greets him with a steely and unwavering gaze from a balcony high above (a haughty Juliet to his sand-blown Romeo), noting that she'll see him "later"; then she retreats into her apartment, where she has been entertaining Mr. Andrews from the railway company (Rhys Williams) with a soft and genteel femininity and an indomitable bottle of port. Soon enough she will show herself to be alternatively motherly and protective, and cold-bloodedly capitalistic and commanding. The heavy lipstick Crawford sports enables her to effect serious dramatic transformations of character merely through slight alterations in the shape of her mouth: the star's (the capitalist's) mouth seemingly has become the character entirely. Jacques Audiberti commended her way of "centering everything in that indefatigable square mouth" (28; my translation). The place is as empty as a grave, Johnny notices, but on command the roulette man Eddie (Paul Fix) has immediately set his ball spinning in that wheel. Around and around and around and around and around it goes, that sound both intoxicating and unnerving hissing out the power of the cycle, the dream of repetition, the prolongation of time. Vienna has established a high-class saloon here, her employees prepared at each instant to be servile and useful to a clientele expected to arrive at any moment (like the Futura in Tennessee Williams's *Camino Real*, a train that stops for only a moment in a forsaken sun-drenched town, to bear anyone who can rush aboard forward and away to a glorious future). Vienna has a little plaster model of the town these strangers will arrive and build—her bartender Frank (Frank Marlowe) polishes the tiny model railway. Soon everyone will get rich: the standard prediction of the gambler who is not rich yet herself. Johnny calmly sips a whiskey, then leaving his guitar on the bar (collateral) retreats into the kitchen where Old Tom (John Carradine), the handyman, will serve him dinner.

Already we have the empty space waiting to be filled, the hungry woman no longer not a man, the infrastructure ready for servility, the surrounding sandstorm to indicate an alien environment ready to erode this saloon to dust.

The peace and quiet of all this potentiality is interrupted by a noisy stir, the arrival of the stage coach with a posse that carries in the body of Smalls, the dead man. He is the town banker, and the brother of Emma Small (Mercedes McCambridge), a fiery young woman whose loathing for Vienna drips boldly from her tar-black eyes. In her dark hatred she partly reflects the interests and attitude of the town's magnate, McIvers (Ward Bond), who wants to own much more than all the cattle and all the land in the neighborhood, which is to say specifically, rights to the railway depot, which Vienna presently claims (claims and affirms in her present conversation with Andrews). Vienna must go, he demands, and Emma, betraying a confused and twisted emotional life, a deep scar, as Vienna can clearly see, outspokenly supports him. "Emma is clearly the origin of the (significantly all-male) community's persecution mania, and she is the character the film works to discredit," observes Jennifer Peterson. "It is she who whips the men into a frenzy, thus underscoring the men's own failed masculinity. . . . Emma is a half-crazed, pathological caricature" (8). Vienna waits on the balcony above this angry crowd, her gun pointed at Emma's head, and staves them off with hard talk about having her rights and not intending to go anywhere. Emma insists—vociferous and uncontrolled—that the Dancing Kid and his gang robbed the stage and killed her brother; furthermore, that Vienna has been harboring them because she is part of that gang. Perhaps the Kid rebuffed her one day. Perhaps he failed to notice when she made eyes at him. Hers is the purely irrational and eruptive anger of a tortured soul who cannot save herself.

The posse is shiftless on the polished floor: among them the sheriff (Frank Ferguson), polite but frightened; McIvers, tough, mean, and cupidinous; the stage driver, who had the sun in his eyes and cannot quite say he really saw who the robbers were; one of McIvers's henchmen (Denver Pyle), his gaze flickering, nervous, off-balance, inexplicably malevolent.

Raucously now, with a random tattoo of gunfire, the Dancing Kid (Scott Brady) and his trio of friends burst into the premises. Bart (Ernest Borgnine) is an impulsive and combative spirit, always looking for a fight. Corey (Royal Dano) is disciplined, loyal, and sage, but degenerating with a case of pneumonia. Young Turkey (Ben Cooper) is half a man, half a boy, decked out in flamboyant yellow and eager to prove how brave he is.

And now with all his principals arrayed in the saloon, indeed spread across the screen, Ray performs an astonishing dramaturgical trick.

It starts with the dense silence that reigns among these types, the shiftless posse, the arrogant and brutal McIvers, the firebrand Emma, the giddy boys in the Kid's gang, and Vienna in a wordless standoff with Emma. The pathetic Corey starts hacking with a cough. He turns abruptly away, into the bar. Seizing the whiskey bottle in a spasm, he pours a glassful, downs it in a single swift gulp, then throws the glass down.

We swoop in for a close shot that shows the gleaming glass as it spins in circles on the wooden bar, a star going around and around in a vast vault. We are reminded instantly of the roulette wheel, its circling, hypnotic sound that Vienna likes so much. (Leo Charney cites Jean Mitry: "Things contained in the frame are literally 'cut,' deprived of all immediate relationship to the outer world. Their links, previously extended in the expanse of space, find that they are turned in on themselves, as if the limits of the frame were reflecting them back to the center like a parabolic mirror" (qtd. in Charney 30). Ray cuts sharply to McIvers's nervous henchman, openly alarmed and triggered as he turns quickly to watch the glass.

We shift back to the glass, which is rotating closer and closer to the lip of the bar. (Around and around, closer and closer.) It slides off into space.

But a hand appears from screen right to catch it, and as we draw back we see Johnny Guitar, emerged silently from the kitchen, with a blue-and-white delftware teacup in his other hand. This is his moment of true introduction, that architectural grounding whereby the principal figure of a film is brought into contact with all of the other primary players: Johnny in the face of the Kid, as a rival for Vienna's affection; Johnny in the face of Emma and McIvers, who want domination of, and trouble for, Vienna; Johnny in the face of the Kid's three friends, who find him inscrutable; Johnny in the face of the Vienna who is the Kid's focus of attention, the Vienna he seems to remember yet may never know again. "I'll take that smoke if you please, friend," he says peaceably enough to the Kid, walking over and slowly removing a cigar from the Kid's hand. Then he strides over to McIvers: "And I'll take a light from you, friend," as McIvers strikes a match for him. It is an attempt to make peace between combatants, sewing the space between the Kid and McIvers through the gesture of the lit smoke, the invocation of *heimliche* hearth. "Some men got the craving for gold and silver, others need lots of land with herds of cattle, and there's those that got the weakness for whiskey and for women. But when you boil it all down, what does a man really need? Just a smoke and a cup of coffee."

All of this so far has been one twisting, pulsing, driving rhythm of chance and happening. The teacup recalls Vienna's plush salon upstairs, her softer side, her culture, even as the shot glass invokes at once the possibility of her business success and a pervasive male sensibility: male customers, male drinking rituals. The carriage of that teacup, as well as Johnny's calculated civilities of language as he addresses the men, show that like Vienna, he may have two sides, combative and civilized, rough and delicate. His sudden materialization in the shot, his move to catch the glass—that is, to save the scene from a moment of trivial destruction—places Johnny Guitar in the center of not only the film (that bears his name) but also the dramatic tension between the vigilante posse, independent Vienna, and the ambiguous Dancing Kid.

Let us see how Ray has set up the pieces for this coup, this slowly developing tension and swift resolution that comprise together the cocking of a springworks of action:

1. Seeing the mountain blasting, Johnny is cued to the development of the railroad. The future is here now; one must race to hop aboard.

2. Johnny watches a holdup from above, as from above Vienna will soon watch him. The event seems remote, disconnected, uninteresting—perhaps he seems this way to her?—and he can have no idea that within moments he will be standing in the middle of the storm it creates. The sandstorm into which he now rides is trivial by comparison.

3. Johnny enters Vienna's and immediately recognizes her prosperity and high hopes (attached to the railroad development). Aside from Eddie at the roulette, Sam at the craps table, and Frank at the bar, the place looks empty—perduringly, hopelessly, yet also attendantly empty. Room to stand, room to grow, room for action. Geoff Andrew calls the place "unreal" (71).

4. Vienna looks down at Johnny from her balcony, just as Old Tom muses, "Somethin' about a tall man makes people sit up and take notice." This is not the first time she is seeing him, we have every reason to think. "Spin the wheel, Eddie, I like to hear it spinning."

5. In her suite handsomely decorated in powder blue Vienna closes a deal to get a railway depot. In the background behind the table is a plaster bust of Ludwig van Beethoven.

6. The stagecoach pulls up in the sandstorm and the posse emerges with the body of Smalls. Vienna sees it all from her balcony: "Keep the wheel spinning, Eddie." (We hear the persistent, even intoxicatingly zippy sound of the metal ball going around and around its trap.) Emma spits out her hatred for Vienna and the Dancing Kid and his

gang. "I'm sorry, Emma," Vienna says peaceably, "Your brother was a very fine man." "How would you know? He was one man who never even looked at you." McIvers, arrogant and decisive: "We're taking you and your men into custody." Vienna looks down at Eddie: "You can stop spinning the wheel." Eddie instantly complies, and Ray holds on this scene, as viewed from the balcony, for three expansive seconds of utter silence before cutting to a floor shot as Vienna walks down the stairs. That spinning wheel was life itself, life and hope and possibility; the silence is mortality, commitment, reality.

7. Vienna sees that Emma and McIvers want to kill the Dancing Kid and evict her. McIvers's stubbornness and Emma's deeply entrenched loathing are carnal, palpable. "You want the Kid and you're so ashamed of it you want him dead," Vienna says, a canny diagnostician. Emma, for her part, needs to broadcast her own unquestionable seemliness. "You're nothing but a railroad tramp; you're not fit to live among decent people." As Vienna steps all the way down the stairs, pistol pointed, and confronts Emma face-to-face, the older, wiser woman clearly could be the other's mother, but is not. "I'm going to kill you!" Emma says. "I know, if I don't kill you first."

8. Eating in the kitchen, Johnny hears the McIvers mob in its row with Vienna, learns of the Dancing Kid and her attachment to him. Perhaps she does not remember or love him at all, perhaps the past has not cycled back to the present, and his situation here is only marginal and utilitarian.

9. The Dancing Kid and his boys arrive, whooping it up after a long day's work at their hidden silver mine. The Kid is a pure narcissist, but friendly.

10. The tension in the room is palpable as the Kid and his cronies stand in wordless confrontation with McIvers and his posse. Corey breaks into a cough, snatches a quick drink to soothe it, and leaves his glass spinning like a roulette ball.

11. Johnny catches the shot glass, and is introduced to the Kid. He tries unsuccessfully to bring peace to a war zone.

12. To prove he is worth his name, Johnny plays his guitar while the Kid circles the room in a mad dance with Emma. She is caught in an inescapable, circular trap, eager to be in his arms but at the same time wanting him dead. The dance is like the rotating roulette ball, or the shiny shot glass falling off the edge of its world. "She practically swoons with suppressed lust," writes Leo Charney (29).

Consider the lines of emotional tension between the characters, and how each and every one implies a backstory neatly indexed—but only indexed—by the present dialogue:

1. Emma and Vienna are rivals for the Kid, the one younger and more impetuous, the other mature and calculating. Emma has a low opinion of Vienna, thinks her a woman of ill repute. Vienna knows that Emma's pristine surface covers a very dark interior. "Joan Crawford and I hated each other," Mercedes McCambridge wrote, "but that's been written about so many times that it bores me stiff" (qtd. in Eisenschitz 206).

2. Vienna has been protecting the Kid, most likely out of affection. The Kid admits to his boys that he is from New York, and possibly this is the origin of his epithet and his gracile style; surely it is partly what makes him attractive to Vienna, who is also from the East.

3. Turkey is emulating the Kid, trying to dress slickly and show himself to be sarcastic and grown up, when he is in truth neither; Johnny sees through this, and Turkey deeply resents the fact that he is so visible.

4. Johnny was once a gunfighter but is now hiding under the guise of a man who is "not the fastest gun west of the Pecos" (which, indeed, he shows himself to be).

5. Vienna's love for Johnny might—or might not—be rekindling. Has he had too many women, and has she had too many men? Will the past catch up with her now that she is successful? He met her first in a saloon—"But this one I own," says she. In what capacity did he meet her, then? A dancing girl? A prostitute? Sterling Hayden would confess to the press at an opening party, "I've had all I want to do with working with Miss Crawford" (207).

Everything discussed thus far takes place in the first fifteen or twenty minutes of this film. We are instantly imbricated in a complex weave of narratives or strains of action, all circling around the emotional tensions of the characters (owing to what has happened before the film began). The quickness of judgment that leads the posse to be ready to hang the Dancing Kid and his gang for a robbery that cannot be proved; the Kid's resentment of both Vienna and Johnny for a relationship he suspects but cannot prove; Emma's loathing of the Kid for a twisted emotional rebuff we did not see and that she cannot swear to; the posse's refusal to believe in the Kid's silver mine, when they have no evidence one way or the other; and that repetitive, almost hypnotizing circling of the roulette wheel when nobody is there to play, the sense of impending chance always pervading the room acoustically as background to the action we see. As a clincher, note that look of panic and anxiety on McIvers's henchman's face as he sees that shot glass about to fall on the floor, as though a broken glass in his enemy's saloon might be traumatic for him, indeed, as though a glass spinning toward a precipice is already a problem, already a threat. These people are all on the edge: every move implicates their futures and dreams; every word is prelude to a move.

That spinning shot glass cannot work dramatically if it is just a glass, just any glass, just the result of somebody having a drink. It must be a glass that contains and radiates with all the tension of this place, the property owners and their resentment against the newcomer, the undetermined innocence or guilt of the Kid, the unresolved nature of Johnny's presence and his relationship with Vienna, Vienna's arduous work in building the saloon and her commitment to independence and freedom, and the sexual tension mounting in Emma because she cannot admit to her own desires and keep what she believes is her dignity. It must be a spinning shot glass because it has been thrown onto the bar by a man beyond his limits, a prospector (or robber, we do not know) sick to death of living in these parts, a man whose lungs cannot bear the tensions of suspended breath they are now forced to endure. The shot glass must be thrown as a result of the entry of the man and his friends into what they expect will be a friendly place but what turns out to be the scene of an ambush. And the ambush must happen as a result of the vituperative hostility between Emma, McIvers, and Vienna, long-standing, growing, ready to explode. All this, of course, in the context of an environment just past the point of being ready to explode, an environment already exploding, and exploding with potential for a technocratic future that will overwhelm the agrarianism that now controls men's lives here—and their fate. And all of this must be happening at a cultural threshold where the civilization represented by refinements and decoration—women's culture—is thrust against rocky landscape, brutal economic domination, the power of personality, and the repressions that make desires hide and crumble. So it must be that when Johnny Guitar catches the shot glass in one hand, the other hand holds the teacup. Not only a teacup, but an elegant teacup, an expensive teacup, a teacup that screams "Europe."

Since Johnny has made a little speech about the supreme value of a smoke and a cup of coffee, and since he typifies the American personality, it is undoubtedly not tea he is drinking from this teacup, yet a teacup it is: soft and delicate, refined, fragile, a marker of culture and civility. Scorsese's astonishing comment that "blue is suppressed in this film"—reflecting Ray's own admission, "We carefully avoided having blues in the field" (qtd. in Eisenschitz 209)—is belied forcefully by the glazing on this little cup, a firm and redolent blue made from cobalt. Delftware was made by partially kilning the clay form until it had "biscuit" consistency, and then dipping it into a glaze of "lead made opaque with ashes or oxide of tin." John Bedford notes that delftware, such as Johnny is carrying, is "neither porcelain . . . nor china . . . nor stoneware" (5). It was specifically designed, from its origins in Spain before 1500, to "emulate" the rarer and more expensive china, porcelain, and opaque glass it could so resemble. This brilliant blue and white teacup suggests high society without actually belonging to it, allowing Emma's assessment of Vienna as a tramp to resonate not only through the dialogue of the film but also through the color design. Named after a European capitol but bearing no ancestral wealth, Vienna has had to clamber and slave for her markers of social status. On this white absorbent surface, writes Bedford, "the decorator paints his pattern or picture *swiftly and irrevocably*, as though he were working in watercolour. The technique calls for a sure instinct" (5; my emphasis). Think about that technique of painting the blue color "swiftly and irrevocably": every moment in this film is swift and irrevocable, explosive, uncompromising—and, in a way, thirsty for that very blue. As Ray puts it, "Every sentence, thought, or phrase that is spoken on screen [sounds] as though it is being spoken for the very first or very last time" (*Interrupted* 76).

A Kiss

Emma Small's conviction in the guilt of the Dancing Kid is indomitable and extreme, played out in her unwavering steely gaze as she confronts Vienna with her certitude. How can she be so sure? Is Vienna right in supposing that deep in Emma is a twisted passion, turned from desire to loathing and suppression? Emma's posture, her ascetic clothing—her black dress is an inverted cassock—her moral rectitude and superior-

Figure 11.3. *Johnny Guitar*: They will struggle verbally, their faces moving in and out of shadow, and then come together and kiss, kiss as though no time has passed, kiss as though there is no tomorrow (frame enlargement).

ity: all these convey an extremity of self-restraint, judgmentalism, and clear-sightedness, clear-sightedness in the negative sense of being able through a morass of complexity and subtlety to determine far too easily the pathway to righteousness. She is sanctimonious in the extreme, and Vienna has pegged her for it. But can Vienna not also be in error? Whatever her emotional relation with the Kid, we have been absent from it, as from Emma's. These two women see the world in contradictory ways, and the Dancing Kid is the symbolic figure on whom they can cast their contradictory philosophies. One is already wealthy and powerful; the other is an upstart who began with nothing and put the saloon together—"every board, plank, and beam"—agony by agony.

Ostracized with her staff, and with the Dancing Kid and his gang, Vienna is left to come to terms with her affections. The Kid has regaled and entertained her, even charmed her, but Johnny is the one who has stolen her heart. As she confides to him late at night, "Once I would have crawled at your feet to be near you." He begs her not to go away:

VIENNA (flatly): I haven't moved.

JOHNNY (hungrily): Tell me something nice.

VIENNA: Sure, what do you want to hear?

JOHNNY: Lie to me, tell me all these years you've waited.

VIENNA (very flatly, as though reading a script, with a rectangle of light on her eyes and the rest of her face in shadow): All these years I've waited.

JOHNNY: Tell me you'd have died if I hadn't come back.

VIENNA: I would have died . . . if you hadn't come back.

JOHNNY: Tell me you still love me like I love you.

VIENNA: I still love you . . . like you love me.

They will struggle verbally, their faces moving in and out of shadow, and then come together and kiss, kiss as though no time has passed, kiss as though there is no tomorrow. But now it is tomorrow, a bright morning, and a far more explosive kiss is on the way. With Johnny driving her into town, the proud Vienna is preparing to remove her funds from Emma's bank, the better to cut off her business relations with her enemy. Because of the brother's funeral the bank is closed, but a teller opens the way for her and she comes in to make her withdrawal, leaving Johnny outside in the eerily quiet, much-too-quiet, empty town.

A wagon rolls up, driven by Turkey. He has money to deposit and cannot wait for the bank to open. Can they hold it for him? As the teller opens the door, Turkey seizes him and throws him into the street in front of Johnny's eyes. The rest of the gang leap from under a tarp and race into the bank with guns drawn. Vienna's jaw has dropped. As Corey and Bart head into the vault, the Kid jaws with Vienna who, struggling between disbelief and confusion, is trying to convince him to give up. She will not say anything, and the teller will not say anything. Stay in town, make a new start, it will all be right. But no, says the Kid, McIvers wants him gone, so he'll take all the money with him. (Is he proving that he is indeed the robber people claim he is, or is he doing this out of bitterness at being falsely labeled?) There is a merciless tension as he keeps hollering to the invisible Corey and Bart to hurry, and Vienna asks point blank what it would take for him to stay. "You," says he bravely, but he knows there's no chance. "Sorry, Kid," says she—almost a legal stipulation her tone is so irredeemably flat, so final. She walks closer, as he warns her he will shoot. Closer still. He is nervous, barks at Corey and Bart to hurry, hurry up, it's time. Closer . . . but he'll shoot. And closer. She is touching him now, gently reaching for his gun, a moment of sexual charge that is weighed with his fear, his urgency, and his lust for mortality. But in a flash the Dancing Kid suddenly becomes a dancer, jumping away from her with the gun intact. He barks at his men, and as they roll out of the bank he steps up to Vienna in a moment that could never occur in any other filmmaker's kind of Western, capping the bank robbery with nothing less than a fierce embrace and a prolonged kiss. Now in half a breath he's gone, out into the air, with Johnny wittily commenting on how he has the best seat for the entertainment.

A kiss to end a bank robbery! Is it recompense to Vienna for taking all her money, the robber expressing gratitude to his victim? Or, is this a bank robbery to establish motive for a kiss? Vienna as an enchantment was all the Kid ever wanted, while Johnny, a different kind of man, was settling for civilization, stasis, a place to stop, a smoke and a cup of coffee. Johnny wanted that teacup and the Vienna who had acquired it. The Kid wanted the momentary woman who was in his arms.

Author's note: With thanks to Ryan Dodge.

12

PAUL ANTHONY JOHNSON

"You Can't Be a Rebel If You Grin"

Masculinity, Performance, and Anxiety in 1950s Rock-and-Roll and the Films of Nicholas Ray

" '[Elvis] knew I was a friend of [James Dean],' said Nicholas Ray, . . . 'so he got down on his knees before me and began to recite whole pages from the script. Elvis must have seen *Rebel* a dozen times by then and remembered every one of Jimmy's lines.'"

—Peter Guralnick (*Lost Highways: Journeys and Arrivals of American Musicians*, 119)

UNLIKE RICHARD BROOKS'S *Blackboard Jungle* (1955), Nicholas Ray's *Rebel Without a Cause* does not feature a rock-and-roll soundtrack, yet it is a film haunted by rock-and-roll. Rock, in turn, became haunted by *Rebel Without a Cause* and the James Dean myth

Figure 12.1. *Rebel Without a Cause* (Warner Bros., 1955): James Dean's Jim Stark simply apotheosizes the typical Nicholas Ray protagonist, creating the most lasting and influential pop iteration of Ray's chronicles of a fracturing American masculinity (frame enlargement).

it helped engender. Produced at the same time that Elvis Presley's first singles were stirring up trouble in Memphis, the film marks the culmination of Ray's reconstruction of American male angst, producing in James Dean the avatar of youthful unrest, and thereby providing a performance model for Presley, Buddy Holly, and Bob Dylan, all of whom borrowed elements of Dean's performance in their own carefully constructed star personas. Rock-and-roll, like Method acting, represented a revolution in American performance practices, and it paralleled and responded to the performances of Brando and Clift and, of course, James Dean. But the clearest sign of the new performance aesthetic emerges less from the inconsistent patterns of an inconsistent star such as Brando than in the consistent excesses and obsessions of an *auteurist* cult figure such as Nicholas Ray.

James Dean's performance in *Rebel Without a Cause* is not *sui generis*—it is simply another addition to the portraits of conflicted manhood Ray had been collecting since the late-1940s. As François Truffaut observed, "Ray's hero is invariably a man lashing out, weak, a child-man when he is not simply a child" ("Certainty" 107). Dean's Jim Stark simply apotheosizes the typical Nicholas Ray protagonist, creating the most lasting and influential pop iteration of Ray's chronicles of a fractured American masculinity.

The mythic power of Dean's performance crystallizes in the film during the pregame confab between Jim and his adversary Buzz (Corey Allen), which precedes the film's crucial chicken run set piece. This scene plays an expected confrontation as something tender, almost like a courtship. Dean affects a beguiling nonchalance as the scene begins, leaning over his car door, his arms crossed and his head nodding compulsively as Buzz approaches. As the two men walk toward their automobiles, Dean indulges in typical Method-influenced bits of seemingly extraneous business, like tugging at the cuffs of his bright red blazer, or looking back attentively toward a rock Buzz obliviously avoids tripping over. The bundle of affectations signals his nervousness and vulnerability, and at this point we have already seen the kind of explosive histrionics that the performance reduces to in popular memory, so the scene has a volatile charge. Dean combines various aspects of previous performances from Nicholas Ray movies, from the awkward diffidence of Farley Granger in *They Live by Night* to the jangled weariness of Robert Ryan in *On Dangerous Ground*, but to this panorama of angst he adds the self-conscious exhibitionism that was the Method's legacy, each excess gesture a telltale distraction for a boy and an actor nervous about being watched and judged, a dilemma all too typical for Ray's heroes and victims. But Dean also manages to convey wistfulness amidst all the anxiety, a resignation that proves haunting. Murray Pomerance describes the mysteries of this scene well: "While the scene is filled with action and angle . . . it is lit and acted with a curious pacificity, an almost gracious self-possession and sociability. There is no boisterousness, only elegance and prowess" ("Stark" 42).

Elvis's worship of Dean's performance suggests recognition of a common strategy, a way of negotiating a balance between exhibitionism and diffidence that plays out in many of Elvis's finest recordings. "Heartbreak Hotel" (1956) does not contain anything that might be mistaken for nonchalance, but it does demonstrate how Elvis could pretend to retreat from his own flamboyance, putting on an operatic display of resentment at one moment and a quavering imitation of shame the next. The recording explodes with Elvis's shout of the first line, "Well, since my baby left me, . . ." signaling a boy on a rant, telling a story directed less at the affronted listener than at the absent lover, the target of the song's venom and despair. But as the song heads from the opening verses to the chorus, Elvis drops down several registers, as the man who came flying out the gate in a nervous rage retreats as if shocked by his own petulance (a tactic Greil Marcus has traced across Elvis's early recordings), and when he mutters the lines, "well, I'll be so lonely baby/I'll be so lonely I could die," the words now sound like the tortured murmurings of a man sobbing alone in a corner (158). Elvis's own collection of Method-like gestures—the vibrato, the stuttering "b" in his utterance of "baby"—parallels Dean's tendency to use excessive gestures to signal vulnerability, tossing off the armor of cool that his performance occasionally assumes to reveal the all-too-human boy inside. Elvis's performance theatricalizes anxiety and confrontation, and makes a romantic, masochistic spectacle out of unearned bravado and shame. It represents the essence of the performance revolution augured by rock-and-roll and the myriad shifts occurring in filmed performance in the 1950s, shifts that Nicholas Ray obsessively documented and partly orchestrated.

In August 1956, Elvis gave an interview in which he claimed he had "made a study of poor Jimmy Dean." He went on to explain, ". . . I know why girls . . . go for us. We're sullen, we're broodin', we're something of a menace. . . . I don't know anything about Hollywood, but I know you can't be sexy if you smile. You can't be a rebel if you grin" (Guralnick, *Last Train* 324). Elvis's words could apply equally well to the leads of any Nick Ray movie, as each film found Ray chronicling the emergence of a new performance paradigm. The shock of a raw, chaotic performance style, rooted in the contradiction of time and place, reverberates across Farley Granger's performance in *They Live by Night*, Robert Ryan's in *On Dangerous Ground*, and Sterling Hayden's in *Johnny Guitar*, as well as Dean's in *Rebel Without a Cause*. It is a style that gets at a vernacular expression of dis-ease, rebellion, and frustration, the same *lingua franca* that came to define rock-and-roll the moment Elvis stepped into a Memphis recording studio in 1954.

Specters of Tomorrow along Nicholas Ray's Lost Highway

By 1949 the stirrings of the Method and its attendant legend were already being felt on American screens, starting with Montgomery Clift's appearances in two movies, Howard Hawks's *Red River* (1948) and William Wyler's *The Heiress* (1949). But what one finds in Ray's movies is a style of acting that though sympathetic with the mystique of the Method, contains its own peculiar cadence.

Nicholas Ray came to filmmaking with an established interest in American folk culture, having worked alongside Alan Lomax collecting field recordings during the Great Depression (see James I. Deutsch and Lauren R. Shaw's chapter herein, "Citizen Nick: Civic Engagement and Folk Culture in the Life and Work of Nicholas Ray," for an exploration of Ray's prefilm activities). This background led producer John Houseman to recommend him for the job of bringing the rural crime novel *Thieves Like Us* to the screen. As Houseman recounted to Bernard Eisenschitz, "'Nick particularly was very familiar with that territory [the south in the 1930s]. He'd been there when he worked with the Lomaxes, he'd been there when he worked with the Department of Agriculture, and so on. And that whole Depression thing was terribly his stuff" (qtd. in 90). *They Live by Night* thus represented an attempt to express a lyrical vision of American rural Depression culture in a manner that Ray himself could tolerate as reasonably authentic, and relatively free of sentimentality or schmaltz. His most daring moves in this direction included use of a free-roaming camera (courtesy of the famous helicopter shot that opens the film) and the two rather green and awkward leads (Farley Granger and Cathy O'Donnell) (97–100). He adapted the film from Edward Anderson's novel, vividly responding to its Depression-era setting and narrative of defeat and desperation. Possessing a kind of outlaw fatalism, the film is often grouped with contemporaneous *noir* films, but its focus on the country rather than the city and its sincere investment in the central love affair (Cathy O'Donnell is about as far from a *femme fatale* as one can get) mark it as something subtly different in American cinema (see Ria Banerjee's chapter herein, "Economies of Desire: Reimagining *Noir* in *They Live by Night*," for an analysis of the unique ways in which the *noir* couple functions in the film). The difference between it and a hard-bitten urban *noir* like *Force of Evil* (Abraham Polonsky, 1948) can be measured by the emotional distance between Charlie Parker and Hank Williams.

At the same time Ray was expressing a new, tender madness on-screen in *They Live by Night*, Hank Williams was on his way to pop martyrdom, producing a new vision of rural authenticity that would prove to be a foreshadowing of rock-and-roll just a few years later. In the same year that *They Live by Night* saw release, Williams recorded "Lost Highway," a song whose lyrics echo Ray's film ("I was just a lad, nearly twenty-two/Neither good nor bad, just a kid like you/And now I'm lost, too late to pray/Lord, I've paid the cost on the lost highway"), and Williams's ragged tenor matches the disarming freshness of Granger's and O'Donnell's performances. Of course, Williams was not quite rock-and-roll, but his image of the hard-living, doomed troubadour anticipates rock's many martyrdom myths and fits nicely with *film noir*'s tales of loserdom and pointless sacrifice, and especially Ray's romantic, fatalistic revision of *noir* convention. Writing about Williams's approach to life in his book *Lost Highway*, pop music historian Peter Guralnick borrowed a line from Faron Young to sum up the Williams myth, one that echoes the most famous line from Ray's *Knock on Any Door*: "Live fast, love hard, and die young" (203).

Ray's treatment of the velocity with which violence alternates with rapture in American life endured on the edge, conveyed so forcefully by the opening helicopter shot and reiterated by a series of eccentric choices regarding camera placement and sound, reflected a turn in American cinema away from studio finesse and toward something more raw and immediate. Already American cinema had followed Italian neorealism outdoors with films such as *The Naked City* (Jules Dassin, 1948), and Ray evinced a feeling for both exteriors and human interiors (contra Philip Kemp's assertion that Ray evinced a talent primarily for exploring the latter) that echoed the vernacular wit and strangeness he had heard in his years collecting field recordings (403). He found new ways to keep his camera alert and mobile, by keeping it either close to the floor or by doing then unheard-of things like placing the camera in a helicopter or in the back of a car. The result makes the film vibrantly coarse and clumsily lyrical, evincing an openness to mistakes that became a deliberate formal practice, such as when he would deliberately choose to cut to a bad match when editing the film (Eisenschitz 101). The aesthetics of "fucking up" went against the grain of the entire Hollywood production process, the fabled genius of the system that elided signs of labor, but Ray's experiences recording the best and most interesting parts of folk culture gave him faith in the raw beauty of the accidental and unpolished. Similar aesthetics could only be witnessed in either Poverty Row filmmaking or in the parts of the recording industry devoted to putting out what the industry referred to as "race" or "hillbilly" records.

The American recording industry at the time was devoted to singers crafting beautifully wrought interpretations of American standards in an assembly-line process devoted to glamour that was as smartly efficient in its workings as the American film industry. But the margins had been moving toward the middle for a long time, and the changes in the recording industry and the instability caused by the 1948 recording strike were helping to accelerate a metamorphosis that would augur Hollywood's own postindustrial conditions a decade later (Wald 136–37). The change occurred in both the conditions of production and in the products themselves because rock-and-roll represented a new sonic philosophy, an investment in youth and sexuality, and an otherworldliness misidentified as authenticity. *They Live by Night*, by its kinetic engagement with location shooting and its rhapsodic handling of the two doomed lovers at the story's core, foreshadowed the turns that would dominate the record industry in the next, produced using a method and a style that would prove transformative.

Robert Ryan's Cold Night of the Soul and the Rockabilly Roundup

In his recordings for the Memphis label Sun Records (produced in 1954 and 1955), Elvis showed an unnerving ability to shift back and forth between casual cruelty and profound tenderness, demonstrating in both kinds of performances an emotional investment in the moment that turns the business of selling a lyric into a deeply personal and immediate affair. His rendition of "That's All Right" reveals a faintly vicious turn in the lyrics not obvious in Arthur Crudup's original recording, as he phrases the last word in the refrain, "That's all right, mama/that's all right for *you*," into something mean and hard (Guralnick, *Lost Highway* 127). In the 1940s, Frank Sinatra had excelled at the intimate address to the listener; one could believe stories of heartbreak and jubilation traced in the lyrics he honored came from a deeply personal place. But when he did anger, it often sounded like a burlesque, and his art always consisted partly of the grace experienced from his ability to pull back from the brink at the last moment, to refuse to give himself completely over to the heartbreak of a lost love or the ecstasy of a new one. Presley gave the impression of having no such limits, giving his recordings an unpredictable and dangerous quality because he was not afraid to sound like a genuinely mean son-of-a-bitch on a song like "That's All Right," just as he was not afraid to sound like a man overwhelmed by orgasmic lust in a song like "One Night of Sin" (1957).

The Method as Brando practiced it in the early 1950s carried with it a similar sense of unbounded emotion, a startling unpredictability that made Brando exciting and superreal, as he redefined authenticity as the melodrama of the lawless. Robert Ryan's bitter performance in *On Dangerous Ground* comes from a similar place, and informed by Ray's lyrical treatment of degradation and redemption, it digs even deeper into the kind of emotional terrain that defined Elvis and would come to define Jerry Lee Lewis, Johnny Burnette, Buddy Holly, and Gene Vincent. Elvis's ability to move between ferocity and tenderness across his early recordings creates a striking performance aesthetic not easily pigeonholed. Both the punk rebel ready to throw down and the sensitive country boy ready to break hearts, Elvis's persona fell in line with new constructions of masculinity in the early 1950s that belie the masculine cold war stereotype of the unemotional man's man unwilling to confront his emotions. A performance such as Ryan's in *On Dangerous Ground* (or James Mason's in *Bigger Than Life*) similarly reflects the contradictions of the epoch; 1940s cool, as epitomized by the Bogart of *To Have and Have Not* (Howard Hawks, 1944) and *The Big Sleep* (Hawks, 1946) or Robert Mitchum in *Out of the Past* (Jacques Tourneur, 1947), gave way to the troubled boy-men of both Ray's movies and rockabilly.

On Dangerous Ground introduces Ryan as a man alone, isolated in his apartment, in contrast to both his partners, one with a girl and a gun and another one with a family and a television set. Ryan's performance contains a flurry of movements, as in his introductory scene when he scurries about reading, finishing a breakfast and getting his gear together for a night on the job, all contained in the same flow of gestures, barely pausing to shift gears from one moment to the next. It is the same logic that underlies Ryan's few tender moments in the early part of the film. He plays his cop as resentment personified, rage constantly boiling just beneath the surface. Even when he gets sweet, Ray and Ryan let the viewer see the danger lurking behind the façade, such as when a flirtatious encounter with a girl behind a soda fountain counter turns bitter and mean the moment her father, the owner of the joint, reveals that the girl has a boyfriend, leading Ryan to swivel away from her in his chair, his face turning from a glad-handing smile to a grimace of fierce distaste, a metamorphosis only the camera witnesses.

Later, Ray frames Ryan's violence as seductive, as Ryan confronts the blonde bombshell girlfriend of a suspect. She tells him he is cute and he plays cool and reserved, the better for the looming threat his tense physicality poses to make itself manifest to the girl. His silence proves both tender and scary, and precisely that tension works its malicious magic on the girl. The violence that remains latent in the scene rises to the surface just a couple of cuts later, when Ryan barges in on the aforementioned boyfriend and begins throwing him across the room like a stuffed doll. What is striking and unnerving here is the way Ray links the vicious and the tender, rendering the two antipodes codependent, so each moment of restraint just builds up the tension that makes the eventual explosion of violence all the more visceral.

Ray's mining of a dark, violent sexuality hinted at by 1950s rock music, while not exactly new to the pop scene, was to become newly omnipresent, particularly as an acknowledged facet of teenage desire and angst. Ray is not cornering the teenage market just yet, but in his portrait of the wound-up menace of Ryan's middle-aged, harried city cop, he is hinting at new contradictions in American performance, where the violence that used to hide behind placid, opaque surfaces now has a way of becoming suddenly manifest and visceral. Ryan's character, in conception and execution, conveys the idea of innocents, poets, and dreamers capable of enormous destructive force, and Ryan's lost, lonely angel of vengeance echoes Farley Granger's doomed boy-hoodlum. Ryan, for all his intelligence, sexual power, and danger, conveys the image of a wounded child, a quality that united him both to the teenager murderer he has to face in the film's climax and the ethos Elvis and those who followed in his wake evoked.

The wounded, tender Elvis pops up in recordings such as his reading of the Rodgers and Hart tune "Blue Moon" or "Tomorrow Night" (both recorded in 1954). In the latter song, his phrasing, drawing out his vowels using a gentle vibrato that allows the words to drift off hauntingly into the reverb, evokes a painful yearning, creating the impression of a profound vulnerability and openness. But the following year, in "Baby Let's Play House," we hear how easily that vulnerable boy transforms into a monstrously possessive man, most infamously in the refrain, "I'd rather see you dead little girl/Than to be with another man." As Greil Marcus observes, Elvis sings the lines with appropriate menace but then backs out into an almost comically syncopated reading of the rest of the lyrics, "as if the venom he'd put into those words struck him at once as ludicrous, and maybe a little frightening" (157).

Part of what distinguishes Ray's delicate antiheroes is the same sense that they live in fear of their own destructive capacities. A sense of hysteria threatens to overcome the leads of Ray's films at crucial moments, such as in the scene in *In a Lonely Place* where Humphrey Bogart simulates strangling a person as a kind of party joke (only in the kind of party people throw in Ray's movies), or in *On Dangerous Ground*, as Ryan almost thrashes an innocent passerby mistaken as a suspect. Ray presents actors who always seem in danger of losing control of their own expressive power, a crucial facet of 1950s performance that separates the acting in most of Ray's films from the far more self-possessed performance styles that had characterized Classical Hollywood up until the late 1940s.

The same sense that control could be lost at any moment characterizes much of the best rock vocal performances from the era, from Little Richard's famous orgasmic yelps in songs like "Tutti Frutti" or the way that Elvis opens a song like "Baby Let's Play House" with a bubbling repetition of the "b" in "baby" (a tic repeated in "Heartbreak Hotel") that almost sounds like an involuntary stutter. Such impressions of chaos help characterize Elvis's vocal persona as playful and exuberant, yet also scary. When he does assert control, the result is usually either an assertion of sexual desire or of control and derision. For example, in "Baby, Let's Play House" he pointedly twists the line "You may go to college, you may go school" into something that sounds like an insult thanks to the stress he places on the word "school," making it come out something like "skewl," a mysterious piece code that sounds like a dagger. What rock brought to popular music performance was then this odd combination of boyish innocence and sheer meanness. It was a mad, bad, dangerous kind of performance, like Ryan crowding a bottle blonde against a doorway, his malice momentarily indistinguishable from desire.

"I'm Stranger Here Myself":
Johnny Guitar and the Delicate Beauty
of "Blue Moon" Boys

Johnny Guitar traffics in the contradictions of grand myth, presenting a burned-out vision of Western conventions reduced to marvelously grotesque caricatures. Sterling Hayden rides into town with his guitar and his gun, ready to growl purple prose at his lost love, not making up his mind whether it is meant as a seduction or a threat, and not knowing or caring about the difference. As such, Johnny Logan (Hayden) fits the mold of rock-and-roll pioneer as well as any nobody who managed his way into a Memphis recording studio in the year of the film's release, 1954.

Johnny Guitar, with its adherence to Western commonplaces played out on well-used Republic pictures sets, offers the opportunity to watch as an explosive, expressive lyrical sensibility toys with the most reified narrative conventions imaginable. The same might be said of what someone like Johnny Cash was doing with the murder ballad in a song like "Folsom Prison Blues" (1955), in which Cash takes the traditional murder ballad and infuses it with a pop wit and sings it with wiseacre enthusiasm that turns murder and malice into grand farce and then back into grand tragedy. In other words, exactly the operating principle at play throughout *Johnny Guitar*, in which Ray underlies Western clichés with a romantic flourish evoked, as Eisenschitz notes, by the film's odd, stark interiors and Victor Young's lush score, and then betrays those clichés with a stylized, high camp approach that keeps everything teetering on the edge of grand farce (201).

At the center of the film's odd flamboyance stands Hayden, whose powerful yet oddly passive gunslinger-hero helps transform the typical gender politics of the Western film and underscores the ambiguous gender identity that would come to be a defining feature of *Rebel Without a Cause*. Such ambiguities also inform the perverse performance practices of Little Richard, Gene Vincent, and even Elvis himself, musicians who played with evocations of femininity that prefigured glam aesthetics twenty years before the fact.

Ray frequently underscores Hayden's femininity in his blocking choices, particularly in the saloon sequence in which Johnny and Vienna attempt to reconnect after years apart. Consistently placed in subordinate positions to Vienna, either sitting in a chair or pleading to Vienna as she either has her back turned to him or assumes stoic, resigned postures, Johnny plays the role of a supplicant, forced to beg and plead using lyrical paeans to the past and their shared pain in order to reach her. It is a highly unusual sequence in a Western, as the new gunslinger in town abandons any pretense toward stoicism and instead becomes a loquacious, emotionally needy figure, a mark of the kind of vision of wounded masculinity that defines all of Ray's heroes.

Early rockabilly, for all its bravado, contained hints of the same kind of vulnerability, either directly or indirectly. In the ballads he recorded for Sun Records, Elvis essays a haunting tenderness, particularly his recording of "Blue Moon," in which his vocals reduce to a soft whisper, and his croon trails off into a mournful whimper that leaves an impression of a singer precariously exposed. It is the same sense Hayden's forlorn Johnny Logan evokes, a performance that benefits from the broken quality that Hayden brought to the role. As Eisenschitz writes, "Hayden no longer gave a damn about his career . . . [and] had no reason to be interested in a role to which he brings so much, precisely through his air of having lost all his illusions and the dreamy detachment with which he delivers his most lyrical lines" (202). Hayden thus created another hero for whom anxiety and frustration were ways of staying relatively sane. In much the same way, Elvis's combination of deep reserves of feeling and unbridled energy provided an image of hysteria transformed into a personal ethos, a way of responding with full awareness to the demands of the world at hand.

Nicholas Ray desperately wanted Elvis to star in his 1957 Western *The True Story of Jesse James*, but studio politics led to Robert Wagner to be cast instead (Eisenschitz 283–88). Ray recognized in Elvis a volatility that he wanted to harness, just as Elvis had seen in *Rebel Without a Cause* an expression of anxiety with which he felt a deep connection. But despite the failure of the two men to come together on a film project, Elvis's recordings contain an aural aura that mirrors the performances of doomed rebellion that dominate the cinema of Nicholas Ray.

13

Robin A. Larsen

Places and Spaces in *Rebel Without a Cause*

REBEL WITHOUT A CAUSE DEEPLY affected teenagers like me, who saw the film at the same age as Jim, Judy, and Plato. We did not realize how peculiar it was to grow up in suburbia during those years of blacklisting and nuclear buildup, but Ray did. The action lines and allusions in the film allow audiences today to keep discovering the spaces and places in the film. *Rebel* visualizes space in compelling ways. Not only do these spaces contain the three stars' action lines, they allude to submerged, semipermanent sociopolitical structures. Still with us, these structures command conformity, obedience, and rapid adaptations to environmental change. *Rebel* still obliquely connects audiences in complex, nonlinear ways to the protagonists' confrontations with these structures.

Ray worked from direct experience and not from techniques and a lexicon (Ray, *Interrupted* xxxix). Earlier experience with Frank Lloyd Wright at Taliesin in Wisconsin during 1933 and 1934 sparked Ray's way of thinking about filmic spaces as lifelike, organic, architectural entities that actively shaped relationships. Ray also imported into the commercial studio environment the intensely collaborative ways of working he had learned from 1932 to 1945 at the Theatre of Action, Group Theatre, Works Progress Administration, and Voice of America (see James

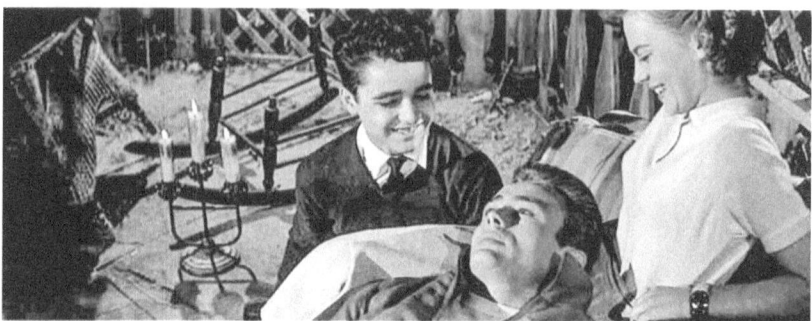

Figure 13.1. *Rebel Without a Cause* (Warner Bros., 1955): After Jim (James Dean) chases Judy (Natalie Wood) as she sprints around the pool edge, they land on a chaise in the gazebo. As Jim puts his head on Judy's lap, she wipes his face with a handkerchief, and Plato (Sal Mineo) continues to play child, rolling on the floor into a sitting position against their legs that indicates they should be his parents (frame enlargement).

I. Deutsch and Lauren R. Shaw's chapter herein, "Citizen Nick: Civic Engagement and Folk Culture in the Life and Work of Nicholas Ray," for an exploration of Ray's prefilm activities). He directed each member of the *Rebel* cast individually, sometimes giving them completely different ideas of what the story was about to foster surprises that made their action lines more genuine. But just as Ray's collaborators formed a sort of temporary family, Ray's own nomadic lifestyle informed his conception of space in *Rebel Without a Cause*; from the time he graduated from high school in 1929 until his death in 1979, he moved every few years. For most of his life he pulled away from the intimacies of family and home.

Ray maintained tight creative control over the visual conception of *Rebel*. He storyboarded dozens of sketches of action to be shot from unique angles within striking spaces in sequences that violated editing conventions. One theory in particular supports Ray's own views on film space and its reception. He wrote and spoke about film as a humanlike, intentional entity. Its three most important elements are experience, love, and truthful knowledge of human connection. To be important a film must be "done within the cradle of love and experience, and with the ability to observe and participate in life at the same time. . . . The whole process of film is catching the essence of a moment, and keeping that alive" (Ray, *Interrupted* 151, 193). Furthermore, Ray suggests that "It is the director who has to find all the properties of the camera, relations to space, time and people, to create a given circumstance that is vital enough that the audience can sense it . . ." (192–93).

Like Ray, Vivian Sobchack argues that audiences experience "cinema as life experiencing life, as experience expressing experience" (5). Thus filmmaker, film, and spectator all mutually experience cinema as "*viewers viewing* what a film's 'acts' are; its *perception of expression* and the *expression of perception*" (5). Regardless which elements of a film someone interprets, a film "assumes and assures its own intelligibility (even if it assumes and assures no single interpretation)" (6). Sobchack's strategy for analyzing a film, which informs this analysis of *Rebel*, is to attend to its phenomena of experiences as they occur, to describe the phenomena, to arrange these phenomena in an equalizing way, and to reduce them analytically to "structures and invariant features" of a film's intended "patterns of experience" (48).

One important structural and invariant feature of Ray films is the memorable moment. To locate these moments, as Murray Pomerance argues, "one must always watch action, not story. Because human action is for him the greatest, most powerful, of mysteries, the cinematic frame must somehow be made equal to capturing every nuance of it" (*Horse* 37). Audiences build their own experiences out of film moments that evoke memorable emotions. Sobchack recommends several strategies for analyzing a film's spectatorship. First, the analyst should describe its "common and cooperative function" within society (166). People are still writing about the impact of *Rebel*'s collaborative production and of Ray's communal way of working with its actors, and to find out what the film is still saying about youth (Slocum 17). Its construction of youth is rooted in Ray's experiences with gangs in action and interviewing youth in juvenile halls giving authenticity to the film's action lines expressing loneliness, paranoia, and meaninglessness. Evidence that middle-class youths on the margins of suburbia were feeling the feelings his protagonists felt appeared in sources he cited for his original story, "The Blind Run." *Rebel* and the rest of Ray's work also ignited *auteurist* ideas of French cinema intellectuals such as Godard, Rivette, and Truffaut, who agree that Ray's individuals face hostile environments which, in the words of J. David Slocum, "cut to the heart of life in contemporary society" (3).

Second, following Sobchack's theory, the analyst should examine a film's "historical activity and teleological accomplishment of human intentional projects and productions" (166). Warner Bros. transformed *Rebel* from a juvenile delinquency cycle product into a quality hit film made with the studio's newest technology. It created three new young stars. It captured the teen market signaled by earlier 1955 releases, *Blackboard Jungle* and *East of Eden*. And today's youth are still enacting the Stark/Dean paradigm. Lastly, the analyst should remain aware that audiences experience a film subjectively and objectively as having its own consciousness. A film has perceptions and actions and then reflects on them (Sobchack 166). *Rebel* still actively participates in history.

Positions on Rebel's Spaces

Two strong positions on the meaning of spaces in *Rebel Without a Cause* have been argued. George Wilson writes that Ray arranges space to reflect pressures arising from "impersonal determinants" in "a field of forces guiding" the characters' bonds "in the face of death, isolation, and sheer nothingness" (117). Plato responds to this field destructively, whereas Jim and Judy are impelled by it to fall in love and reconcile their issues with their parents. Similarly, Blaine Allan writes that visual conditions and elements in Ray's films stress existential aspects of significant moments. Moments of violence, for example, are the result of conditions that "give rise to and complicate" patterns of living (21). Two patterns that develop from this treatment of space are the protagonists' chronic problems with being unable to make themselves understood, and feeling confused about why they cannot feel as if they belong. The moment at the end of *Rebel* confirms the value of the family, but its existential lesson is that some family members must be sacrificed so others can move on to an uncertain future. When Plato dies there is no one to blame; according to this view, Plato's death resonates because this death is simply a part of life.

An opposing position is that *Rebel*'s spaces are creatively expansive and convey what Jonathan Rosenbaum calls "utopian promise." Though they juxtapose couples with "anarchic movement erupting into violence," the violence unfolds in "a spectacular form of choreography" with elements "intensely articulated, yet 'distanced' into a sort of abstraction" ("Circle" 127). As Rosenbaum goes on to point out, in *Rebel*'s "framework of romantic futility" (127) we find "a strong empathy for adolescents, a particular flair for color and CinemaScope," and his recurrent desire to film a musical (128). *Rebel*'s contribution to widescreen space construction involved architectural balance in character construction and *mise-en-scène* that accentuated erotic dynamics between couples (for a further consideration of this aspect of Ray's work, see Harper Cossar's chapter herein, "Ray, Widescreen, and Genre: *The True Story of Jesse James*"). The vivid and singular performances of the actors in his films undercut the notion that his spaces frame experience as futile and bleak.

Both of these positions are reflected in James Dean's presence in the film, which exudes both existential despair but also a sense of utopian promise. Ray instilled in Dean an urgent and desperate need to be possessed by the Jim Stark character. According to Bernard Eisenschitz, Ray's direction of actors involves the filmmaker's ability "to extract elements of a film out of real-life conflicts" by being very close to an actor over time to draw on "a variety of aspects of one's innermost self" (243). In an interview for *Cahiers du cinéma* in 1958, Ray said that "a very satisfactory way" of getting an actor to improvise a scene was to give contradictory instructions. He invited Dean over to his bungalow where he coached him to evoke the feelings that led him to attack his father so violently. Ray told Dean, "first to go upstairs without being heard, and then, at the same time, to feel the irresistible need to talk to somebody" (Bitsch 122). Consider, though, that this "somebody" Dean has to improvise wanting to talk to is the powerful Ray: his director, father figure, or lover, or perhaps all three. Dean's particular choice for his line of action in the scene practiced in Ray's bungalow can be interpreted ironically, as the infantilized son wanting to be bottle-fed by an inadequate father.

Two judgments on the Dean/Stark persona Ray's direction and Dean's acting created stand out. Elia Kazan sensed the existential despair behind the persona, but argued that it was inauthentic. He never lost his contempt for Ray's role in fostering the Dean legend. According to Kazan, "In contrast to these parent figures, all youngsters were supposed to be sensitive and full of 'soul.' This didn't seem true to me. I thought them—Dean, 'Cal,' and the kid he played in Nick Ray's film—self-pitying, self-dramatizing, and good-for-nothing" (539).[1] In such a view, Dean's persona became an empty cliché rather than an authentic existential statement.

Yet the "utopian promise" we find in one position on Ray's spaces is also echoed in one critical perspective on Dean. For these critics, the Dean persona motivated his generation to want to reinvent the role of the adolescent within the family. Quoting Dean, who said "*I need creatures who resemble me*," David Dalton calls the persona "a freak, a sport of nature who must play two roles at once," roles involving both looking back and moving forward (341). His posthumous success has much to do with how he used the Stark persona to drive toward "the future of the new species" (342). In fighting against adult timidity, conformity, secrecy, and hidden hostilities, Dean's Stark showed his generation how to empower itself to create a new culture out of the ashes of "the decaying organism" cold war America had become (340). Likewise, Ray's goal in directing the Jim Stark role was to expose the destructiveness of the unit rooted in the film's spaces, the nuclear family (Dickstein 2). The "cool" of Dean's legacy epitomized youth's defense in the 1950s against adult inauthenticity and insincerity.

If Dean's presence, as read through these critical perspectives, embodies both the existential angst and utopian promise that critics have perceived in *Rebel*'s spaces, the spaces of the film nevertheless function autonomously as organic, architectural entities, and these are perhaps more memorable than their stars or genres. Without space there can be no action, and for Ray the aim of all action is expressing the need to connect. All of his spaces are architectural, and architecture was for him the "backbone of all arts" (Bitsch 121). Architecture became for Ray a way of looking for underlying structures and for "connecting the void, space and time with the need for people to connect," which "comes out of aloneness, the aloneness that different spatial alignments or counter-themes create, or set the stage for, or help to dramatize" (Ray, *Interrupted* 26). Ray spoke of the need for connecting in these spaces as a kind of energy. A space can heighten tension in action, can say "no man is an island" (106), and can show a state of mind (136). At first, Ray constructed spaces out of the way they looked in comic books, as action seen from extreme angles, as jumps from close-ups to extreme long shots, and by positioning an object in the center of a long shot to lead viewers out of one space and into another. Eventually he learned to make editing follow an "inner logic," which freed his direction to allow "for life and breadth and change, for accident, inspiration, and the sudden impulse that is a mistake of beauty" (42). In the film's spaces, the camera invites audiences to stare at the protagonists from varying angles with shifting degrees of closeness.

Rebel's crowded, de-centered spaces also serve to contain intense, repressed, and taboo emotions. Their images are intended for audiences to get in touch with their own suppressed emotions. Ray's architectural focus also permits a film to generalize about human action's more permanent aspects. Viewers of *Rebel* discover these abstractions through multiple points-of-view of spaces alive with shifting shadows, colors, lights, and movement. Ray's architectural way of looking also accounts for *Rebel*'s triangular groupings. Conflicts change when the triangles turn into single lines or circles. The price for Plato's death, however, is that it "serves no one"—Jim has the bullets. Its "existential void" is passed on to the audience (Allan 36).

In spaces and places of institutional authority, audiences are positioned in complicity with how white male authorities judge Jim, Judy, and Plato. They witness the trio with some detachment, perhaps embarrassment. Blocking and camera positions make us comfortably "look around the corner" at them. Our first gaze at Judy is in profile through two walls of glass, as if a patient in a clinic. As adults do, we look askance at how uncontrollably she plays out her feelings about her father and mother. Similarly, we look down at Plato's bowed head from the vantage of his interviewer and agree with him when he says Plato needs a psychiatrist.

The station houses unsympathetic interrogators and traps the trio under its low ceilings and crowded offices. As George Wilson has observed, the station space is an almost "palpable medium" in which camera setups and editing have "the power to slice and manipulate" audience perceptions, also to make Jim and Judy "blow up in rage and frustration" (113–14).

But the station also affords empathic moments. The first images of the protagonists show they are emotionally damaged and lonely, but appealingly so. Jim mimics siren noises when more police arrive, and imitates trumpets from "The Ride of the Valkyries" when his matriarchal family shows up. We look over his shoulder sympathetically at the huddled, shivering Plato to whom he offers his jacket. We peer with Jim around the corner at Judy in her blazing red Easter suit. We see an intimacy unfold between Jim and Ray Fremick (Edward Platt) after Jim's shocking fistfight with the desk.

If the police station oscillates between authoritative and empathic positions, the function of the planetarium later in the film is more mysterious, shifting across various identities. The film's screenwriter, Stewart Stern, likened the planetarium to Greek temples: "The way the steps came down from its great doors reminded me of the skene that used to stand in front of the back wall of ancient Greek theaters—where they did the sacrifices" (39–40). With its ceiling shot out of earth ending "in a burst of gas and fire," the planetarium recalls the apocalyptic rhetoric of the Atomic Energy Commission during the cold war in an April 19, 1954, *Life* article about the hydrogen bomb explosion at Eniwetok (qtd. in Broderick 154). At other times the planetarium acts like a live monster surveilling the perimeter. When Buzz vandalizes Jim's car and Jim and Plato watch from above, its dome pops up on the screen in an odd insert that triangulates the action. It rears its ugly, truncated shape again in the amphitheater at the end, when Jim punches its light switches to corner Plato. As Plato silently rises behind Jim's back, the projector rises too and creepily nods to Plato's left. The planetarium also takes on the guise of a mausoleum. Echoes of voices in the planetarium foyer make it reverberate like a Mycenaean tholos. This association with a huge burial chamber (linked to the themes of sacrifice suggested by Stern) hints at not just the death of earth but that of one of the lecture's audience.

Wilson reads collective action on the steps of the planetarium at the end of the film as "effects that arise from factors beyond mere psychology and . . . causes of desires that unconsciously guide their actions throughout the symbolic day" (123). Had Ray been able to persuade the studio to permit Plato and Jim to climb the dome and Jim to fail to prevent Plato from falling to his death, the planetarium would certainly convey a much darker vision of Plato's sacrifice. But Ray had difficulty with endings. Like the less violent, more indeterminate meaning he recreated for *In a Lonely Place*, *Rebel*'s ending leaves open more positive possibilities. The final, high-angle long shot of the planetarium can be read as a depiction of a space now dedicated to science with the potential for better ways of seeing the world. The shot affords audiences a long look that dwarfs the police car procession and the figure of Ray himself, who walks toward the building. Viewed as an abstraction, the planetarium is also there to remind audiences about the circularity of human existence, of Plato ducking down in terror between the amphitheater seats and then fleeing back into the amphitheater to die at dawn.

While the police station and the planetarium have important functions in the film, Ray's primary focus in *Rebel* is with the meaning of the home. In a publicity interview for *Rebel*, Ray indicated the film's purpose was "to put what happens in the home—the middle-class home—ahead . . . of slum conditions. These things are taking place on all social, economic, and cultural levels, wherever young people feel they are 'out of attention'" (qtd. in Michaud 45). In his original story for *Rebel* called "The Blind Run," Ray describes the home of one suburban teen as "non-distinctive. Neither gauche, flashy nor poor or unkempt. They just move a lot. Hoping to improve, but not doing much, in fact, to achieve it" (Ray, *The Blind Run* 4). This sounds like Jim's home. Crowdedness, factory-made décor, and colors of beige, tan, brown, cream, pink, and mint green cause nauseating feelings of being suffocated, bored, frustrated, and depressed. Doorways, hallways, and landings create spaces where everyone can watch everyone else but no one connects. In every home scene, someone expresses a taboo emotion: incestuous desire, feelings of patricide, feelings of matricide, desolation of being left out, rage at being ignored.

Class, sexual, and political markers are visible in the three home spaces. Gendered antagonism in *film noir* is said to have occurred in response to how white male power and privilege reasserted itself after the war. With this reassertion came efforts to define masculinity and femininity as private and individualized. At the same time, the state invaded and surveilled private homes. The response in *noir* melodramas like *Rebel* was contradictory: male figures at home were drawn as incomplete, misogynistic, and "right-thinking," and female figures at home were presented as hysterical and aggressive (Breu 201–02). From the rigid manner of Judy's father, the crossed swords on the wall behind him, Beau's toy machine gun at dinner, and his violence to Judy, we infer he is a militaristic father with sexual problems, a common coding for fathers in this genre. Robert Genter points out that in the wake of sexuality scares associated with political subversion both McCarthyism and earlier changes in gender roles generated, the authoritarian male was thought to have "the same psychological failings as other 'sexual deviants' such as gays and psychopaths" (144). On the other hand, Jim Stark's father lacks manliness and avoids conflict and decision-making, which implies that his confused gender role was rooted in the postwar corporate managerial masculinity that David Riesman criticized for its fearful conformity in *The Lonely Crowd*. In an interview for *Cahiers du cinéma* in 1956, Ray shows he was aware of cold war gender confusion. The 360–degree tilt showing Jim's mother and house upside down, he said, "came to express my feeling toward the entire scene: here was a house in danger of tipping from side to side. It was organic to the scene" (qtd. in McGilligan 291). Plato's more affluent mother, with the means to live in a more elaborate house with its own full-time maid, is another sexually deviant figure in 1950s melodrama: the independent middle-class woman. As Genter notes, she is willing to put "the stability of the family in question" (144).

The space of the chickie run, meanwhile, affords a cluster of memorable moments with contrasting allusive meanings. The chickie run fails as a ritual for proving the youth are invincible because one of them dies; meanwhile at home and in school, they remain unprotected from emotional and physical damage. Nonetheless, a creative expansiveness exists in the chickie run, making it a site of liberation relative to the home, the police station, and the planetarium. With panoramic views of clusters of excited spectators, close-ups of Buzz, Jim, and Judy, revving motor sounds, and a grid of cars and lights that create a wide, shining race path, the cliff is a space where moments of real change occur. Before the run begins, the gang pauses at the edge. This is a moment when they reflect on the run's worst outcome. Then the action shifts to a panorama. A second shift back to the edge turns the bluff into a space for male intimacy. However, the camera, as it looks at Buzz and Jim from a point dangerously beyond the edge, underlines their discussion of the run's lack of meaning. A fourth shift in perspective transforms the scene into that of a battlefield. In a series of backlit aerial shots, Judy semaphores the start, the racers nearly hit her, and a centered shot of her back as she seductively swirls her circle skirt alludes to the sexual excitement of the chickie run. After Buzz dies, the meaning of this space changes again, now becoming a crime scene from which almost everyone flees. Only the trio remains, where they enact one of the film's most memorable moments. Jim holds out his hand to Judy, which holds her back from the edge. Though the bluff costs Buzz his life, it affords Jim a chance to shift into a more responsible role.

Yet this responsibility leads to yet another of the film's spaces, the abandoned mansion. After Judy, Jim, and Plato assemble at the mansion,

Plato initiates the family ritual by lighting a candelabra to usher the couple on a tour of his "castle." Judy and Jim play married consumers looking for a way to show off their millions. Then they play the children playing in the "nursery" that is the empty pool, as they execute acrobatics and dashes in and around it: after Jim chases Judy as she sprints around the pool edge, leaping over shrubs and walls, they land on a chaise in the gazebo. As Jim puts his head in Judy's lap, she wipes his face with a handkerchief, and Plato continues to play the child, rolling on the floor into a sitting position against their legs that indicates they should be his parents. Their conversation drops into a languorous rhythm as Plato slides face down on the patio, with Judy encouraging him to sleep by humming Brahms's "Lullaby." Quietly the couple sneaks off to be alone, an impulse that Plato sees as a betrayal after his rare moment of happiness for feeling included. The betrayal makes him explode in violence. The mansion changes from a utopian setting into a nightmarish ambush.

As this consideration of the various spaces in the film shows, one of *Rebel*'s most striking existential truths is that protagonists become aware of their limitations and how these affect their relationships with their environments, truths which they, in turn, teach to audiences. As Allan suggests, "The exorbitant price Ray heroes pay for education is loss. Understanding is gained only through trauma and reconciliation" (35). Abrupt shifts in *Rebel*'s spaces, with their rituals and rhythms, are intended to center and de-center audiences. The shifts move audiences back and forth between perceiving and reflective points of view. Much as real-life individuals either approach or avoid moments of crisis, *Rebel* alternates scenes of "anarchic movement erupting into violence" with scenes conveying "intensely articulated" cinematic elements. In this way, audiences can either intensely engage in a *Rebel* moment or experience it as a "distanced abstraction."

Interpreting architectural and sociopolitical aspects of *Rebel*'s spaces also helps explain why Judy and Plato and other characters can be viewed as "different facets of a single personality" facing the same dilemmas, that is, as arenas of forces to be grappled with collectively rather than individually. Jim's bonding with Buzz hints at how he could have been Buzz going over the edge. Viewed now in a less sexually repressed time, moments of male bonding show Jim could have chosen either Plato or Buzz as lovers instead of Judy. The parents' repetitive, near-involuntary outbursts of anxiety and anger show us now how tightly connected they were to a political environment that threatened personal persecution and nuclear annihilation.

Ray said several times that he wanted this film about youth to be viewed by youth. I think the film now speaks on a mythic level to both youth and adults. In spaces that afford youth and adult characters multiple points of view, in the flexible movements from space to space, audiences cannot avoid becoming uncomfortable parties to both sides of *Rebel*'s generational gap between confused, self-destructive protagonists and disingenuous, soul-destroying adults.

The question of whether *Rebel* is ultimately a story about existential angst or utopian promises remains. *Rebel*'s spaces, however, allude to pressures to retain the status quo that today's audiences still face: sexual and emotional repression, geographical modernization, materialism, and bureaucratically distributed power and authority. John Kreidl claims Ray sought to have *Rebel*'s audiences confront America's national "nervous system" and not fall back on "Hollywoodized methods" (14). Existential motifs arising from pulp literature and comic books found their way into *noir* melodramas like *Rebel*: the nonheroic hero; the widespread alienation and loneliness; unavoidable choices; sentences of death; a sense of meaninglessness or purposelessness; instances of chaos, violence, and paranoia; and resorts to sanctuary, ritual, and order. These motifs add up to an existential attitude that still resonates. Authentic, complexly rendered spaces in *Rebel* make this dual existential attitude of despair and hope understandable for today's audiences.

Note

1. Dean starred as Cal Trask, another troubled youth, in Kazan's *East of Eden*.

14

Susan White

Nicholas Ray's Wilderness Films
Word, Law, and Landscape

Nicholas Ray's films are frequently structured around parallel and competing wildernesses, but certain of Ray's works examine the dynamics of wilderness more overtly than, say, *Rebel Without a Cause* or *On Dangerous Ground*. *Bitter Victory*, *Wind Across the Everglades*, *The Savage Innocents*, and the made-for-television "High Green Wall" (1954) conjoin and elaborate significant issues related to wilderness. The first is the question of terrain, whether jungle, desert, frozen wasteland, or swamp. For Ray, terrain is as much psychological as visual, almost always linked to questions of rivalry and the success or failure of men to create a common relationship to the land. Ray's peculiar brand of cultural relativism is also expressed in these films through an intricately rendered presentation of spoken and written word, placed in the context of human actions in the wilderness setting. Books and written documents serve in the wild as cultural remnants, fetishes, and motivations for human action. But words also produce laws, both through oral tradition and in the form of written documents. These laws, whether fashioned by colonizing societies, by indigenous peoples, or by nature itself, may be depicted as perverse, as catalysts of mental disease, as a means of preserving or destroying cultures and individuals, or as simply implacable. Thus, both

Figure 14.1. Joseph Cotten as Henty in "High Green Wall" (Revue Productions/ *General Electric Theater* series, 1954): Henty has left "the jungle of the civilized world," the sole survivor of a doomed expedition into the Amazon (*General Electric Theater* press release/Susan White Collection).

the spoken and the written word are frequently instruments of violence. Laws, whether they are passed down through oral traditions, books, or nature, also move across time. The endurance of the word, the law, is inextricably bound up with its moral status in Ray's wilderness films.

"High Green Wall"

In 1954 Ray directed "High Green Wall" for the *General Electric Theater* television series; it was an adaptation of Evelyn Waugh's 1933 story, "The Man Who Liked Dickens." Whether Ray suggested the text to be adapted or if he simply accepted it as an assignment is not clear (Eisenschitz 221), but certainly the program iterates many of the themes examined in greater depth elsewhere in Ray's *oeuvre*. The program differs not only from Waugh's story, but also from the text Charles Jackson wrote, particularly in the works' treatment of Dickens's prose.[1] Waugh's novel includes no citations of Dickens whatsoever, while "High Green

Wall" uses Dickens's words both as devices to further the plot and as a means of underscoring themes otherwise expressed visually.

"High Green Wall" is set in a minimally rendered Amazonian jungle. Joseph Cotten, as Henty, stumbles dazed and sick into a jungle complex ruled by a half-Indian, half-white man appropriately named McMaster (Thomas Gomez). Henty has left "the jungle in the civilized world," the sole survivor of a doomed expedition into the Amazon. McMaster's "paternal" reign is backed by the power of a rifle. He nurses Henty back to health, drawing on the knowledge of jungle potions imparted by his Indian mother. McMaster, it seems, refused to learn how to read from his white missionary father, but has carefully preserved the latter's extensive collection of Dickens novels, and is desperate to acquire a "guest" who will read the books aloud. Henty is at first quite willing to take on this task. The previous reader, a well-educated Venezuelan, is buried nearby, his grave hinting broadly at Henty's fate.

Gomez's simultaneously languid and menacing performance—often surprisingly agile and childlike—is marked by alternately fierce and dreamy eyes. Cotten's shifting emotions—anxious, reflective, indignant, hopeful, and melancholy—provide an excellent counterweight to Gomez's performance. As he awakens much weakened after four days of serious illness, Henty struggles with his bed's mosquito netting, held in check by even this gossamer material. Suspicious that McMaster is in fact holding him prisoner, his body tenses and the camera lingers more than once on his face, creased with worry.

Unlike Waugh's story, the specific tribe of the silent Indians is named "Sirians," Venezuelans whom McMaster describes as "shy." Their shyness is heavily tinged with fear because they most often slip away from McMaster when he appears. Like Cottonmouth (Burl Ives) in *Wind Across the Everglades*, McMaster is well-adapted to his environment. Whenever Henty explores his surroundings, McMaster suddenly and mysteriously appears, commenting first on Barnabas's grave as Henty gazes upon it, then interrupting him as he attempts to induce the Indians to build a boat. He must await the rainy season in order to leave the jungle. Renewed hope mellows Henty, who admits, upon reading a moving Dickens passage, as the camera pulls to a slight high-angle that emphasizes the importance of the moment, that "our civilized world does produce some wonderful things." But when the rainy season arrives, McMaster informs him that he "forgot" to disclose that superstition prevents the Indians from building boats during the rainy season. Henty demands his release, but McMaster points out that he is not actually a prisoner: he simply needs help out of the jungle, which the latter is not willing to provide.

The arrival of a Frenchman renews Henty's hope for escape. Aubert (Maurice Marsac) mentions that, like Henty, Barnabas always had a book in his hand. In one of the most significant moments of the program, Henty slips a page torn from one of McMasters's books into the departing Aubert's hand, hoping that the Frenchman will recognize the printed words as an appeal for help. And, indeed, American explorers arrive. But McMaster arranges for the Indians to put on a celebration before, during which Henty gazes with interest at the wild gyrations of the Indian woman dancing around the fire, a spectacle McMaster no doubt directed. Henty allows himself to relax, drugged with a honeyed concoction, noting that he believes he is better equipped to cope with the civilized world, and that in the future he will "think fondly of this place."

The explorers arrive while Henty is drugged, and naively read the "message" to McMaster: "Release me from this prison of horror, for I find every hour nearer to destruction" (a rephrased quotation from *A Tale of Two Cities*). McMaster announces that Henty has died, and gives the explorers Henty's watch as a keepsake, which he has thoughtfully wound, first when Henty was sick, and now when the latter is in the induced coma.

All is revealed to Henty when he awakens. McMaster's cajoling voice acts as another drug, lulling Henty into a despairing resignation: "We won't read today, but tomorrow—and the day after that, and the day after that. And then we'll begin *The Tale of Two Cities* again. There are certain passages in that book I can never hear without the temptation to weep." Henty listens to these devastating words from behind the screened door. Earlier he had thrown a book through this door, but now he only dully stares. After a cut, the camera pulls back and pans to reveal thatched roofs and Indians walking through the jungle. Animals cry out. In voiceover, Henty begins reading again, his voice echoing strangely: "It was the best of times. It was the worst of times." Cotten's face, simply looking up from the book, not reading aloud, is superimposed over the jungle.

The inclusion of Dickens's unmistakably beautiful prose in "High Green Wall," especially insofar as that prose usually reflects McMasters's states of mind, implies a more complex relationship to Dickens and to the status of culture than is usually recognized. Dickens provides Henty with words of hope, with laments, with words that plead for his release. And yet the written word itself (as Derrida often observed) is treated with suspicion. It represents an idiosyncratic religious cult for McMaster (who comments that Dickens believed in God), the "wonderful things" of the civilized world. In refusing to learn to read, McMaster straddles the two worlds of the Indians and his white father (whose place, ironically,

Henty takes insofar as his excellent reading voice reminds McMaster of his father's).

Except during the celebration, the Sirians are mostly mute, cyphers. We cannot know whether McMaster has invented the superstition about building during the rainy season, if any of the Indians are indeed his "children," or even why he is so profoundly addicted to Dickens. The book represents the passing of years and seasons for McMaster. It takes two years to work through all the volumes. The renewal of the cycle of life occurs for McMaster when they arrive once again at *A Tale of Two Cities*. The stacks of books in the background act as an hourglass, as the unread stack diminishes and the read one grows. But the cycle of rainy seasons, the endless rotation of Dickens's novels, are not linked to renewal. Like the watch McMaster keeps wound, the "cycle" is a metonym only for death, "alive" as it ticks, and then only as an inert "keepsake." Half-white and half-Indian as he claims to be, McMaster hopelessly obscures our look at the Sirian culture. The paradox (the best of times and worst of times) reveals itself as chiasmus: civilization as jungle, jungle as civilization, and finally as the crosspiece marking Barnabas's real and Henty's virtual grave.

Bitter Victory

The script for *Bitter Victory* diverges significantly from the Rene Hardy novel, *Amère victoire*, and the film itself differs from the script. The producers rushed the filming, and some members of the cast strongly disliked Ray. Nevertheless, Ray managed to develop a close working relationship with Richard Burton, using rehearsals as springboards for powerful improvisational acting moments and important *trouvailles* for the script. (For example, the alteration of a line from the novel—from "I polish off the wounded and save the dead" to "I kill the living and save the dead"—creates much stronger and more to the point dialogue, as well as words more characteristic of Leith, who speaks them).

From the beginning the dynamics of words—written and spoken— establish the rivalry between the film's protagonists. Terrain—including the specific cultural formations that exist against this landscape, and the "turf" implied by military rank, the possession of a woman, and so forth—is paramount. The film reverses the usual foregrounding of military action in war films. Like the violent vision of the cosmos revealed in *Rebel Without a Cause*'s planetarium, the desert as represented in *Bitter Victory* proves to be a force that renders human concerns insignificant.

Curd Jürgens's Brand is a paper-pusher, a major who has never seen action. Introduced shuffling papers and accompanied by the sound of offscreen typewriters, Brand paces nervously until an Arab man, Mokrane (Raymond Pellegrin), exits Major General Paterson's office. Under the unyielding eye of the General's assistant (Lieutenant Colonel Michael Callander [Alfred Burke]), Brand self-consciously puts out his cigarette, dons his cap, and places his swagger stick under his arm, stiffly "performing" his role as military officer. The Command is seeking an officer to attack the Nazis' Benghazi headquarters and to steal documents vital to Rommel's North African campaign. Paterson: "I know you've always wanted action. Well, you may be the man to command this operation. It is paperwork, after all. [Sardonic reaction shot from General's assistant.] Do you speak Arabic?" Brand replies, "I'm afraid I'm not very good at languages. I left South Africa but I never got rid of my accent." The caricature of a narrow-minded British officer, Paterson subtly insults Brand by describing the mission as "paperwork."

Exiting, Brand catches sight of Captain James Leith (Burton), presented in an extreme low-angle shot, perched on a chair straightening a fan for the General. Leith is immediately called into the General's office by the Lieutenant Colonel, whom he addresses as "Mike," while the latter addresses him as "Jimmy." Leith is a man of action, willing to express friendship through small acts of consideration. This conventional display of dominance through camera angle is undercut: he is dominant insofar as he moves easily among the men who understand him. The codes of masculinity are manipulated in Leith's favor, but his willingness to serve other men foreshadows what critics have described as his masochism. Leith adjusts his cap and stick with firm gestures and walks unflinchingly into the General's office. But when a typist informs Brand that his wife is on the base, his face changes completely; he is almost embarrassingly excited by the news. As he leaves to meet her, the typist shakes his head ever so slightly.

Leith, an archaeologist who volunteered for the army, speaks Arabic and, as Callander points out, knows the desert and its people. The General, shown in a diminishing high-angle, argues that Leith is "hardly civilized," "an intellectual"—"and besides, he's Welsh." Brand, Paterson asserts, will know (presumably because he is a career paper-pusher) all about those documents. Callander is clearly put off by his superior officer's lack of judgment, but rank prevails and, while both men will be assigned to the mission, Brand will be in command.

Brand is left in a state of confusion about Leith, a confusion that will only deepen as he meets his wife, Jane (Ann Todd), for a drink. Brand and Leith enter together, Leith immediately realizing that Brand's wife (who has been kept "top secret") is his own former lover. An awkward shot–reverse shot sequence ensues. Brand's confusion, weakness, and suspicion are etched on his twitchy, baggy-eyed face. Leith, on the other hand, calmly eyes Jane, who, like him, is presented in glamorizing close-ups. She is witty and careless, while Leith's handsome eyes burn with love, self-contempt, and his ongoing existential crisis. A conversation full of innuendo follows, Brand realizing that he and Leith are up for the same assignment, even as the latter reproaches his wife for "mixing drinks," an obvious allusion to her interest in Leith. The turf battle will intensify in the enveloping desert.

Leith knows the desert, but, as an archeologist, he especially knows the desert of the deep past. And, of course, his knowledge of and feelings for Jane inhabit another past in which he demonstrated his cowardice in love, but where his abrupt departure left behind an unmistakable allure. Both Brand and Leith show cowardice, but Leith's is more abstract—it is more available to him for private self-torment, while Brand's is only too public, and known not only by a woman but also by other men. While Brand will fail many times in the field, most pointedly when he fails to kill a sentry and Leith must do the job, Leith's lack of moral fiber was only to leave forever waiting (at the British Museum) a woman whose love frightened him. And yet—he has won the woman. As he shouts (borrowing from Walt Whitman) while throwing his body over Brand's to prevent the Major from being smothered in a sandstorm: "I contradict myself." Indeed.

The mirroring relationship between Brand and Leith is no less compelling for its lack of subtlety. Brand's filmic lesson has the familiar chiasmatic form: winning is loss; loss is winning. Nobility is not in the win or the medal, but in gesture, language, and a manliness revealed most of all in a loving respect that is certainly homosocial if not actually homosexual, forged over years of men working a terrain together. Ironically, Brand's final gesture in the film, marking the futility of success and the absurdity of war's "bubble reputation," is most demonstrative of integrity. His admission of being a stuffed shirt, a straw man, when he pins his medal onto the dummy, betrays a self-knowledge that Leith should envy.

Jane is readily and early on conflated with the mission itself. After having had a row with her jealous husband, Jane returns to the base, where some of the soldiers are muttering at having their leave canceled on Brand's orders. One soldier comments: "The only thing that Major Brand has slept with is the book of rules." Overhearing, Jane asks the sentry to see Brand. "Who are you?" "The book of rules," is her sharp reply. In Ray's films women at their best and worst often *do* function as books of rules. In *Bitter Victory*, the drama acted out in a gorgeously filmed desert where men play the most important roles, also involves a sacrifice, but does not lead to the establishment of a family. The film's ending is piquant in its refusal to conform to that norm, even if (as in *Rebel Without a Cause*) the Hollywood family group generally faces a sadly conformist future.

The book of rules segues into the pursuit of documents whose acquisition will foil Rommel's Northern African campaign. In an act of derring-do, during which Leith is as willing to be killed as to kill at close range, the British soldiers succeed in breaking into the safe containing the military plans. During this sequence, the group acts as a familiarly Rayish band of outlaws, depending on the safe-cracking skills of the obviously crooked Private Wilkins (Nigel Green).

The men slog along with the sacks of documents, metaphorizing the conflict over book-of-rules Jane. But the real triangle is among men. When Leith is left behind to await the rescue or, more likely deaths, of the men wounded in a skirmish with the enemy, Mokrane takes off. This is a strange reconfiguration of Leith's having left Jane to wait at the British Museum, drawn together again only because Jane joins the military to be close to her husband. The wilderness of sand is a more enduring place of waiting than even the British Museum. As the men arrive, against odds, at the ruined city, where they were to have been met with camels and reinforcements, Leith declares his allegiance to the past: "This must have been quite a city. Berber, I think. Tenth century. Built, I suppose, to protect themselves from Arab invasions. I'm not very good on this period. Too modern for me." Brand later allows Leith to be lethally stung by a scorpion, but of course Leith has already committed himself to being left to wait eternally, as the sand blows across his beautifully etched features, at one with the natural law that commands our deaths.

Even as Leith rots under the desert sun, the now "victorious" Brand almost loses the all-important documents to a fire their German prisoner of war (taken in the earlier skirmish) set, as the men excitedly run to meet their army unit. The fire is extinguished, and the singed papers survive and Brand gets his medal. But in the process, the "rule book" walks away, leaving behind only a decorated dummy.

Wind Across the Everglades

Although Ray was exhausted and broke by the time *Bitter Victory* wrapped, it did not prevent him from quickly entering into a partnership with Budd and Stuart Schulberg to film the former's screenplay about life in the Everglades. The concerns of the film mesh in even more intimate ways with the concerns of Ray's other "wilderness" films because it is organized around how "primitive people," both Indians and white Southerners, and "civilized" people confront nature through complex figurations of word, custom, and law.

The film is also a swan song for the outlaw's way of life. The ragtag outlaws are a particularly problematic group, bearing subtle allegiance to the defunct Confederacy, if only in Cottonmouth's (Burl Ives) disparaging use of the word "Yankee." While no significant black presence is found in the film (with the exception of one terrific scene featuring the African-American pianist and singer Rufus Beecham), it demonstrates nostalgia not only for the "noble savages" that whites have so nefariously impacted, but also for the "savage" whites who are competing for control of the swamp. Both groups are ultimately endangered by the vast consumer society of the United States. As bonded to Cottonmouth's band as Audubon Society warden Walt Murdock comes to be, he knows that the outlaw group the contradictions of American culture created must be destroyed.

After an elegiac opening montage of sunset and birds, a voiceover speaks of Florida as a new frontier, and laments the ecological damage wrought on the birds of the Everglades because of the feather hat craze across the United States. We see these hats on the train that carries Murdock (Christopher Plummer) to a bare-bones turn-of-the-century Miami. The "wonderland of wildlife" that Murdock sees from the train is "a refuge no longer." Feather poachers shoot and shout lustily, flash pans following their vigorous movements across the screen, bringing their "bloodstained cargo in open defiance of the law," to the "sleepy" town, having preserved the valuable plumes between "the musty pages of books, or sometimes even a Holy Bible."

Murdock has been hired to work as a nature teacher for the local high school, and immediately reacts to the bloody fad evident even in the train of women wearing enormous feathers and even entire birds on their hats. Soon after he steps down from the train, Murdock grabs feathers on a woman's hat ("How would you like it if this bird wore *you* for a decoration?"). Local officials promptly fired him from his job as a schoolteacher. Members of the Audubon Society are impressed by Murdock's feisty defense of the birds and offer him the dangerous position of game warden for the swamp—his sentence has been "commuted" to becoming a badge-wearing warden for the Audubons.

From man of (nature) books, Walter Murdock becomes an outlaw/man of the law. After having been jailed for the feather incident, he journeys into the Everglades' heart of darkness. Using a bulky period camera, Walter is taking a photo of a bird, when the image of the film's heavy, Cottonmouth (Burl Ives), appears upside down in the lens, a startling apparition with his red-bearded, vital rotundity. Cottonmouth (who has not yet introduced himself) declares that he has a thousand places in the Glades, that he was born here and will die here with the seeds of a swamp cabbage in his gut, and that a tree will grow from his body. Indeed, Cottonmouth (so called because he holds in his pocket at all times a cottonmouth snake by the name of Curly) is in his way "indigenous" to the swamp—for there are degrees of indigenousness in the film, and his troublesome presence, along with the other swamp rats, is at the heart of Schulberg's and Ray's meditation on the Americas as occupied wilderness.

After Cottonmouth vanishes, Walter posts the letter of the law on a tree, warning passersby that this bird sanctuary is protected by federal and state law, as well as the Audubon Society. As he drives in the last nail, shots ring out (a bullet figuratively shot into the text of the law). The bird slaughter has begun, accompanied by the whoops and hollering of Cottonmouth's crew. Walter confronts Cottonmouth, vowing to uphold the law. With a laugh at Walter's badge, Cottonmouth recedes into the Glades, leaving behind broken birds and a sorrowful game warden. The audience is left wondering what to feel about Cottonmouth.

In Cottonmouth's domain his word is law. The swamp rats in their muddy settlement dance with one another and call out women's names (the gender norms of their society are obviously complex). A vivid moment occurs when two escaped convicts arrive and (guffawing at the notion that they might be marshals—"Do we look like the law?"), are invited to fight for a shack. The strangely assorted crew looks on, Cottonmouth reigning supreme from his chair, snake in hand. This fight, like the knife fight in *Rebel*, has rules forged by the outlaws, but this skirmish is more humorous, in keeping with the ambiguous representation of the swamp rats. Magnificent low-angle shots of Ives, red beard against the blue sky, show him tenderly picking up the tiny jockey, "Loser," from the mud.

On return from the swamp to the home of the Nathansons (a local merchant whose daughter, Naomi [Chana Eden], is Walter's love interest), Murdock is pronounced "changed," "almost wild." This is the beginning of Walter's "going native": he gives a beautiful speech about the Glades—how a river becomes a prairie; the grass and water running together. While Nathanson would like to see the swamp cultivated, Murdock wants to keep this "empire" a sanctuary. They are caught, however, between the "land pirates" in Miami, and the pirating poachers.

The most important emotional arc involves Walter's powerful bond with and "sacrifice" of Cottonmouth for the greater good (of what, we cannot be sure). Cottonmouth attempts to kill Walter indirectly, by assigning Billy One-Arm (played by Seminole Chief Cory Osceola, a very important member of the Seminole community) to the job. But hearing Walter talk about the Seminole and the birds, Billy is taken with the warden and cannot bring himself to kill him. Confronted with the fact that he has lied to Murdock (who "thought the Seminole didn't lie"), Billy (in halting English) explains that he has been expelled from his tribe for lying. As they paddle down river Billy and Walter pass by the wife and child he has been forced to leave behind. The plight of the Seminole is touched on only briefly, but the fact that Billy will be, in effect, burned to death by Cottonmouth's gang, tied to the scalding, poisonous manchineel tree, and this glimpse of the family to whom he can speak no more, give the Seminole's understated presence great power. At his "trial," before he is sentenced to die, Billy declares that he has learned from Walter (a "Yankee," of course) that "Seminole like all the birds, and white men not all the same." The colonizer's fantasy of being able to teach the "savage" to live with the invader in harmony is, indeed, an alluring fool's paradise.

Like the Confederates who seem to have spawned him (and, yes, "Dixie" is played in Cottonmouth's compound), Cottonmouth is beyond redemption. But for Ray, even the reprehensible, if they are members of an "authentic" culture, must have their moment of enjoying the "sweet-tasting things of this world" (as Cottonmouth says). The fundamental law of the Glades that he enunciates, in what is perhaps the film's most interesting scene (and one that Ray definitely shot before he was banned from the set) is stated thusly: "I eat the birds; the birds eat the fish; and someday something will eat me, too. We don't need your ten commandments. We do all right in the Glades with one. Eat or be et [sic] is the law of the glades." As Walter, under threat of death, participates with gusto in a bacchanalia with the outlaws, Cottonmouth becomes wildly enthusiastic, and says: "He's a-joinin' us!"[2] Truly, Cottonmouth loves Walter and the feeling seems to be reciprocated. But Walter (not entirely in vain) points out to Cottonmouth that he does not understand "the balance of nature" as Walter does. The "Perfessor" and Cottonmouth summarize their opposition to the "whole overgrown spider web of civilization" in one single word—one that Ray understands: "Protest." Cottonmouth stands like a mountain in his birthplace, but his presence is an aberration. As the film ends, with Cottonmouth dying of snakebite, he finally sees the beauty of the birds, and the necessity for his own annihilation.

Wind Across the Everglades is a compendium of competing systems of law, from the Bible perverted by poachers as a place for pressing their bloody feathers, to the Seminole interdiction of lying that has caused Billy One-Arm to be ostracized. Law is written and law is oral tradition or convenient local custom. The sheriff of Miami only partially enforces the law (the brothel where Gypsy Rose Lee holds sway is out of his jurisdiction and functions as neutral ground); the law of Moses and the laws of the United States are strangely mixed; Cottonmouth and Walter are both outlaws and lawmakers and enforcers. The only meeting ground is in drunken revelry, but that only leaves one lying in the mud with a ferocious hangover.

The Savage Innocents

Wind Across the Everglades' outlaws, including Billy One-Arm, are in a sense irredeemable. *The Savage Innocents* depicts what, unfortunately, may be seen as the "noble savage," who may be able (temporarily) to escape the real and symbolic violence of dominant culture. But the Inuit of *The Savage Innocents* are presented as people who struggle with their own laws and customs, even without the interference of white intruders, and show resiliency in the face of such temptations as acquiring modern weapons. The film depicts the clash of laws and culture, pitting the symbolic violence of the white man's book-dominated law, which, perversely, irrevocably (from the point of view of the Inuit) outlasts its human authors and permits no negotiation. The Inuit people, on the other hand, have adapted their civilization and legal system to the realities of their environment. As an "anthropological" look at Inuit life, *The Savage Innocents* runs the risk of parody (although it is clearly meant to be a respectful and moving depiction of the Inuit people). Anthony Quinn plays Inuk, the Inuit protagonist of the film, and is both childish and a little vague about the world (his baby is born with no teeth and he plunges into despair). But Inuk is an anomaly in his own culture, and cannot be taken as its stereotypical representative.

As implied earlier, the Inuit are shown to share the human affliction of violence disconnected from the natural world. The nature of this culpable violence is complex and constantly being reassessed. At one point in the film, Inuk decides to kill another Inuit man for possession of the woman he desires. Somewhat mysteriously he changes his mind at the last moment and decides to keep as his wife the woman he had considered less desirable (Asiak [Yoko Tani]). Inuk makes a moral decision, perhaps based on tribal law, that to kill with sexual desire as a motive is wrong. (As he says, "a man is not a seal.") Later in the film Inuk does kill, motivated by a clash of cultural norms. He offers his wife's sexual favors and other prized possessions to a visiting missionary and is, he feels, rudely refused. When he reacts by bashing the missionary's head against a wall, Inuk is surprised by the fragility of the man's skull because the action (which we have seen Inuk perform before without such dire consequences) kills the man and makes Inuk a murderer according to white law—although not according to Inuit law. He is from this point a hunted man. Peter O'Toole plays a trooper who must bring Inuk to "justice." O'Toole's character tries to explain to Inuk the astonishing fact that the white man's law will live on even if the individuals involved may die.

Because of this attempt to make its laws and cultural norms universal absolutes, the civilization that O'Toole represents seems to Inuk—and perhaps to the viewer of the film—an incomprehensible perversion in a world of contingency. The law, in imposing itself as an absolute, corrupts the human spirit and imposes its system of symbolic violence, in Pierre Bourdieu's sense, on those who come under its sway. The trooper, whose life Inuk has saved during the course of the narrative, practices a kind of street justice, finally allowing Inuk to remain free. But despite Inuk's temporary reprieve, the future of the Inuit is writ large in the film. We see it in the pathetic reality of the trading post where Inuk and his wife went earlier in the film to trade fox pelts for a rifle (the sheer volume of pelts needed for human ornamentation, as in *Wind Across the Everglades* regarding feathers, marks white culture as lost in the excesses of capitalism). Rock music, normally not a particularly terrible thing in Ray's films, blares out in the wilderness, a shocking contrast to the world of the Inuit. Disgusted with the ridiculous behavior at the post, Asiak gives away Inuk's rifle. Rifles, book-bound laws, and commodity culture will continue to invade the North.

The "psychological terrain" of the Arctic, as much a product of the behavior of wildlife as that of humans, can only be more and more the struggle of the Inuit to continue to maintain an intact culture, even as they adapt to the white man's crazy laws.

Notes

1. For a further discussion of the relationship between "High Green Wall" and its literary antecedents, see Andrew (84–89).

2. This is not the only time that the Old Testament is invoked; for example, Nathanson is a Jew; his daughter gives Walter a Star of David to protect him in the wild; and the name of "Cain" is invoked.

15

WILL SCHEIBEL

Bigger Than Life

Melodrama, Masculinity, and the American Dream

As A POPULAR FILM GENRE, melodrama originated from the "blood and thunder" spectacles of the late nineteenth and early twentieth centuries known for their thrilling sensationalism. Film reviews and the motion picture trade press continued using the term in reference to an action genre, whereas film theory and criticism of the 1970s and early 1980s rediscovered the disparaged "woman's picture" as the quintessence of the American film melodrama. In this latter realm, neo-Marxist and feminist-psychoanalytic critics saw romantic and domestic films about the bourgeois family as sites of deconstruction that exposed the social, psychological, and sexual conflicts of post–World War II American culture.[1] Melodrama therefore came to signify "feminine" emotion rather than violent action and suspense, which led to an interest in passionate and sentimental Hollywood "weepies" by Max Ophüls, Vincente Minnelli, Douglas Sirk, and Nicholas Ray. According to the critical consensus, such films laid bare ideological tensions through excessive, self-reflexive, and ironic aesthetics of *mise-en-scène*. These poststructuralist critics often linked what they regarded as subversive textual politics and Freudian

Figure 15.1. The marketing and reception of *Bigger Than Life* (Twentieth Century-Fox, 1956) as an exploitative social problem movie about prescription drug addiction can be read as an attempt to conceal or repress the more unspeakable (or "melodramatic") social problem the film wants to address: masculinity in crisis (frame enlargement).

themes either to an *auteurist* style or to the artifice and conventions of melodrama as a progressive film genre.[2]

Ray's *Bigger Than Life*, like his *Rebel Without a Cause* released a year earlier, is an example of male melodrama. Unlike *Rebel*, however, it fared poorly both at the box office and with reviewers of the time. Through an analysis of the film in the context of its genre and critical reception, I argue that the cultural work of *Bigger Than Life* destabilizes the already precarious position of American masculinity in the 1950s, a position informed by contemporary discourses on gender that ran through popular culture. Moreover, I show how the marketing and reception of the film as a social problem movie about drug addiction can be read as an attempt to conceal or repress the more unspeakable (what I call "melodramatic") social problem the film wants to address: masculinity-in-crisis.

Substance abuse thus becomes a way to render masculine insecurities legible to a mainstream audience on-screen. The negative critical reception suggests that *Bigger Than Life* fails as a realist social problem movie, as if to rein in the film to a more socially acceptable register. If the film has been acclaimed since 1956 as Ray's critique of the postwar domestic ideal in suburban America, I also want to point out that the film is symptomatic of a larger ideological process in constructing a particular conception of manhood. I therefore comprehend melodrama not as a genre in the traditional structuralist or formalist sense, but, to use Linda Williams's words in her essay "Melodrama Revised," as a mode. Furthermore, I maintain that it often articulates the construction of masculinity itself in the mass cultural landscape of 1950s America.

Melodramatizing the Male

Before proceeding, I should explain this understanding of melodrama in detail. Williams contends, "Melodrama is the fundamental mode of popular American moving pictures," and "supposedly realist cinematic *effects*—whether of setting, action, acting or narrative motivation—most often operate in the service of melodramatic *affects*" (42). This phenomenological definition asserts that melodrama, not classical realism, serves as the foundation for American screen narratives across a range of films, genres, media, and historical periods. Despite film scholarship's take on melodrama as an oppositional excess of classical realist norms, Williams views melodrama at the heart of any text that strikes specific emotional chords. In particular, she claims that melodrama "invites us to feel sympathy for the virtues of behest victims, if the narrative trajectory is ultimately more concerned with a retrieval and staging of innocence than with the psychological causes of motives and action" (42).

This dialectic of pathos for the suffering victim-hero and the proceeding action organizes what Williams describes as the "basic vernacular of American moving pictures" (58). Her framework is useful for liberating melodrama not only from strict historical periodicity, but also from the confines of a single film genre that consists of a select group of texts adhering to rigid aesthetic criteria. The shifting definitions of melodrama, from an industrially-defined genre of "blood and thunder" at the turn of the century to a critically-defined genre in the 1970s and 1980s of passion and sentiment, speak to the limitations in thinking of melodrama and classical filmmaking as mutually exclusive. Pushing melodrama beyond aesthetic film practice, we can also think of it in Christine Gledhill's terms as "a way of viewing the world" ("Introduction" 1). In this manner, I am positing melodrama as a lens or reading strategy we can map onto the discourses of 1950s popular culture at large. How then can we read *Bigger Than Life* in conversation with the cultural negotiations of postwar masculine identity, and how are those discourses themselves part of a uniquely melodramatic cultural form?

Adapted from Berton Rouechés 1955 *New Yorker* story "Ten Feet Tall," *Bigger Than Life* focuses on the plight of middle-aged schoolteacher Ed Avery (James Mason). Working part-time as a switchboard operator for a taxi company, Ed tries to compensate for his low wages as a teacher in order to foster the "all-American life" in the suburbs with his wife Lou

(Barbara Rush) and his son Richie (Christopher Olsen). After suffering from exhaustion, dizzy spells, and severe pain for the past six months, he is diagnosed with *periarthritus nodosa*, a rare, degenerative inflammation of the arteries, and learns he may only have a few more months to live. When he agrees to begin taking an experimental new "miracle drug" called cortisone, his condition improves practically overnight, but he soon develops a crippling addiction and becomes an abusive, paranoid despot. The doctors warn him of cortisone's side effects, and at first Lou and Rickie grow worried over his erratic behavior and mood swings. Ed's friend Wally (Walter Matthau), the school gym teacher, even notices a strange transformation. Eventually forcing Richie to follow a militant educational and athletic regime, Ed devises a "revolutionary" new concept in pedagogy and goes as far as mentally divorcing Lou for "undermining" his project. This patriarchal megalomania climaxes in his attempt to murder Richie for trying to dispose of the cortisone, but Wally overpowers him, coming to the Averys' rescue in a last minute *deus ex machina*. The film ends with Ed awakening in his hospital bed, sedated, and unable to remember these recent events. Finally reconciling with Lou and Richie, he realizes he must regulate his use of cortisone in order to live with his illness.

Bigger Than Life wrestles with the social constructions of gender and the identity crises men face as they attempt to perform and conform to culturally correct masculinity in a domestic environment. Yet, as a male melodrama, it also blurs the lines between traditional masculine and feminine roles. Tom Lutz conceives the male melodrama as a gendered inversion of the woman's film, explaining that the 1950s was the heyday of the "male weepie," a type of film that paralleled the social revisions of male roles after World War II. Lutz notes:

> [T]he male melodramas of the 1950s were responding not to the long history of patriarchy but to contemporary developments. The male weepies tried to evaluate this refashioning of male roles in complex ways, ways that can be called neither revolutionary resistance to nor reactionary reinforcement of patriarchy as such, but instead provided new symbolic role models that attempted to respond to both traditional and contemporary pressures. (195)

Bigger Than Life certainly questions the traditional male roles of the period, but its tension between advocating for conformity *and* rebellion is never entirely resolved. Like other male melodramas of the time, the melodramatic affect derives from an anguished expression of these masculine anxieties and an attempt to work through their contradictions. Ray depicts Ed as the suffering, feminized victim-hero, whose addiction to cortisone and drug-induced tyranny stand in for his difficulty living up to the expectations of a successful and still ordinary husband, father, and American man. Recast as an embodiment of pathos instead of power, the male engenders action to restore order while sorting out Manichean binaries of moral legibility: he is virtuous because he endures the burdens of masculinity modern institutions place on him.

The film invites identification and sympathy with Ed as one of these men whom Lutz refers to as "rebels without fully articulated causes" (201). Lutz claims that men weep in relief when at the end of the hero's rebellion, he finds a new role fulfilled with more important social values than what he had originally rebelled against. In other words, Lutz concludes, "the men represent at best transitional compromises in relation to their own desire for change" (201). The woman's film and the male melodrama can therefore be read as gendered variations on the same vexed theme: the desire to rebel *in order to conform*. Fringe characters transgress their socially prescribed gender roles as part of a larger attempt to find solace in social acceptance—to be a part of the regular community from which they were marginalized at the beginning of the film.

Bigger Than Life interrogates hegemonic masculinity from a male (and paternalistic) point-of-view, caught in the push-pull between resisting and achieving the traditional values of the American dream from a place of suffering victimhood. Ed battles with his own world to form an individual identity by violently striving to rise above conformity, and yet his want to become extraordinary—"bigger than life" and "ten feet tall"—is actually a self-destructive mission of masculine hyperconformity, bringing the myth of the suburban family ideal to its logical fascist extreme. Once he begins taking the drug, Ed's efforts to rebel against "petty domesticity," what he perceives to be the mediocrity of bourgeois life in the suburbs, only upholds and heightens everything that Eisenhower-era American culture held dear: consumerism, athletics, education, Christianity, and so forth. Through this new "program," Ed is able to reclaim his normative position both in and outside the home. Ed is a radical *paterfamilias* and, in accord with the conformist cold war climate, an average husband and father like everyone else. "What strikes one as the true pathos is the very mediocrity of human beings involved," observes Thomas Elsaesser in his influential essay on the American family melodrama, "putting such high demands upon themselves trying to live up to an exalted vision of man, but instead living out the impossible contradictions that have turned the American dream into its proverbial nightmare" (67).

When we turn our attention just outside the film to popular discourses surrounding the sexual economy of middle-class labor, family, and domestic space, we find a similar play of melodramatic situations. In fact, *Bigger Than Life* emerged at the same moment of outcry over American masculinity voiced in magazines as disparate as *Reader's Digest*, *Nation's Business*, *American Mercury*, *Esquire*, and *Playboy*.[3] Perhaps the most culturally revealing of this rhetoric is a triptych of sociological essays *Look* published in 1958 that aimed to intervene in threats to postwar manhood. J. Robert Moskin's article advances the misogynistic thesis that male fatigue, passivity, anxiety, and impotency are direct results of the economic and sexual demands a woman places on her husband in her new rank in the family home. In a follow-up piece, George B. Leonard addresses the male pressures to conform, cautioning men to stay true to their individuality when "The Group" insists on assimilation. Echoing Moskin's argument, William Attwood's conclusion chides American wives for their "keeping up with the Joneses" mentality that urges their husbands to facilitate a family lifestyle of constant consumption. Alongside this debate, *Bigger Than Life* appears less like a social problem film about prescription drug addiction than an additional symptom of a more fundamental psychosexual problem: the uncertainty of what it means to be a "normal" American man in the 1950s. The "decline of the modern American male" as a subject opens the door for a variety of melodramatic engagements with love, sex, family, sacrifice, desire, and repression.

The "Social Problem" of *Bigger Than Life*

As the film's producer for Twentieth Century-Fox, James Mason hired Cyril Hume and Richard Maibaum to write the screenplay after Ray struck a deal with the studio to adapt the *New Yorker* article. Bernard Eisenschitz reports that Ray was attracted to the material for its leftist indictment against "keeping up with the Joneses" and the underpaid salary of public schoolteachers, but was unsatisfied with Hume and Maibaum's medical case history (meanwhile, he struggled with his own substance addictions). Their treatment was faithful to the article, so much so that Ray found it hampered by a passé "documentary approach" representative of Fox's postwar "important subjects" films (271–72). Ray brought in British author and critic Gavin Lambert as a script doctor,[4] and then reworked the screenplay with the help of playwright Clifford Odets. Odets villainized Lou as a social climbing housewife who drained the Avery account with her spendthrift habits, forcing Ed to overwork, but Ray and Lambert eschewed this reductive characterization. According to Eisenschitz, however, Odets opened up a new perspective in the writing through pessimistic themes about the unconscious "shrinkage of idealism" (273).

Advertisements for the film emphasized its controversial "social problem" aspects of drug abuse to circumvent the more taboo and less commercially appealing problem of male anxiety among the American middle class. The interior crisis of masculinity in this regard is therefore the social problem that must be policed and disguised. For example, a full-page ad in *Variety* refers to it as another one of Fox's "biggest controversial money-makers" in the vein of *The Snake Pit* (Anatole Litvak, 1948), a film about mental illness; *Gentleman's Agreement* (Elia Kazan, 1947), a film about anti-Semitism; and *Pinky* (Elia Kazan, 1949), a film about racism. The self-important trailer markets the film as a sensational, ripped-from-the-headlines exposé with plenty of exploitation potential. Introduced by Mason dressed in a tuxedo, it foregrounds scenes of Ed popping pills and terrorizing his family played over a series of cautionary taglines. Mason authoritatively states that "the human issues involved are of the sort that might reasonably crop up in the everyday lives of all of us."

Reviewers in publications ranging from mainstream newspapers such as the *New York Times* and the *Washington Post* to middlebrow literary magazines such as the *New Yorker* and *Saturday Review* to conservative Catholic periodicals such as *Commonweal* and *America* were not sold on Mason's pitch. Despite the film's nomination for the top prize at the Venice International Film Festival and its enthusiastic praise from French critics, U.S. reviewers deemed it a failed "issue" movie for its hysterical exaggerations, slow pace, heavy-handed message, and general lack of realism or believability. Leading the charge was Bosley Crowther of the *New York Times*, who declares, "to ask a paying audience to sit for almost an hour and watch somebody . . . go through a painfully slow routine of becoming intoxicated from taking too much cortisone is adding a tax of tedium to the price of admission" ("Tax of Tedium" 11). John McCarten of the *New Yorker* excoriated the film on similar grounds. "Obviously, with hypochondriacs outnumbering the robustious by two to one," he quips, "this picture should churn up a lot of interest" ("So Sad" 50). In his *Saturday Review* column, Arthur Knight criticizes the cast for rarely rising above the "melodramatic approach of the script," but places most of the blame on the adaptation of Rouché's article. Knight writes, "While the film is based on fact, the writers . . . have failed either to make their facts significant enough or their people sufficiently interesting to justify a picture that runs almost two hours. We learn from it that cortisone is indeed a miracle drug if taken as prescribed. This is controversial?" (24).[5]

What this critical reception makes visible is the aesthetic bias toward downbeat social realism and reportage over stylized family melodrama.

Broad characters and emotions, or stories that stretch conventional standards of plausibility, would have had more in common with Douglas Sirk's critically maligned tearjerkers than a liberal humanist film such as *Gentleman's Agreement*, which prospered from its controversy, timeliness, and "good taste." The reception of *Bigger Than Life* as lowbrow claptrap demonstrates how it was read only on the literal level and dismissed for its alleged shock value and melodramatic exaggerations (Ray's flamboyant use of color along with his baroque angles and dynamic camera movements only further distance the film from the realism of controlled docudrama). For most critics of the time, melodrama is not only the bad object as a genre, but also the unacceptable mode of expression for male distress; in either inflection, melodrama remains associated with the feminine domestic.

A closer analysis of the film shows how it diagnoses masculinity itself as a social problem under the superficial guise of a medical case history, displacing latent psychosexual issues onto an external cause of concern. Contra the traditional phallocentric Oedipal narrative of Classical Hollywood cinema, *Bigger Than Life* never allows Ed to reach a unified, masculine ego ideal. He suffers in his alternately passive and active attempts to disavow the feminine, as a self-professed "male school marm," and take his proper place in the Symbolic Order. The *periarthritus nodosa* and cortisone addiction both become somewhat arbitrary plot devices that merely exteriorize Ed's masculine discontent in which the film seems more seriously invested ("It isn't anything physical," he cries in one scene, "I wish to god it were!").

Ray wastes no time establishing Ed's physical illness, his body wincing, hunching, and doubling over from a mysterious pain in the first scenes, but Ray also quickly alludes to Ed's feeling of emasculation *before* his addiction takes over. Ed gazes longingly at his flirtatious, *haute couture* colleague Pat, a younger and unmarried woman with whom Lou suspects he may be having an affair. Clearly humiliated by moonlighting as a taxi dispatcher (we see him surrounded by female operators when he takes his seat at the switchboard), he lies to his family that he has been meeting with school board members after hours. When Ed returns home, he is reminded that the water heater still needs repairing, as it sits rusting in the middle of their cramped kitchen, a signifier of his consumerist obligations to his family. The film shifts into biting domestic satire during the evening's bridge game, consisting of banal small talk among the Averys' friends that includes a discussion about whether to have a baby or buy a vacuum cleaner. After the guests leave, we follow Ed and Lou through their living room as the camera reveals maps and travel posters of exotic destinations that they can only dream of one day visiting. When they climb the stairs to the bedroom, Lou refers to their friends as "dull," and Ed replies that they are no different as a couple, asking, "Can you tell me one thing that was said or done by anyone here tonight that was funny, startling, imaginative?" As if to punctuate his cynical assessment, he collapses on the floor and is rushed to the hospital.

Critics who have championed *Bigger Than Life* understand it not as a warning about the horrors of drug addiction, but as a film about a more elusive psychosis. François Truffaut insists, "The cortisone wasn't responsible for Avery's megalomania, it simply revealed it" (*Films* 145)[6]. Elaborating on this point, Robin Wood looks at Ed's attempts to reclaim his position as "man of the house" even before he begins taking the drug. The simple act of switching off the lights in the house takes on an air of menace as he quietly stalks Lou while she tidies up after the bridge game. Furthermore, raising his son to be a "real man" allows Ed to live vicariously through Richie. Wood argues, "The role of the drug in the film is in fact purely functional: it removes all inhibitions and releases the urges that are already present in Ed. His illness can be read as the product of the inner tension built up by their frustration; it is the illness of man-in-society rather than of a particular individual" (59).

Ed's first step in rising above "dull" conformity is taking Lou shopping, not at her regular frock shop, but at an upscale designer clothing store downtown. Demanding that she try on dress after dress, he watches Lou model a series of outfits for him. Later that evening, still running on high energy and nostalgic for his teenage past as a star athlete, Ed works up a sweat playing tackle football with Richie in the house. The turning point in the film comes when Ed stares at himself in the medicine cabinet mirror after swallowing a cortisone pill, wrapping a towel around his neck like a cravat and coolly puffing on a cigarette before bed, as if to admire his grand ambitions and superior stature erected over the past twenty-four hours. Ed opens the mirror again, asking Lou to pour another kettle of hot water in the bathtub, only to stare back at his cracked reflection when she slams the mirror shut in frustration.

The second half of the film is considerably darker, focusing on Ed's "mission" after he exceeds his prescribed dosage. Although the details of his project are never made entirely clear, we learn that they involve him writing a series of magazine articles that espouse his unorthodox theories of education, which will lead to a new type of television programming for adults. At a Parent-Teacher Association meeting, he delivers a speech to a mortified group of parents about his pedagogical philosophy: "childhood is a congenital disease and the purpose of education is to cure it." Richie becomes his first test subject at home, forced to run math drills in his bedroom past dinner time while Ed towers above him, barking instructions and casting monstrous shadows on the boy's wall. Ed continues to bully Richie in their backyard, where he trains him to play football to the point of exhaustion. On Easter Sunday, the film brings us to the fullest extent of Ed's delusions with his attempt to murder Richie after he tries to dispose of the cortisone. Both contemptuous of religious authority and striving to usurp it, Ed decides to slay his son ritualistically when they return home from mass, inspired by the biblical story of Abraham and Isaac. When Lou reminds him that God stopped Abraham, he snaps back with the film's most famous line—"God was wrong!"—and then threatens to kill Lou along with himself. Only when Richie presents Ed with his football, a gift to his son and symbol of his youth and innocence, does Ed temporarily snap out of his murderous craze.

Bigger Than Life leaves us essentially right where we started, with Ed lying in his hospital bed, this time awakening from a dream. This *Wizard of Oz*–like coda equates the preceding events not with a dream of escape, but with nightmarish containment within "the American Dream." Deploying melodramatic affects of pathos and action, the film's construction of masculine identity and individuality has worked itself out by coming to terms with a compromised position. This position lies not only between the dialectic of rebellion and conformity, but also between madness and authority, apropos of David N. Rodowick's reading of the Hollywood domestic melodrama of the 1950s. Rodowick tells us that the film demonstrates how "the relationship between madness and authority was in a sense, two expressions of the same term. Either pathetically castrated, or monstrously castrating, the figurations of patriarchal authority completely failed the social and sexual economies of the melodramatic narrative and the structure of conflict in which they found form" (278). By also tapping into postwar American mass culture, *Bigger Than Life* operates under the same mode as the popular discourses on masculine insecurities of the period. Less a reflection of these discourses than a critique of their normative prescriptions, this ambivalent film ultimately neither acquiesces to social norms nor completely dismantles them. Rather, it finds an unhappy medium.

Notes

1. See Neale 179–204 for a comprehensive intellectual history of melodrama in Hollywood cinema.
2. See Klinger for more on "the progressive genre."
3. See Barth; Kilgallen; Lowry; Schlesinger "Crisis"; and Wylie, "Abdicating."
4. Lambert, who also contributed to the script for Ray's *Bitter Victory*, became his lover at this time (McGilligan 332–334).

5. For equally harsh reviews that marshal similar attacks, see also see also Coe, "Dopey"; Hartung; and Walsh, "*Bigger.*"

6. Truffaut's colleague at *Cahiers du cinéma*, Éric Rohmer, gave a similar evaluation. See Rohmer 140–46.

16

Harper Cossar

Ray, Widescreen, and Genre
The True Story of Jesse James

"Nicholas Ray is one of those who fight it out to the finish, and can exhaust the possibilities of a development."

—Jacques Rivette ("Imagination" 105)

❦

WHEN A VIEWER CONJURES AN image of a Nicholas Ray film, she is likely to evoke some canonical shot from *Rebel Without a Cause*, *Bigger Than Life*, or even an earlier film such as *In a Lonely Place*. While all of these films bear the Ray trademarks, they are first and foremost genre films (juvenile delinquency/social problem film, domestic melodrama, and *film noir*, respectively). While we may think of Ray as rebel, a visionary, or both, we must also recall Ray was usually a studio director working within standard production trends. In fact, what makes Ray's *oeuvre* so significant and exciting is that he often made controversial (and sometimes risqué) films within the confines of the late studio system. Because of Ray's position as a studio director,

Figure 16.1. In *The True Story of Jesse James* (Twentieth Century-Fox, 1957), Ray fashions the CinemaScope format toward more laterally oriented set-ups, whereas *Johnny Guitar*'s outdoor shots rely on more vertical compositions that emphasize height rather than width (frame enlargement).

he was often beholden to whatever decisions a studio executive or the studio as a whole made. Therefore, when Ray is working for various studios during the late 1940s and early 1950s, he will inherit the shift to widescreen cinema in 1953.

In his excellent and comprehensive survey of Nicholas Ray's films, Geoff Andrew writes, "no director . . . has used the unwieldy format of the CinemaScope frame so expressively or beautifully as did Ray" (19–20). Andrew admires Ray's technique and posits that Ray is doing something different and superior to that of his peers working within the 'Scope frame. However, like Charles Barr before him, Andrew stops short of a detailed textual analysis revealing specifically what Ray's technique is comprised of and how it functions within his films. Widescreen aesthetics have often gone underdefined within scholarly examinations of film style. While scholars have devoted considerable attention to Ray, comparatively little has been written with regard to how Ray's visual poetics change in the widescreen era (that is, post–1953).

This chapter examines how Ray's filmmaking style changes and adapts to the onset of widescreen by comparing two of Ray's Westerns, *Johnny Guitar*, a prewidescreen Academy ratio (1.33:1) film, and *The True Story of Jesse James*, a CinemaScope (2.35:1) film. *Jesse James* is significant for myriad reasons. First, it is alternately overlooked, devalued, or both within the Ray catalog of films because (like many Ray films) he lost control over the postproduction of the film. Second, and perhaps more important, this film represents Ray's fourth Western and his fifth widescreen film. As chronicled in my book *Letterboxed: The Evolution of Widescreen Cinema*, I propose that examinations of *auteurs* working in studio genre films (such as the Western) reveal their widescreen style and aesthetics in ways that more "personal" films cannot. Thus, how does Ray serve the tropes and strictures of the Western genre within the newly widened CinemaScope frame? Does he approach stylistic choices in a different manner than his previous Academy ratio Westerns such as *The Lusty Men* or *Johnny Guitar*? If so, how are these shifts represented within the 'Scope frame when dealing with close-ups, landscape shots, camera angles, camera movement, or a combination of these techniques? This chapter questions whether Ray's widescreen filmmaking style was forced to adapt and change his approach to the Western genre within the newly adopted widescreen frame. The focus here is limited to the close inspection of close-ups, landscape shots, camera angles, and camera movement that occur in (1) opening sequences, (2) interior conversation set-ups, (3) outdoor vistas, and (4) complex camera movements (defined as more than a tilt or pan).

Why limit this examination of film style to these narrow parameters? First, this systematic methodology of inquiry provides a rubric so that Ray's Academy ratio and widescreen films can be equally evaluated. Opening sequences function as a site for a filmmaker to explore new parameters for widescreen poetics, and thus create a kind of primacy effect to prepare the spectator for innovative viewing strategies that may be different from those of the Academy ratio era. Interior scenes often rely on close-ups, but practitioners and scholars alike have suggested that widescreen "progresses" beyond the need for close-ups so an interrogation of the texts is warranted. Due to the extra width of the CinemaScope frame,[1] canted or extreme camera angles were said anecdotally to be jarring to audiences. Finally, camera movement is reportedly minimized in early 'Scope films because scenes can be taken in "naturally" by long shot without the use of "distracting" cuts. By establishing these ground rules, the analysis here focuses on both aesthetic and narrative aspects present in Ray's Western genre films both before *and* after widescreen. Additionally, this analytical form allows for consistent inquiry across the board and not simply doting on novel scenes of "attraction" or spectacle.

A Few Words on Widescreen Criticism

During the early 1950s and the shift to widescreen a subtle dance occurs between new technologies and the subsequent aesthetic strategies that "debut" simultaneously. A shift emerges between the stylistic and exhibition norms of the Academy ratio screen and the new CinemaScope frame. In addition, the newly widened frame was also a radical challenge to the home television screen that Academy ratio dimensions also governed. CinemaScope was marketed as something *different from* the "old" screen and television ("Breathtaking CinemaScope!"). The impetus is therefore very strong for the early CinemaScope-era filmmakers to use the unique framing possibilities in ways that oppose the Academy ratio's potentialities.[2] However, there is very little common ground with regard to specifically *how* widescreen changed studio filmmaking practices when it "debuted" in the earlier 1950s. Cinema after widescreen's introduction foregrounds the new norm of exhibition, and therefore the production and stylistic practices must adapt and stabilize. In short, if cinematic history can be compared to painting, then prior to the 1953 advent of widescreen filmmaking, cinema existed as a portrait-*only* operation with a premium placed on vertical compositions. Feature films before 1953, with very few exceptions, were composed in only one shape: the almost square Academy ratio. Before 1953 cinema's shape is that of portraiture; after 1953 the shape of filmmaking is more akin to that of landscape. Widescreen was quite simply a break from previous stylistic norms because the shape of the frame itself was radically reconfigured.

Widescreen's aesthetic cornerstone, according to critics, is that it restores "continuity of both time and space" that was absent or "latent" in the Academy ratio (Bazin, *Cinémascope* 683). Several preeminent scholars have wrestled with isolating particular areas of widescreen criticism and analysis throughout cinematic history. Charles Barr's "CinemaScope: Before and After" argues that widescreen cinema challenges spectators to be "alert," but that widescreen filmmakers should strive for a "gradation of emphasis" regarding its implementation. His assumption is that widescreen cinema (and particularly CinemaScope) offers the possibility of "greater physical involvement" for the spectator and a "more vivid sense of space" (11). Barr suggests that wide films represent a *different* experience than that of Academy ratio films by composing action laterally with fewer edits. Given the wider field of vision as well as the wider screens in exhibition sites, Barr suggests that widescreen filmmakers may now compose scenes of expanded width and scope that demand greater attention on the part of the spectator to discern details of performance, composition, narrative significance, and so forth.

David Bordwell in *The Classical Hollywood Cinema* surveys earlier scholars' critiques (including Barr's) of the poetics of widescreen cinema and presents a slightly underwhelmed assessment of widescreen's impact on filmmaking practices and reception. Bordwell and others argue that widescreen filmmaking may have caused a slight experimental bump in the road for the Classical Hollywood studio system, but that technicians and filmmakers quickly adapt to the newly widened frame with little difficulty. John Belton in *Widescreen Cinema* offers both a cultural and ideological critique of the industrial and social factors present in widescreen's adoption. While Belton's book serves as an informative and indispensable guide to the diffusion of widescreen technologies and formats, Belton stops short of offering specific terminology and/or a typology for aesthetic criticism with regard to widescreen.

As the above survey indicates, critical reactions to widescreen and its importance to the film canon are, at best, conflicted. Other scholars have examined widescreen practices with regard to lens characteristics, exhibition practices, or advertising strategies, all of which contributed to CinemaScope and widescreen's ultimate success. James Limbacher, Barry Salt, James Spellerberg, Richard Hincha, and Leo Enticknap among others have attended to these areas satisfactorily. More recently, editors John Belton, Sheldon Hall, and Stephen Neale have examined the worldwide exhibition practices of widescreen films beyond Hollywood.

A Few Words about Authorship

According to David Bordwell, directors establish their narrative voice via a systematic use of devices and techniques that vivify their narrative and visual style. Janet Staiger suggests that authorship "as origin" occurs when "the author is conceptualized as a free agent, the meaning is a direct expression of the author's agency" (30). Among other issues, this simply presumes a "grouping on the basis of the historical body of the individual's" work (33). Specifically with regard to the transition to widescreen, Bordwell posits that "we can learn a great deal about cinematic technique, particularly staging and composition, by studying how talented directors managed the distended image" of CinemaScope (*Poetics* 283). How do filmmakers adapt and challenge the distinguishing traits of their existing visual style to the new norms of widescreen? What interplay occurs with issues of generic formula, authorial voice, and the need for differentiation and foregrounding of the CinemaScope frame? In short, do directors continue to apply the same techniques as they had in the Academy ratio frame, or do they experiment within the new CinemaScope proportions and forge new norms to signify their presence and fulfill generic aims?

Overall, after the adoption of widescreen, Nicholas Ray uses extreme close-ups where other directors shy away from or fear them. This serves what we know about Ray's desire for tortured introspection with most of his protagonists. Therefore, while many directors resist the close-up after widescreen's adoption for fear of "shocking" the audience or because they deem the practice no longer necessary, Ray uses the close-up as a generic and authorial device. Second, Ray's widescreen camera is lower overall than in his Academy ratio films. I suggest in *Letterboxed* that this is an overall tendency for widescreen directors not only to stress the lateral nature of widescreen, but also because sets must be made wider and therefore lower overall. In many of Ray's postwidescreen films, he tends to move the camera in novel ways only to "justify" the new screen's width, which at times seem forced and perhaps even gimmicky. Also, Ray joins other widescreen *auteurs* such as Otto Preminger, Douglas Sirk, and even Vincente Minnelli in adopting the two-shot as the new norm for widescreen conversation sequences. However, Ray continues cutting his conversation sequences into familiar shot–reverse shot patterns that Preminger and other directors seem to regard as belonging to the Academy ratio era. Additionally, Marshall Deutelbaum suggests that a common strategy for composing in (anamorphic) widescreen was to compose the screen elements in thirds (that is, 33% left, 33% center, 33% right) to accommodate the expanded dimensions of widescreen. While this is true for many widescreen filmmakers such as Preminger, Sirk, Minnelli, and others, Ray often centers single figures in the 'Scope frame, which creates awkward compositions that seem to float in a kind of book-ended negative space. Rather than compose in thirds, more often than not, Ray seems comfortable breaking the wide and rectangular 'Scope frame into essentially *two Academy ratio frames*. This may be seen as Ray's experimental attempt to normalize and adjust to the new format: break the new wide frame down into familiar and composable parts. Bruce Block suggests that such widescreen framings "not only place the actor in a new, smaller area of the frame, but also helps confine the audience's attention to one portion of the overall frame. . . . [This composition] controls and limits the audience's ability to visually roam the frame" and "acts like a visual fence" (63). This confinement and "fencing" is useful for Ray's authorial impetus; Ray wants the viewer to feel his character's sense of entrapment. Ray is not so much forging new norms as he is shoehorning his Academy ratio tropes into the elongated CinemaScope frame.

This chapter begins with an epigraph from *Cahiers du cinéma* author (and film director) Jacques Rivette. The *Cahiers* group was among the first to adopt Ray as something *other* than a studio director; they felt Ray was to be lauded as one of Hollywood's true *auteurs*. Andrew suggests that Ray's work found great favor with the *Cahiers* critics because Ray's themes and style aligned with European emigrant directors such as Fritz Lang, Billy Wilder, Douglas Sirk, Alfred Hitchcock, and Otto

Preminger who "cast a detached and critical eye over the mores of their adopted country" (9). If a Nicholas Ray film is said to have a stock set of narrative and stylistic ingredients—"shock" close-ups, a solitary group of characters facing some internal turmoil, and so forth—then how does Ray adapt these signature elements after widescreen? After the following examination of consistent visual elements between *Johnny Guitar* and *The True Story of Jesse James*, certain conclusions can be drawn about Ray's film style after 1953.

By comparing the opening sequence of *The True Story of Jesse James* with that of Ray's earlier Academy ratio Western *Johnny Guitar*, significant changes are observed in Ray's cinematic style and choices. Both films begin with a wide shot to align with Western's generic expectations of open spaces, man's exploration and taming of nature, and the vastness and emptiness of the wilderness. Observing the opening sequences, Ray is clearly using a different aesthetic and stylistic approach for the two films. The illustrations from *Johnny Guitar* (left column) suggest that Ray is more comfortable with vertical framings, severe high- and low-angle shots and generally using greater depth in composition. However, the illustrations from *The True Story of Jesse James* (right column) show that Ray is favoring a much lower camera overall, and composing his shots with more lateral width.

Interestingly, widescreen films are said to have lower overall average shot lengths due to widescreen's expanded screen size. Anecdotally, editors and filmmakers believed that "fast cutting" in 'Scope would disorient viewers unaccustomed to the newly wide and vast images, and thus shots should remain longer.[3] In this sequence, Ray's cutting of the CinemaScope film is *more* rapid than that of *Johnny Guitar*. This film could be said to be more contemplative or even ruminative as Johnny (Sterling Hayden) surveys the lawless Arizona town where Vienna's (Joan Crawford) saloon resides. Both films open with Ray's trademark violence, but Ray uses quick edits, a lower and more lateral camera and less severe angles to vivify the Western narrative world in *The True Story of Jesse James*. Also of note is that while *Johnny Guitar* is cinematographer Harry Stradling Sr.'s final Academy ratio film, *The True Story of Jesse James* is cinematographer Joseph MacDonald's twelfth widescreen film and his second with Ray. This points to the notion that neither Stradling Sr. nor MacDonald were in any way "experimenting" with new technology; both cinematographers had ample experience with their equipment and thus were not limited in their efforts by any stylistic or technological barrier that may occur with "new" filmmaking practices.

As striking as the differences are between the opening sequences in the two films, a strong correlation exists in the way Ray handles

Figure 16.2. *Johnny Guitar* (frame enlargement).

Figure 16.3. *Johnny Guitar* (frame enlargement).

Figure 16.4. *Johnny Guitar* (frame enlargement).

Figure 16.5. *The True Story of Jesse James* (frame enlargement).

Figure 16.6. *The True Story of Jesse James* (frame enlargement).

Figure 16.7. *The True Story of Jesse James* (frame enlargement).

Figure 16.8. *The True Story of Jesse James* (frame enlargement).

Figure 16.9. *Johnny Guitar* (frame enlargement).

Figure 16.10. *Johnny Guitar* (frame enlargement).

Figure 16.11. *Johnny Guitar* (frame enlargement).

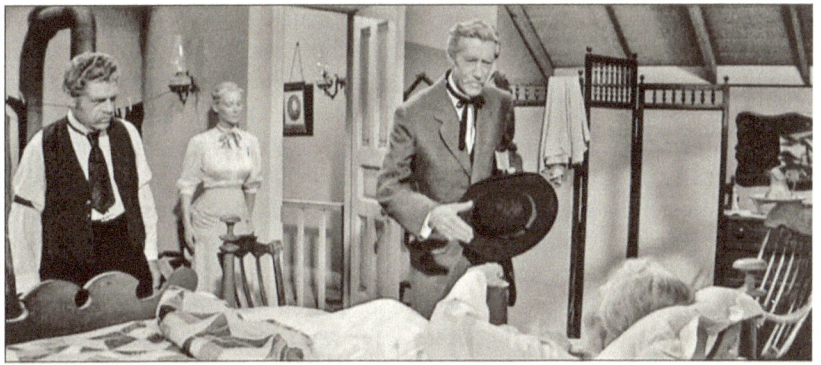

Figure 16.12. *The True Story of Jesse James* (frame enlargement).

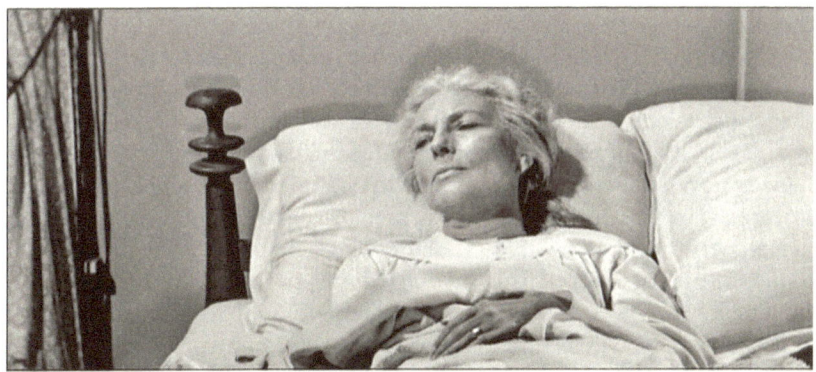

Figure 16.13. *The True Story of Jesse James* (frame enlargement).

Figure 16.14. *The True Story of Jesse James* (frame enlargement).

his conversation sequences regardless of format. In both *Johnny Guitar* and *The True Story of Jesse James*, Ray relies on the standard continuity editing structure of shot–reverse shot. While Ray will establish the narrative space with a wide shot for spatial reference, he then begins cutting alternately between two ends of the 180-degree axis regardless of format. Thus, the interior conversation sequences look quite similar in both films. This seems to be more a Ray stylistic trademark than anything that may need adjusting with the shift to widescreen. Ray usually relies on the continuity system of a master shot followed by alternating singles throughout his career when representing an interior conversation sequence. This is most likely due to Ray's fondness for "interiority" with regard to his narrative structure. Regardless of genre, Ray's narratives tend to feature tortured outcasts who are introspective and brooding. Given this narrative recipe, then, we are not surprised that that Ray does not stray far from convention because he wants the conversation to be the focus rather than the style.

Within the *Johnny Guitar* sequence Vienna tries to persuade Mr. Andrews (Rhys Williams) to back her efforts to bring the railroad through the town, which will bring the wrath of the town on Vienna and her associates. Ray begins with the establishing shot, and then alternates between over-the-shoulder point-of-view shots. This practice commonly features stand-ins for actors, and is meant to extract the very best individual performances from each actor whose lines may be shot out of sequence and assembled later in the editing process. Notice that Ray's camera in *Johnny Guitar* is well above table height for the master shot and the shot of Mr. Andrews. Moreover, once Ray cuts to the reverse shot of Vienna, the camera is raised to an even higher angle. This variance of camera height is more common in Academy ratio films because of the more vertical nature of the format. The depth of *mise-en-scène* is also accentuated in the *Johnny Guitar* sequence due to the Academy ratio style of representation and set design.

In contrast, the conversation sequence from *The True Story of Jesse James* is noticeably "flatter" in its composition, although the shot–reverse shot pattern is repeated. When Reverend Bailey (John Carradine) visits the ailing Mrs. Samuel (Agnes Moorehead) to discuss Jesse's whereabouts and his past, Ray first offers the master shot and then cuts along the axis of action. Of interest here is how the wider 'Scope frame necessitates the preproduction decision of overall lower set construction. Thus, the camera angles are lower overall throughout this shot–reverse shot pattern. While everyone in the room can be taken in via the master shot, Ray leaves Mrs. Samuel alone "floating" almost centered in the wide frame. However, the reverse shot allows Ray to accommodate both

Reverend Bailey and Zee (Hope Lange) into one shot, although still quite low overall with regard to camera height. Unlike the sequence in *Johnny Guitar*, here the two shot is used in a way that will not only affect individual performances, but also facilitates a more "natural" look according to widescreen critics. While the *Johnny Guitar* sequence may seem artificially crafted out of individual takes, the conversation sequence in *The True Story of Jesse James* appears to have a stronger verisimilitude with regard to its blocking and staging of both actors and *mise-en-scène*.[4]

A comparison of outdoor vistas in the two Westerns here suggests that Ray perceives the differences between the CinemaScope and Academy formats and makes aesthetic adjustments. Curiously, the landscape shots in *Johnny Guitar* appear more awe-inspiring than those of *The True Story of Jesse James*. The usual line of criticism is that CinemaScope was good for "snakes and funerals" but not people.[5] However, an inspection of these two Westerns reveals that Ray was more comfortable in outdoor spaces with the Academy ratio format than that of widescreen. Like the opening sequences, Ray fashions the CinemaScope format toward more laterally oriented set-ups, whereas *Johnny Guitar*'s outdoor shots rely on more vertical compositions that emphasize height rather than width.

Andrew comments that "one of the main strands of symbolism in [*Johnny Guitar*]" is "the natural elements" (71). This is true from the opening sequence of the film and resonates throughout as the violence between Vienna and the townspeople escalates. In a sequence where the Dancing Kid's (Scott Brady) gang is en route to their secret hideout, a series of explosions shatter the peaceful Sedona vista. Interestingly, Ray and Stradling Sr. accentuate the vertical nature of the Arizona landscape and harshness of the terrain. Ray vivifies the tension throughout *Johnny Guitar* via extreme angles and stark contrasts between the barren desert and Vienna's extravagant saloon. While *The True Story of Jesse James* has violent shoot-outs and expanses of Western locales, Ray and MacDonald are using CinemaScope in ways quite different from the outdoor shots we see in *Johnny Guitar*. In the final shot of *The True Story of Jesse James*, a blind beggar sings the "Ballad of Jesse James" after James (Robert Wagner) has been killed by Robby (Bob) Ford (Carl Thayler).[6] Ray and MacDonald take in the long procession of the beggar-singer in one take as he proceeds past the horrified townspeople. Rather than "shock cut" to accentuate the violence of James's death, Ray shows the final moments of the film with a low camera and a single take. While *Johnny Guitar* is filled with rapid edits to illustrate violence and action, *The True Story of Jesse James* unfolds a bit more lyrically as the widescreen frame accentuates the slow progression down the sidewalk. As Barr states, this ability was available in the Academy ratio format, but remains

Figure 16.15. *Johnny Guitar* (frame enlargement).

Figure 16.16. *Johnny Guitar* (frame enlargement).

Figure 16.17. *Johnny Guitar* (frame enlargement).

Figure 16.18. *The True Story of Jesse James* (frame enlargement).

Figure 16.19. *The True Story of Jesse James* (frame enlargement).

Figure 16.20. *The True Story of Jesse James* (frame enlargement).

"latent" until someone like Ray chooses to "activate" the potentialities of the wide frame with pastoral compositions such as the final shot in *The True Story of Jesse James*.

The final analytical comparison between the two films is perhaps the most revealing of all, although not in its comparison of film style, but due to the *lack* of elements to compare. A preponderance of complex camera moves (more than a pan or tilt) occurs in *The True Story of Jesse James*, but not one exists in *Johnny Guitar*. Again, this speaks to the disparity between the two formats, in that Ray uses bravura camera moves repeatedly in *The True Story of Jesse James* but keeps the camera vertically anchored in *Johnny Guitar*. By definition, *Johnny Guitar* is thus more vertical and stationary, whereas *The True Story of Jesse James* is more horizontally oriented. Because *Johnny Guitar* has no complex camera moves, this analysis examines one of the many from *The True Story of*

Figure 16.21. *The True Story of Jesse James* (frame enlargement).

Figure 16.22. *The True Story of Jesse James* (frame enlargement).

Jesse James. In this long tracking shot, James is conversing with Zee about the future, family, and what Jesse envisions with regard to such ideas. As the couple strolls along the wide lane of the frontier town, Ray and cinematographer MacDonald allow the wide 'Scope frame to take in the entire expanse with a long take in excess of 90 seconds. These illustrations represent points along the tracking shot, but no edits "disrupt" the couple's interaction.

As with the earlier conversation sequence with Reverend Bailey and Mrs. Samuel, Ray here uses the two-shot as the *lingua franca* of the new era of CinemaScope. Again, Ray uses a low camera throughout the take and frames no closer than a medium shot. Thus, the airiness of the frame is fluid and allows for such longer and more introspective exchanges about the existential qualities of the life on an outlaw. Like other "early" widescreen directors of the mid-1950s, Ray maintains a

Figure 16.23. *The True Story of Jesse James* (frame enlargement).

Figure 16.24. *The True Story of Jesse James* (frame enlargement).

lower overall camera because the horizon (the camera's top and bottom framing lines) has effectively been lowered. Thus, sets are lower, action is more planimetric rather than composed in vertical depth, but Ray allows the camera to be more mobile and dynamic. While *Johnny Guitar* is more extreme with its use of angles and verticality of design, *The True Story of Jesse James* is more laterally limber and fluid.

A consideration of an *auteur*'s style across a historical arc of time can be elusive. We often consider Ray as a director of psychologically intense melodramas and perhaps even quirky Westerns, but he is also a studio director whose "personal style" must adapt and change to stylistic and technological innovations regardless of genre. As observed herein in the textual analysis, we see how Ray, while working under studio constraints and limitations, addressed the absorption of widescreen. Ray is quite familiar with the Western genre by the time of *The True Story of Jesse James*, and thus his changes are stylistic rather than narrative. While we may think of Ray as being the rebellious and eccentric *auteur*, like other studio directors, he was forced to navigate industrial innovations such as color and widescreen, and adapt his filmmaking practices accordingly.

Notes

1. Ray is quoted as saying, "I like the horizontal line, and . . . I like the 'Scope format very much; and when I am free to use it as I please, as in *Rebel*, I get great satisfaction from doing so." The telling point here is that Ray feels he was not allowed to use CinemaScope as he pleased on films after *Rebel Without a Cause*. Perhaps this suggests that Ray would have been more creative and innovative with his 'Scope compositions if not impeded by studio executives who wanted widescreen film style to not threaten box-office potential (Bitsch 121). Of course, Ray may have also been thinking of parallel shooting of Academy ratio and widescreen films. This practice was common when widescreen debuted in 1953. Studio filmmaker Douglas Sirk told Jon Halliday that he was "required to shoot so that the film [*Sign of the Pagan*, 1954] would fit both the new CinemaScope screen and the old-size screen. You had one camera and one lens, but you had to stage it so that it would fit both screens" (117).

2. Twentieth Century Fox's Darryl F. Zanuck famously noted after widescreen's introduction: "Our actors now can move without fear of moving out of focus. Relatively they've been moving in handcuffs and leg irons and so has everything else on the screen, from jet planes to alley cats. CinemaScope is an Emancipation Proclamation on the sound stages. Like all freedoms it must be exercised soberly and intelligently" (157).

3. Leon Shamroy, cinematographer on *The Robe* (Henry Koster, 1953), describes a similarly framed scene: "A Roman archer in the left foreground pulls his bow and sends an arrow into the heart of actor Dean Jagger standing with Richard Burton and Victor Mature, 75 yards away. Yet the audience sees all of

this in virtual close-up—the arrow leaving, the arrow traveling, the arrow hitting its target, the pain of surprise on the actor's face, the actor falling. On any other film medium this cavalcade of action would have required a half-dozen different camera set-ups and a half-dozen confusing film cuts. We did this in one smoothly flowing, life-like scene, thanks to . . . CinemaScope" (178).

4. I am not suggesting here that *The True Story of Jesse James* is not artificial in its constructedness as a Hollywood film that would include myriad creative and thus nonnatural production techniques. I am merely offering that the CinemaScope sequence may appear less produced as a characteristic of the format itself.

5. Fritz Lang actually says CinemaScope "wasn't meant for human beings. Just for snakes and funerals" in Jean-Luc Godard's *Contempt* (1963). Lang is also quoted as saying CinemaScope is "a format for a funeral, or for snakes, but not for human beings: you have a close-up, and on either side, there's just superfluous space" (qtd. in Higham and Greenberg 122).

6. Interesting legends abound regarding the production of *The True Story of Jesse James*. Bernard Eisenschitz (and others verify) reports that Ray originally wanted to cast Elvis Presley as Jesse James, but went with contract players instead (284). Christopher Anderson claims that *The True Story of Jesse James* was made because Fox wanted to reuse stunt footage from Henry King's *Jesse James* released in 1939 (50). A fantastic stunt from the earlier film is "blown up" for CinemaScope, and Patrick McGilligan quotes Ray as saying "the whole picture [*The True Story of Jesse James*] was made to use that scene again. We matched the clothing and everything. A lot of the same buildings were still around" (343).

17

Adrian Martin

Disequilibrium, or:

Love Interest (On *Party Girl*)

In Alain Bergala's indispensable book *Godard au travail*, an on-set photo of Jean Seberg and Jean-Paul Belmondo, about to be filmed in a small room, bears this caption: "The first great 'insular' scene of Godard's cinema: twenty minutes of 'chamber cinema,' free figures far from the sound and fury of the police story" (27, my translation).

So there is a narrative—a public, generic, Hollywood-style narrative that sweeps the characters, and us, all the way to either death or redemption at the end—and then there is, opposed to it, "chamber cinema." And this chamber cinema is, for many filmmakers such as Godard, always the same thing: a man and a woman alone in a small room. For as much of the movie as possible—eight minutes of *À bout de souffle* (1960), even longer in *Le mépris* (1963) or *Prénom: Carmen* (1983). Didn't Philippe Garrel indeed once assert that a man, a woman, and a room are all that one needs to make a film? Maybe that could be the motto of the *nouvelle vague* as a whole.

But this time of intimacy, in a small room, tends to be precious and fleeting, and thus tense. Something always menaces it: the world outside the apartment, the march of history, the demands of the plot. Many years after the *nouvelle vague*, Bernardo Bertolucci in *The Dreamers* (2003)

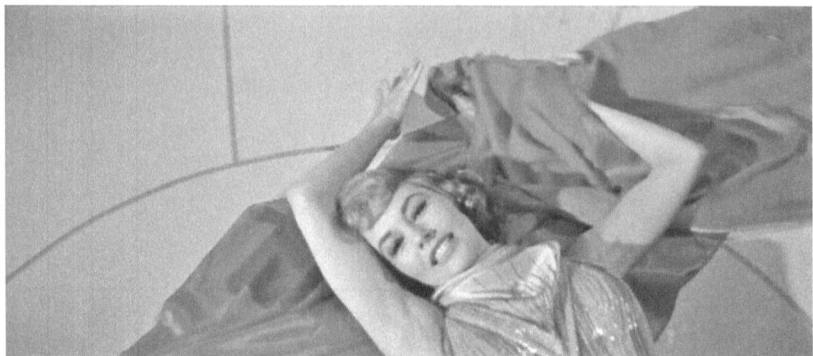

Figure 17.1. *Party Girl* (Metro-Goldwyn-Mayer, 1958): Nicholas Ray is a director who is dear to many cinephiles, but he proves hard to get a grip on. . . . We cannot tell, sometimes, whether we are really watching the films themselves or the images we project onto them . . . (frame enlargement).

will pay his homage to the cinema of the 1960s—and what changed it in 1968—with his image of the riots in the street literally throwing up rocks that smash the windows of a secluded chamber and force the young characters back out into the world, after the *Jules et Jim*-type experimental paradise they have enjoyed within those walls. The free figures must reenter history, and join a new, collective narrative.

But all of this begins further back, in the late 1940s, with Nicholas Ray.

Aren't all of Ray's greatest films—*They Live by Night, In a Lonely Place, On Dangerous Ground, The Lusty Men, Johnny Guitar, Rebel Without a Cause*, and others of each cinephile's own choosing—about an exquisitely elongated, tense, doomed passage of intimacy between a man and a woman? Characters who find themselves alone with each other in a hotel room, an apartment, a cabin, a hideout, a planetarium—under stars real or artificial? Down the decades, many fine critics (from Victor Perkins and Victor Erice to Jonathan Rosenbaum and Jacques Rancière) have tried to nail down the central, thematic nucleus of Ray's cinema; they have used evocative words like the hunt, solitude, twilight, violence, all of which capture something true to its texture of incidents and atmospheres. . . .

But rewatching *Party Girl* anew in the twenty-first century, after all the modern cinema that has come after Nicholas Ray and that he, in a crucial sense, helped prepare the ground for, I am convinced that what he tried to get to, again and again—and what was impossible to hold onto—was the simple dream of a man and a woman in a room.

In his brilliant biography of Ray, Bernard Eisenschitz stresses the theme of *risk* in Ray's approach to filmmaking. There always had to be something incomplete, off-balance, out-of-kilter in the material he was working with—some margin not yet filled in, some space left for a sudden yet decisive intervention or improvisation, but also the constant possibility of error or outright failure—in order for him to be fully, creatively engaged. A creativity mixed with a gamble, a constant flirtation with chaos, mess, self-destruction or destruction of the work at hand.

One sees this even at the level of the shots: certain images strike the viewer—even in the midst of so much professional, classical, studio-enforced glamour and gloss—as having been seemingly caught on-the-fly: the camera is too close to the actor, a gesture has not been entirely captured within the frame, superbrief insert shots are uncertain blurs or swishes of action, the sound has had to be resynched (often clumsily) later—there is a moment like this very early in *Party Girl* when one showgirl dips into another's face cream and the camera participates in the chaos. In such clearly risked moments, which Ray must have sometimes fought to retain in the final cut (or else no one was bothering to take them out), we see the beginnings of John Cassavetes, of Godard, of Maurice Pialat, of Kathryn Bigelow, of Abel Ferrara, and so many others. The beginnings of a kind of action-filmmaking (like abstract-expressionist action-painting), a cinema of energies, of emotional frustrations and explosions, breakthroughs and short-circuits.

Yet for all the literal violent action in Ray's films—the wars, the fights, the murders, the attacks, the cowboys (and cowgirls) and cops—he was not, in the conventional sense of the term, a typical action filmmaker. He was a softie, a lyricist, a romantic. Love was what he craved: love as utopia, love as a sweet, blessed escape from the world. Ray's life was full of all kinds of sex, but in the movies of the 1940s and 1950s, of course, sexuality had to be merely suggested and in fact extravagantly sublimated: the bisexual passions and complex relationship-entanglements of this modern artist had to be purified into an acceptably mythic story form. And, like the typical decadent pop star of the 1950s or early 1960s who could only channel his or her energy and experience into songs about holding hands at the drive-in on a Saturday night, Ray came to embrace this cover-up—not as a lie to be exposed with irony (that is not Ray's register), but as an intense, trembling, touchingly innocent strategy of make-believe that ultimately bears witness to the most profound truth. Hence Ray's return, again and again, to that corny old Hollywood convention that, in his hands, promised, every time, to break every Hollywood convention: the romantic idyll of a man and a woman.

If there is risk in Ray's cinema, there is also tension, disequilibrium. Some feeling, some longing that can never find a place of rest, never just settle in or settle down. We must imagine that this feeling—whatever its specific and no doubt changing content over time—was central to Ray's life and his art. The precious scenes of intimacy in Ray are like extremely precarious moments of equilibrium, of balance and grace, amidst the wildly raging storms of society, history, and community. Scenes of rest that are, very soon, about to slip agonizingly out of kilter—which is the pain, the ache, the tragedy we all wait for, every time, in Ray's films (that's what Gloria Grahame's final recitation of the poem in *In a Lonely Place* is all about). These chamber scenes freeze the narrative, or rather delay its onward march for as many minutes and seconds as possible. Passages of passionate time and intimate space that are far shorter, and far more abbreviated, than the eight minutes or more of chamber cinema that Godard could linger with in the 1960s (or the1980s). And therefore even more precious.

We count these seconds in Ray as spectators, we feel their virtual depth, their ephemerality. And we catch their intensity. Because it is as if we can feel the weight of the entire Hollywood machine—its screenwriters, producers, editors, publicists—bearing down with its onerous complaint: *What are you doing wasting time with this? Get on with the plot! Haven't we had enough of the "love interest"?* Ray had to claw out every moment of this one-on-one screen intimacy from every force of the system that was trying to hurry him on. Because that film-industry phrase used the world over, in every studio and by every script editor and mogul—*love interest*—tells us a lot: it tells that love is an optional, sometimes necessary, ingredient in the narrative, but it must never be all-consuming—never anything like the *amour fou* that it can be in real life. This was particularly so in the genres—essentially, masculine action genres (despite the early stopover for *Born to Be Bad* with Joan Fontaine)—in which Ray mainly found himself employed in the 1950s. He was pulling, in a sense, toward a type of melodrama typically labeled female—but even that would not (and did not) provide a full outlet for the juices that drove him.

Nicholas Ray is a director who is dear to many cinephiles, but he proves hard to get a grip on, beyond the superficialities of his recurrent themes (shared by a hundred other filmmakers: city and country, hunter and hunted, generational and familial dysfunction) and his ostentatious stylistic flourishes (the red of dresses and flames, the blows or blasts that are thrown at, near or from the camera/audience range). He is a myth, a cult, and thus more than a little mystified, obscured. We cannot tell, sometimes, whether we are really watching the films themselves or the image we project onto them, after all our reading of *Cahiers du cinéma* or *Movie* magazines or books like Colin McArthur's *Underworld U.S.A.* from 1972—which fondly introduced me to Ray when I was fourteen years old. (On the Internet, blogger Christopher Funderburg testifies that: "Reading Godard's words and seeing in them my own sentiment about Ray made me wistful and happy and confused—like seeing an old girlfriend after years of estrangement"). And after all our viewing, so many years later, of Godard and Truffaut and Jarmusch and Wenders and Pedro Costa—all those filmmakers who were themselves captured by the Ray myth, and fashioned that fantasy into their own, very different kinds of cinema.

By the time Ray had become a firmly entrenched cult in the 1960s, his much-loved and even fetishized Hollywood career had already come to a sad and definitive end, and he had turned his ever-more ragged energies to the radical, experimental counterculture: McArthur ends his chapter on Ray with the ambivalent declaration that "his early return to the commercial cinema is earnestly to be hoped for, though hardly to be expected" (137). Ray had become a walking contradiction by then, but a newly reromanticized and enabling type of contradiction: the maverick who the system had expelled, the rebel who no longer had the constraints of formula or genre to push against. It was a kind of free fall (with magnificent moments of a totally new kind of work in many areas: video, teaching, theater) for Ray, as it was for many of his generation, once the studio system collapsed underneath them.

What we need to be able to grasp today, in retrospect, is how profoundly Ray was a *transitional* figure in 1950s American cinema. Like, in different ways, Kazan and Fuller and Losey and even Cukor, his work embodied the possibility, and offered fugitive glimpses, of a new kind of cinema, then only dimly imaginable or possible (the burgeoning art cinemas of other countries were still, in so many ways, so far away, so utterly foreign, and so unassimilable)—and it was precisely this vision, this crack that let in some light from the future, that made him so special to budding filmmakers like Godard and Truffaut. And yet this vision and these signs are not always easy to see or discern, when we look back today (and many dull viewers and reviewers could not see or sense them at all back then): the spectator needs a certain, intoxicated leap of faith to see *into* the films, to catch the true intensities, to register the traces of Ray's special, personal intervention into the material. Because everything is, on many levels, still so rule-bound, conventionalized, and formulaic: those with dull eyes and minds see only just another Western or gangster movie or melodrama or war movie. . . . And even as we warm to the films and get close to them, even then we can sometimes only see the flaws, the oddness, the clunky bits, the ill-fittingness of the parts: all the material that was struggling to be reborn into a cinematic modernity, but was not yet in the right place or time or cultural situation. . . .

My claim here is a bigger or different one to the old *auteurist* wisdom (as Paul Willemen has diagnosed it) that the cinephile taste for a director such as Ray necessarily requires "a form of cinema that is perceived as being highly coded, highly commercial, formalised and ritualised. For it is only there that the moment of revelation or excess, a dimension other than what is being programmed, becomes noticeable" (238). What I am pointing to has more to do with the drama, at once cultural and biographical, personal and political, of the uneasy and uneven transition between classical and modern cinema—and how special films, moments in or aspects of them, give certain people (cinephiles, critics, but perhaps especially budding filmmakers) glimpses, flashes, intuitions, and intimations of what is to become of their art.

For Eisenschitz, *Party Girl* is not the movie to go to in looking for the visionary, combative, risk-taking Ray who still inspires us today. With access to the production documents, he can see how tiny Ray's space of control and interference was; he knows how little the project meant to MGM (a retro 1930s gangster movie when the genre was no longer hot, starring two players—Robert Taylor and Cyd Charisse—at the end of their contracts and maybe their careers); he has the proof that the zany musical numbers were handled (as was the studio custom) by someone else. He knows well that Ray remembered and regarded it as a "shit film," and he basically (a few fine, well-orchestrated passages like a murder montage aside) concurs. Even the do-or-die pronouncements of *Cahiers* critics in the 1950s, much quoted by Ray aficionados and derided by nonbelievers ever since ("*Party Girl* gives me a glimpse of the kingdom of heaven": Fereydoun Hoveyda [127]) are presented by Eisenschitz as hollow and rather misguided, mere fan projections.

But something in the movie insists; there is—somehow—some magical alchemy left in it still to intoxicate our senses and inflame our critical passions. To begin with, it is a film that sits uneasily within a single genre, or even an amalgamation of diverse genres—for the revolutionary spark of Ray's man-and-woman-in-room dramas is that this precious, beating, secret heart of the movie is quietly pulling free from the orbit of all genres, resisting all the conventions. Like all filmmakers trying to slip away from the comfort and the trap of genres (Robert Altman, Monte Hellman, Bob Rafelson), Ray moves swiftly between various generic references and templates, shuffling the deck in order to eventually stage his getaway.

Party Girl begins in an opportunistic mishmash of gangster film and musical. The credit sequence and snappy theme tune recall a Technicolor Frank Sinatra hit like *Pal Joey* (George Sidney, 1957) or *Guys and Dolls* (Joseph L. Mankiewicz, 1955). Yet the gangster trappings, in color, are already well and truly retro in 1958 (as those musicals certainly were), and the stage dance numbers, at least at the start, have a tawdry, world-weary air reminiscent of a French hit of the 1950s like Becker's *Touchez pas au grisbi* (1954) with its hilarious "meat market" parade of feathered female flesh. An odd and unforgettable bit of plot invention intervenes: a lovesick gangster shoots the photo of the star actress who has never even met him! Soon we are into a backstage conversation between showgirls that evokes gritty, female centred "working girl" melodramas such as *Our Blushing Brides* in 1930, directed by Harry Beaumont, or (more up-market) *The Women* in 1939, directed by George Cukor (both with Joan Crawford), and even—in its harshest implications of the rape suffered and recalled, allusively, by Cyd Charisse's character Vicki Gaye—another, later beyond-genre shuffle, Cassavetes's *The Killing of a Chinese Bookie* (1976 and 1978 versions).

And then it becomes a courtroom drama, with more than a touch of Otto Preminger, as we observe how Tommy Farrell (Taylor) seduces and swings a jury with his act and his tricks. Women's melodrama of a kind more keyed to the corporate 1950s emerges in the bitchy face-off between Vicki and Tommy's wife (Claire Kelly). Back, now and again, to being a gangster film, with a classic scene of Rico Angelo (Lee J. Cobb), this Capone-style mobster, and the violence he inflicts with a baseball bat, an iconic spectacle replayed (in various ways and keys, up and down cinema history) in Corman's *The St. Valentine's Day Massacre* (1967), in Wilder's *Some Like It Hot* (1959), and in De Palma's *The Untouchables* (1987)—but here with the indelible touch of a miniaturized, although still lethal, bat in silver! A film of all genres (seemingly), in order to be, finally, of no genre at all.

Then there is the love interest. In the 1950s, the signs of modernity creeping slowly into Hollywood production had less to do with narrative construction or *mise-en-scène* (although Ray did outstanding things on these levels, too) than with elements of acting and, hand in glove with that, a changing conception of character psychology. This is something that, again, we often have to read between the cracks of the given stereotypes and conventionalized performance modes—which is as true of *Party Girl* as it is of Fuller's *House of Bamboo* (1955) or Kazan's *East of Eden* (1955) or Cukor's *A Star is Born* (1954). Alain Masson has remarked in a *Positif* essay from 1980 that, in relation to Hollywood's depiction of personality and emotion, where the 1930s was a decade of lighthearted "vivacity," and the 1940s (thanks to Jean Renoir, Fritz Lang, Joseph Mankiewicz, Douglas Sirk, and others) ushered in a mysterious, ghostly, mercurial set of presences even at the heart of naturalist drama, the 1950s were a period of "wrenching conflicts" particularly informed by the growing cult of popular psychoanalysis (26–32).

Ray, who was famous for mixing trained and untrained actors (the bald guy who gets beaten with the bat was a Buddhist of Ray's acquaintance who would not flinch as he anticipated the blow!), was fixed on bringing out peculiarities of unique, frequently damaged personality types, especially in wordless, unusual physical gestures (of which *Party Girl* boasts many); indeed, when he once declared that his heroes needed to be as screwed up as he or the average spectator in order to be successful figures in a drama, he indirectly confessed that all his characters (whether nominally good or evil according to their stereotype) were neurotics of one shade or another.

How do we ever get to the love interest between such neurotic cases? That was always Ray's question, and his drive. In his films, love is the miracle that survives—and briefly overcomes—mutual suspicion, rigid personal defenses, bitter memories, and a history of relationship failures. Colin McArthur sensitively sums up *Party Girl* as being about "scarred and mutually hostile people being humanised by loving each other" (132). Scar is the word: pushing metaphor as close as it can go to the literal in 1958, Tommy's injury (the result of larking around on a bridge—the only location-shooting touch Ray could introduce—in childhood) is transparent code-speak for sexual impotence or difficulty (his body disgusts his wife, we are told); while Vicki's understandable lack of fondness for man-woman intimacy, her "icy exterior," is hooked to a constant aura of menace horribly threatening her physical beauty (the acid that Rico and his crony Louis [John Ireland] frighteningly wield). Let us note a very small, fleeting but striking gesture: when Vicki recalls her rape, and presumed loss of virginity, she is sewing up a dress!

In this circuit of suggestions and substitutions, certain gestures take on an enormous power of implication and affect: Louis being too close for comfort to Vicki in her dressing room; Vicki's sexual invitation, or gesture of abandon, in letting her fur drop to the floor in Tommy's apartment. But the room is not yet right for their love. . . .

Something uncanny here passes or is mysteriously, even prophetically, transmitted into the life-long careers of the *nouvelle vague* filmmakers who worshipped Ray as one of their heroes: issues of impotence; of crippling or disfiguring injury; of illness, old age, and death, especially as they afflict men, will come to haunt the works (and sometimes the lives) of Godard, Truffaut, Chabrol, Demy, and most of the rest of that crew. There is even something of Ray's necessary, Hollywoodian sublimation of explicit sexual passion recreated in Godard's no-kissing policy, Truffaut's genre-cushioned chasteness, Rohmer's Marivaudage and medievalism, Demy's hetero-only romances, and Rivette's fairy-tale ambiences. And what a strange echo or rhyme (Eisenschitz notices it) between the shocking scene of Vicki in face bandages, peeled off to reveal her still intact, and the Brechtian tale that Jean-Pierre Léaud spins as he unwraps a similar mask in Godard's *La Chinoise* (1967).

The worship by cinephiles of Nicholas Ray has certainly taken its place in the history of polemical struggles that have, here and there, found it necessary (and fun) to make use of exaggerations, hyperbole, and absolutist claims to drive a wedge into cultural taste and make a decisive, generation-forming alliance around a shared, endangered object. (No wonder, as Frieda Grafe points out, that the cult of film in the 1950s was also a *cult de femme* and that Charisse's perfect beauty does a dance here with an ever-present bottle of disfiguring acid). Of *Bitter Victory*, Godard once (in)famously wrote that it "is not a reflection of life, it is life itself turned into film, seen from behind the mirror where cinema intercepts it. It is at once the most direct and most secret of films, the most subtle and the crudest. It is not cinema, it is more than cinema" (*Godard on Godard* 66). But: this magic, poetic talk of mirrors and interception, of secrets and crudeness. But: "*Party Girl* gives me a glimpse of the kingdom of heaven." Are these such outrageous, merely provocative statements, after all? Is that all they are?

These lovers of cinema, and of Nicholas Ray's cinema, were trying, in their flamboyantly dandified way, to pierce something that is hard to see, hard to point to with a remote-control freeze-button, hard to put into words. Something that is not mystical or transcendent, but only half-formed, shrouded in the fog of the present and trying to evade the weight of the past, something that is moving in a blur of disequilibrium, something struggling to settle down and fill the time and space of an eternal scene. Something like tomorrow; something like love.

18

Jason McKahan

King of Kings and the Politics of Masculinity in the Cold War Biblical Epic

ONCE DISMISSED AS A CRITICAL failure, *King of Kings* in subsequent years has been reclaimed in Nicholas Ray's *oeuvre*, and it is perhaps one of the most compelling films about Christ ever made. Ray considered the film a great accomplishment, even if he was disappointed with the film's editing and reception, which he attributed to the realities of Hollywood filmmaking and a chain of negative reviews at the time of its theatrical release (Eisenschitz 375). However, the dominant critical discourse of Ray's Christ was framed in terms of another mythic cult figure, James Dean. In the forefront of this interpretive framework, *Time* magazine characterized *King of Kings* as "the corniest, phoniest, ickiest and most monstrously vulgar of all the big Bible stories Hollywood has told in the last decade," and its casting of Jeffery Hunter as the central protagonist as resulting in a "teenage Jesus" ("Sign of the Cross" 55). This left an indelible mark on subsequent evaluations of *King of Kings*. *Time* magazine's criticism, grounded in *auteurism* and gender anxiety, failed to take into account the social, political, and religious conditions of production and reception that shaped the *King of Kings*.

Figure 18.1. Ultimately, the realization, marketing, and reception of *King of Kings* (Metro-Goldwyn-Mayer/Samuel Bronston Productions, 1961) was grounded in the filmmakers' effort to gain respectability among religious middle-class audiences by forging a humanist image of Christ, and simultaneously, increase filmic appeal by engaging the gospel text from a contemporary worldview (Jason McKahan Collection).

This chapter situates *King of Kings* within historical, intellectual, cultural, and religious tensions—and its production as a dialogic process of negotiation and resistance among the film industry, filmmakers, critic-arbiters, religious authorities, and church people. Ultimately, the realization, marketing, and reception of *King of Kings* was grounded in the filmmakers' effort to gain respectability among religious middle-class audiences by forging a humanist image of Christ and simultaneously increasing filmic appeal by engaging the gospel text from a contemporary worldview.

From Atonement to Incarnation

King of Kings originated as *Son of Man* in the mind of director John Farrow. A Hollywood director, Papal Knight, and devout Catholic, Farrow had spent World War II at sea in the Canadian Navy, writing his history of the papacy, *Pageant of the Popes*, and went on to write biographies of

Saint Damien of Hawaii and Sir Thomas Moore. Farrow saw *Son of Man* as a nonsectarian effort to spread the Christian commandment ("love one another"), as a force to save civilization from the atomic bomb (Muir; Wright). Farrow had in mind a striking style for the film—a contrast of classically trained actors and neoimpressionistic acting and sets. Ecclesiastic artist Rouault was first suggested as art designer, later Salvador Dali. *Son of Man* would combine music, dance, theater, art, and widescreen cinema in a *Gesamtkunstwerk* (Notes; Farrow; "Press Release"). The face and figure of Christ in *Son of Man* would never be turned fully toward the camera, as was the custom in Hollywood. Farrow explained, "the human frame that housed The Savior—his hands, his voice, all the things of flesh—are shown, except that which is the private vision of every man—HIS FACE" ("Press Release").

A string of production deals with major and minor studios emerged and then unraveled between 1948 and 1956. Only in the collaboration with the movie mogul of Madrid, Samuel Bronston, during the production of *John Paul Jones* in 1958, did it become certain Farrow's production would finally go before cameras ("New York Sound Track" 7). Bronston signed a three-picture deal with Farrow and they formed an independent company, Brofar Productions. Farrow and Bronston had their disagreements. Farrow wanted the film to adhere faithfully to the Gospels in text and character, filmed as a series of miniatures, rather than in the style of the biblical spectacle—"DeMille's thousand donkeys and extras with jugs on their heads" (Unidentified clipping). Bronston derided miniatures as "toys," and in the tradition of DeMille, planned to build colossal sets (eventually 396 sets and some 20,000 extras) (*Anthologie Du Cinéma* 233). Bronston felt Farrow's script did not have a story, just, "all Thee and Thou and everything else" (qtd. in Eisenschitz 361). Farrow felt Bronston wanted "guts, gore, and a fictional frame" (Ried). When a news release unexpectedly announced the split of Brofar, Farrow was surprised and puzzled ("Report" 15).

Bronston had an option on the script and had decided to replace Farrow. Several directors were considered, including King Vidor, before Nicholas Ray was selected. In December, Ray and writer Phil Yordan began a rewrite of the screenplay and soon changed the title to *King of Kings*. Bronston and Yordan initially planned to conceal the face of Christ, but the focus on Christ as "human" began to permeate the production. There had been an incarnationalist tendency in Hollywood biblicals, in which the humanity of Christ and other biblical figures was emphasized, reflecting a post-Victorian shift in theology from Christ's Atonement for sin to his Incarnation (Hilton 35). Humanistic portrayals complemented the Classical Hollywood narrative system, grounded in the human protagonist and human conflict. Humanism accentuated a universal condition, while masking a film's ideological adherence to any particular religious doctrine. With the growing controversy over existence of God in the late 1950s, religious filmmakers committed to the Western struggle against communism sought to dramatize the living Christ. Ministers and other religious leaders called for an incarnate Christ: "They want to see him smile, even laugh, in the picture" (Spiro X5). In 1954, Dr. James K. Friedrich, producer of *Day of Triumph*, responded to protests against showing Christ's face: "He can no longer remain a hollow voice or a shadow" ("Of Local Origin" 26).

Similarly, Ray was reconstructing the Gospels for the audience's imagination so that, "all of the Biblical characters, including the role of Christ, will have more vitality and will be more actively involved than those put on the screen before" (Johnson, "Jeffrey Hunter" 3). Ray suggested that unless the actors could capture the "basic humanity" of the Apostles, "they will be nothing more than wax figures" (qtd. in Eisenschitz 368). Moreover, Ray saw *King of Kings* as primarily a film about and made for youths. Jesus was only thirty-three years old when he died on the cross, and his Apostles were all young men in their teens to thirties. Previous films, such as *They Live by Night*, *Knock on Any Door*, and *Rebel Without a Cause*, adopted a worldview that focused on the sociological and psychological roots of youthful rebellion (White 58). In Ray and Yordan's "Superwesterns" *Johnny Guitar* and *The True Story of Jesse James*, the mythic structure of the Western becomes a vehicle for highlighting cold war neurosis, social conformity, gender relations, and institutionalized violence (Kreidl 173).

King of Kings would similarly refocus the mythic structure of the Gospels to create a "superbiblical" touching on cold war consensus, youth, and their struggle for belief and understanding (McGilligan 417). Ray received technical advice from Reverend George Dunbar Kilpatrick, a professor of Exegesis of Holy Scripture at Oxford University, who suggested that religion had to be contemporaneous if it were to mean anything to young people today. The cumulative effect of Ray's attempt to humanize the Gospels, "as though they were happening before us for the first time," bothered associate producer Alan Brown, who believed that such humanization diminished the divine nature of Christ (Eisenschitz 368).

From Incarnation to Anxiety

Slavoj Žižek notes how humanization in Hollywood cinema draws attention to the uncertainties, weaknesses, doubts, fears, and anxieties of characters. What is generally left unexamined is the connection between humanization, storytelling, and the structure of society. Humanization constructs a false binary between "private" identities ("Who I really am") and "public" identities (the symbolic determinations and responsibilities "I" assume in public life) (40). The "private" is fundamentally a screen, a false distance, "to save my appearance, to render palpable (accessible to my imaginary narcissism) my true social-symbolic identity" (40). By stripping away the pretense of the "inner life" we see that the humanizing strategy that would make *King of Kings* meaningful to contemporary audiences was grounded in the transposition of cold war ideology upon the social-symbolic identities of biblical figures.

In his preparation for the role of Judas, Rip Torn worked with Theodor Reik (a former student of Sigmund Freud) and began to conceive of Judas as an alter ego of Christ. Reik's famous analysis proposed that the social-symbolic messiah figure was born out of Israel's subjugation, its feminine-masochist internalization of subjugation as the price of Israel's sins against Yahweh and the yearning for a rebellious force of resistance to domination and the feminine-masochist attitude toward Yahweh (3). Reik contended that Judas and Christ were two complementary parts of a single psychological individuality, separated by a splitting mechanism. Judas as an alter ego bears the responsibility for the characteristics and tendencies of Jesus that early Christians repressed and did not wish to see in Christ, namely the guilt feelings associated with Christ's "personified projection of the revolutionary impulse against Yahweh" (qtd. in Luz 487). The Barabbas figure is another antipode that stands for the conflicting impulses and ideals in one and the same person (Reik 10). Barabbas is an alter ego of Jesus, a robber and rebel, whom the people released while Christ died (Malmquist and Meehl 149).

The overlapping of biblical and cold war social-symbolic identities in *King of Kings* is striking. The cold war presented an analogous set of circumstances in which the feminine-masochistic state was consumed by the constant threat of the Soviet Union from without and gender inconformity from within. The Roman occupation of Judea presented an analogue to the Soviet Union, and reflected the "agency panic," which Timothy Melley describes as the overarching insecurity of the cold war, characterized by the displacement of individualism onto anonymous social or corporate forces (57). U.S. audiences would identify with the Hebrew-Christians subjected to Roman occupation in the context of cold war nationalism, which equated "Americans" and "subject peoples" (McAlister 67; Wyke 131).

Christ and John the Baptist are "liberators" whose principal crime is being "different and refus[ing] to act like the others." The Christ-rebel personifies the existentialist tendencies of resistance to the cold war consensus and brings partial liberation from middle-class conformity; he reminds us of the profound role of war and genocide in the structuring of cold war consensus (Davidson 9). Barabbas and Jesus represent two parts of a single psychological individuality—as Judas tells the high priests, "Jesus and Barabbas were the left and right hands of the same body." Expanded into a Messiah of War in *King of Kings*, Barabbas gives full meaning to the personality of Christ, the Messiah of Peace (Guarner 86). Barabbas is an alter ego of the rebel: the "organization man," a product of the bureaucratic and militaristic order, lacking individualism and prone to indifference to the violence that resides in social structures of the cold war consensus (Whyte 48). The "organization man" stands in and assumes the attributes and tendencies people do not wish to see in the rebel. He is the scapegoat embodying all of the aspects of corporate Western life that the rebel abhors. Barabbas is the "patriot" (a name associated with hawkish politics), who believes that the Jewish people need "more fighters and less prophets." Barabbas has no use for prophets except to appropriate them to win over the people. Barabbas is the antipode who survives while Jesus perishes, so that "violent death is a sacrificial ritual that will permit the remaining characters to find a more peaceful way of life" (White 68).

Judas, who was traditionally represented as demonic traitor and associated with *feminized* corruption linked to money and Judaism (Kaplan and Cohen 123), is transformed in *King of Kings* into another alter-ego of the rebel. Judas represents all of the feminine characteristics people do not wish to see in the rebel. Judas is unbalanced and dependent on others—the narration introduces him as a "man seeking answers." His lack of male authority and emotional emancipation (he faints at the sight of the cross) constructs a type of effeminate masculinity associated with "momism," a class of contemporary mothering characterized by the repression of the family by an overprotective, domineering Mother. Opined by Philip Wylie in his misogynistic *Generation of Vipers*, "momism" produces dependent and infantile men, who are easy targets for corrupting forces such as sexual maladjustment and communist ideology (Medovoi 44; Rogin 9).

Always lurking in the background of cold war discourses on masculinity was the threat of demonic femininity, variously embodied in the homosexual, the *femme fatale*, or the female enemy agent. The Oedipal triad of Herod Antipas, Herodias, and Salome also personifies "momism," in which Herod Antipas is encircled by domineering women. Herodias taunts Antipas to prove whether he is a "king or a puppet" and at the seductive prompting of Salome, Antipas calls for John the Baptist's head on a silver platter. Salome's demonic femininity is conveyed through Miklos Rozsa's orientalist music score and her sadistic gaze, which repeatedly takes John the Baptist as the fetishistic object of a sociopathic sexual fantasy.

Circulation and Response

Only a couple weeks after production began, Joe Vogel and other MGM executives visited the shoot in Madrid. Impressed with the sets, they acquired distribution rights and a significant $5 million ownership of *King of Kings*. MGM was "worried" about Ray directing an epic film of Christ's life, and Ray found himself gradually losing control of the direction of the film (McGilligan 401). MGM executive associate Bernard Smith remained in Spain and oversaw creative control. At the insistence of MGM, Hunter's portrayal of Christ's rebellious humanism was minimized; through intricate dubbing of new dialogue to lip movements of the original footage, Hunter now spoke in "the traditional, religious quietness of Christ" (Johnson, "Filming of 'King of Kings'" 5). Harry Guardino suggested that MGM chose action over depth of character, cutting important scenes and reducing his portrayal of Barabbas to "one big swashbuckling guy" (qtd. in Johnson, "Actor Disappointed" 4). MGM's cuts had created a lack of cohesion in the narrative, so Ray Bradbury was hired to pen a narration and Orson Welles to provide a voice-over.

King of Kings would be a roadshow "super production," exhibited in key cities at individual or group performances with advance ticket sales, just as other epics recently had been distributed, including *Ben-Hur* (William Wyler, 1959) and *Spartacus* (Stanley Kubrick, 1960). At regional sales meetings with exhibitors, MGM focused on roadshow engagements, especially group-selling activities directed toward schools and religious organizations of all faiths. Exhibitors were excited about the potential of *King of Kings*. A sneak preview of the film held in Scottsdale, Arizona, brought an "enthusiastic" audience reaction.

King of Kings' advertising and promotion campaign would reach national magazines, trade publications, newspapers, radio, television, regional supplements, and religious publications. Window and counter displays could be seen at airline offices, bus terminals, bookstores, department stores, and music shops. The Wise Men with their camels from *King of Kings* joined in the annual Parade of Stars that opened the Santa Claus Lane in Hollywood. The year-end holiday season campaign would include children carolers to appear nightly in the theater forecourt of the Egyptian Theatre; the rear of the forecourt held a huge Nativity. MGM arranged to mail from Bethlehem 100,000 Christmas cards depicting the film's Nativity scene. MGM's policy of sending a troupe of the studio's "new faces" on tour with each of its important films launched Ray and Bridgette Bazlen, who played Salome, on a whirlwind tour of interviews and screenings in support of *King of Kings* (McGilligan 416).

MGM ran a national program of speakers and filmstrip showings that involved schools, churches, service clubs, women's organizations, and other groups. Special morning performances for students and seminars for high school newspaper editors were held, as were essay and art contests based on the film. Preceding the New York premiere of *King of Kings*, benefit screenings were held for the volunteer workers of the Cardinal's Campaign and the Protestant Council of the City of New York. Before the film's opening at the Egyptian Theatre in Los Angeles, a special advance screening for the Catholic archdiocese of southern California was organized. Critics of the recent deluge of biblical films were not blind to Hollywood's efforts to co-opt religious authorities, politicians, and other civic leaders for public support and official endorsements of *King of Kings* (Walsh, "Christ" 71).

The film's world premiere was on October 11, 1961, at Loew's State Theatre in New York City. Film critics were mixed in reception. Some championed its educational value; its sincerity, dignity, and reverence; and its passionate story, which seemed to avoid the excesses of recent sandal and sword epics (Winsten 64; '*King of Kings*,' *Filmfacts* 251; 'Liked the Book" 5). Others described the film as picture pretty but ineffective in providing a living personality to Christ (Crowther, "Good" SM10; Mosley D2). Some identified Ray's unmistakable effort to present Christ as both human and divine (Cameron). Critics who questioned the profit-seeking motives of the film doubted whether Ray knew "how to deal with the divine in human form or, alternatively, the human shrouded in divinity" ("Sign of the Cross" 55; Rae 16). Critics also recognized the connotative topicality of *King of Kings* in an age confronted by the prospect of nuclear self-destruction (Spear 15).

For the most part, civic organizations and councils commended *King of Kings* as a family-friendly film. The National Screen Council (comprised of women's clubs and civic and educational organizations) bestowed on *King of Kings* the Blue Ribbon Award "as not only outstanding but suitable entertainment for the whole family" (Sykes 15). "The Green Sheet," published by the Film Estimate Board of National Organizations, placed *King of Kings* in the family class ("Green Sheet" 5). The California Federation of Women's Clubs presented honors to the film ("Calif. Women's Clubs" SE–1).

Church groups were divided on the Christ-human angle. *King of Kings* met with the approval of *L'Osservatore Romano*, the semiofficial newspaper of the Holy See, perhaps because the film's human and psychological dimensions were so immediately accessible to the viewer (Guarner 86). The Ecclesiastical Advisor of the Office Entertainment of the Vatican called *King of Kings* "a praiseworthy message of love and peace in our restless world" ("*King of Kings* in Catholic Italy" 5). The Catholic Cinematographic Center, the branch of the Vatican that reviews movies for morality, approved the picture for all ages. However, the Catholic Legion of Decency rated the film "theologically, historically and scripturally inaccurate," and because of doctrinal reservations, placed it in a new "separate classification" in an attempt to caution without condemning ("Jesuit Weekly's Rap" 24; "Censorship Regarded" ME–4). The Jesuit weekly, *America*, found the film "dis-edifying and even anti-religious. . . . Christ is there as a physical presence, but his spirit is absent" (Walsh, "Christ" 73). Catholic critics in Italy noted the film's "evident attempt to reduce the Saviour's drama to simple human terms" ("*King of Kings* in Catholic Italy" 5).

The Mainland Baptist Convention gave its apparent approval by putting *King of Kings* on the front and back cover of its Christmas edition of the *Maryland Baptist* ("Baltimore" E–4). However, the Interfaith Committee for Better Entertainment in Columbus omitted *King of Kings* from its listing of films suitable for the whole family ("Film Classification" ME–2). Reverend Eugene Carson Blake, chief executive officer of the United Presbyterian Church, criticized the marketing of the film "to make use of religious interests to entice people to Biblical pictures which are basically sex-oriented and pseudo-historical" (Archer 36). Episcopal vicar Reverend R. DeWitt Mallary Jr. was "embarrassed" by the film and denounced the Protestant Council of the City of New York for endorsing it. Mallary lamented the "complete white-washing of the Jews"—the producers had leaned over backward in the attempt not to offend modern audiences ("Cleric" 5). The Protestant publication *Christian Century* mocked the film's humanist presentation of Christ as a true American with auburn hair and lovely blue eyes, and red-baited *King of Kings*: "I think if it is shown in the uncommitted countries it will hasten their commitment . . . to Marxism" ("Epitaph" 1303).

Jewish commentators recognized Ray's effort to eschew the negative portrayal of Jews associated with earlier Christ films, such as DeMille's *King of Kings* (1927) (Ohad-Karny 190). The *Canadian Jewish Chronicle* noted that in Ray's *King of Kings*, Judas and Caiaphas are not the conventional wild-eyed, intolerant, and vengeful figures DeMille portrayed them as (Luft 67). The *Jewish Daily Forward* was thankful and hoped that Christians would finally accept the Roman responsibility for Christ's crucifixion (qtd.in Komar). Rabbi William F. Rosenblum supported the film's "tender and sympathetic portraiture of the struggles of the Jewish people when they were under the tyranny of Rome" ("In Defense" 69). Rabbi Louis M. Lederman appreciated the message of comfort and hope in Ray's *King of Kings*: "The constant conflict between Communism and Christianity has yet to be resolved. And as you can imagine, the Jewish people are just as concerned. Communism will eventually be wiped out for all time ("Movie on Christ" 11).

Religious authorities were especially critical of the fictionalization of Barabbas and Judas, the lack of stress on the divinity of Christ, and the omission of any responsibility of the Scribes and Pharisees for Christ's crucifixion, yet they were generally more approving in their responses to the film than secular critics ("*King of Kings*," *Filmfacts* 251). *Weekly Variety* observed a curious phenomenon of "unexplained resentment and attack" in some reviews of *King of Kings* and suggested that this tendency was a culmination of a backlogged resentment against the spate of biblical-themed films ("Liked the Book" 5). Jose Guarner, writing in the Spanish film journal *Film Ideal*, could not understand how film critics who had passed over DeMille's gigantism and bizarre reworkings of the Bible without the slightest flinch were now "tearing their clothes" (86). To be sure, contemporary critics were more absorbed with the morality of biblical films and their treatment of subject matter; only recently in the late 1950s and early 1960s did critics begin to consider the broader religious or theological issues raised in biblical films (May viii).

Perhaps as Susan White suggests, Ray's refocusing of popular myths toward contemporary social issues and his emphasis on social origins of violence got him labeled a "liberal" (54). Ray's socialist background was well known (he had joined the Communist party in the mid-1930s) and mysteriously avoided the wrath of the McCarthy witch hunt, even though many of his friends on the Left were denounced and blacklisted (McGilligan 174; Krutnik 70). When Ray transposed the McCarthy witch hunt on the Western genre in *Johnny Guitar*, critics not only assailed the film's generic excesses, but also the "perverted pleasure" of a film that scrutinized cold war gender and sexual norms (Corber 126). Now with *King of Kings*, Ray had directed a cold war *roman à clef* on the life of Christ—an act that was certain to make some enemies. Criticism of *King of Kings* was embedded in broader discourses regarding gender, religion, and the conservative disdain for Ray's public persona and the political ideology of his films.

In the retelling of *King of Kings*' production and reception, Ray himself appears a Christ-rebel, an outcast of Hollywood, the defiant antipode of the showman Bronston, betrayed by the Judas Yordan. To be sure, the romantic *auteurism* of Ray, as a rebel pitted against the monolithic studio system, was an attractive "author function" ready-made for middle-class white males in a society of unbridled corporatism and "crisis" of masculinity (White 57). Judas was another icon of the age, a personification of the obsession with discourses of treason. The Rosenbergs were convicted and executed for selling nuclear secrets, an act of treason likened in the press to "the sin of Judas" (qtd. in Neville 53). Director Elia Kazan became a traitor when he appeared as star witness for the House Un-American Activities Committee, which led to the blacklisting of actors, writers, and directors. Samuel Bronston was now being called the "Judas" of runaway production for outsourcing Hollywood jobs in Spain.

King of Kings was the product of the confluence of these various forces, including the vagaries of studios, financiers, producers, filmmakers, exhibitors, film critics, religious authorities, and audiences of various faiths. What *King of Kings* would have been without MGM's influence is still not clear. What is clear, however, is that Ray was not interested in adhering to the convention of presenting Christ and the Apostles in a series of dioramas; rather he sought to dramatize "the story of a minor prophet of the first century" (Lederer 62). My analysis suggests that changes in theological discourse in the late-1950s were reflected by the growing interest of religious officials and church peoples in seeing a more "human" Christ in the movies. Ray sought to humanize the Gospels and make Christ meaningful to young, contemporary audiences. Using the genre of the biblical film, Ray's humanization of Jesus was both incarnate (close-up shots of the face, Hunter's piercing blue eyes) and social-symbolic (postwar masculinity, the rebel, alter ego).

19

Larysa Smirnova and Chris Fujiwara

"As Surely as a Criminal Would Die"

Nicholas Ray's *The Doctor and the Devils*

For Nicholas Ray, the personal debacle of *55 Days at Peking* in 1963 marked the beginning of a mode of activity marked by the failure to complete projects. Some films that Ray announced or tried to make were canceled or trailed off into limbo; work on *We Can't Go Home Again* became coterminous with Ray's life. Nevertheless, *We Can't Go Home Again* exists as a film. Among the projects that failed to attain this status, *The Doctor and the Devils* has a unique significance for several reasons.

As Bernard Eisenschitz writes, *The Doctor and the Devils* was "Ray's last important project in Europe, the one which came closest to fruition" (394). The film would have been Ray's adaptation of an original screenplay by Dylan Thomas. Published in 1953, *The Doctor and the Devils* is based on the true story of nineteenth-century Edinburgh surgeon Robert Knox (renamed Rock in Dylan Thomas's version), who, hampered by laws limiting the use of human cadavers for scientific purposes, turned to the help of grave robbers. This practice became a public scandal and a criminal case when two of Knox's suppliers, William Burke and William

Figure 19.1. Ray's attraction to *The Doctor and the Devils*, then, can be seen as a stage in his progressive approach to theme of the artist's death, including also his acting role as the American ambassador who abstains—that is, withdraws, or plays dead—in *55 Days at Peking* (Samuel Bronston Productions, 1963) (frame enlargement).

Hare, were discovered to have murdered numerous people and delivered the bodies to Knox.[1]

Avala Film of Yugoslavia was to produce Ray's film, on which he worked throughout much of 1964 and 1965. Production headquarters were established in Zagreb, where Ray lived for some time. First Laurence Harvey, and then Maximilian Schell was to play the lead role (now spelled Rok), and Susannah York, Geraldine Chaplin, Barbara Steele, and Tanya Lopert were cast at various times. To adapt Thomas's text, Ray collaborated with a succession of writers, the last of whom was Gore Vidal. Working in Rome, Vidal and Ray produced four draft scripts, which are preserved in the Vidal collection at Houghton Library at Harvard. Although the early-nineteenth-century time period was retained, the Yugoslav production setup motivated a shift in locale from Edinburgh to the capital of a German Grand Duchy. For reasons that remain unclear, and that may have been due as much to Ray's own self-doubts as to the unreliability of the Yugoslav producers, the film was canceled shortly before its projected start date.[2]

Among other additions to Thomas's script, Ray and Vidal incorporated two striking prologues that are expressive of Ray's ambitions for the project. The film was to begin with a modern-day sequence in Zagreb, with a film director, his script girl, and an assistant scouting locations. After visiting a house that the director says reminds him of Ulysses S. Grant's house in Galena, Illinois, they go to a cemetery where a group of children "are playing as if they were on any ordinary playground." The script girl finds this shocking, but the director corrects her: "My dear, they are fortunate. They'll never be impressed by all the mysterious bugaboo. I wish a graveyard had been my playground—I wouldn't have been afraid of death."[3] Years later, Ray remembered this opening:

> I couldn't help but feel how healthy this could be: here were kids who were going to grow up without any illusions about death. These children would not believe all the fairy tales, or create importances for themselves beyond their abilities. They would know they could not win enduring life by whatever great deeds they accomplished, that they were going to die as surely as a criminal would die. (*Interrupted* 181)

This message is the main theme of *The Doctor and the Devils* as Ray reimagined it. Perhaps it was also a lesson he felt he needed to learn himself.

This prologue is followed by a battlefield scene that takes place fifteen years before the main narrative, in the aftermath of a battle between Napoleon's Grand Army and that of the Austrian Alliance. Here occurs the first encounter between Rok, at this point still a medical student, and his future helper Philo (as Burke is renamed in Ray and Vidal's version), a soldier in the Austrian army. Because of the shortage of medical personnel in the improvised hospital, Rok is allowed to operate on Philo's neck wound. As a result of Rok's surgery, Philo is saved but slightly disfigured. Years later, Rok attributes this surgical mistake to his lack of practical experience because of the shortage of cadavers. The relationship between past and present in Ray's treatment of the story is not linear; present, past, and future are mixed together. Rok's former patient, the victim of Rok's inability to gain surgical experience, fills up that lack by supplying bodies, which will help Rok's future patients and those of his students.

Ray planned to use a multiple-image process for *The Doctor and the Devils*. He named this process "mimage"—probably his own coinage. Vladimir Novotny, whom Ray requested as cinematographer on the strength of his work on Oldrich Lipsky's *Lemonade Joe* (1964), shot some test footage with a system that produced multiple images directly in the camera, using mirrors and filters (Eisenschitz 396). In *Don't Expect Too Much* (2011), Susan Ray's documentary of the making of *We Can't Go Home Again* at Harpur College, Ray says, "I want to break the rectangle." The rectangle is broken only partially by the multiple-image process used for *We Can't Go Home Again*, in which the larger rectangle of the projected image encompasses smaller rectangles that remain, for the most part, fixed (although perhaps we are to conceive of simultaneity as the power that can break the rectangle). According to Susan Ray in her recent article "Out of the Box," practical limitations prevented Ray from realizing his full vision of mimage for *We Can't Go Home Again*:

> Ultimately Nick intended to dissolve the hard edges of all the frames completely. He also wanted to run an animated strip up one side of the film. A watercolor he painted of how he wanted the film to look now hangs in my living room. As one artist assessed it, it is a painterly vision, subtly textured and layered. (24)

In his spoken teaching, as recorded in *Don't Expect Too Much*, Ray insists on the priority of the contents of the frame (above all, the actor) over the frame itself: "If you don't have content within that goddamn camera, and all you have is composition, you have nothing." The hostility to the frame that can be felt in this remark in part explains Ray's attraction to mimage.

In *Don't Expect Too Much*, Nicholas Ray says to his Harpur students: "It's impossible to describe multiple image to anybody. I worked on it for ten, eleven years, [and] I've never been able to describe it to anybody so they [sic] would understand it. You have to see it." If Ray's timeline is accurate, then he had started working on the multiple-image process as early as 1960, the year of the production of *King of Kings* (which in fact features some shots filmed with a split-diopter lens focused at two distances at the same time), or as late as 1963, the year after Ray's departure from *55 Days at Peking* (for which he envisioned using multiple images) (Eisenschitz 380–81). Years before, he had also conceived of shots for *Rebel Without a Cause* that would use multiple images, although these plans were abandoned before production (Eisenschitz 239). Forerunners or analogues of mimage can be found throughout Ray's work, including the use of rearview mirrors as internal frames in shots in *In a Lonely Place* and *The Lusty Men*, the police station scene in *Rebel Without a Cause*, with Jim, Judy, and Plato framed separately in different zones of a single composition, and Avery's reflection in the broken mirror in *Bigger Than Life*.

Ray and Vidal's scripts for *The Doctor and the Devils* specify three uses of the multiple-image process, designated variously by the words "multimage," "mimage," or "split screen." The first is a scene in the city square on Sunday: Rok detaches himself from the university chancellor and some colleagues in order to greet the disreputable pub singer Jennie. The script is not explicit on how the multiple-image process is to be used here, although one may imagine that Ray might have shown simultaneously in two images the conversation between Rok and Jennie and the reactions of his startled colleagues. In the second scene, as Rok enters his half-empty lecture hall, another screen shows some of the worthies of the city debating Rok's future. The multiple image—the moment of the most intense dramatization—appears when Rok's students lose faith in him and desert the classroom. This disintegration of the student-teacher relationship is juxtaposed and contrasted with the assembly of another group (those who detain power). Finally, multiple image would have been used in the climactic courthouse sequence (like many Ray films, *The Doctor and the Devils* moves its narrative to the point where the characters must account for themselves before the law), possibly to juxtapose images of Rok's trial with images of the crowd gathered ominously outside.

The figure of the teacher links *The Doctor and the Devils* to Ray's future work—not only *We Can't Go Home Again*, but also the teaching activities that occupied much of the final period of his life. The problematic of teaching in Ray's work is too complex to be summed up by any single example, but a memorable question from *Rebel Without a Cause* may provide an entrance to it. Jim asks his father, "What can you do when you have to be a man?" Although most viewers of the film have probably felt that the father is held up as a figure of pronounced inadequacy in the shot that shows him stumbling in a vain attempt to answer it, Jim's question may well be an unanswerable one, perhaps *the* unanswerable one. It is important that Jim asks it in this way, "What can you *do* . . ."—and not "how can you *be* . . ."—making it a question about doing rather than being. Years later, introducing his key concept to his students, Ray says, "An actor has to act. To act means to do. . . . What do I want? How do I overcome my problem? Why am I here? What do I want to do? Action implies desire and will. . . . Forget the state-of-being school of acting. It leads to no place. A state of being is not something you can utilize as an actor" (*Interrupted* 15). Rather than for a discussion of being, of essence, Jim is asking his father for his action; more than that, he is asking him for the theory of the conditions of action ("what *can* you do . . .").

Learning what you can do means learning about death. In the Libyan expedition of *Bitter Victory*, Leith and Brand find out what they are capable of, in matters of life and death, only through the experience of doing it. In *Rebel Without a Cause*, Jim is forced to assume adulthood through his duel with Buzz and his attempt to save Plato. In *Johnny Guitar*, Vienna tells the adolescent Turkey, "Boys who play with guns have to be ready to die like men"; in other words, Turkey, having usurped the symbolic guise of adulthood, therefore must assume the knowledge of death that constitutes full adulthood. To be a man is to accept that you must die. To Jim's question, "What can you do when you have to be a man?" then, his father might have answered, "You must take your death upon yourself." *We Can't Go Home Again* concludes with an assumption of death that can be read as a pedagogical act: Nicholas Ray, the teacher, hangs himself in a quasi-accident before the eyes of his students. Is this suicide a lesson, or is it a theft of death from the other, of the other's responsibility for dying? Ray's death in *We Can't Go Home Again* repeats Jeff's death at the end of *The Lusty Men*, another intentionally ambiguous suicide, another death taken on so that the student (in the case of *The Lusty Men*, this student is Wes, who has learned from Jeff the technique and the world of rodeo) may go on living.

Avery in *Bigger Than Life* is a limit figure because he is both a teacher and a person in a special relationship with death: his disease places him close to death, and, at the climax of the film, he becomes convinced that he must kill his son, Richie. In accepting the responsibility of Abraham, enjoined by God to sacrifice Isaac, Avery takes on what Jacques Derrida describes as Abraham's courage: "You had the courage to behave like a murderer in the eyes of the world and of your loved ones, in the eyes of morality, politics, and of the generality of the general of your kind. And you had even renounced hope" (72). In contrast, Leith in *Bitter Victory* is a "coward," and is berated as such by the man whose life he tries to save because in this act he manifests the refusal to accept the responsibility of death: he "saves the dead" after having first "killed the living"—he is committed to a course of failure.

That Rok in *The Doctor and the Devils* is a teacher who is in a special relationship with death is obvious. When he first turns his face toward the camera in the battlefield prologue, we see that "his right eye has been shot away, but there is no bleeding now, only the empty socket and the scar." Asked whether he can see and operate properly with only one eye, Rok replies that "in the land of the blind the one-eyed medical student is king," positioning himself (characteristically for a Ray protagonist) as a solitary—but royal—figure. Rok's one-eyed-ness suggests the incompleteness inherent in anyone who takes on the role of authority.

Rok carries with him, on his face, the visible sign of death, in the form of a black eyepatch. (The eyepatch is also a sexually attractive trait. As Jennie explains, it signifies a lack that women feel invited to complete). This sign has multiple resonances in Ray's work. Like Jeff in *The Lusty Men*, Davey in *Run for Cover*, and Tommy in *Party Girl*, Rok is wounded. His missing eye more directly recalls Chickamaw in *They Live by Night*: he has one dead eye that he leaves uncovered, staring with bleak hostility, and is angered when he is referred to in newspaper articles as "One-Eye." (There are also blind characters in *On Dangerous Ground*, *The True Story of Jesse James*, and *King of Kings*). The eyepatch is also a signature of Nicholas Ray, who suffered an embolism in his right eye while editing *Conspiracy* in Chicago in early 1970. As Bernard Eisenschitz writes, "the loss of sight in his right eye remained a mystery which he fostered, pretending he could see" (419). According to Christopher Plummer, the director had begun wearing an eyepatch as early as the production of *Wind Across the Everglades* in 1957 (Plummer 255).

Ray's single eye is the mark of a special insight. In *We Can't Go Home Again*, his role is that of the one who gets others to reveal their secrets: Tom Farrell shaving his beard, Leslie Levinson discussing her plan to prostitute herself in order to raise money for the film. Rok in *The Doctor and the Devils*, analogously, is the one for whom the dead reveal their secrets: his one eye is the eye that can see into the secrets of the body (perhaps if he had two he would not be granted this vision).

At the end of *The Doctor and the Devils*, Rok's effigy is hanged and burned, whereupon the face of the effigy "becomes" the face of the film director from the beginning of the film, reappearing in a final epilogue. Rok's staged death within the narrative becomes a metaphorical death for the character of the film director. The identity between these two figures is established in the prologue when the script girl tells the director, "If you don't stop acting the reincarnation of Dr. Rok, I'll quit." The mob's symbolic killing of Rok is thus a symbolic suicide by Ray, an approach to the hanging of Ray in *We Can't Go Home Again* and the apparent death of the preacher in *The Janitor* (Ray's episode in *Wet Dreams*) and to Ray's actual physical death as depicted in *Lightning Over Water*. Ray's attraction to *The Doctor and the Devils*, then, can be seen as a stage in his progressive approach to the theme of the artist's death (compare, too, his acting roles as the supposedly dead painter in *The American Friend* [1977] and the American ambassador who abstains—that is, withdraws, or plays dead—in *55 Days at Peking*). Perhaps it is the second crucial stage in this approach, following his premonition during the making of *55 Days at Peking* that he would never make another film—a premonition that provided the initial theme for *We Can't Go Home Again*, which constituted the third stage.

The lesson Ray leaves his students in *We Can't Go Home Again* is prefigured in *The Doctor and the Devils*. In Thomas's script, only professional gravediggers rob the graves; in Ray and Vidal's version, they are helped (and actually compete with) Rok's students. The first lesson Rok teaches them is to have a pragmatic relation to death. When the prefect visits Rok to warn him to stop his students from robbing graves ("You defile our dead, Rok"), the doctor replies: "If I have defiled the dead, it is to help the living." This inverts Leith's chiasmus in *Bitter Victory* ("I kill the living and save the dead"). Unlike Leith, Rok uses the dead to save the living. Rok is the Leith who succeeds in directing his knowledge for the use of humanity. He has no particular attraction to death; its function is purely instrumental. Like the children playing in the cemetery, Rok is familiar with death and not afraid of it. Advocating in the Parliament for the repeal of the Burial Act, he says: "Let the dead serve the living. Gentlemen, I beg you, choose life." Advising Charlotte against abortion, Rok explains: "there is so much death in the world, yet you can now make life." During a dissection session, Rok comments on one of his students' "bad work": "the object of this exercise is not to amputate but to protect and preserve, to heal and restore." To heal and restore could be Ray's testament, a lesson for young filmmakers. A seemingly destructive activity—to dissect the flesh, to break the rectangle—is justified when it has this purpose. Many of Ray's own late-career projects started as a kind of therapy. *The Doctor and the Devils* itself was one of the occupational-therapy projects suggested to Ray by Dr. Barrington Cooper, to whom Ray went on Joseph Losey's recommendation to seek a cure for his drug addiction. The project of the film that was eventually completed as *Lighting Over Water* also seems to have begun as a form of therapy.

The encounter between Ray and the younger generation in *We Can't Go Home Again* also takes the form of a therapy, with Ray assuming the role of an analyst before his students. Ultimately, he can play this role fully only by dying in place of one of them, Tom Farrell. This death is one of several deaths in Ray's films that bring to an end the cycle of exchanges that run through their narratives. The structure of exchange in Ray's cinema is not infinite: there is one act of exchange with which the exchanges stop, relieving the other characters of responsibility and permitting them to leave the circuit. This is also the case with Jeff's death in *The Lusty Men*, arguably with the sacrificial deaths of Danny in *On Dangerous Ground* and Plato in *Rebel Without a Cause*. Cottonmouth's death in *Wind Across the Everglades* and Leith's death in *Bitter Victory* can also be said to fulfill this function. In *The Doctor and the Devils*, the exchange that ends exchange is the bargain that allows Rok to escape punishment while an effigy is burned in his place: an equivalence that recalls the last shot of *Bitter Victory*, Brand pinning his medal on the dummy.

Generally in Ray's work, the woman has no role in the sacrificial play: she can neither intervene to stop it, nor can she insert herself into the sacrificial structure as victim, sacrificer, or the god to whom the sacrifice is made. Ray's cinema repeatedly visualizes the exclusion of the woman from the sacrificial structure as spatial exclusion: in *Rebel Without a Cause*, Judy waits outside the planetarium while Jim talks Plato into leaving; in *Bigger Than Life*, Lou is locked in a closet while Avery threatens Richie; in *Bitter Victory* and *Wind Across the Everglades*, women are left behind while the men go off on dangerous expeditions that lead to sacrificial conclusions. The structure of sacrifice is a structure of law. For Ray, the woman stands outside this structure, as someone not intimate with it, who can regard it only with suspicion. Here we would have to hear again Asiak's line in *The Savage Innocents*: "when you come to a strange land, you should bring your wives and not your laws."

Ray and Vidal's script of *The Doctor and the Devils* places greater importance on women than Thomas's script. If Thomas's text uses female characters mostly for the characterization of its protagonist (for example, Rock's unequal marriage with a woman from the lower class goes along with his rebellion against social norms and conventions) and limits women's tasks to motherhood or housekeeping (Rock's wife and sister) and prostitution (Jennie), Ray and Vidal's version suggests new roles—professional, emotional, ethical—that allow the female characters to emerge as more complex individuals.

The figure of Jennie goes through important transformations: she is now a singer, not a prostitute, even though she "is in love with love," "a hero of love" who would like to make love "thousands of thousands of times" and is promiscuous as self-expression and out of personal choice, not financial necessity. Ray's Jennie "is not the most beautiful girl in the world, . . . but in her warmth she seems to be." Jennie's innocence is stressed by her sacrificial function: it takes her death and the death of the young Billy (another addition to the gallery of Ray's doomed children; significantly, Ray gives the same name to the seventeen-year-old filmmaking apprentice who accompanies the film director in the prologue) to make Rok see the ethical problems with his traffic in cadavers.

Rok crosses paths on several occasions with the smart, ambitious, and lucid Charlotte, the daughter of his professional rival. Like Jennie, she enjoys sexual freedom, refusing to marry the father of her unborn child because she does not respect him. Trained in medicine together with her father's medical students, she defiantly aspires to become a doctor to the puzzlement of both her retrograde father and the rebel scientist Rok ("A *woman* doctor?" he exclaims). Charlotte's "masculine" brain and attitude win her the respect of medical students who note—in terms reminiscent of one of Vienna's staff in *Johnny Guitar* ("Never seen a woman who was more like a man: she thinks like one, acts like one, and sometimes makes me feel like I'm not.")—that she is more of a man than her father. Yet, in Rok's presence, Charlotte becomes docile and submissive and assumes "feminine" tasks that he imposes on her (following Rok's advice, she goes on with her pregnancy instead of getting an abortion and, sacrificially, starts working as a nurse in a poor district with an epidemic of birth fevers). Having followed Rok's advice to keep her baby—"there is so much death in the world yet you can now make life"—she becomes a figure of future life and salvation, a mother figure not only to her future child but also to Rok (who, like most Ray's characters, needs a woman to resolve his inner conflicts) and maybe even to science (which she preserves by protecting Rok).

Charlotte's decision to accompany Rok in exile is one of several aspects of Ray and Vidal's scripts that make the story less morbid and more optimistic than Thomas's version. There are no real losses in the script: Charlotte takes Jennie's place, Billy's sacrifice is not in vain. While the effigy of Rok burns, Charlotte affirms the triumph of life over death and destruction and expresses the promise of a new beginning: "Not a good likeness. . . . Don't worry, we shall survive." Her final words resonate with Ray's parting words in *We Can't Go Home Again*: "Take care of each other. It is your only chance for survival." Both that film and *The Doctor and the Devils* express frustration with the stubborn forces of stagnation and reaction and advance the idea that survival is possible only with collective effort. (The same themes underlie *55 Days at Peking*, a coincidence that suggests that the relevance of that film to the main body of Ray's work is currently underrated.) The ending of *The Doctor and the Devils* also repeats, and carries further, the ending of *The Savage Innocents*: the characters cast out of the law, out of history, and ultimately out of the narrative (as the nineteenth-century narrative of Rok gives way to the modern-day narrative about the film director). The alibis and protections of fiction are progressively discarded as Ray moves farther away from Hollywood and closer to *We Can't Go Home Again*. In this process of denudation and self-inquiry, *The Doctor and the Devils* marks a crucial, if abandoned, stage.

Notes

1. The story of Knox, Burke, and Hare had inspired several previous films, notably Robert Wise's *The Body Snatcher* (1945) and John Gilling's *The Flesh and the Fiends* (1960). Thomas's script was eventually filmed under its original title by Freddie Francis in 1985.

2. For accounts of Ray's *The Doctor and the Devils* project, see Eisenschitz 395–400 and McGilligan 443–49.

3. All references to *The Doctor and the Devils* in this chapter are from Ray and Vidal's drafts.

Steven Rybin

The Pedagogical Aesthetics of *We Can't Go Home Again*

Nicholas Ray's *We Can't Go Home Again* premiered in its earliest public form at the Cannes Film Festival in May 1973. The context of this screening, as described by attendee Jonathan Rosenbaum, was hardly auspicious. On the final afternoon of the festival, Rosenbaum observed a weary audience attending a difficult and demanding work that went virtually unnoticed by the festival press ("Circle" 125). Combining 16mm, 35mm, and Super 8 footage, as well as images processed through a video color synthesizer that were then transferred back to film, *We Can't Go Home Again* was—and remains, in a version newly restored by Susan Ray in 2011—a challenging mosaic of sight and sound.[1] As many as five separate images—all projected separately on a pro-filmic screen and then refilmed in a composite image by a 35mm camera—crowd the frame for attention at any one time, splintering a loose narrative about the struggle of a cinema professor (played by Ray) and his students to make a movie in the midst of political and personal turmoil. As tiring as it may have been for the Cannes audience to process this unexpected experiment by a Hollywood *auteur*, their weariness could not match the director's own: after an exhausting effort to assemble a print of the film in time for the journey to Cannes, Ray fell asleep during the screening (Eisenschitz 446).

Figure 20.1. Both dressed in red (the signature color of rebellion in Ray's cinema, after the red jacket James Dean wears in *Rebel Without a Cause*), Tom Farrell and Ray are united not only by their costumes but also by the fact that both of them are blind in their right eye (frame enlargement).

What Ray was presenting to the Cannes audience, more than a decade after his departure from Hollywood, was a fundamentally new kind of cinema. This new cinema was not a part of the industry in which Ray made the masterpieces for which he is celebrated, and is only loosely related to the larger context of the American cinema's avant-garde. The film was, rather, the product of Ray's new job as a teacher. This joint effort between Ray and his film students at Harpur College, part of the State University of New York at Binghamton, began two years prior to the Cannes screening. Filmmakers Larry Gottheim and Ken Jacobs (the founders of the Harpur film program) invited Ray to work as a visiting professor of cinema in fall 1971, following a successful guest appearance earlier that year. But Ray's students would not be in store for more lectures. Ray's course would involve the production of a film, initially titled *Gun Under My Pillow* (a reference to the character Sal Mineo plays in *Rebel Without a Cause*) and then changed to *We Can't Go Home Again* (an allusion to the title of Thomas Wolfe's posthumous novel *You Can't Go Home Again*). The original narrative scenario Ray devised involved a story about a film director who wakes up one night with a strong premonition that he will never make another movie. The film would refract Ray's original conception through a highly experimental formal play with multiple moving images (a process that Ray coined "mimage"). But this was not to be a mere exercise in form. *We Can't Go Home Again* is a uniquely and radically pedagogical film—a film about the teaching of the making of images, with a story and shape that reflects, as one of Ray's students observed, the conditions of its own making (Eisenschitz 432).

Rosenbaum astutely describes the work as "cinema at the end of its tether" ("Circle" 126). Ray's struggle to make films during the final years of his life, indeed, finds its reflection in the disjunctive, moving, and often puzzling collage of imagery on the screen. Most critics have relied on *auteurism* as the lens through which to tame the film's unwieldy contours. Rosenbaum, although astutely aware of the film's larger political and social context, links the "the framework of romantic futility" undergirding Ray's earlier narratives to *We Can't Go Home Again*, seeing an explicit structural manifestation of the psychodrama at work, on a more subtle level, in Ray's earlier features. For Rosenbaum, the shattered mirror of a medicine cabinet Lou (Barbara Rush) slams shut in *Bigger Than Life* finds its "structural equivalent" in the shards of imagery Ray presents for us in his final film ("Circle" 132). Rosenbaum's words throw into relief more purely *auteurist* interpretations. Geoff Andrew, for example, remarks that the film functions as "a summation of themes that had haunted [Ray's] career from its very beginning," including the difficulty of communication, the injustice of society, and the innocence of youth (154). And Cullen Gallagher, in a recent reappraisal of the film, suggests that it "just might be the most direct, unfiltered expression of 'Nicholas Ray' on film."

As invaluable as the *auteurist* approach is, Ray's own writing suggests *We Can't Go Home Again* exists for reasons other than self-expression. In a posthumously published essay on the film (which also serves as part of the opening voice-over of the restored version of the film), Ray describes himself, in the third person, as a retired director with the "full intention of growing a goatee, buying a crooked cane, walking a crooked mile, and impressing his students with his rhetoric and ponderosity, meanwhile completing his autobiography" (*Interrupted* 203–04). But Ray quickly recognized that the traditional lecture format would not work: "The students had also retired from the conflicts of the late 60s, and submerged themselves in what they thought a safe and serene womb, where no outside voices could be heard, least of all that of a Hollywood director" (204). Far from functioning as cinematic lecture from a retired director who has already learned everything he has to teach about his subject, *We Can't Go Home Again*—in both its earlier Cannes cut and its recent digital restoration—is about the struggle to create a context in which a collective expression might occur.

The *auteurist* approach to writing about *We Can't Go Home Again*, then, while invaluable for linking Ray's final effort to the implicit and explicit social and aesthetic concerns of his earlier films, tames (a little too much) the difficulties this film poses to any critic seeking to transpose its fractured images into critical discourse. The limits of *auteurism* are, after all, evident in the film's mode of production. The students rotated responsibilities on the set every two weeks, trying their hands at directing, lighting, acting, and sound at various points throughout the production (Eisenschitz 430). The film's focus on a social context that goes beyond the individual *auteur* mirrors this collective mode of filmmaking. The first sequence presents images from the documentary footage Ray shot in Chicago in the 1960s during the Chicago Seven trials, as well as images from the 1968 Democratic Convention and shots of political activists such as Jerry Rubin and Abbie Hoffman. One of the students, Tom Farrell, reads a voice-over to accompany these images in the Cannes version. Farrell outlines his involvement in the Students for a Democratic Society and his experience of watching the Chicago Seven trials on television. (In the version Susan Ray restored, Farrell's voice-over is replaced by Ray's own, perhaps bringing the restoration closer to an *auteurist* statement.) This prologue serves to situate the film loosely, as Andrew points out, in the zeitgeist of the period, locating Ray's struggle to make another movie, and his students' own grappling with the personal and the political, in a larger social context.

The film then goes on to question the suitability of Ray's authorial persona, and indeed the university system itself, as a frame through which this social turmoil might be understood. Ray frames his arrival at Harpur College as an intervention into the increasingly corporate structure of public education: "Education is very big business," Ray says in a voice-over, as shots of students paying tuition bills unfold on the image tracks. The subsequent staging of Ray's first encounter with the students reminds us of the director's own past in "big business," the Hollywood industry. In the film, the director is warily greeted by the younger generation. The students can, of course, vaguely recall *Rebel Without a Cause*, *They Live by Night*, *Johnny Guitar*, and even (as one student calls it) "that Eskimo movie with Anthony Quinn," *The Savage Innocents*. But they regard their memories of these films with ambivalence. And they wonder why a celebrated Hollywood director—who must have a lot of money—is slumming in the professorial ranks. Initially, Ray's image is separated, on the right side of the frame, from the images of the students, who are often figured in group shots while Ray is framed alone, in close-up. Nam June Paik's color video synthesizer distorts Ray's image, twisting the director's self-portrait into an electronic swirl of blues, greens, and whites. As the students enter the same shot as Ray (which, for a moment, is the only image on the screen), the synthesizer's colors paint them in turn. Ray then christens them in the name of cinema, referring to one of his young students, Leslie Levinson, as "Lola Montes," an apt point of reference for the multiring circus of images *We Can't Go Home Again* is to become. (This line is also a sly foreshadowing of a later moment in the film, in which Levinson's character admits to Ray she has turned to prostitution in order to find funding for the movie.)

Despite the film's ostensibly collective mode of production, some of Ray's students (including several interviewed in Susan Ray's 2011 documentary on the film's making) recall their frustration with Ray's insistence that the technical crew remain waiting on the set for interminable hours while he and his actors discussed motivation and rehearsed the actions that would eventually be filmed. To what extent *We Can't Go Home Again* successfully functions as a work of collective authorship, especially in light of the ambivalence that remains in some of Ray's collaborators to this day, is indeed a question the film itself asks. As one of the students declares in a moment prior to the scene introducing Ray: "I don't even know why I came back to school. These dumb machines are just making noise at me. Is this what I have to do to graduate? Get a job somewhere?" Given that cinema always might become just one more of "these dumb machines" (Ray's own disregard, in a number of interviews, for several of his genre efforts in the Hollywood system comes to mind here), *We Can't Go Home Again*, despite its ambivalence, becomes an experiment in investing the collective act of cinema production with pedagogical value. Here the film emerges as a dialogue between a filmmaker hoping to make a movie with a makeshift film crew and a group of students facing their own uncertain futures.

In this respect, the film is also a participant in the relationship that developed between experimental cinema and film studies pedagogy on college campuses in the 1960s and 1970s. As Michael Zryd points out, groups committed to experimental cinema "were instrumental in developing student demand for film courses and programs at many universities" (184). At Harpur College, the development of just such a program was already in progress under the auspices of Gottheim and Jacobs, who founded the cinema department at the college in 1969. As Gottheim recounts, a rift eventually developed between Jacobs and Ray (with Jacobs accusing Ray of monopolizing the film equipment), prompting students to pledge loyalty to one or the other of the two directors. But for Gottheim, what united Ray and Jacobs were their similar attitudes toward pedagogy: "Just as Nick's own living persona would itself be a performance to pull people magnetically into his own aura in order for them to finally become more of themselves, as well as creatures of his own imagination, this was also Ken's role as a teacher" (95). Even if, ultimately, Ray's conflict with Jacobs ensured the temporary nature of his position at the school, Ray and Jacobs were like-minded in their teaching methods; both used the *auteur*'s personality not as an end in itself but a means to enable students to discover their own creativity.

Perhaps the most salient intervention *We Can't Go Home Again* makes into the tradition of experimental, and pedagogical, cinema is in its combination of Ray's approach to acting with the associational form of experimental filmmaking that the film itself embodies. The viewer of the film does not merely see a student playing a role. Rather, the viewer is the witness to a student actor finding his or her "action," a key idea in Ray's theories of acting during the period (as captured in his posthumously published body of essays, *I Was Interrupted*). And just as the student performer in the frame works to find his or her action, the film itself joins them in the process, combining multiple images to open a space for the viewer's own negotiation of the meaning of the actions on the screen. In a scene that is first projected on the top left of the screen (it shortly shifts to the center of the frame), an argument involving a female student's refusal to submit to sex and cook her male partner dinner unfolds on a staircase. On the bottom right, a slightly larger image records a conversation between a couple against the black backdrop of what is presumably one of the studio spaces at Harpur (this scene will soon shift to the top right of the frame and decrease in size as the scene on the staircase begins to take precedence; and as the sequences come to an end, the two scenes are then superimposed, the imagistic blending of the two projected images ultimately commanding as much interest as the dramatic content of either scene). The associational arrangement of the images invites viewers to become part of the process of making the film's meaning. The performances, in turn, are themselves also ragged and unfinished, inviting viewers to witness the transformation of students into actors and adults, a painful process of becoming that complements the personal struggles of the characters the students are playing.

Because the psychodrama that is occurring here might be said to be happening not within either of the frames projected before us but between them, a structuralism, echoed in other experimental work of the period, informs the film. The director, professing his desire to conceive of a cinema not determined by the compositional limits of the horizontal frame ("I had dreamed for years of being able to destroy the rectangular frame," Ray said; "I couldn't stand the formality of it"), created with the mimage of *We Can't Go Home Again* a radical sundering of cinematic structure (qtd. in Eisenschitz 433). As a result, the film provides a tentative, abstract shape to the constantly fluctuating set of interpersonal, existential, and pedagogical situations depicted in the separate images.

Ray is himself a central figure in the images that comprise the film, an aspect that places this work in the larger avant-garde tradition of portraiture. However, Ray and his students depart from the norms of the portrait film in ways that are consistent with his rejection of *auteurism* as a mode of production. As Paul Arthur points out, the portrait film typically "is among the most literal, or nontropic, of genres," tending toward "fewer instances of radically disjunctive editing or denaturing of the image than in other avant-garde idioms" (25). These portraits, exemplified by Jonas Mekas's films, particularly *Walden: Diaries and Sketches* (1969), also place the individual's portrait in a larger social context that, for experimental filmmakers, includes other filmmakers, artists, poets, painters, and dancers. *We Can't Go Home Again* develops just such a context, beginning with Ray's arrival at the SUNY–Binghamton campus and ending with his symbolic death, a portrait of the director inseparable from the relationships with his students that develop in, and around, the movie. But unlike the films Arthur cites, which rely on a certain literality of image in their portraits, the portrait of Ray that emerges in the film is inseparable from the film's disjunctive juxtapositions and treatment of image.

The film's disjunctions, indeed, offer pointed reflections on Ray's role in the lives of these students and come in a handful of scenes between the director and one of the film's main actors, Tom Farrell. Their first scene together unfolds in a single image on the bottom right corner of the frame (all other images are removed from the film during this sequence, ensuring the audience's focus on this narrative event). In the scene, Ray makes a pointed comment about his disgust for police officers. Farrell, like Ray, is indeed a leftist; elsewhere in the film he reveals his disgust over Nixon's nomination for the presidency and his own involvement with the Students for a Democratic Society. But he also reveals that his father is a cop, and he does not take kindly to Ray's glib generalizations about police officers. Farrell tells Ray that his father should not be crudely characterized because he has, in Farrell's words, "talked a lot of people out of committing suicide." To this Ray's character retorts with a philosophy straight out of Albert Camus's *The Myth of Sisyphus* (one of Ray's assigned texts in the class), inferring that Farrell's father has interfered with the existential destiny of those he saved. Farrell then admits his own suicidal thoughts, revealing that he has pointed his father's gun at his head numerous times, and reacts with anger at Ray for bringing up the subject: "You're just like the other professors, you always talk and you never listen to people. You think you know it all just because you made movies, and you're old?" Farrell here articulates the very problem *We Can't Go Home Again* attempts to express on a filmic level: How will an *auteur*, instead of expressing, teach?

The most powerful moment between Farrell and Ray comes later in the film. Farrell, having returned from a traumatic journey to Florida for the Democratic National Convention in which he was beaten by a gang of thugs who despised his appearance as a "hippie," makes the decision to shave the scruffy beard he has sported throughout the film. As Farrell makes clear, the beard is indissolubly linked to his political and social identity, and the decision to shave it is a crucial gesture in a film that is in large part about the painful transition from college student to socially responsible adult. Ray, in keeping with the pedagogical spirit of this work, not only captures this important moment in the life of his student on film, but also encourages his pupil to make meaning out of a performative moment that finds an "action" that emerges from the most painful and personal depths. As Farrell cuts his beard (breathing heavily, trembling, and struggling to prevent the scissors from cutting his cheek), Ray whispers to his protégé from offscreen (words heard in the newly restored version): "Tom, talk to me, will you? Just talk. Make me believe you. . . . Don't give it to me in morality, Tom. Just say what it means to you."

Regardless how much he is encouraging his students to translate their real lives into the stuff of cinema, Ray is clearly treading on dangerous territory here. In the earlier moment between Farrell and Ray, the theme of suicide was introduced, and in the scene of the shaving of the beard, Farrell appears highly unstable (blood is even visible on his cheek). But Farrell's remarkable performance is consistent with the ideas at work in Ray's course. In *The Myth of Sisyphus*, Camus outlines an absurd world in which the absence of God triggers the existential struggle for meaning in every individual. Ray's own efforts in making *We Can't Go Home Again*, a film he struggled to shape into final form up to his death, are, of course, Sisyphean in nature. However, Ray seems to be using Camus's philosophy less as a means to explore his own subjectivity and more as an inspiration for his students to realize and enact their own personal struggles in the form of cinema, as exemplified in the scenes with Farrell. Shortly after mentioning his conflict with his father earlier in the film, for example, Ray and Farrell turn it into drama, casting Farrell as a security officer who chases a couple out of the school's pool after hours. While clearly connected to the profession of Farrell's father, the scene also has a psychosexual dimension: in another image, another security officer (which a different student, Richie Bock, plays) flirts with Levinson, a character who has earlier in the film declared her desire for Farrell. But instead of acting on his desires, Farrell plays the role of authorial father, chasing a couple out of a swimming pool after hours while dressed as a cop.

If this scene echoes the love triangles in earlier Ray films, such as *Johnny Guitar* and *Rebel Without a Cause*, Ray ultimately encourages his actors to grapple with these psychological conflicts in personal, rather than *auteurist*, terms. Ray's *auteurism* does not provide the frame that his students simply fulfill, but is rather a point of departure enabling his students to negotiate personal and political meaning. If the philosophical backbone of *We Can't Go Home Again* is linked to the existentialism of the 1940s and 1950s, the film also shows the ethical dilemma Ray creates for himself by involving his students in his own struggle to create a film. Ray's feeling of failure as a teacher is one of the film's motifs ("don't expect too much of a teacher," Ray says later in the film, a quote that gives the title to Susan Ray's 2011 documentary on the film's making). During a confrontation with Levinson later in the film, she voices her personal drama to Ray, asking him for help because of his role as teacher. "Who can teach?" Ray says in voice-over, a hesitation about the value of his pedagogy. Later, after the students discover Ray sitting alone in a shed (and fearing he has committed suicide), Ray tells them he has been at a faculty party. His dilapidated condition is clearly meant to convey his lack of comfort among other teachers (perhaps reflective of his falling out with Jacobs). The scene inscribes Ray's suggestion that he has failed in his teaching as a possible reason for his character's potential suicide.

Ray himself most likely did not entertain suicidal thoughts while making the film. Instead, the theme of suicide seems here to function as death does in many of Ray's films, as the sacrificial opening of a space that others must work to fill. Herein lies a key aspect of Ray's pedagogical act. As Blaine Allan has discussed, death in Ray's films, often accidental, is an opening through which other characters, and indeed the viewers, make meaning: "The cost of a single life becomes for Ray an indicator of value on a larger scale. If a single life is sacrificed for others, the trauma and hell that led to that death, the pain and suffering because of the loss, are supplanted by the potential for development and learning" (35–36). Allan's linkage of the space opened by death to the acts of development and learning echoes Ray's symbolic death in *We Can't Go Home Again*, in which we see Ray, dressed as Santa Claus, accidentally run over by a car (as if to link this death to the act of cinematic pedagogy that is this film, Ray's dead body is then covered with spools of celluloid, the gift Ray gives his students to negotiate their identity). Although this death is related to the director's recurring theme of sacrificial death, and is thus in that sense of a piece with his body of work as an *auteur*, Ray nevertheless effectively erases the *auteur* in this image, calling on his students to forge their own struggles to make meaning.

Ray would later take the theme of sacrificial death to its existential and bodily limits in his collaboration with Wim Wenders, *Lightning Over Water*. The film was initially conceived as the story of an American painter who attempts to bring together the loose strands of his life before dying. But very quickly *Lightning Over Water* became a collaborative documentary about Ray's own last days. The film is a final testament to Ray's pedagogy and to the way he was able to open up experiential spaces in which his actors, collaborators, and indeed viewers would generate self-made meaning. As with *We Can't Go Home Again*, the Wenders film is in part a collaboration with Tom Farrell, whose involvement with the project Ray insisted on. Farrell shoots video footage of Wenders and Ray and appears in the film as himself.

In several of his appearances in the first half of *Lightning Over Water*, Farrell is depicted at Ray's editing table, attempting to cobble together the images and sounds of *We Can't Go Home Again* (which Ray was still editing at the time of his death). At one point in *Lightning Over Water*, Farrell projects *We Can't Go Home Again* for Ray, Susan Ray, and Wenders. This version, which includes Ray's voice-over in lieu of Tom Farrell's, is closer to the version Susan Ray restored in 2011. But while this later version of *We Can't Go Home Again* is perhaps a more "personal" film than the earlier cut, for Farrell, Nicholas Ray's most important role in this work clearly has been as teacher, not as *auteur*. As Tom, Nick, Susan, and Wim watch *We Can't Go Home Again* in the film, another scene with Ray and Farrell unfolds, this time in a single image comprising the entire frame. Both dressed in red (the signature color of rebellion in Ray's cinema after the red jacket James Dean wears in *Rebel Without a Cause*), Farrell and Ray are united not only by their costumes but also by the fact that both of them are blind in their right eye. *Lightning Over Water* then cuts to a close-up of Farrell watching himself in the film he helped Ray make six years earlier. Here Ray's personal signature does not occupy the space between Farrell and the screen. This space is instead the gift of the most personal kind from teacher to student, as it is for any viewer who learns how to see and respond to cinema through watching the films of Nick Ray.

Note

1. Susan Ray's 2011 release of the film, which was showcased in September and October 2011 at the Venice Film Festival, the New York Film Festival, and the Turner Classic Movies cable channel, is a digital restoration, adding yet another moving image technology to Ray's cinematic mix. It was released on DVD and Blu-Ray in 2012 by Oscilloscope.

Postscript

The Class: Interview with Nicholas Ray

BILL KROHN

THE OFFICIAL FILMOGRAPHY OF Nicholas Ray ends in 1963, with *55 Days at Peking*; it was not until I read in *Pariscop* that a film by Nick Ray and Max Fischer called *Wet Dreams* was being shown at the Cinémathèque during the summer of 1973 that I began to suspect the existence of the "other" films. I had arrived in Paris one day too late to see *Wet Dreams*, so when a friend informed me a year later that sections of a work-in-progress called *We Can't Go Home Again* were to be shown at the First Avenue Screening Room in New York, I resolved to investigate.

The theater was packed. Elia Kazan and Nick's old producer John Houseman were there, along with a number of backers who were considering investing in the film. We were all disappointed—the screening lasted only a few minutes before the First Avenue's projector suffered a mysterious breakdown. But the few minutes we saw were worth the price

---

Editor's note: This interview was conducted by the author in late 1977, the same period during which Ray taught classes at the Strasberg Institute and, later, New York University. Krohn, who also observed Ray's teaching at Strasberg, originally published this interview in French, in the May 1978 issue of *Cahiers du cinéma* (vol. 288, pp. 62–67). This is the original English transcript of the interview, republished with the author's permission. It has never before been published in English.

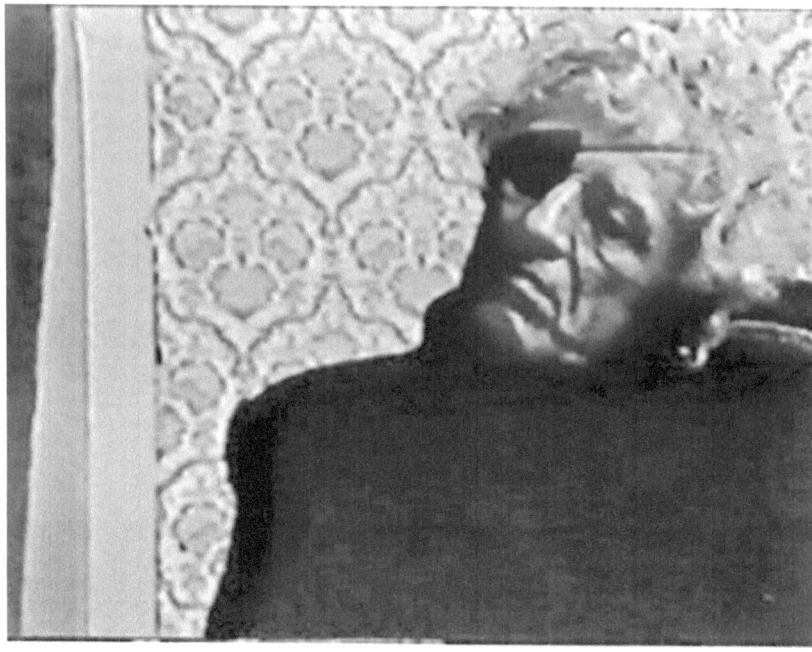

Figure P.1. Ray in the short film *The Janitor* (Film Group One, Amsterdam, with Cinereal Films, West Berlin, 1974; frame enlargement).

of admission, for *We Can't Go Home Again* turned out to be a radically experimental work employing what appeared to be television screens of various sizes imbedded in still photographs of an old frame house, a T.V. set, a city street. Nick's appearance when he spoke before the screening also left a strong impression: it was the Nick Ray of *The American Friend* (1977), sporting an eye-patch and accompanied by the collective of students from Harpur College with whom he had been working on the film since 1971.

That fall *Variety* reported on the progress of an independent feature starring Norman Mailer and Rip Torn, based on Bruce Jay Friedman's novel *Murphy*, which was abandoned before shooting began because of a disagreement between Nick and his producer. But it seems there were already a number of other films made for the most part outside the normal production system: an unfinished film made on an island in the North Sea in 1968 (see interview); the short shown at the Cinémathèque, which was Nick's contribution to an anthology film made in Amsterdam in 1974; an unfinished film starring the Chicago Seven which was subsequently incorporated into *We Can't Go Home Again*; another multiple-image work made in Czechoslovakia, which Nick mentions in passing in a long interview accorded to the Canadian film magazine *Take One* in 1974. . . .

These films are like flying saucers—you catch glimpses of them or hear about them from people who've seen one. Most of my information about *We Can't Go Home Again* comes from conversations with one of the Harpur students, Danny Fisher, and an editor who worked on the project in New York. There is also a documentary about the making of the film by David Helpern, Jr., called *I'm a Stranger Here Myself* (1975)—the working title, according to Nick, of every film he has ever made.

In the documentary he speaks of the Chicago Seven trial, which lured him back to the U. S. in 1969 after an absence of ten years, as a "circus of bigotry" which pitted the feeble adolescent humor of the defendants against a Court that insisted on taking them seriously. One of the Seven even asked Nick to bring in Groucho Marx as an expert witness, "to explain our sense of humor." Then in 1971, abandoning one archetypal Ray scenario for another, Nick started teaching a film class at Harpur College in Binghamton, New York, out of which grew the collective that made *We Can't Go Home Again*. "This is a method of teaching," he explains to the documentary camera. "That we've come out of it with a film is, we hope, a lucky accident." Nick's method of teaching, like his way of making films, did not fit comfortably into an institutional framework; the class adopted a communal lifestyle and was obliged to move to a farm Nick had purchased outside of Binghamton, where the work continued for another two years before the first version of *We Can't Go Home Again*, with a running time of nine hours, was ready to be screened at Cannes in 1973.

The subject of the film is the class itself; the story developed out of scenes improvised by Nick and the students and was continually expanded to incorporate new events in the life of the class—the decision of one of the actors to shave off his beard, for example, or the death of a poet who had acted in a couple of scenes and was subsequently run over by a truck while hitchhiking in upstate New York, dressed, according to the newspapers, as Santa Claus. Nick insisted on commemorating the event with a full-scale reenactment, playing the role of the victim himself. The story which developed in this way is, in Nick's words, one of mutual betrayal. At the end, after a confrontation with the students in which he is accused of exploiting them, the director fashions a noose and hangs himself; the students decide to let him die.

The film was shot in 35mm, 16mm, 8mm, and super-8, and the 2-inch, 1-inch, and 1/2-inch videotape; more recently, for the sake of completeness, additional footage was shot in Amsterdam using super-16. Some of the videotape footage and 16 footage which had been transferred to video was reworked in an optical synthesizer; all of the video sequences were then transferred to 16 before the final transfer to the multiple-screen format, which was itself an inspired piece of bricolage: sequences which were to be mounted together were projected onto a back-projection screen, with as many as five projectors operating simultaneously, and filmed with a 35mm camera. The womb-like photographs which serve as frames for the different assemblages produced in this way were an afterthought of Nick's, added either in the camera or in the laboratory. The number of screens varies from one section to another, but the basic format employs four: a large screen for 16mm at the lower left corner of the frame, two smaller 16mm screens in the upper left and lower right corners, a smaller screen in the upper right corner for 8mm and video footage, and in some cases a 35mm image intermittently superimposed over the whole assemblage.

In spite of the staggering complexity of the conception, the form of the film is linear and narrative, with the large screen in the lower left corner carrying the story-line and the smaller screens playing, in Nick's words, a "supplementary" role. In the one sequence which I remember, the large screen shows Nick's leading lady Leslie Levinson telling the story of her quest for "corruption" in New York's East Village, while Nick (wearing two eyepatches) listens coolly, occasionally smoothing his hair and munching on a tomato. When the actress finishes her story, Nick hits her with a tomato, and the action is duplicated by dramatic rhymes on the smaller screen: a group of students throwing tomatoes while Nick directs them like an orchestra conductor; another group in a room with a bright red carpet being machine-gunned by a Chinese actor named Stanley Loo; and in the upper right corner, images from Picasso's *Guernica*. It was this format or an earlier, simpler one which Godard probably saw and adapted to his own purposes in *Numéro Deux* (1975) and *Ici et ailleurs* (1976), in the process producing something quite different, which Nick could only view as the result of a "misunderstanding."

We Can't Go Home Again was financed initially with a grant of $28,000 from the state of New York and then with the director's own money. To this day it is still unfinished, for financial reasons, it would seem. "We'll finish this one," Nick says in the documentary, remembering all the experiments which have been left unfinished, "And the next one. . . ." One thinks of Orson Welles, who has been nursing a body of works-in-progress for so long that the title of one of them—*The Deep*—has been stolen by a Hollywood super-production, and the title of another has been changed from *The Adventures of Don Quixote* to *When*

Are You Going to Finish Don Quixote? Like Ray, Welles has released only one film in the seventies, the little essay-film *F for Fake* (1973), where we see him meditating bemusedly about the general inflation of the value of the signature, which he was the first to put into play in the American cinema with *Citizen Kane* (1941).

Welles's *We Can't Go Home Again* is a mammoth film called *The Other Side of the Wind*, about a director who returns to Hollywood after twenty years of wandering and finds it drastically changed. Thanks to a televised American Film Institute tribute to Welles a few years ago, strangely reminiscent of the abortive screening I attended in New York the same year; I was able to see a few minutes of that film as well. In the scenes I remember, Edmond O'Brien, playing the Great Man's stooge, screens footage from the work-in-progress for a pompous young producer, reportedly modeled on Robert Evans. The footage—something about a boy, a girl, and a bomb—is in the soft colors of a seventies Hollywood romance, but the producer and the stooge are in black-and-white. The producer is trying unsuccessfully to figure out the plot; the stooge's pathetic efforts to please only garble the matter further. Finally the producer divines the horrible truth: "You can't fool me—there isn't any plot. He's making it up as he goes along!" Stooge (fiercely proud): "He's done it before!" We should really invent a new category for these films, which are the work of directors who have in a sense been missing for years, but missing in action (MIA).

Which is not to say that they have been invisible. Welles has been appearing a lot on television, telling stories and doing magic tricks, and his voice haunts countless commercials for airlines, soft drinks, and frozen peas. Nick, for his part, has been an increasingly visible presence for the last few years in New York's artistic community, a kind of fourth network where every inhabitant does double duty as a portable video camera. You hear more incredible stories about him than about anyone else, and most of them are first-person accounts. Nick is not exactly inaccessible these days, but he doesn't respond well to formalized situations; so it was only after two chance encounters, the first of which took place in a little bodega in Soho, that I was able to wangle an invitation to the class he has been teaching at the Lee Strasberg Institute for the Dramatic Arts.

The Strasberg Institute is the present-day successor of the old Actors' Studio, where Ray and Elia Kazan, along with several generations of American theater artists, absorbed Stanislavski's theories of acting and put them to work in ways that revolutionized theater and film in the two decades after the War. It is the most prestigious acting school in New York, and what strikes me first about the students with whom Nick is working today is the contrast with the unruly gang he had around him when I first sighted him in the early seventies. These kids, many of whom have come from Europe to study at the Institute, are well-groomed, well-behaved, well-heeled, and almost intimidatingly soft-spoken. With his new glasses Nick looks a little bit like Barry Goldwater, and what he seems to be teaching, apart from the time-tested precepts of the Method, is discipline, orderliness, and professionalism. A far cry from the wild tales of the Harpur days, which reminded one observer I spoke to of something out of the novels of Joseph Conrad. What's going on? I decide to go back one more time to find out, and when I do, Nick is making another film.

The new film, a 16mm short, is being shot in two sections: improvised scenes in which the students play criminals who have been caught in a police dragnet, and scripted scenes about a character named Marco. The first day of shooting is devoted to booking the students, each of whom has been assigned to a crime as the basis for his improvisation, in keeping with Nick's theory that anyone is capable of becoming a criminal. The technicians on the crew are not novices—Danny Fisher, for example, has been with Nick off and on since the Harpur days, and the cameraman is Robert Locativo, one of the founders of Newsreel. But because of the inadequate wiring at the Institute, the lights keep blowing every three minutes, and shooting conditions on the cramped stairway outside the Marilyn Monroe Room are difficult, as one student after another mounts the steps and stands before the desk-sergeant while Gerry Bamann, a New York theater director who is helping Nick with the class, reads off the list of crimes. By six o'clock the shooting is already half a day behind schedule; Nick makes a stern speech berating the students for their habitual lateness and enjoins them to report in at twelve o'clock sharp the next day.

Assuming that the injunction does not apply to journalists, I come at four o'clock, and Nick shows up an hour after me. By this time (calculation?) most of the class has gone home, leaving just the crew, a few observers, and the three actors who will be performing in the scripted scenes: a New York actor named Jim Ballagh and a Mexican television director named Ned Motolo, who will both play cops; and a gifted young Italian actor named Claudio Mazzatenta, who will play a character named Marco who walks into the police-station in a state of shock and confesses to the most horrible crime of all. The shooting takes place from six in the evening until two in the morning in a little classroom that has been done over to look like a police interrogation room. By the time the crew has finished setting up, the atmosphere is very much like a police station late at night: dead silence, stale cigarette smoke, tired men doing their job, almost no women. No one pays any attention to Claudio, who sits in a kind of trance at the center of all the activity in the last stages of what Stanislavski calls the actor's "preparation," while Nick works with Ned and Jim, explaining to them how policemen think.

He talks about the month he spent researching the phenomenon of police virulence for *On Dangerous Ground* by riding in a patrol car with the Boston Violence Squad—three cops who had all gone to night-school and become lawyers in order to defend their own cases in the Boston courts. One night when Nick was on patrol with his subjects, stopping to take a piss in a vacant lot, one of them pointed to the Brinks building across the street and said, "That's where the money is." A week later the St. Augustine Gang pulled their famous Brinks job, and Nick, who had already gone back to Hollywood, learned that his friends on the force had put a make out on him, on the remote possibility that he might have been a plant. "Very cultivated men, a lot of contradictions. . . ." Going ahead of them on another occasion to observe how they walked into a bar, he noticed that they were immediately identifiable from the fact that they didn't take their hats off, for fear that someone would get the drop on them; when they did take their hats off, it was a bit of business to cover a conversation with the hatcheck girl, who was inevitably a stoolie. Stoolies: "The real stoolie is a professional, not a hysterical amateur. There's a news-dealer on the corner of Washington and 4th who even turned in his own son." Cops. . . . "The good-cop bad-cop routine is as old as the hills. Producers like the Warner brothers used it; so did the best agents in Hollywood, the Bergs. And married couples do it to everyone, when they aren't doing it to each other. . . ."

It's getting to be the time of night when everyone reminds you of somebody else. Complimenting Iris the script-girl on her intuitive sense of protocol, Nick talks about his script-girls in Hollywood, and then tells her a story about Fanny Brice, whom she resembles. Just before the shooting begins, he tells Gerry and some of the crew about the editor of *They Live by Night*, who encouraged him to try things like shooting double-reverses—a violation of an inflexible rule among Hollywood technicians. "Go ahead, he'd say, do it! Fuck 'em! He was a frustrated director, so people wouldn't hire him. Same thing with Ernst Haller, my cameraman on *Rebel Without a Cause*. Warners had fired him because Joan Crawford didn't like the way he lit her in some picture. I didn't really like the tests he'd shot for me, but I hired him anyway because I hated Warners. They were so perverse." Gerry: "*They* were?" Nick: "They started it."

For the next few minutes Nick moves around the room with a hand-held camera, seeing how the shots line up, and then the scene begins. Almost on cue Claudio starts to erupt like a man coming out of shock and having an hysterical breakdown. Nick continues to work with Ned and Jim, who are responding too slowly, and calls again and again for re-takes. He looks like a bloodhound on the scent, prowling around the room, talking to Claudio in a low voice between takes, crouching behind the camera and making drawn-out gestures with his fists, always attentive to the framing, the composition, the relationship of the actors in space. By the time Ti-Vo starts shooting close-ups Claudio is in a state of near-collapse, rolling his eyes and sobbing wordlessly, and the other actors are finding their rhythm by responding to him. When the emotion gets too big, Nick darts in and cradles Claudio in his arms, whispering instructions to him. Finally he gets a perfect take—everybody is good. Nick is exhausted by jubilant: "Print 'em all!" About twenty takes.

The shooting is interrupted, and I am left alone in the room with Claudio, who stays in his chair, working to bring the emotion down to the level he will need for the next scene. I have no urge to talk to him; he might as well be on another planet. After an hour the crew drifts back in and starts setting up to film Claudio's confession. At the last minute Nick decides to try something: "I want to break a rule. When they touch him on the shoulder and walk away, zoom in slowly on that. A zoom-in not on a movement breaks a rule, but there's an emotional movement, so I think it'll work." After Claudio makes his confession, the two cops will look at each other, get up and walk out of the shot, leaving him alone in front of the camera. "Just leave him there," Nick explains to them. "He's not going anywhere. Where's he going to go?" The crime to which "Marco" has confessed is infanticide, the murder of his own infant son.

The scene goes faster, in a quieter mood. After several takes Nick is satisfied, but Claudio wants to try it again. Nick gives him a piece of technical advice: "To get the last beat, you might go back and use a part of your preparation that you haven't used yet tonight, so that when you leave it's a new kind of pain." The next take is not quite audible, so Nick tells Claudio to bring it up a little and calls for one more. In spite of the rawness of the emotions evoked by the actor and the director, I have the impression that what I've been watching is a technique which has been brought to such a peak of perfection that it can dispense with the quasi-religious aura which surrounded the Method when people first started using it in the forties and fifties. As the crew is packing up to go home, Nick comments to the little group that has been watching: "In my early days as a director I thought it was uncouth, and a violation of the Method, to say 'Louder.' I had to go circuitously through motivation and so on to avoid saying 'More voice.' Those were the days of the Swami. . . ."

It took several weeks, and a third chance encounter in a newsstand on Lexington Avenue, before Nick finally succumbed to a combination of harassment and moral blackmail on my part and graciously accorded me a brief interview. Our conversation took place in Ray's Famous Pizza Parlor (no relation), which in my opinion makes the best pizza in New York City; fans of "supplemental information" should note that Ray's juke-box, which is also the best in New York, was playing "When I'm Sixty-Four" as we sat down to talk. During the intervening weeks I had heard from people in the business that Nick was getting ready to make his first commercial feature in fifteen years—a note in *Take One* informs me that the title of the film will be *The Sea Horse*. But on the day of the interview, Nick was not very forthcoming about his new project.

Nick Ray Interview

Q. Could you tell us something about what you're doing these days?

A. No, I don't want to talk about it. I've been writing the new script, and we plan to go into production in June or July. In the meantime I'm taking a little holiday from that and going out to play a part in *Hair*, a very small part.

Q. A wizard?

A. No, a general. I kind of like to do acting once in a while, to see if what I'm teaching other actors to do still works for me, you know. And it works out well.

Q. I saw a Wenders film last night. . . .

A. Which one?

Q. *Goalie*.

A. It's a good film.

Q. I wondered if his working methods were in any way related to what I saw you teaching.

A. Well, he does some of the stuff instinctually which I do, and . . . while one may be trained in Method, nevertheless not all the actors you work with are trained in Method, and you have to use entirely different vocabulary and techniques with them.

Q. I heard that Robert Mitchum hated the Method, but you made a very good picture with him.

A. Yeah, but he doesn't know what he's hating. It was just fashionable to say that. When I went to Hollywood, if you mentioned Method or improvisation, they'd think you were artsy-fartsy from. . . .

Q. From New York. . . .

A. From New York, and that included Mitchum. But without his knowing it, just by using different terms than "improvisation," terms like "we'll ad-lib this one, or "we'll play around with it and see what comes," or whatever, you're using the same technique, without using the language.

Q. I had the impression watching *Goalie* that some of the things I'd been reading about Stanislavski, he was using, but reduced to the bare bones—just the objects, just the line of development of a part from one object to another, but it had a real inner intensity.

A. It does have, and Wim has a very intense inner emotional and intellectual life. He's a very bright man. But you mustn't forget that the Stanislavski method evolved out of Stanislavski's observance of all the great actors and directors of his time. He went back-stage to find out what they were doing. All of the elements of the Method existed before Stanislavski.

Q. Are you going to be shooting here?

A. I'll be shooting here and in Ohio and Canada. Very briefly in Canada. Maybe a little bit in Georgia, a little bit in Florida.

Q. Can we talk about *We Can't Go Home Again*? I saw a little bit of it in a public screening a few years ago, and I've never forgotten it.

A. Quite a few people keep asking me about it, but it's . . . I've just never finished it. I ran out of money. It's all intact, I still have it. Someday I'll get around to it.

Q. Did that develop out of the Chicago Seven film you were working on?

A. It developed out of my work at Harpur's. But that was very close to the Chicago experience, so it was still in the consciousness of the students at Harpur's. So they all kind of blended together—I used the footage of what I shot in Chicago as well.

Q. Were you shooting public events in Chicago during the trial?

A. Yes.

Q. But that's not the film that was screened a few years ago at the Cinémathèque as *Wet Dreams*.

A. No.

Q. I'd sort of like to find out where all these things are in time. . . .

A. That's a short one I made in Amsterdam in just a couple of days, right after I'd taken *We Can't Go Home Again* to Cannes film festival. My film got lost—lost or stolen.

Q. Did Godard see *We Can't Go Home Again* at Cannes? Did you talk to him about it?

A. I didn't talk to him about it, but he obviously has seen some of my work in multiple image, and I know he'd seen some stuff I did in England a long time ago, my first work in that.

Q. When did you get interested in multiple-image?

A. I've always been interested in it, but then I determined to experiment: I was living on an island in the North Sea. I know Jean-Luc saw it because I was using his cameraman.

Q. What was the subject of that one?

A. High-school students. . . . A couple of private-school students who come into Paris at the time of the riots.

Q. '68? How many screens?

A. Just a couple—I never finished it.

Q. What's the dramatic function of having action going on in different areas of the screen? You don't even need to have multiple screens to do that, of course—you can divide the image up in other ways.

A. That's supplemental information which is peripheral to our thinking very often. Our thinking is not just pure straight-line thinking. There are other associations which are going on at the same time, and it helps fulfill that. Very often I use just a certain color, an area of the screen just in color that has no story significance, but it supplements my feeling about what the feeling is.

Q. I remember a sequence where you're working with an actress, and she's telling a sort of Baudelarian story about how she deliberately contracted a venereal disease, and you're smoothing your hair and munching on a tomato or something. And at the same time things are going on here and here and here—I don't even remember what they were because I was focused on the central story.

A. Right—but it doesn't make any difference whether you can see it—it helps the composite impression.

Q. And then you throw the tomato at her, and the screen goes to opticals. Was that a judgment on the performance or on the philosophy?

A. It was an interpretation of how she expected society to treat her. And so my comment was on the person who would scorn, and don't you realize you're setting yourself up to be spit on.

Q. Have you seen any of Godard's work with multiple screens?

A. No, I've just heard about it.

Q. Did you see *Ici et ailleurs* down at the Bleecker?

A. Oh yes I did. I thought it was dull as hell. Pedantic. He didn't really understand what I was doing.

Q. He was using it for a didactic purpose.

A. And if it's dull it's not good teaching.

Q. He's been influenced by Brecht's theories of acting—for example, that the actors should do what you call "indicating. . . ."

A. I worked with Brecht! He was a very complete man—he was just so fucking complicated that people misinterpret him.

Q. You do acknowledge an interest in teaching in your own films, though.

A. Yes—but I leave it open for anybody else to draw their own conclusions.

Q. That came up in an interview, and I thought it was strange you'd say the only content of those films was the emotional experience.

A. I didn't say that.

Q. "A heightened sense of being."

A. A heightened sense of being—that's the function of the director to provide to an audience. Now that certainly embraces learning, disclosure, illumination, insight—that's all included in the heightened sense of being. Heightened experience—that doesn't mean a strictly emotional experience, because what's going to trigger the emotion can be intellectual. It can be physical. It can be spiritual.

Q. A lot of European directors renounced drama in their films at a certain point—Godard is just one of them.

A. Godard is also fading off the earth! I have great love for Jean-Luc. I'd just wish he'd stop denying himself the pleasure of making a film. His essays bore me.

Q. You've been working with my generation a lot in the last few years—you've been teaching. What do you make of us?

A. Well my interest is there—I wouldn't be devoting my time to it if I didn't think there was hope. But the conformity and the achievement syndrome is very disturbing to me. And I think it's settling for less. I think the material gain world has begun to mean everything. And I think it's bullshit.

Q. Did you like the people you were working with in Chicago—Jerry Rubin and so on? That was the other direction.

A. That isn't the other direction—I think he's a charlatan. But he was making the best of what he had, and I think he's somewhat better informed than most of the people of this generation.

Q. You're already talking about the generation after mine. . . .

A. Right. The illiteracy is astounding. The lack of knowledge, the restricted areas of information—isn't it shocking?

Q. Maybe it has to do with what we did in the sixties—the idea of tearing everything down.

A. Well it seems to be a reaction against it. The achievement thing is certainly that. But you see, people interpret the need for spontaneity, which is essential in art, as the need to "do things my way." And the privilege of not being prepared, and not knowing a goddam thing. Not learning how to use the tools that are available to you.

Q. Isn't it possible that some of the anti-intellectualism you're talking about came out of the Method, and the impact that had?

A. Oh, no—if it came out, it came out as a misinterpretation, because you take Lee Strasberg—he's one of the most knowledgeable people I know. And every actor or theater person that

I know of my generation is pretty fucking well-grounded, not only in the arts, but in politics and sociology as well. And all of the arts combined. . . . Shit, man, you know we would start our day at nine o'clock in the morning with body-movements, dance, and if we had ten cents for subway fare, we'd spend our lunch at a museum. And steal, beg, borrow, and get ways to concerts. And be constantly reading, and being involved in the events of the day. And then into working in our exercises, in our Method: training, training, training. It's certainly not out of. . . . Maybe out of the drop-outs who wanted to prove they were right.

Q. And the best people, the encounter groups.

A. That came a little later.

Q. So much of that looks to me like a parody of acting exercises.

A. Yeah, a lot of it does, doesn't it?

Q. You seem more interested now in the story-telling art again in its traditional forms. The picture I saw you making at the Institute had a story, and it was centered on the actor. Did you get away from that when you were experimenting in the sixties and seventies?

A. No, I always have a strong narrative line. However, if you take a film like *Rebel Without a Cause*, there is no story, there is no plot. There's not a convention. I don't make any rules like that, because the material, the content determines the form.

Q. I was thinking of the contrast with something like *We Can't Go Home Again*, where the form is very fragmented.

A. But there's a story-line.

Q. The director and the students.

A. And disintegration.

Q. And betrayal—do you feel that those kids were betrayed?

A. I think it was a mutual betrayal. You see, I don't care much for my generation. I think my generation flaked out. And even now I only care to associate with a very few people—Houseman, Kazan, a few scientists. . . . I gotta go.

Q. One more question. Jean-Louis Commoli wrote a number of years ago that when you made *55 Days at Peking*, and finally packed your bags and left, you had divorced your art to begin your life. Is that accurate? I have the impression that you've been doing a lot of interesting work. . . .

A. I have, and I've ventured into areas that I wanted to. It's been very costly to me, because of. . . . What the hell do you say to something like that?

Q. So the work hasn't suffered?

A. Well, the quantitative product has, and I regret or resent that. And I dislike the whole *55 Days* experience. But I knew that I was getting ready, and that I would need the money to. . . . I was getting ready for perhaps the most creative part of my life, and it was good; but that I regret.

Nicholas Ray: Chronological Filmography

They Live by Night (RKO Radio Pictures, 1948)
Knock on Any Door (Santana Productions/Columbia Pictures, 1949)
A Woman's Secret (RKO Radio Pictures, 1949)
Born to Be Bad (RKO Radio Pictures, 1950)
In a Lonely Place (Santana Productions/Columbia Pictures, 1950)
Flying Leathernecks (RKO Radio Pictures, 1951)
On Dangerous Ground (RKO Radio Pictures, 1952)
The Lusty Men (Wald-Krasna Productions/RKO Radio Pictures, 1952)
Johnny Guitar (Republic Pictures, 1954)
"High Green Wall," from *General Electric Theater* (Revue Productions/Columbia Broadcasting System, 1954)
Run for Cover (Paramount Pictures, 1955)
Rebel Without a Cause (Warner Bros., 1955)
Hot Blood (Howard Welsch Productions/Columbia Pictures, 1956)
Bigger Than Life (Twentieth Century-Fox, 1956)
The True Story of Jesse James (Twentieth Century-Fox, 1957)
Bitter Victory (Transcontinental Films/Robert Laffont Productions/Columbia Pictures, 1957)
Wind Across the Everglades (Schulberg Productions/Warner Bros., 1958)
Party Girl (Metro-Goldwyn-Mayer, 1958)
The Savage Innocents (Gray Films/Joseph Janni-Appia Films/Magic Film/Play Art/Société Nouvelle Pathé Cinéma/Paramount Pictures, 1960)
King of Kings (Samuel Bronston/Metro-Goldwyn-Mayer, 1961)
55 Days at Peking (Samuel Bronston/Metro-Goldwyn-Mayer, 1963)
"The Janitor," from *Wet Dreams* (Cinereal Film/Film Group One/P. Greulich and H. Freitag, 1974)

Marco (filmed at the Lee Strasberg Institute, 1978)
Lightning Over Water, co-directed with Wim Wenders (Road Movies Film Produktion/Viking Film/Wim Wenders Productions; 1980)
We Can't Go Home Again (filmed at the State University of New York at Binghamton; completed, restored, and reconstructed by Susan Ray, 2011)

Works Cited

Allan, Blaine, ed. *Nicholas Ray: A Guide to References and Resources*. Boston: Hall, 1984.
Allen, Michael. *Rodeo Cowboys in the North American Imagination*. Reno: U of Nevada P, 1998.
Anderson, Christopher. "Jesse James, the Bourgeois Bandit: The Transformation of a Popular Hero." *Cinema Journal* 26.2 (1986): 43–64.
Andrew, Geoff. *The Films of Nicholas Ray: The Poet of Nightfall*. London: BFI, 2004.
Anthologie Du Cinéma 11. Paris: L'Avant-scène, 1983: 233.
Archer, Eugene. "Hollywood and the Bible." *Show* 4.11 (Dec. 1964): 30–36; 98–100.
Arthur, Paul. *A Line of Sight: American Avant-Garde Film since 1965*. Minneapolis: U of Minnesota P, 2005.
Atkinson, Brooks. "The Play: WPA Journalism." *New York Times* 25 July 1936: 16.
Atkinson, Michael. "Crossing the Frontiers." *Sight and Sound* 4.1 (1994): 14–18.
Attwood, William. "The American Male: Why Does He Work So Hard?" *Look* 4 Mar. 1958: 71–74.
Audiberti, Jacques. "Billet VII." *Cahiers du Cinéma* 46 (Apr. 1955): 25–29.
"Baltimore." *Boxoffice* 1 Jan. 1962: E-4.
Barr, Charles. "CinemaScope: Before and After." *Film Quarterly* 16.4 (Summer 1963): 4–25.
Barth, Ramona. "What's Wrong with American Men?" *Reader's Digest* Nov. 1949: 23–25.
Bazin, André. "*Le Cinémascope sauvera-t-il le cinéma*." *Esprit* 12.10–11 (Oct.–Nov. 1953): 672–83.
Bedford, John. *Delftware*. New York: Walker, 1966.
Belton, John. *Widescreen Cinema*. Cambridge: Harvard UP, 1992.
Belton, John, Sheldon Hall, and Stephen Neale. *Widescreen Worldwide*. Bloomington: Indiana UP, 2010.
Bergala, Alain. *Godard au travail. Les années 60*. Paris: Editions Cahiers du Cinéma, 2006.

Bigger Than Life, dir. Nicholas Ray. Advertisement. *Variety* 1 Aug. 1956: 17.
Bitsch, Charles. "Interview with Nicholas Ray." Trans. Liz Heron. *Cahiers du Cinéma, the 1950s: Neo-Realism, Hollywood, New Wave*. Ed. Jim Hillier. Cambridge, MA: Harvard UP, 1985. 120–24.
Block, Bruce. *The Visual Story: Seeing the Structure of Film, TV, and New Media*. Boston: Focal P, 2001.
Bordwell, David. "The Bounds of Difference." *The Classical Hollywood Cinema: Film Style and Mode of Production to 1960*. New York: Columbia UP, 1985. 70–84.
———. *Poetics of Cinema*. New York: Routledge, 2008.
———. "Widescreen Aesthetics and *Mise-en-scène* Criticism." *Velvet Light Trap* 21 (Summer 1985): 118–25.
———. "Widescreen Processes and Stereophonic Sound." *The Classical Hollywood Cinema: Film Style and Mode of Production to 1960*. New York: Columbia UP, 1985. 358–64.
Bordwell, David, Janet Staiger, and Kristin Thompson. *The Classical Hollywood Cinema: Film Style and Mode of Production to 1960*. New York: Columbia UP, 1985.
Breu, Christopher. "Radical *Noir*: Negativity, Misogyny, and the Critique of Privatization in Dorothy Hughes's *In a Lonely Place*. *MFS Modern Fiction Studies* 55:2 (Summer 2009): 199–215.
Broderick, Mick. "Armageddon without a Cause: Playing 'Chicken' in the Atomic Age." *Rebel Without a Cause: Approaches to a Maverick Masterwork*. Ed. J. David Slocum. Albany: State U of New York P, 2005. 149–70.
"Bronston Decides on *King of Kings* Title." *Hollywood Reporter* 26 Jan. 1960, miscellaneous clipping, MS 104/6/11. John Villiers Farrow Papers. American Catholic University Archives, Washington, DC.
Browne, Nick. "The Spectator-in-the-Text: The Rhetoric of *Stagecoach*." *Movies and Methods*. Vol. 2. Ed. Bill Nichols. Berkeley: U of California P, 1985. 458–75.
Cagle, Chris. "Two Modes of Prestige Film." *Screen* 48.3 (2007): 291–311.
"Calif. Women's Clubs Vote Honors to *King of Kings*." *Boxoffice* 16 Apr. 1962: SE–1.
Cameron, Kate. "*King of Kings* Is Reverent Biblical Film." *New York News* 12 Oct. 1961, clipping, *King of Kings* file. Pacific Film Archive, Berkeley, CA.
Camus, Albert. *The Myth of Sisyphus*. New York: Knopf, 1961.
Campbell, Neil. *Post-Westerns*. Lincoln: U of Nebraska P, forthcoming.
"Censorship Regarded as Parental Duty." *Boxoffice* 27 Nov. 1961: ME–4.
Charney, Leo. "Historical Excess: *Johnny Guitar*'s Containment." *Cinema Journal* 29.4 (Summer 1990): 23–34.
"Cleric vs. Cleric in re *Kings*." *Variety* 8 Nov. 1961: 5.
Coe, Richard L. "Dopey Hyde and Jekyll." Rev. of *Bigger Than Life*, dir. Nicholas Ray. *Washington Post* 22 Sept. 1956: 63.
———. "Life Is Rugged on Rodeo Circuit." Rev. of *The Lusty Men*, dir. Nicholas Ray. *Washington Post* 6 Nov. 1952: 29.

Comolli, Jean-Luc, and Jean Narborni. "Cinema/Ideology/Criticism." *Film Theory and Criticism.* Ed. Leo Braudy and Marshall Cohen. 7th ed. Oxford: Oxford UP, 2009, 686–93.

Corber, Robert J. *Cold War Femme: Lesbianism, National Identity, and Hollywood Cinema.* Durham, NC: Duke UP, 2011.

Cossar, Harper. *Letterboxed: The Evolution of Widescreen Cinema.* Lexington: UP of Kentucky, 2010.

Crowther, Bosley. "The Good Book Is a Great Script." *New York Times* 31 Dec. 1961: SM10.

———. "*Lusty Men,* Tale of Rodeo Riders with Robert Mitchum, Makes Debut at Criterion." Rev. of *The Lusty Men,* dir. Nicholas Ray. *New York Times* 25 Oct. 1952: 12.

———. "Screen: The Everglades: Schulbergs' Film Has Debut at Mayfair." Rev. of *Wind Across the Everglades,* dir. Nicholas Ray. *New York Times* 12 Sept. 1958: 21.

———. "Screen: Tax of Tedium: *Bigger Than Life* Has Debut at Victoria." Rev. of *Bigger Than Life,* dir. Nicholas Ray. *New York Times* 3 Aug. 1956: 11.

———. "The Screen: Three Films Make Their Bows." Rev. of *In a Lonely Place,* dir. Nicholas Ray. *New York Times* 18 May 1950: 46.

———. "The Screen in Review: Humphrey Bogart, John Derek Seen in *Knock on Any Door,* New Tenant at Astor." Rev. of *Knock on Any Door,* dir. Nicholas Ray. *New York Times* 23 Feb. 1949: 31.

———. "The Screen in Review: *Johnny Guitar* Opens at the Mayfair." Rev. of *Johnny Guitar,* dir. Nicholas Ray. *New York Times* 28 May 1954: 19.

———. "The Screen in Review: *On Dangerous Ground,* Story of Detective Turned Sadist, Opens at the Criterion." Rev. of *On Dangerous Ground,* dir. Nicholas Ray. *New York Times* 13 Feb. 1952: 35.

Cumings, Bruce. *The Origins of the Korean War: Liberation and the Emergence of Separate Regimes, 1945–1947.* Princeton, NJ: Princeton UP, 1981.

Dalton, David. *James Dean: The Mutant King.* Chicago: A Cappella, 2001.

Davidson, Michael. *Guys Like Us: Citing Masculinity in Cold War Poetics.* Chicago: U of Chicago P, 2004.

Davis, Evan. "Sly Precursors to Gay Liberation: *Born to Be Bad.*" Mubi.com, 27 July 2009: <http://mubi.com/notebook/posts/851>.

Deleuze, Gilles. *Cinema 1: The Movement-Image.* Trans. Hugh Tomlinson and Barbara Habberjam. London: Continuum, 2005.

Derrida, Jacques. *The Gift of Death.* Trans. David Wills. Chicago: U of Chicago P, 1995.

Deutelbaum, Marshall. "Basic Principles of Anamorphic Composition." *Film History* 15 (2003): 72–80.

Dickstein, Morris. "Besieged: The 1950s at War and at Home." *Dissent Magazine,* 2 July 2010: <http://www.dissentmagazine.org/atw.php?id=197>.

Donaldson, Sarah. "Filmmakers on Film: Neil Jordan." *Daily Telegraph* 22 Feb. 2003: 10.

Dyer, Richard. "Postscript: Queers and Women in *Film Noir*." *Women in Film Noir*. Ed. E. Ann Kaplan. New ed. London: BFI, 1998. 123–29.

Eisenschitz, Bernard. *Nicholas Ray: An American Journey*. Trans. Tom Milne. London: Faber and Faber, 1993.

Elsaesser, Thomas. "Tales of Sound and Fury: Observations on the Family Melodrama." *Home Is Where the Heart Is: Studies in Melodrama and the Woman's Film*. Ed. Christine Gledhill. London: BFI, 1987. 2–15.

Enticknap, Leo. *Moving Image Technology*. London: Wallflower P, 2005.

"Epitaph for an Epic." Christian Century 1 Nov. 1961: 1302–03.

Erice, Victor, and Jos Oliver, eds. *Nicholas Ray y su tiempo*. Madrid: Filmoteca Española/Instituto de la Cinematografia y las Artes Audiovisuales, 1986.

Eyles, Allan. *John Wayne and the Movies*. London: Tantivy P, 1976.

Farrow, John. Letter to Harry Cohn. n.d. MS 104/6/15. John Villiers Farrow Papers. American Catholic University Archives, Washington, DC.

Filene, Benjamin. *Romancing the Folk: Public Memory and American Roots Music*. Chapel Hill: U of North Carolina P, 2000.

"Film Classification Step to Censorship." *Boxoffice* 21 Jan. 1963: ME-2.

Flanagan, Hallie. *Arena: The History of the Federal Theatre*. New York: Duell, Sloan and Pearce, 1940.

Frascella, Larry, and Al Weisel. *Live Fast, Die Young: The Wild Ride of Making Rebel Without a Cause*. New York: Simon and Schuster, 2005.

Funderburg, Christopher. "Nicholas Ray." Thepinksmoke.com, <http://thepinksmoke.com/nicholasray12.htm>.

Gallagher, Cullen. "Not Coming to a Theater Near You: *A Woman's Secret*." Notcoming.com, 18 Aug. 2008, <http://www.notcoming.com/reviews/awomanssecret>.

———. "Not Coming to a Theater Near You: *We Can't Go Home Again*." Notcoming.com, 8 Sept. 2008. <http://www.notcoming.com/reviews/wecantgohomeagain>.

Genter, Robert. "'We All Go a Little Mad Sometimes': Alfred Hitchcock, American Psychoanalysis, and the Construction of the Cold War Psychopath." *Canadian Review of American Studies*. 40.2 (2010): 133–162.

Gledhill, Christine, ed. *Home Is Where the Heart Is: Studies in Melodrama and the Woman's Film*. London: BFI, 1987.

———. "Introduction." *Home Is Where the Heart Is: Studies in Melodrama and the Woman's Film*. Ed. Christine Gledhill. London: BFI, 1987. 1–4.

Godard, Jean-Luc. "Beyond the Stars." Trans. Tom Milne. *Cahiers du Cinéma, the 1950s: Neo-Realism, Hollywood, New Wave*. Ed. Jim Hillier. Cambridge, MA: Harvard UP, 1985. 118–19.

———. *Godard on Godard*. London: Secker and Warburg, 1972.

Goodwin, Michael, and Naomi Wise. "Nicholas Ray, Rebel!" *Take One* 5 (Jan. 1977): 7–21.

Gottheim, Larry. "Bigger than Life: Between Ken Jacobs and Nicholas Ray." *Optic Antics: The Cinema of Ken Jacobs*. Ed. Michele Pierson, David E. James, and Paul Arthur. Oxford: Oxford UP, 2011. 89–95.

"Green Sheet Lists 5 Films in Family Class." *Boxoffice* 25 Dec. 1961: 5.
Guarner, Jose Luis. "Rey De Reyes, De Nicholas Ray." *Film Ideal* (Madrid, Spain) 89.1 (1962): 85–87.
Guralnick, Peter. *Last Train to Memphis: The Rise of Elvis Presley*. New York: Little, Brown, 1994.
———. *Lost Highway: Journeys and Arrivals of American Musicians*. Boston: Goldine, 1979.
Halberstam, David. *The Coldest Winter: America and the Korean War*. New York: Hyperion, 2007.
Hall, Stuart. "When Was the Postcolonial: Thinking at the Limit." *The Post-Colonial Question: Common Skies, Divided Horizons*. Ed. Iain Chambers and Lidia Curti. London: Routledge, 1996. 242–59.
Halliday, Jon. *Sirk on Sirk: Conversations with Jon Halliday*. London: Faber and Faber, 1997.
Hartung, Philip T. "The Screen: The Malady Lingers On." Rev. of *Bigger Than Life*, dir. Nicholas Ray. *Commonweal* 64 (Aug. 1956): 466–67.
Harvey, James. *Movie Love in the Fifties*. New York: Knopf, 2001.
Harvey, Stephen. "The Road Movie: Versatile Vehicle for a Portrait of Society." *New York Times* 22 June 1980: 17.1.
Harvey, Sylvia. "Woman's Place: The Absent Family of Film Noir." *Women in Film Noir*. Ed. E. Ann Kaplan. New ed. London: BFI, 1998. 35–46.
Higham, Charles, and Joel Greenberg. *The Celluloid Muse*. London: Angus and Robertson, 1969.
Hill, John. "The British 'Social Problem' Film: *Violent Playground* and *Sapphire*." *Screen* 26:1 (2002): 1–26.
Hillier, Jim, ed. *Cahiers du Cinéma, the 1950s: Neo-Realism, Hollywood, New Wave*. Cambridge, MA: Harvard UP, 1985.
———. *Cahiers du Cinéma, the 1960s: New Wave, New Cinema, Reevaluating Hollywood*. Cambridge, MA: Harvard UP, 1986.
Hilton, Boyd. *The Age of Atonement*. Oxford: Clarendon P, 1991.
Hincha, Richard. "Selling CinemaScope: 1953–1956." *Velvet Light Trap* 21 (Summer 1985): 44–53.
Houseman, John. *Front and Center*. New York: Simon and Schuster, 1979.
———. *Unfinished Business: A Memoir*. London: Chatto and Windus, 1986.
Hoveyda, Fereydoun. "Nicholas Ray's Reply: *Party Girl*." *Cahiers du Cinéma, the 1960s: New Wave, New Cinema, Reevaluating Hollywood*. Ed. Jim Hillier. Cambridge, MA: Harvard UP, 1986. 122–31.
"In Defense of a Film." *New York Times* 12 Nov. 1961: 69.
"Jesuit Weekly's Rap." *Weekly Variety* 18 Oct. 1961: 24.
Johnson, Erskine. "Actor Disappointed in *King of Kings* Role." *Times Daily* 2 Dec. 1961: 4.
———. "Filming of *King of Kings* Has Story Inside the Story." *Florence Times* 26 Nov. 1962: 5.
———. "Jeffrey Hunter Gets Big Chance in Role of Christ." *Ocala Star-Banner* 22 Aug. 1960: 3.

Kaplan, E. Ann, ed. *Women in Film Noir*. Ed. E. Ann Kaplan. New ed. London: BFI, 1998.
Kaplan, Leonard V., and Charles Lloyd Cohen. *Theology and the Soul of the Liberal State*. Lanham, MD: Lexington Books, 2010.
Kazan, Elia. *Elia Kazan: A Life*. New York: Knopf, 1998.
Kemp, Philip. "Ray, Nicholas." *The St. James Film Directors Encyclopedia*. Ed. Andrew Sarris. Detroit, MI: Visible Ink Press, 1998. 402–04.
Kilgallen, Dorothy. "The Trouble with Men." *Nation's Business* 39.7 (July 1951): 30–32; 68–69.
"*King of Kings.*" *Filmfacts* 4 (10 Nov. 1961): 251–54.
"*King of Kings* in Catholic Italy." *Variety* 8 Nov. 1961: 5.
Kirgo, Julie, and Alain Silver. "*In a Lonely Place.*" *Film Noir: An Encyclopedic Reference to the American Style*. Ed. Alain Silver and Elizabeth Ward. 3rd ed. Woodstock, NY: Overlook P, 1992. 145.
Klinger, Barbara. "'Cinema/Ideology/Criticism' Revisited: The Progressive Genre." *Film Genre Reader III*. Ed. Barry Keith Grant. Austin: U of Texas P, 1986, 1995, 2003. 75–91.
Knight, Arthur. "SR Goes to the Movies: It's Controversial." Rev. of *Bigger Than Life*, dir. Nicholas Ray. *Saturday Review* 39 (28 July 1956): 24.
Komar, George. "*King of Kings*: Rediscovering the Film and the Score." *Film Score Monthly*. 2009. <http://www.filmscoremonthly.com/notes/king_of_kings2.html>.
Kouvaros, George. *Famous Faces Not Yet Themselves: The Misfits and Icons of Postwar America*. Minneapolis: U of Minnesota P, 2010.
Kreidl, John Francis. *Nicholas Ray*. Boston: Twayne, 1977.
Krutnik, Frank. "'A Living Part of the Class Struggle': Diego Rivera's *The Flower Carrier* and the Hollywood Left." *"Un-American" Hollywood: Politics and Film in the Blacklist Era*. Ed. Frank Krutnik, Steve Neale, Brian Neve, and Peter Stanfield. New Brunswick, NJ: Rutgers UP, 2007. 51–78.
Laderman, David. "What a Trip: The Road Film and American Culture." *Journal of Film and Video* 48.1–2 (1996): 41–57.
Lambert, Gavin. *Natalie Wood: A Life*. New York: Knopf, 2004.
Lederer, Joseph. "Film as Experience: Nicholas Ray—The Director Turns Teacher." *American Film* 1.2 (Nov. 1975): 60–64.
Leonard, George B., Jr. "The American Male: Why Is He Afraid to Be Different?" *Look* 4 Feb. 1958: 95–104.
"Liked the Book Better than Pic." *Weekly Variety* 18 Oct. 1961: 5.
Limbacher, James. *Four Aspects of the Film*. New York: Arno, 1978.
Loftin, Clinton Scott. "Seeing the Past: Jesse James and American History in Motion Pictures." Thesis. U of Maine, 2000.
Lomax, John A., and Alan Lomax. *Our Singing Country: A Second Volume of American Ballads and Folk Songs*. New York: Macmillan, 1941.
Lowry, Robert. "Is This the Beat Generation?" *American Mercury* Jan. 1953: 16–20.
Luft, Hubert G. "The Jewish Year in Hollywood." *Canadian Jewish Chronicle* 28 Sept. 1962: 67–71.

Lüscher, Max. *The Lüscher Colour Test*. Trans. and ed. Ian A. Scott. London: Cape, 1967.
Lutz, Tom. "Men's Tears and the Roles of Melodrama." *Boys Don't Cry: Rethinking Narratives of Masculinity and Emotion in the U.S.* Ed. Milette Shamir and Jennifer Travis. New York: Columbia UP, 2002. 185–204.
Luz, Ulrich, et al. *Matthew: A Commentary*. Minneapolis: Augsburg, 1989.
Lyon, Christopher. "'A Unique Loneliness': The Existential Impulse in Art of the Forties." *MoMA* 6 (1991): 3–7, 20.
Maland, Charles J. "*Film Gris*: Crime, Critique, and Cold War Culture in 1951." *Film Criticism* 23 (Spring 2002): 1–26.
———. "The Social Problem Film." *Handbook of American Film Genres*. Ed. Was D. Gehring. New York: Greenwood, 1988. 305–30.
Malmquist, Carl P., and Paul E. Meehl. "Barabbas: A Study in Guilt-Ridden Homicide." *International Review of Psycho-Analysis* 5 (1978): 149–74.
Marcus, Greil. *Mystery Train: Images of America in Rock 'n' Roll Music*. New York: Plume, 1987.
Masson, Alain. "*Un passé Romanesque: Sur huit films Américains inédits*." *Positif* 228 (Mar. 1980): 26–32.
May, John R. *New Image of Religious Film* Kansas City, MO: Sheed and Ward, 1997.
McAlister, Melani. *Epic Encounters*. Berkeley: U of California P, 2001.
McArthur, Colin. *Underworld U.S.A.* London: Secker and Warburg, 1972.
McCarten, John. "The Current Cinema: Kill or Be Killed." Rev. *Johnny Guitar*, dir. Nicholas Ray. *New Yorker* 5 Jun. 1954: 62–63.
———. "The Current Cinema: So Sad, So Sad." Rev. of *Bigger Than Life*, dir. Nicholas Ray. *New Yorker* 11 Aug. 1956: 50.
McGilligan, Patrick. *Nicholas Ray: The Glorious Failure of an American Director*. New York: HarperCollins, 2011.
McNiven, Roger D. "The Middle-Class American Home of the Fifties: The Use of Architecture in Nicholas Ray's *Bigger Than Life* and Douglas Sirk's *All That Heaven Allows*." *Cinema Journal* 22.4 (Summer 1983): 38–57.
Medovoi, Leerom. *Rebels: Youth and the Cold War Origins of Identity*. Durham, NC: Duke UP, 2005.
Melley, Timothy. "Agency Panic and the Culture of Conspiracy." *Conspiracy Nation: The Politics of Paranoia in Post-War America*. Ed. Peter Knight. New York: New York UP, 2001. 57–81.
Michaud, Michael Gregg. *Sal Mineo: A Biography*. New York: Crown Archetype, 2010.
Mitry, Jean. *Esthétique et psychologie du cinéma*. Vol. II. Paris: Éditions Universitaires, 1965.
Moskin, J. Robert. "The American Male: Why Do Women Dominate Him?" *Look* 18 Feb. 1958: 77–80.
Mosley, Leonard. "British Writer Describes *King of Kings* as Flop." *Albuquerque Tribune* 24 Nov. 1961: D2.
"Movie on Christ Stirs up Storm; Responses Varied." *Lawrence Daily Journal-World* 20 Feb. 1962: 11.

Muir, Florabel. "Florabel Muir Reporting." *Los Angeles Examiner* 28 Jul. 1950, miscellaneous clipping, MS 104/6/10. John Villiers Farrow Papers. American Catholic University Archives, Washington, DC.

Neale, Steve. *Genre and Hollywood*. New York: Routledge, 2000.

Neville, John F. *The Press, the Rosenbergs, and the Cold War*. Westport, CT: Praeger, 1995.

"New Films." *Newsweek* 10 Nov. 1952: 108–09.

"New York Sound Track." *Weekly Variety* 4 Jun. 1958: 7.

Nogueira, Rui, and Nicoletta Zalaffi. "*Recontre avec* Robert Ryan." *Cinema 70* (1970): 145.

Notes re: *The Son of Man*, n.d., MS 104/7/4. John Villiers Farrow Papers. American Catholic University Archives, Washington, DC.

"Of Local Origin." *New York Times* 23 Nov. 1954: 26.

Ohad-Karny, Yael. "'Anticipating' Gibson's the Passion of the Christ: The Controversy over Cecil B. DeMille's *The King of Kings*." *Jewish History* 19.2 (2005): 189–210.

O'Hara, Maureen, and John Nicoletti. *'Tis Herself: A Memoir*. New York: Simon and Schuster, 2004.

"1000 Films to See Before You Die: *The Silence of the Lambs* to *Three Colours* Trilogy." *Guardian* 29 June 1997: 7.

Palmer, James W. "*In a Lonely Place*: Paranoia and the Dream Factory." *Literature/Film Quarterly* 13.3 (1985): 200–07.

Palmer, R. Barton. *Hollywood's Dark Cinema: The American Film Noir*. Boston: Twayne, 1994.

Park, Robert E., Ernest W. Burgess, and Roderick D. McKenzie. *The City*. Introd. Morris Janowitz. Chicago: U of Chicago P, 1967.

Patterson, James T. *Grand Expectations: The United States, 1945–1974*. Vol. 10 of *Oxford History of the United States*. New York: Oxford UP, 1996.

Perkins, V. F. "The Cinema of Nicholas Ray." *Movie Reader*. Ed. Ian Cameron. New York: Praeger, 1972. 64–70.

"Press Release," n.d., MS 104/7/6. John Villiers Farrow Papers. American Catholic University Archives, Washington, DC.

Peterson, Jennifer. "The Competing Tunes of 'Johnny Guitar': Liberalism, Sexuality, Masquerade." *Cinema Journal* 35. 3 (Spring 1996): 3–18.

Plummer, Christopher. *In Spite of Myself: A Memoir*. New York: Knopf, 2008.

Polan, Dana. *In a Lonely Place*. London: BFI, 1993.

———. "On the Bad Goodness of *Born to Be Bad*: *Auteurism*, Evaluation, and Nicholas Ray's Outsider Cinema." *Bad: Infamy, Darkness, Evil, and Slime on Screen*. Ed. Murray Pomerance. Albany: State U of New York P, 2004. 201–11.

Pomerance, Murray. *The Horse Who Drank the Sky: Film Experience beyond Narrative and Theory*. New Brunswick, NJ: Rutgers UP, 2008.

———. "Stark Performance." *Rebel Without a Cause: Approaches to a Maverick Masterwork*. Ed. J. David Slocum. Albany: State U of New York P, 2005. 35–52.

Quinn, Susan. *Furious Improvisation: How the WPA and a Cast of Thousands Made High Art Out of Desperate Times*. New York: Walker, 2008.

Rae, Norman. "Kinquering Congs." *Sunday Gleaner* 15 Apr. 1962: 16.
Rancière, Jacques. *Film Fables.* Trans. Emiliano Battista. New York: Berg, 2001.
Rathgeb, Douglas L. *The Making of* Rebel Without a Cause. Jefferson, NC: McFarland, 2004.
Ray, Anthony. *English Delftware Pottery in the Robert Hall Warren Collection, Ashmolean Museum Oxford.* London: Faber and Faber, n.d.
Ray, Nicholas. "The Blind Run" (outline), 18 Sept. 1954, Warner Bros. Archives. University of Southern California, Berkeley.
———. *I Was Interrupted: Nicholas Ray on Making Movies.* Ed. Susan Ray. Berkeley: U of California P, 1993.
———. Letter to Dr. Harold Spivack[e]. 30 Oct. 1939. American Folklore Center, Library of Congress, Washington, DC.
———. South Dakota Recordings, Mitchell, South Dakota, Oct. 1939. American Folklife Center, Library of Congress (3673–83), Washington, DC.
Ray, Susan. "Out of the Box." *Cinema Scope* 48 (Fall 2011): 21–25.
Reik, Theodor. "Der Eigene Und Der Fremde Gott." *American Imago* 25.1 (Spring 1968): 3–15.
Ried, Howard. "Portrait of an Unknown Australian." *Sydney Morning Herald* Jun. 1962, miscellaneous clipping, MS 104/6/10. John Villiers Farrow Papers. American Catholic University Archives, Washington, DC.
"Report Puzzles Farrow." *Daily Variety* 14 Oct. 1959: 15.
Riesman, David. *The Lonely Crowd.* New Haven, CT: Yale UP, 1961.
Riis, Jacob. *How the Other Half Lives: Studies among the Tenements of New York.* New York: Dover, 1971.
Rivette, Jacques. "Notes on a Revolution." Trans. Liz Heron. *Cahiers du Cinéma, the 1950s: Neo-Realism, Hollywood, New Wave.* Ed. Jim Hillier. Cambridge, MA: Harvard UP, 1985. 98–101.
———. "On Imagination." Trans. Liz Heron. *Cahiers du Cinéma, the 1950s: Neo-Realism, Hollywood, New Wave.* Ed. Jim Hillier. Cambridge, MA: Harvard UP, 1985. 104–06.
Robertson, Pamela. "Camping under Western Stars: Joan Crawford in *Johnny Guitar.*" *Journal of Film and Video* 47.1/3 (Spring-Fall 1995): 33–49.
Rodgers, Lawrence, and Jerrold Hirsch. *America's Folklorist: B. A. Botkin and American Culture.* Norman: U of Oklahoma P, 2010.
Rodowick, D. N. "Madness, Authority, and Ideology in the Domestic Melodrama of the 1950s." *Home Is Where the Heart Is: Studies in Melodrama and the Woman's Film.* Ed. Christine Gledhill. London: BFI, 1987. 268–80.
Rogin, Michael. "Kiss Me Deadly: Communism, Motherhood, and Cold War Movies." *Representations* 6 (1984): 1–36.
Rohmer, Eric. *The Taste for Beauty.* Trans. Carol Volk. Cambridge: Cambridge UP, 1989.
Rosenbaum, Jonathan. "Circle of Pain: The Cinema of Nicholas Ray." *Movies as Politics.* Berkeley: U of California P, 1997. 125–33.
———. *Essential Cinema: On the Necessity of Film Canons.* Baltimore, MD: Johns Hopkins UP, 2004.
———. "Guilty by Omission." *Film Comment* 27 (Sept.-Oct. 1991): 42–46, 50.

Roueché, Berton. "Ten Feet Tall." *New Yorker* 10 Sept. 1955: 47–77.
Royle, Nicholas. *The Uncanny*. Manchester: Manchester UP, 2003.
Salt, Barry. *Film Style and Technology: History and Analysis*. 2nd ed. London: Starwood, 1992.
Sarris, Andrew. *The American Cinema: Directors and Directions, 1929–1968*. New York: Simon and Schuster, 1973.
"Savagery in the Swamps." *Newsweek* 8 Sept. 1958: 94–95.
Schlesinger, Arthur M., Jr. *The Coming of the New Deal*. Boston: Houghton Mifflin, 1959.
———. "The Crisis of American Masculinity." *The Politics of Hope*. Cambridge, MA: Riverside, 1962. 237–246. Reprinted from *Esquire* (Nov. 1958).
Shamroy, Leon. "Filming *The Robe*." *New Screen Techniques*. Ed. Martin Quigley Jr. New York: Quigley, 1953. 177–80.
Short, James F., Jr., with Lorine A. Hughes. "Criminology, Criminologists, and the Sociological Enterprise." *Sociology in America: A History*. Ed. Craig Calhoun. Chicago: U of Chicago P, 2007. 605–38.
"Sign of the Cross." *Time* 27 Oct. 1961: 55.
Slocum, J. David, ed. Rebel Without a Cause: *Approaches to a Maverick Masterwork*. Albany: State U of New York P, 2005.
Sobchack, Vivian. *The Address of the Eye: A Phenomenology of Film Experience*. Princeton, NJ: Princeton UP, 1992.
Spear, Ivan. "King of Kings." *Boxoffice* 16 Oct. 1961: 15.
Spellerberg, James. "CinemaScope and Ideology." *Velvet Light Trap* 21 (Summer 1985): 26–34.
Spicer, Andrew. *Film Noir*. Harlow, Eng.: Longman, 2002.
Spiro, J. D. "Hollywood Canvas: Musical Version of 'Rain' Now Planned—Independent Betty Hutton—Addenda." *New York Times* 27 Jul. 1952: X5.
Staiger, Janet. "Authorship Approaches." *Authorship and Film*. Ed. David A. Gerstner and Janet Staiger. New York: Routledge, 2002. 27–57.
Stanush, Claude. "King of the Cowboys." *Life* 13 May 1946: 59–64.
Suid, Lawrence H. *Guts and Glory: The Making of the American Military Image in Film*. Rev. and exp. ed. Lexington: UP of Kentucky, 2007.
Sutherland, Edwin. "Edwin H. Sutherland: The Development of Differential Association Theory." *The Origins of American Criminology*. Ed. Francis T. Cullen et al. *Advances in Criminological Theory*. Vol. 16. New Brunswick, NJ: Transaction, 2011. 37–57.
———. *Principles of Criminology*. 4th ed. Chicago: Lippincott, 1947.
Sykes, Velma West. "*King of Kings* (MGM) Is Voted November Blue Ribbon Award." *Boxoffice* 11 Dec. 1961: 15.
Szwed, John. *Alan Lomax: The Man Who Recorded the World*. New York: Viking Penguin, 2010.
Tannenbaum, Frank. *Crime and the Community*. Boston: Ginn, 1938.
Taubman, Howard [H. H. T]. "Screen: Jesse James. Outlaw Returns in a Well-Made Movie." *New York Times* 23 Mar. 1957: 17.
Thomson, David. "The Nick Ray I Hardly Knew." *Guardian* 18 Apr. 1999: 4.
———. "Review: Arts: The Poet of Nightfall." *Guardian* 27 Dec. 2003: 16.

Tinee, Mae. "Film for Your Do Miss List: *Hot Blood.*" Rev. of *Hot Blood*, dir. Nicholas Ray. *Chicago Tribune* 29 May 1956: A4.

Truffaut, François. *The Films in My Life*. Trans. Leonard Mayhew. New York: Simon and Schuster, 1978.

———. Letter to Helen Scott, 20 Aug. 1965. *Letters*. Ed. Gilles Jacob and Claude de Givray. Trans. Gilbert Adair. London: Faber and Faber, 1989. 278–82.

———. "A Wonderful Certainty." Trans. Liz Heron. *Cahiers du Cinéma, the 1950s: Neo-Realism, Hollywood, New Wave*. Ed. Jim Hillier. Cambridge, MA: Harvard UP, 1985. 107–10.

Unidentified clipping, n.d., MS 104/6/11. John Villiers Farrow Papers. American Catholic University Archives, Washington, DC.

Vidal, Gore, and Nicholas Ray. *The Doctor and the Devils*, draft scripts (1965). Gore Vidal Collection, Houghton Library, Harvard University, Cambridge, MA.

Wald, Elijah. *How the Beatles Destroyed Rock 'n' Roll: An Alternative History of American Popular Music*. New York: Oxford UP, 2009.

Walsh, Moira. "Christ or Credit Card?" *America* 21 Oct. 1961: 71–74.

———. "*Bigger Than Life*," rev. of *Bigger Than Life*, dir. Nicholas Ray. *America* 11 Aug. 1956: 452.

Warshow, Robert. *The Immediate Experience: Movies, Comics, Theater, and Other Aspects of Popular Culture*. Enlarged ed. Cambridge, MA: Harvard UP, 2001.

Wenders, Wim. *On Film*. London: Faber and Faber, 2001.

White, Susan. "'You Want a Good Crack in the Mouth?': *Rebel Without a Cause*, Violence, and the Cinema of Nicholas Ray." *Rebel Without a Cause: Approaches to a Maverick Masterwork*. Ed. J. David Slocum: Albany: State U of New York P, 2005. 53–87.

Whyte, William Hollingsworth. *The Organization Man*. New York: Simon and Schuster, 1956.

Willemen, Paul. *Looks and Frictions: Essays in Cultural Studies and Film Theory*. London: BFI, 1994.

Williams, Linda. "Melodrama Revisited." *Refiguring American Film Genres: History and Theory*. Ed. Nick Browne. Berkeley: U of California P, 1998. 42–88.

Willis, Gary. *John Wayne's America*. New York: Touchstone, 1997.

Wilson, Colin. *The Outsider*. New York: Putnam, 1956.

Wilson, George M. "Nicholas Ray's *Rebel Without a Cause*." *Rebel Without a Cause: Approaches to a Maverick Masterwork*. Ed. J. David Slocum. Albany: State U of New York P, 2005. 109–30.

Winsten, Archer. "*King of Kings* at Loew's State." *New York Post* 12 Oct. 1961: 64.

Wood, Robin. "On *Bigger Than Life*." *Film Comment* 8.3 (Sept.-Oct. 1972): 56–61.

Works Progress Administration Central Files: State, 1935–1944. South Dakota 651.3163. Record Group 69, MLR number PC 37 12–46. National Archives, College Park, MD.

Wright, Cobina. "Society As I Find It." n.d., miscellaneous clipping, MS 104/6/10. John Villiers Farrow Papers. American Catholic University Archives, Washington, DC.

Wyke, Maria. "Projecting Ancient Rome." *The Historical Film: History and Memory in Media*. Ed. Marcia Landy. New Brunswick, NJ: Rutgers UP, 2001. 125–42.

Wylie, Philip. "The Abdicating Male and How the Gray Flannel Mind Exploits Him through His Women" *Playboy* 3.11 (Nov. 1956). 23–24, 50, 79.

———. *Generation of Vipers*. New York: Holt, Rinehart and Winston, 1955.

Zanuck, Darryl F. "CinemaScope in Production." *New Screen Techniques*. Ed. Martin Quigley Jr. New York: Quigley, 1953.

Žižek, Slavoj. *First as Tragedy, Then as Farce*. London: Verso, 2009.

Zryd, Michael. "Experimental Film and the Development of Film Study in America." *Inventing Film Studies*. Ed. Lee Grieveson and Haidee Wasson. Durham, NC: Duke UP, 2008. 182–216.

Contributors

Ria Banerjee is a doctoral candidate in English at the Graduate Center, City University of New York, with a concentration in film studies. Her areas of specialization are literary and filmic modernism, especially *film noir*. She currently teaches English and film classes at City College.

Chris Cagle is assistant professor in Temple University's Film and Media Arts Department. He has published articles on the history of the American cinema in recent edited volumes, and his article, "Two Modes of Prestige Film," was the 2006–2007 winner of the *Screen* journal award. He is currently working on a book-length study on the Hollywood social problem film.

Neil Campbell is professor of American studies and research manager at the University of Derby, UK. His major research project is an interdisciplinary trilogy of books on the contemporary American West: *The Cultures of the American New West*, *The Rhizomatic West*, and the recently published *Post-Westerns*.

Harper Cossar is Visiting Lecturer in film studies at Georgia State University. He is the author of *Letterboxed: The Evolution of Widescreen Cinema*.

James I. Deutsch is a curator at the Smithsonian Institution's Center for Folklife and Cultural Heritage, where he has helped plan programs and exhibitions on the Peace Corps, Apollo Theater, National Aeronautics and Space Administration, Mekong River, U.S. Forest Service, Silk Road, and White House workers. In addition, he serves as an adjunct professor—teaching courses on American film history—in the American Studies Department at George Washington University.

Alexander Doty (1954–2012) was professor in the Departments of Gender Studies and Communication and Culture at Indiana University–Bloomington, the latter of which he also chaired. He wrote *Making Things Perfectly Queer: Interpreting Mass Culture* and *Flaming Classics: Queering the Canon*, as well as coedited *Out in Culture: Gay, Lesbian, and Queer Essays on Popular Culture*, and edited two special "diva" issues of *Camera Obscura*.

Chris Fujiwara is the artistic director of the Edinburgh International Film Festival, the author of *Jerry Lewis*, *The World and Its Double: The Life and Work of Otto Preminger*, and *Jacques Tourneur: The Cinema of Nightfall*, and the editor of *Defining Moments in Movies*. He is also the editor of *Undercurrent*, an online magazine of film criticism. He has taught and lectured on cinema at Tokyo University, Yale University, and elsewhere.

Paul Anthony Johnson is a Ph.D. candidate in the English Department at the University of Florida. He is currently completing a dissertation that analyzes the performances of Charlie Chaplin and Louis Armstrong.

Bill Krohn has been the Hollywood correspondent of *Cahiers du Cinéma* for more than twenty years.

Robin A. Larsen is professor emeritus of communication studies at California State University–San Bernardino. She has published on early cinema and censorship in the pre-Code era, and is the recent recipient of a Fulbright scholarship to teach in Poland in 2001, where she returned in 2009 to conduct interviews with Polish women filmmakers.

Adrian Martin, associate professor, teaches in film and television studies, and is codirector of the Research Unit in Film Culture and Theory, Monash University (Australia). He has authored six books, hundreds of essays, and thousands of reviews since 1979. He is the coeditor of the online film magazine *LOLA*.

Joe McElhaney is a professor in the Department of Film and Media Studies at Hunter College and in the Theatre Program at the City University of New York Graduate Center. His books include *The Death of Classical Cinema: Hitchcock, Lang, Minnelli*; *Vincente Minnelli: The Art of Entertainment*; *Albert Maysles*; and the forthcoming *A Companion to Fritz Lang*. His essays have appeared in numerous collections and journals.

Jason McKahan is an assistant professor in communication and new media at Shepherd University. He received his Ph.D. in mass communications from Florida State University in Tallahassee, Florida. He is currently area head of digital filmmaking at Shepherd University and finishing a manuscript on political and religious protest and violence in Hollywood action films.

R. Barton Palmer is Calhoun Lemon Professor of Literature and director of Film Studies at Clemson University. He is the author, editor, or coeditor of more than forty volumes on various literary and cinematic subjects.

Murray Pomerance is professor in the Department of Sociology at Ryerson University and the author, editor, or coeditor of more than two dozen books, including *Alfred Hitchcock's America*; *The Eyes Have It: Cinema and the Reality Effect*; *Michelangelo Red Antonioni Blue: Eight Reflections on Cinema*; *The Horse Who Drank the Sky: Film Experience Beyond Narrative and Theory*; *Johnny Depp Starts Here*; *An Eye for Hitchcock*; *The Last Laugh: Strange Humors of Cinema*; and *Cinema and Modernity*. He is editor of the "Horizons of Cinema" series at SUNY Press and the "Techniques of the Moving Image" series at Rutgers University Press, and with Lester D. Friedman and Adrienne L. McLean, respectively, coeditor of the "Screen Decades" and "Star Decades" series at Rutgers.

Jonathan Rosenbaum, former film critic for the *Chicago Reader*, is the author of numerous books on film, including most recently, *Discovering Orson Welles* and *Goodbye Cinema, Hello Cinephilia: Film Culture in Transition*. He currently writes at jonathanrosenbaum.net.

Steven Rybin is an assistant professor of film at Georgia Gwinnett College. He is the author of *Michael Mann: Crime Auteur* and *Terrence Malick and the Thought of Film*. He is currently writing a book on the performance of courtship in classical Hollywood cinema.

Steven Sanders is professor emeritus of philosophy at Bridgewater State University in Massachusetts. His work in film and philosophy appears in *The Philosophy of Film Noir*; *The Philosophy of Science Fiction Film*; *Film Noir: The Encyclopedia*; *The Blackwell Companion to Film Noir*; and *Miami Vice*, a critically acclaimed monograph on the 1980s television series. He is currently coediting a volume of philosophical essays on the films of Michael Mann.

Will Scheibel teaches in the Department of Communication and Culture at Indiana University–Bloomington. He is currently working on a reputation study of Nicholas Ray.

Lauren R. Shaw is a research associate at the German Historical Institute in Washington, DC, and an alumnus of the College of William and

Mary. She has served as an intern at the Smithsonian Center for Folklife and Cultural Heritage and recently completed a two-year Fulbright Teaching Assistantship in the southern Austrian town of Völkermarkt.

Larysa Smirnova holds her Ph.D. in French literature from Yale University. Her dissertation dealt with Roland Barthes and his relationship with the theatrical and theoretical legacy of Bertolt Brecht. She currently lives in Boston, teaching French Literature and Film at Boston College.

Susan White is professor of film and literature in the Department of English at the University of Arizona, and film editor for the *Arizona Quarterly*. She is the author of *The Cinema of Max Ophuls*, and many essays on gender theory and cinema, with special focus on the works of Alfred Hitchcock, Stanley Kubrick, Nicholas Ray, and Anthony Mann.

Tony Williams is professor and area chair of film studies in the Department of English at Southern Illinois University at Carbondale. He has written several books, including *John Woo's Bullet in the Head*. His *George A. Romero: Interviews* was published by the University of Mississippi Press in 2011 and the second edition of *The Cinema of George A. Romero* is forthcoming. He is currently coediting a collection on Hong Kong Neo-Noir with Esther Kau.

Index

55 Days at Peking (Ray film), 3, 10, 78, 231, 234, 237, 240, 251, 266
Aldrich, Robert, 20, 71
Allan, Blaine, 95n, 120–121, 153, 160, 249
Allen, Corey, 140
All the King's Men (Rossen film), 47
Altman, Robert, 71, 214
Amère victoire (Hardy novel), 167
The American Friend (Wenders film), 13, 16, 237, 252
Anderson, Christopher, 207n
Anderson, Edward, 31, 80, 143
Andrew, Geoff, 1, 59, 70, 75, 85–86, 87, 100, 117–118, 130, 175n, 190, 194, 243
Astor, Mary, 38
Atkinson, Brooks, 112
Atkinson, Michael, 39n
Atomic Energy Commission, 157
Attwood, William, 182
Audiberti, Jacques, 127
Auteurism, 1, 5, 41, 46, 47, 49, 51, 71, 73–74, 75, 76–77, 78, 85–86, 153, 177–178, 194, 206, 214, 219, 228–229, 243, 244, 246, 247, 249
Authorship in film, 7, 41, 51, 52, 193–195, 245

Baby Face (Kazan film), 60
Back Where I Came From (CBS music program), 115
Bad Day at Black Rock (Sturges film), 107n
Bacall, Lauren, 65
Backus, Jim, 19
Bagdasarian, Ross, 118
Ballagh, Jim, 256
Bamann, Gerry, 256, 257
Baxter, Les, 118
Bazlen, Bridgette, 226
Barr, Charles, 190, 192, 201
Barth, Ramona, 186n
Battleground (Wellman film), 88
Bazin, André, 192
Beaumont, Harry, 215
Becker, Jacques, 215
Bedford, John, 134
Beecham, Rufus, 171
Begley, Ed, 26
Belmondo, Jean-Paul, 209
Belton, John, 193
Ben-Hur (Wyler film), 225
Benedek, Laslo, 14, 16, 17
Bergala, Alain, 209
Bertolucci, Bernardo, 209
Bezzerides, A.I., 75, 81, 83
Big Country, The (Wyler film), 120
Big Knife, The (Aldrich film), 71

285

Big Sleep, The (Hawks film,), 145
Bigelow, Kathryn, 211
Bigger Than Life (Ray film), 1, 2, 3, 6, 9, 10, 22, 24, 41, 42, 79, 145, 177–187, 189, 234, 236, 239, 243
Bitter Victory (Ray film), 3, 6, 27, 32, 87, 124, 163, 167–170, 186n, 217, 235, 236, 238, 239
Bogart, Humphrey, 4, 14, 24, 43, 64, 65, 69, 70, 76, 81, 145, 147
Blackboard Jungle (Brooks film), 139, 153
Blake, Reverend Eugene Carlson, 227
Body Snatcher, The (Wise film), 240n
Bond, Ward, 22, 75, 90, 128
Bonnie and Clyde (Penn film), 39n
Bordwell, David, 46, 192, 193
Borgnine, Ernest, 128
Born to Be Bad (Ray film), 3, 4, 22, 49–52, 58–61, 79, 212
Botkin, Benjamin, 113, 119, 120
Bourdieu, Pierre, 175
Boy with the Green Hair, The (Losey film), 31
Bradbury, Ray, 225
Brady, Scott, 51, 128, 201
Brando, Marlon, 118, 140, 145
Breathless (*Á bout de souffle*) (Godard film), 209
Brecht, Bertolt, 263
Breen, Joseph I., 31
Bresson, Robert, 15
Brice, Fanny, 257
Bridges at Toko-Ri (Robson film), 90
Brighton Rock (Greene novel), 77
Bronston, Samuel, 10, 221, 228, 247
Brooks, Richard, 20, 139
Brown, Alan, 222
Browne, Nick, 47n
Burke, Alfred, 168
Burnette, Johnny, 145
Burton, Richard, 167, 206n
Butler, Gerard, 75, 77, 78, 79–80

Cahiers du cinéma, 12, 20, 32, 73, 82, 85, 99, 100, 155, 159, 187n, 194, 213, 214, 251n

Camus, Albert, 247, 248
Cannes International Film Festival, 11, 241, 253, 261
Can You Hear Their Voices? (Flanagan play), 121n
Carradine, John, 127, 200
Carter, Janis, 94
Cash, Johnny, 148
Cassavetes, John, 211, 215
Catholic Legion of Decency, 227
Cayette, André, 41
Chabrol, Claude, 217
Chambers, Marilyn, 16
Chandler, Raymond, 63, 80, 81
Chaplin, Geraldine, 232
Charisse, Cyd, 24, 214, 215, 217
Charney, Leo, 129, 132
Child, James, 113
Conspiracy Trial ("Chicago Seven"), 11, 15, 237, 244, 252–253, 261
Chinoise, La (Godard film), 217
CinemaScope, *see* widescreen
Citizen Kane (Welles film), 32, 255
City Blues (unrealized Ray project), 16
City of Fear (Lerner film), 47
Classical Hollywood Cinema, The (Bordwell, Staiger, Thompson book), 46, 192
Clift, Montgomery, 140, 142
Cobb, Lee J., 23, 215
Coe, Richard L., 187n
Columbia Pictures, 12, 47, 118
Commoli, Jean-Louis, 47n, 266
Company She Keeps, The (Cromwell film), 81
Conlin, Jimmy, 25
Conrad, Joseph, 256
Contempt (*Le mepris*) (Godard film), 209
The Conversation (Coppola film), 12
Conway, Jack, 60
Cooke, Alastair, 65
Cooper, Barrington, 238
Cooper, Ben, 128
Coppola, Francis Ford, 12
Corman, Roger, 215

Index

Costa, Pedro, 213
Cotten, Joseph, 164n, 165–166
Crawford, Joan, 123, 126, 127, 132, 195, 215, 257
Crime film, 2, 31–33, 43–46, 63
Criss Cross (Siodmak film), 29
Cromwell, John, 34, 81, 85
Crossfire (Dmytryk film), 31
Crosby, Robert "Wild Horse Bob," 116
Crowther, Bosley, 47, 81–82, 120, 123, 183
Crudup, Arthur, 145
Cukor, George, 213, 215
Cumings, Bruce, 95n
Curtiz, Michael, 49

Dali, Salvador, 221
Dalton, David, 155
Dano, Royal, 128
Dark Corner, The (Hathaway film), 59
Dassin, Jules, 144
De Palma, Brian, 215
Dead End (Wyler film), 45
Dead Reckoning (Cromwell film), 34
Dean, James, 6, 7, 13, 16, 19, 51, 52, 118, 139–142, 153, 154–155, 161n, 219, 250
Deleuze, Gilles, 100
DeMille, Cecil B., 221, 227, 228
Demy, Jacques, 217
Derek, John, 43, 51
Derrida, Jacques, 166, 236
The Devil, Probably (Bresson film), 15
Dickens, Charles, 164–165, 167
Dmytryk, Edward, 31, 45, 78
The Doctor and the Devils (unrealized Ray film), 7, 15, 231–240
Donoghue, Roger, 118
Donnell, Jeff, 51, 70
D'Onofrio, Vincent, 71
Don't Come Knocking (Wenders film), 107n
Don't Expect Too Much (Susan Ray film), 233–234
Dornbush, Adrian J., 112

Double Indemnity (Wilder film), 29, 34, 39
Douglas, Gordon, 47
Douglas, Melvyn, 53
Dowdell, Ethel M., 114
Down in the Valley (Jacobson film), 107n
Dreamers, The (Bertolucci film), 209–210
Driver, The (Hill film), 71
Duelle (Rivette film), 15
Duras, Marguerite, 15
Dwan, Allan, 88
Dyer, Richard, 59
Dylan, Bob, 140

East of Eden (Kazan film), 153, 161n, 215
Eden, Chana, 171
Ehrenstein, David, 61n
Eisenschitz, Bernard, 1, 15, 24, 86–87, 92, 95n, 116, 117, 119, 125, 142, 148, 149, 154–155, 182, 207n, 211, 214, 217, 231, 237, 240n
Eisenstein, Sergei, 32
Elsaesser, Thomas, 181
Enticknap, Leo, 193
Erice, Victor, 210
Erotic Dreams (anthology film), see *Wet Dreams*
Evans, Jean, 112, 113, 115, 117
Evans, Robert, 255
Evans, Walker, 117
Eyles, Allan, 95n

F for Fake (Welles film), 255
Fadiman, William, 80, 81
Farrell, Tom, 14, 237, 238, 244, 247–248, 250
Farrow, John, 220–221
femme fatale, 29, 33, 35, 52, 56, 58, 60, 143, 224
Ferguson, Frank, 128
Ferrara, Abel, 211
Ferrer, Mel, 52

Filene, Benjamin, 113
film gris, 46–47
film noir, 2, 4, 29–39, 46, 47, 49, 52, 55–59, 61, 63, 66, 69, 71–72, 76, 78, 79, 87, 105, 143, 158, 161, 189
Fischer, Max, 251
Fisher, Danny, 256
Fix, Paul, 21, 127
Fixed Bayonets (Fuller film), 90
Flanagan, Hallie, 111–112, 121n
Flesh and the Fiends, The (Gilling film), 240n
Flippen, Jay C., 90
Flying Leathernecks (Ray film), 3, 5, 85–95
Flying Tigers (Miller film), 95n
Fontaine, Joan, 49, 58, 78, 212
Force of Evil (Polonsky film), 47, 143
Ford, John, 88, 90, 98, 125
Forman, Milos, 16
Foster, Norman, 78
Francis, Freddie, 240n
Frankenheimer, John, 71
Frascella, Larry, 61n
French New Wave (*nouvelle vague*), 6, 12, 71, 209, 216
Freud, Sigmund, 223
Friedan, Betty, 103
Friedman, Bruce Jay, 252
Friedrich, James K., 222
Fuller, Samuel, 20, 90, 213, 215

Gallagher, Cullen, 54, 243
Gamet, Kenneth, 89, 95n
Garmes, Lee, 99, 117
Garnett, Tay, 30
Garrel, Philippe, 209
gender, 4, 7, 51–61, 101, 105, 140, 148, 158–159, 172, 178, 180, 219, 222, 223, 228
General Electric Theater (CBS television series), 6, 164
Generation of Vipers (Wylie), 224
Genter, Robert, 158–159

Gentleman's Agreement (Kazan film), 183, 184
Gilda (Vidor film), 59
Gillette, Ruth, 67
Gilling, John, 240n
Gledhill, Christine, 179
Goalie's Anxiety at the Penalty Kick, The (Wenders film), 259–260
Godard au travail (Bergala book), 209
Godard, Jean-Luc, 6, 12, 32, 99, 153, 207n, 209, 211–213, 217, 254, 261, 262, 263, 264
Gomez, Thomas, 165
Goodwin, Michael, 113
Gottheim, Larry, 242, 245
Grafe, Frieda, 217
Grahame, Gloria, 4, 24, 49, 53, 57, 64, 69, 71, 76, 77, 212
Grainger, Edmund, 88, 89, 95n
Granger, Farley, 6, 25, 31, 51, 141, 142, 143, 146
Grant, James Edward, 89, 90
Great Depression, 2, 15, 106, 107, 116, 120, 142–143
Green, Alfred E., 60
Green, Nigel, 170
Greene, Graham, 77, 79
Griffith, D. W., 32
Group Theatre, 151
Guardino, Harry, 225
Guarner, Jose, 228
Guralnick, Peter, 139, 143
Guthrie, Woody, 31, 113, 115–116
Guys and Dolls (Mankiewicz film), 215

Hair (Forman film), 16, 259
Halberstam, Davidm 95n
Halliday, Jon, 206n
Halls of Montezuma, The (Milestone film), 88
Hall, Sheldon, 193
Hall, Stuart, 99
Haller, Ernst, 257
Hampton, Fred, 16
Hanson, John, 12

Index

Hardy, Rene, 167
Harpur College (State University of New York at Binghamton), 10–11, 14, 233, 234, 242, 244, 245, 246, 247, 252, 253, 256, 261
Hart, Lorenz, 146
Hartung, Philip T., 187n
Harvey, Laurence, 232
Harvey, Stephen, 39n
Harvey, Sylvia, 31
Hawks, Howard, 1, 21, 98, 125, 142, 145
Hayden, Sterling, 6, 125, 132, 142, 148–149, 195
Hayward, Susan, 21, 103
Heart of the Matter, The (Greene novel), 77
Heiress, The (Wyler film), 142
Hell's House (Higgin film), 44
Hellman, Monte, 214
Helpern, Jr., David, 253
Higgin, Howard, 44
"High Green Wall" (episode of *General Electric Theater* directed by Ray), 6, 163, 164–165, 175n
Hill, John, 43
Hill, Walter, 71
Hincha, Richard, 193
Hirsch, Jerrold, 118
Hilton, James, 78
Hitchcock, Alfred, 1, 2, 14, 23, 71, 194
Hoffman, Abbie, 244
Holden, William, 90
Holly, Buddy, 140, 145
Hot Blood (Ray film), 3, 51, 109, 118
How the Other Half Lives (Riis book), 44
House of Bamboo (Fuller film), 215
House Un-American Activities Committee (HUAC), 65, 95n
Houseman, John, 15, 23, 30, 31, 74, 76, 79, 80, 81, 83, 113, 115, 116, 142, 251

Houston, Penelope, 12
Hoveyda, Fereydoun, 214
Howard, Trevor, 78
Hughes, Dorothy B., 63, 64, 82
Hughes, Howard, 32, 49, 85, 87, 89, 90, 91, 95n
Hume, Cyril, 182
Hunter, Jeffrey, 27, 51, 219, 225, 229
Huston, John, 29

I'm a Stranger Here Myself (Helpern film), 253
Ici et ailleurs (Godard film), 254, 263
In a Lonely Place (Ray film), 1, 2–3, 4–5, 9, 14, 24, 29, 31, 51, 63–72, 76, 77, 79, 80, 81, 82–83, 92, 124, 147, 158, 189, 210, 212, 234
In Between Time (unrealized Ray film), 15
India Song (Duras film), 15
Injunction Granted (Living Newspaper production), 111–112
Ireland, John, 21, 92, 216
Irving, Richard, 25
Ives, Burl, 115, 116, 119, 120, 165, 171

Jackson, Aunt Molly, 113
Jackson, Charles, 164
Jackson, William Henry, 126
Jacobs, Ken, 242, 245–246, 249
Jacobson, David, 107n
Jagger, Dean, 207n
The Janitor (Ray short), 18, 237
Jarmusch, Jim, 213
Jerome, General Clayton, 88
Jesse James (King film), 207n
Johnny Guitar (Ray film), 1, 3, 5, 9, 11, 18, 21, 32, 51, 79, 83, 92, 119, 120, 123–137, 142, 148–149, 190–191, 195–206, 210, 222, 228, 235, 239, 244, 249
Jones, James, 11
Jules and Jim (Truffaut film), 210

Jürgens, Curd, 167

Kazan, Elia, 115, 116, 155, 161n, 183, 213, 215, 229, 251, 255, 266
Kazan, Molly, 115
Kelly, Claire, 215
Kemp, Philip, 144
Kemper, Charles, 25
Kennedy, Arthur, 21, 103
King, Henry, 89, 207n
Killing of a Chinese Bookie, The (Cassavetes film), 215
Kilpatrick, George Dunbar, 222
King of Kings (Ray film), 3, 6–7, 10, 27, 51, 78, 90, 219–229, 234, 237
Kings of the Road (Wenders film), 107n
Kiss the Blood Off My Hands (Butler novel), 78
Klinger, Barbara, 186n
Knight, Arthur, 183
Knock on Any Door (Ray film), 3, 4, 14, 23, 32, 41–47, 51, 143, 222
Koster, Henry, 206n
Kouvaros, George, 98, 104
Kramer, Stanley, 41
Krasna, Norman, 116
Kreidl, John, 31–32, 33, 39n, 161
Kubrick, Stanley, 225

Laderman, David, 39n
Lambert, Gavin, 12, 61n, 182, 186n
Lancaster, Burt, 78
Lang, Fritz, 21, 33, 194, 207n, 216
Lange, Hope, 201
Lasky, Jesse, Jr., 118
Laura (Preminger film), 59
Lawless, The (Losey film), 47
Lawrence, Atwood, 105
Lay Jr., Bernie, 89
Lead Belly, 113, 115
Léaud, Jean-Pierre, 217
Lederman, Louis M., 228

Lee, Gypsy Rose, 174
Lee, Will, 25
Lemonade Joe (Lipsky film), 233
Leonard, George B., 182
Lerner, Irving, 47
Levinson, Leslie, 237, 245, 248, 249, 254
Lewis, Jerry Lee, 145
Life Magazine, 116, 157
Lightning Over Water (Wenders and Ray film), 10, 14, 16, 99, 237, 238, 250
Limbacher, James, 193
Lindner, Robert, 79
Lipsky, Oldrich, 233
Little Richard, 147, 148
Litvak, Anatole, 183
Living Newspaper, 111, 121
Locativo, Robert, 256
Lomax, Alan, 112–113, 114, 115, 117, 119, 142
Lomax, Elizabeth, 113
Lomax, John, 113, 117, 142
Lone Star (Sayles film), 107n
Lonely Crowd, The (Reisman book), 159
Loo, Stanley, 254
Lopert, Tanya, 232
Losey, Joseph, 31, 47, 111, 112, 213, 238
Lovejoy, Frank, 66
Lowry, Robert, 186n
Luddy, Tom, 12–13
Ludwig, Edward, 95n
Lupino, Ida, 22, 75
Lüscher, Max, 91, 95n
The Lusty Men (Ray film), 3, 5, 21, 23, 24, 41, 85, 97–107, 109, 116–117, 120, 191, 210, 234, 236, 238
Lutz, Tom, 180, 181
Lux Radio Theater, 78

Macao (von Sternberg film), 85
MacDonald, Joseph, 195, 201, 205

MacMurray, Fred, 36
Mad with Much Heart (Butler novel), 75, 77, 78–79, 80
Maibaum, Richard, 182
Mailer, Norman, 253
Maland, Charles, 45
Mallary Jr., Reverend R. De Witt, 227
The Maltese Falcon (Huston film), 29, 38
Mankiewicz, Herman J., 49
Mankiewicz, Joseph L., 215, 216
Mann, Anthony, 88, 125
Marco (Ray short), 7, 256–258
Marcus, Greil, 141, 147
Marlowe, Frank, 127
Marsac, Maurice, 166
Marx, Groucho, 253
masculinity, 5–6, 7, 54, 87, 89, 100, 103, 128, 139–149, 158, 159, 168, 177–186, 219–229
Mason, James, 6, 24, 145, 179, 182, 183
Masson, Alain, 215
Matthau, Walter, 180
Mature, Victor, 207n
Mauriac, François, 80
Mazzatenta, Claudio, 256, 257–258
McArthur, Colin, 213, 216
McCambridge, Mercedes, 21, 127, 132
McCarten, John, 183
McCarthyism, 89, 158
McShane, Jim, 118
McGilligan, Patrick, 1, 31, 32, 61n, 73, 112, 117, 119, 120, 207n, 240n
McNiven, Roger D., 47n
Mekas, Jonas, 247
Melley, Timothy, 223
melodrama, 6, 42, 52, 57, 61, 63, 79, 81, 145, 158, 159, 161, 177–187, 189, 206, 212, 213, 215
Men in War (Mann film), 88
Method acting, 5, 140, 141, 142, 145, 256, 257, 258, 259–260, 264, 265

Methot, Mayo, 69
MGM (Metro-Goldwyn-Mayer), 12, 31, 214, 225–226, 229
Michaud, Michael Gregg, 61n
Mickey One (Penn film), 71
Mildred Pierce (Curtiz film), 49
Milestone, Lewis, 88
Miller, David, 95n
Mills, John, 78
Milne, Tom, 15
Mineo, Sal, 19, 61n, 242
Minnelli, Vincente, 177, 194
mise-en-scène, 18, 51, 55, 58, 83, 99, 103, 126, 154, 177, 200, 201, 215
Mitchum, Robert, 23, 36, 99, 145, 260
Mitry, Jean, 129
Moore, Cleo, 25
Moorehead, Agnes, 200
Moskin, J. Robert, 182
Motolo, Ned, 256
Murnau, F. W., 32
Murphy (unrealized Ray film), 252
Must You Conform? (Lindner book), 79
Myth of Sisyphus, The (Camus book), 247, 248

Naked City, The (Dassin film), 144
Narboni, Jean Paul, 47n
Neale, Stephen (Steve), 186n, 193
Nixon, Richard, 247
North, Edmund, 82
Northern Lights (Hanson film), 12
Novotny, Vladimir, 233
Numéro Deux (Godard film), 254

O'Brien, Edmund, 255
Odets, Clifford, 182–183
O'Donnell, Cathy, 25, 35, 51, 143
O'Hara, Maureen, 49, 53, 54, 57
Olsen, Christopher, 178
On Dangerous Ground (Ray film), 3, 4, 5, 9, 15, 22, 23, 24, 25–28, 73–83, 85, 91, 124, 141, 142, 144–147, 163, 210, 237, 238, 257

Ophüls, Max, 49, 177
Osceola, Chief Cory, 172–173
Osterloh, Robert, 126
Other Side of the Wind, The (unfinished Welles film), 255
O'Toole, Peter, 175
Our Blushing Brides (Beaumont film), 215
Our Singing Country (Lomax brothers volume), 117
Out 1, 15
Out of the Past (Tourneur film), 36, 145

Pacific Film Archives, 12
Pageant of the Popes (Farrow book), 220
Paik, Nam June, 244
Pal Joey (Sidney film), 215
Palmer, James W., 64, 65, 68
Palmer, R. Barton, 34
Paramount Pictures, 12
Paris Cinémathèque, 10
Parker, Charlie, 143
Party Girl (Ray film), 3, 6, 9, 21, 23, 24, 92, 209–210, 214–217, 236
Patterson, James T., 45–46
Pellegrin, Raymond, 168
Penn, Arthur, 39n, 71
Perkins, Victor (V. F.), 210
Perry, Susan, 43
phenomenology, 6, 153–154
Pialat, Maurice, 211
Pinky (Kazan film), 183
Platt, Edward, 157
Player, The (Altman film), 71
Plummer, Christopher, 237
Polan, Dana, 1, 49, 63
Polonsky, Abraham, 47, 143
Pollock, Charles, 112
Pollock, Jackson, 112
Pomerance, Murray, 5, 141, 123–137, 153
Postman Always Rings Twice, The (Garnett film), 30
Preminger, Otto, 59, 194, 215

Prénom: Carmen (Godard film), 209
Presley, Elvis, 139–142, 144–147, 207n
Principles of Criminology (Sutherland book), 45, 46
Production Code Administration (PCA), 31, 37, 60
Pyle, Denver, 128

Quinn, Anthony, 174, 244
Quinn, Susan, 111

Rackett, The (Cromwell film), 85
Rae, Norman, 226
Rafelson, Bob, 214
Rancière, Jacques, 19–20, 210
Rank, J. Arthur, 78
Rathgeb, Douglas L., 61n
Ray, Nicholas
  as architecture student, 11, 15, 17, 151, 156
  as teacher, 3–4, 7, 10–11, 16–17, 213, 233–234, 241–250, 251n, 252–253, 253–255, 255–258, 261, 264
  at RKO Radio Pictures, 30–33, 49, 76–81, 85, 116–117
  in Europe, 9–10, 15–16
  marriage to Gloria Grahame, 69, 71, 76
  New Deal federal service, 5, 109–121, 142–144, 151–152
  reception as *auteur* at *Cahiers du cinéma*, 12, 20–21, 22, 32, 41, 73–74, 75, 76, 83, 85, 99–101, 104, 123, 124, 140, 153, 155, 159, 183, 185, 187n, 194–195, 214, 216–217
  sexuality, 51, 59, 155, 211, 212–213
  work with actors and performance, 5, 91, 123–137, 139–149, 151–152, 154–156, 235, 246, 252, 253, 255–258, 259–260, 264–265
Ray, Susan (Susan Schwartz), 1, 16, 233, 241, 245, 249, 250

Index

Rear Window (Hitchcock film), 23
Rebel Without a Cause (Lindner book), 79
Rebel Without a Cause (Ray film), 1, 2, 3, 6, 9, 11, 12, 13, 19, 20, 22, 23, 24–25, 28, 41, 51, 79, 92, 118, 139–142, 148, 151–161, 163, 170, 172, 178, 189, 206n, 210, 222, 234, 235, 238, 239, 242, 244, 249, 257, 265
Reckless Moment, The (Ophüls film), 49
Red-Headed Woman (Conway film), 60
Red River (Hawks film), 142
Reid, Carl Benton, 67
Ried, Howard, 221
Reik, Theodor, 223
Reisman, David, 159
Renoir, Jean, 32, 216
Republic Pictures, 12, 148
Riis, Jacob, 44
Rimbaud, Arthur, 10
Rio Grande (Ford film), 88
Rivette, Jacques, 2, 4, 12, 15, 20–21, 73–74, 75, 76, 83, 99–101, 104, 153, 189, 194, 217
RKO Radio Pictures, 12, 32, 46, 78, 80, 81, 85, 92, 94
"road movie," 39n
Robe, The (Koster film), 206n–207n
Robertson, Pamela, 127
Robinson, Earl, 115–116
rock-and-roll, 5–6, 139–149, 175
Robbins, Tim, 71
Rodgers, Richard, 146–147
Rodowick, David N., 186
Rohmer, Éric, 12, 22, 99
Rogell, Sid, 80
Rogin, Michael, 224
Romeo and Juliet (Shakespeare play), 11
Roosevelt, Eleanor, 112
Roosevelt, Franklin D., 110–111, 115
Rosenbaum, Jonathan, 4, 9–18, 51, 154, 210, 241, 243

Rosenbaum, Rabbi William, 227–228
Rossellini, Roberto, 19–20, 32
Rossen, Robert, 47
Rouault, Georges, 221
Royle, Nicholas, 107
Rozsa, Miklos, 225
Rubin, Jerry, 244, 264
Run for Cover (Ray film), 3, 24, 51, 120, 236
Rush, Barbara, 24, 180, 243
Ryan, Robert, 6, 22, 27, 74, 81, 85, 87, 88–89, 90, 91, 94, 95n, 141, 142, 144–147

St. Valentine's Day Massacre, The (Corman film), 215
Salt, Barry, 193
Sands of Iwo Jima, The (Dwan film), 88, 89, 92, 92–93, 94, 95n
Sarris, Andrew, 1, 41–42
Savage Innocents, The (Ray film), 3, 6, 9–10, 22, 27, 51, 120, 163, 174–175, 239, 240, 244
Sayles, John, 107n
Scorsese, Martin, 123, 124, 134
Schaefer, Jack, 104
Schary, Dore, 31 49
Schell, Maximilian, 15, 232
Schlesinger, Arthur M., 186n
Schnee, Charles, 31
Schulberg, Budd, 119, 170, 172
Schulberg, Stuart, 119, 170
Schwartz, Susan, *see* Susan Ray
Sea Horse, The (unrealized Ray film), 259
Seberg, Jean, 209
Seconds, 71
Seeger, Charles, 112, 113
Seeger, Pete, 113, 116
Settlement and Resettlement (Ray play), 112
Shahan, Ben, 112
Shamroy, Leon, 206n
Shane (Stevens film), 104, 126
Short, James F., Jr., 45

Sidney, George, 215
"Simple Art of Murder, The" (Chandler essay), 63
Sievernich, Chris, 14, 15–16
Silver, Alain, 69
Sinatra, Frank, 145, 215
Siodmak, Robert, 29
Sight and Sound (magazine), 11
Sirk, Douglas, 184, 194, 206n, 216
Slocum, J. David, 1
Some Like It Hot (Wilder film), 215
Smith, Art, 68
Smith, Bernard, 225
Sniper, The (Dmytryk film), 45
social problem film, 4, 31, 41–47, 189
Solt, Andrew, 64, 81–82
Son of Man, see *King of Kings*
So Well Remembered (Hilton novel), 78
Spartacus (Kubrick film), 225
Spear, Ivan, 226
Spellerberg, James, 193
Spicer, Andrew, 52
Spiro, J. D., 222
Spivacke, Harold, 114
Stagecoach (Ford film), 47n
Staiger, Janet, 193
Stamp, Terence, 15
Stanislavski, Constantin, 255–256, 257, 260
Stanush, Claude, 116
Star Is Born, A (Cukor film), 215
Steele, Barbara, 232
Steel Helmet, The (Fuller film), 90
Stern, Stewart, 157
Sternberg, Joseph von, 85
Stevens, George, 104
Stewart, James, 23
Stewart, Martha, 66
Story of G. I. Joe, The (Wellman film), 88
Stradling, Sr., Harry, 195
Strasberg Institute, 7, 255, 264–265
Sturges, John, 107n, 125
Suid, Lawrence H., 88
Sun Records, 144

Sunset Boulevard (Wilder film), 71
Sutherland, Edwin, 44, 45, 46
Syder, William, 86
Sykes, Velma West, 226

Tale of Two Cities, A (Dickens novel), 166, 167
Taliesen studio, 11
Tani, Yoko, 174
Tannenbaum, Frank, 44
Taylor, Robert, 21, 51, 214, 215
Tchalgadjieff, Stéphane, 15
Technicolor, 86, 87, 215
"Ten Feet Tall" (Roueché story, 179)
Thayler, Carl, 201
Theater of Action, 111, 151
They Live By Night (Ray film), 1, 2, 4, 9, 12, 15, 23, 25, 28, 29–39, 41, 51, 80, 92, 93, 113, 116, 120, 141, 142–144, 210, 222, 236, 244, 257
They Were Expendable (Ford and Montgomery film), 88, 89, 90
Thieves Like Us (Anderson novel), 31, 80, 142
Thomas, Dylan, 7, 10, 15, 231, 232, 237, 239, 240
Thomson, David, 32
Todd, Ann, 168
To Have and Have Not (Hawks film), 145
Torn, Rip, 16, 223, 252
Touchez pas au grisbi (Becker film), 215
Touch of Evil (Welles film), 71
Tourneur, Jacques, 36, 145
Treasury of American Folklore, A (Botkin volume), 119
Truffaut, François, 2, 12, 21, 32, 99, 123, 124, 140, 153, 185, 213, 216–217
True Story of Jesse James, The (Ray film), 3, 6, 51, 109, 118–119, 149, 189–191, 195–207, 222, 237

Index

Tuesday in November (Office of War Information film), 111, 116
Turner Classic Movies, 250n
Twelve O'Clock High (King film), 89
Twentieth Century-Fox, 118, 182, 183, 206n
Twisted Road, The, see *They Live By Night*
"Tutti Frutti," 147

Underworld U.S.A. (McArthur book), 212
Untouchables, The (De Palma film), 215

Valiant, Margaret, 112
Venice International Film Festival, 183, 250n
Vertigo (Hitchcock film), 23, 71
Vidal, Gore, 7, 15, 232, 233, 234, 237, 239, 240
Vidor, Charles, 59
Vidor, King, 221
Vincent, Gene, 145, 148
Vogel, Joe, 225
Voice of America, 115

Wagner, Robert, 51, 149, 201
Wake of the Red Witch (Ludwig film), 95n
Wald, Jerry, 116
Walden: Diaries and Sketches (Mekas film), 247
Walk a Crooked Mile (Douglas film), 47
Walk in the Sun, A (Milestone film), 88, 90
Walsh, Moira, 187n
Walsh, Robert, 125, 226, 227
war movie, 85–95, 213
Warner Bros., 12, 15, 43, 153, 257
Warshow, Robert, 31
Warwick, Robert, 66
Waugh, Evelyn, 163
Wayne, John, 86, 87, 88–89, 90, 94, 95n

We Can't Go Home Again (Ray film), 1, 7, 10–11, 12, 13–14, 231, 233–234, 235, 236, 237, 238, 240, 241–250, 251, 252–253, 253–255, 260–261, 265–266
Weisel, Al, 61n
Welles, Orson, 32, 71, 225, 254–255
Wellman, William, 88
Wenders, Wim, 10, 13–14, 16, 97, 99, 100, 107n, 213, 240, 259, 260
West Side Story (Wise film), 11
Western, 5, 97–107, 116–117, 118–119, 123, 124–125, 126, 148, 189–191, 195–207, 213, 222, 227
Wet Dreams (anthology film), 12, 18n, 237, 251, 261
White, Josh, 116
White, Susan, 6, 163–175, 222, 224, 228, 229
Whyte, William Hollingsworth, 224
Whitman, Walt, 169
Widescreen, 6, 189–207
  CinemaScope, 6, 119, 154, 189–207
Wilde, Cornell, 51, 118
Wild One, The (Benedek film), 14
Wilder, Billy, 29, 71, 194, 215
Willemen, Paul, 214
Williams, Hank, 143
Williams, Linda, 178–179
Williams, Rhys, 127, 200
Williams, Sumner, 26, 51, 75
Williams, Tennessee, 127
Willis, Gary, 95n
Wilson, Colin, 79
Wilson, George, 154, 157
Wind Across the Everglades (Ray film), 3, 6, 27, 51, 109, 116, 119–121, 163, 165, 170–174, 237, 238, 239
Winsten, Archer, 226
Wise, Naomi, 113
Wise, Robert, 240n
Wizard of Oz, The (Fleming film), 186

Woman in the Window, The (Lang film), 33
Woman's Secret, A (Ray film), 3, 4, 49–61
"woman's picture," 3, 49, 52, 55–56, 177, 180, 212, 215
Women, The (Cukor film), 215
Wong, Anna May, 22
Wood, Natalie, 24, 51
Wood, Robin, 185
Wright, Cobina, 221
Wright, Frank Lloyd, 11, 15, 17–18
Wyke, Maria, 223
Wyler, William, 45, 120, 142, 225
Wylie, Philip, 186n, 224

Yordan, Philip, 221, 222, 228
York, Susana, 232
Young, Faron, 143
Young, Victor, 148
Your Red Wagon, see *They Live By Night*

Zanuck, Darryl F., 206n
Žižek, Slavoj, 222–223
Zryd, Michael, 245

www.ingramcontent.com/pod-product-compliance
Lightning Source LLC
Chambersburg PA
CBHW022057230426
43672CB00008B/1199